SIXTH EDITION

Operating Systems
A Systematic View

William S. Davis • T. M. Rajkumar

Miami University, Oxford, Ohio

PEARSON

Addison
Wesley

Boston San Francisco New York
London Toronto Sydney Tokyo Singapore Madrid
Mexico City Munich Paris Cape Town Hong Kong Montreal

Executive Editor: Susan Hartman Sullivan
Senior Acquisitions Editor: Michael Hirsch
Project Editor: Katherine Harutunian
Senior Production Supervisor: Juliet Silveri
Production Services: Dartmouth Publishing, Inc.
Cover Designer: Joyce Cosentino Wells
Marketing Manager: Michelle Brown
Print Buyer: Caroline Fell

Cover Photo © 2004 Sami Sarkis/Photodisc

Access the latest information about Addison-Wesley titles from our World Wide Web site:
http://www.aw-bc.com/computing

Many of the designations used by manufacturers and sellers to distinguish their products are claimed as trademarks. Where those designations appear in this book, and Addison-Wesley was aware of a trademark claim, the designations have been printed in initial caps or all caps.

The programs and applications presented in this book have been included for their instructional value. They have been tested with care, but are not guaranteed for any particular purpose. The publisher does not offer any warranties or representations, nor does it accept any liabilities with respect to the programs or applications.

Library of Congress Cataloging-in-Publication Data
Davis, William S.
  Operating systems : a systematic view / William S. Davis, T.M. Rajkumar. -- 6th ed.
    p. cm.
  ISBN 0-321-26751-6
    1. Operating systems (Computers) I. Rajkumar, T.M. II. Title.

QA76.76.O63D38 2004
005.4'3--dc22
2004044323

For information on obtaining permission for the use of material from this work, please submit a written request to Pearson Education, Inc., Rights and Contracts Department, 75 Arlington St., Suite 300, Boston, MA 02116 or fax your request to 617-848-7047.

2 3 4 5 6 7 8 9 10—PH—0605

To Cathy

Contents

3 Application Software and Data   43

4 Linking the Hardware Components   69

PART 3: COMMUNICATING WITH THE OPERATING SYSTEM   145

7   MS-DOS Commands   147

8   The Microsoft Windows User Interface   177

PART 4: OPERATING SYSTEM INTERNALS   249

10 The Intel Architecture   251

14 Macintosh OS X Internals   343

15 MVS Internals   365

PART 5: NETWORKS   391

16 Data Communication and Networks   393

Preface

◼ Philosophy and Perspective

The first edition of *Operating Systems: A Systematic View* was published in 1977. In those days, one company, IBM, dominated the computer industry. The first edition reflected that reality, but times have changed. Today, a typical computing environment consists of multiple computers from multiple vendors linked to form a network, and that new reality is a key driving force behind this sixth edition.

Although numerous changes have been made, *Operating Systems: A Systematic View* remains an *applied* introduction to operating systems. This is not a theoretical text. It is aimed at those who are interested in using (rather than designing) computers, operating systems, and networks. The intent is to show *why* operating systems are needed and *what*, at a functional level, they do.

The early editions of this book looked at operating systems from the perspective of an application programmer. Like the fifth edition, this edition expands that perspective a bit to include experienced users who may or may not know how to program. As before, the book assumes little or no mathematics beyond high school algebra. The only prerequisites are a reasonable understanding of basic computer concepts and a sincere interest in knowing what goes on beneath the surface of a computer application.

◼ Changes from the Fifth Edition

In addition to technological updates throughout the text, a chapter on Macintosh OS X (14) has been added to the sixth edition, the Windows chapters (8, 12, and 19) have been updated to reflect the most current versions of this popular operating system, additional coverage of Linux has been integrated into the UNIX/Linux chapters (9, 13, and 20), and Part 5 has been substantially rewritten to incorporate the evolving communication infrastructure and network principles (Chapter 16), the Internet (Chapter 17), and the client/server model and security implications (Chapter 18).

Gone from the new edition is the fifth edition chapter on virtual machines (19), although key virtual machine concepts have been incorporated into other chapters. Additionally, the chapters on OS/JCL (11 and 12) have been merged and streamlined to form a new Appendix D, and the contents of fifth edition Chapters 17 (Principles of Operation) and 18 (IBM MVS) have been merged to form a new Chapter 15 on MVS. For interested instructors, fifth edition Chapters 11, 12, 17, 18, and 19 are available for downloading on the book's companion Web site.

◼ Sixth Edition Contents

The new edition retains the pace, level, and writing style of the earlier editions. As before, numerous illustrations closely follow the narrative and visually reinforce the concepts. The book also retains such chapter-level pedagogical features as learning objectives, summaries, key word lists, and review questions, and adds a set of thought-provoking exercises designed to encourage the student to think beyond the book.

Part 1 (Chapters 2-4) reviews essential computer concepts. The primary purpose of these three chapters is to ensure that all students start with a consistent technical base before moving on. Some students might find at least some of this material familiar.

Part 2 presents an overview of key operating system concepts. Chapter 5 discusses the user interface, the file system, and device management. Chapter 6 moves inside the operating system and introduces the more transparent memory and processor management functions. The intent of this section is to present a high-level, generic map of an operating system's primary functions. Later in the text when you begin reading about the internals of several different operating systems, these two chapters will help you make sense of the details.

Users and programmers communicate with an operating system through a user interface, the subject of Part 3. The primary focus of this section is using an interface or a command language to create and manipulate files. Chapters 7, 8, and 9 are presented as interactive tutorials on MS-DOS, Windows XP, and UNIX/Linux respectively. If possible, they should be read while you are sitting in front of a computer and following along, step by step.

Part 4 moves inside the computer. Chapter 10 introduces the Intel Pentium architecture, useful (though not essential) preparation for Chapters 11 (MS-DOS) and 12 (Windows XP). The material in Chapter 13 (UNIX and Linux Internals) is independent of the underlying hardware architecture. Chapter 14 is a new chapter on Macintosh OS X internals. Chapter 15 introduces selected principles underlying the traditional IBM mainframe architecture and describes the IBM MVS dispatching process.

Part 5 covers network operating systems. Chapter 16 introduces the communication infrastructure and key networking concepts, Chapter 17 describes the Internet and the World Wide Web, and Chapter 18 covers key client/server network concepts and explores security implications of networks. Chapters 19, 20, and 21 show how the concepts introduced in Chapter 18 are implemented using Windows 2003, Linux, and Novell NetWare respectively.

◗ Supplements

The following supplementary materials are available to assist instructors and students:

- *Online Instructor's Manual:* Lecture/discussion suggestions and solutions to textbook review questions and exercises.
- *Test Bank:* Sample examination questions.
- *Online PowerPoint presentations:* An average of 27 slides per chapter, including virtually all the textbook figures.
- *Online, downloadable copies of selected fifth edition chapters:* Chapters 11 and 12 (IBM's OS/JCL), Chapter 17 (Traditional IBM Mainframe Operating Principles), Chapter 18 (IBM MVS), and Chapter 19 (Virtual Machines).

The Instructor's Manual, Test Bank, and PowerPoint presentations are available only to instructors through your Addison-Wesley sales representative, or e-mail Addison-Wesley (aw.cse@aw.com) for information on how to access them.

◗ Acknowledgements

We'd like to thank our editor, Michael Hirsch, and our project editor, Katherine Harutunian. Juliet Silveri managed the production process. Elizabeth Hopwood was our primary contact at the production subcontractor, Dartmouth Publishing, Inc., Mary Alice Richardson, our copy editor, asked many excellent questions, and Shoreh Hashemi of the University of Houston prepared the instructor's manual. Additionally, we would like to acknowledge the following reviewers for their many valuable insights and suggestions:

William T. Anderson, *Northwood University, Midland Campus*
Francis Kofi Andoh-Baidoo, *Virginia Commonwealth University*
Peter de Luca, *DeVry Institute of Technology*
Shohreh Hashemi, *University of Houston, Downtown*
K. Niki Kunene, *Virginia Commonwealth University*
Michael Kusheba, *Kilgore College*
Nipul Patel, *Purdue University, Calumet*
Michael Stanton, *ITT Technical Institute*

We're excited about this new edition, and we sincerely hope it meets your needs.

WSD, Sarasota, Florida
TMR, Oxford, Ohio

CHAPTER 1

What Is an Operating System?

When you finish reading this chapter you should be able to:

▶ Define the term operating system.

▶ Identify an operating system's interfaces.

▶ Define the term service.

▶ Explain how the operating system serves as a platform for constructing and running application programs.

▶ Describe an operating system's environment in terms of layers of abstraction.

▶ Relate the black box concept to the layering concept.

▶ List and briefly describe the primary services provided by a modern operating system.

▶ Explain how a complex system can be constructed by plugging together a set of layers.

▶ Distinguish between open source and proprietary.

◼ Basic Operating System Functions

An **operating system** is a set of system software routines that sits between the application program and the hardware (Figure 1.1). It defines a set of standard interface rules, provides numerous services, and serves as a platform for running and developing application programs.

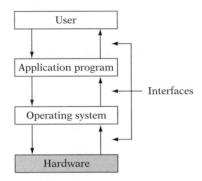

FIGURE 1.1
The operating system sits between the application program and the hardware.

The Interface Function

An **interface** is a point of connection or linkage between two components. Note that there are three interfaces pictured in Figure 1.1: The user communicates with the application program, the application program communicates with the operating system, and the operating system communicates with the hardware. The operating system incorporates logic that supports interfaces with both the application program and the hardware. All application programs access the hardware *through* the operating system following rules imposed *by* the operating system. A modern computer literally cannot function without an operating system in place.

Services

The operating system's internal routines can be viewed as small, single-function programs that perform key support **services** such as communicating with peripheral devices and accepting and carrying out such user commands as launch a program, copy a file, create a directory, open a file, save a file, and so on. A service is a software routine that runs in support of another program.

For example, imagine using a word processing application to write a paper. Most of the time you are working directly with the application logic, but occasionally you encounter a need to perform an input or output operation such as saving a file. Although such tasks seem simple, they are in reality deceptively complex. They are also common to virtually all applications, and it makes little sense to duplicate them in each and every program. The operating system's central position makes it an ideal repository for these common, shared system services because all application programs access the hardware through the operating system. Thus, when you tell your application (via the user interface) to save a file, your application program calls the operating system's file save routine. The application program resumes processing after the requested service is completed.

Platforms

At the hardware level, computers distributed by different manufacturers are often incompatible, perhaps using different rules for communicating with peripherals and other hardware components. Consequently, a program written for one brand of computer might not work on a competitive machine. However, if both computers support the same operating system they can probably run the same application software. Because different brands often imply different hardware, the operating system routines that communicate directly with the hardware might be quite different, but the routines that interface with the application program present a consistent **platform** (Figure 1.2) to the programs running on both machines. Because all communication with the hardware goes through the operating system, the programmer can ignore the hardware differences and the software developer can market the same application program to users of numerous computer brands.

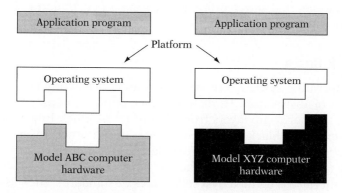

FIGURE 1.2

The operating system is a platform for executing application programs.

Layers of Abstraction

Figure 1.1 shows the user, the application program, the operating system, and the hardware as four linked layers. Each of those layers represents an **abstraction,** a simplified view of an object that ignores the internal details. (For example, standardized controls make it possible for an experienced driver to operate virtually any automobile.) The advantage of using layers of abstraction is that you can focus on the details of any given layer without losing sight of the other layers.

The idea behind viewing a system as a set of layers of abstraction is derived from an old architectural concept called **layering.** For example, imagine that a major retailer has decided to construct a new superstore. Given a choice between locating the new store near a major interstate highway interchange and developing a more remote site, the retailer is likely to choose the former because tapping into the existing transportation infrastructure (the interstate highway system) is far less expensive than building new access roads to bring customers to an outlying site. Moving on to the construction phase, rather than creating new electric power generation, communication, water, and sewer systems, the contractor will almost certainly adopt the standards documented in the local building codes and tap into the existing infrastructures provided by the local electric, communication, water, and sewer utilities. Creating a new building would be prohibitively expensive without layering.

Black Boxes

An operating system's environment can conveniently be viewed as a set of layers of abstraction. Think of the user, application program, operating system, and hardware layers from Figure 1.1 as **black boxes** (Figure 1.3). The contents of a black box are unknown to the other boxes, so each layer is functionally **independent.** Two black boxes communicate with each other only through a shared interface or point of linkage (Figure 1.4). Generally, the interface is defined by a set of rules or standards, such as a list of parameters. Black box A follows those standards to deliver content to the interface. Black box B follows those same standards to accept that content from the interface.

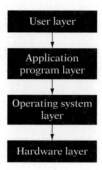

FIGURE 1.3
View each layer of abstraction as a black box.

Viewing each layer of abstraction as an independent black box is useful because it allows you to work with the layers one at a time. Because the other layers are independent of the user, anyone who understands the application program's user interface can access the system. Because the application program layer is independent, the program can be modified, updated, and patched transparently. Because the operating system layer is independent, it is possible to upgrade the operating system without affecting the other layers. Because the hardware layer is independent, it is possible for the top three layers to run, almost literally without change, on a new computer. The only requirement is that the rules imposed by the interfaces must be followed. That is why modern information systems are designed as a series of independent layers of abstraction linked by clearly defined interfaces.

FIGURE 1.4
Two black boxes communicate through a shared interface.

A Modern Operating System's Primary Services

Another advantage of the layered approach is that it gives you the ability to focus on the contents of a given layer while essentially ignoring the other layers. For example, by exploding (adding detail to) the application program layer, you can clearly show that an operating system can support multiple application programs (Figure 1.5).

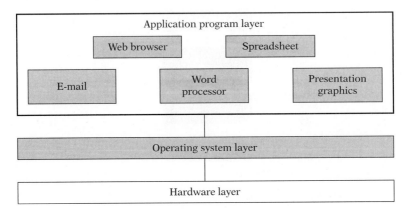

FIGURE 1.5

An operating system can support many application programs.

Similarly, it is possible to explode the operating system layer and iden-tify the operating system's primary services (Figure 1.6). The **user interface**, sometimes called the **shell**, provides a mechanism for the user and applica-tion programs to communicate with the operating system and request oper-ating system support. An operating system's file management and device management functions are closely related. The **file management** function, sometimes called the **file system**, incorporates routines that allow the user or programmer to create, delete, modify, and manipulate files logically, by name. The **device management** function is responsible for controlling communications with the system's physical peripheral devices, such as the keyboard, the display screen, the printer, and secondary storage.

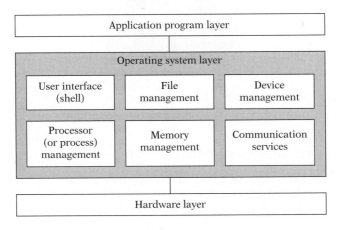

FIGURE 1.6

A modern operating system contains these primary components.

An operating system's processor and memory management functions are more transparent to the user. **Processor** (or **process**) **management** is concerned with efficiently managing the processor's time. **Memory management** is concerned with managing the system's memory resources as the computer runs, allocating space to applications as needed and ensuring that those applications do not interfere with each other.

Inter-layer and Intralayer Communication

You can also show how logic flows between layers and within a layer. For example, Figure 1.7 shows the steps required to carry out a user request to open a file. When the user clicks on the *Open* icon, the application program responds by calling the open routine in the operating system's shell. The shell passes the open file request down to the file management layer, which determines exactly where the requested file is located. If the file is on the local computer, the file management layer passes the request down to the device management layer, which communicates with the hardware layer.

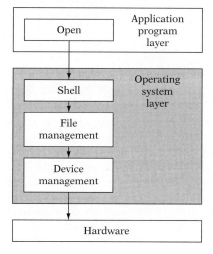

FIGURE 1.7

Opening a file.

Intercomputer Communication

In today's distributed computing environments, applications are often spread over two or more computers, with each computer performing part of the application task. Intercomputer communication is enabled by

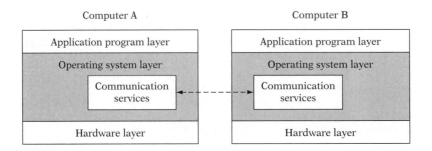

FIGURE 1.8
Intercomputer communication is enabled by communication services installed on both machines.

communication services software installed on both machines (Figure 1.8). Note that each of the two interconnected computers has its own operating system with its own shell, file management, device management, memory management, and processor management services. Note also that the same (or at least compatible) communication services must be installed on both computers.

Operating System Evolution

Operating systems have evolved over time, with new features constantly being added to reflect technological change. Often, those features begin as application programs, demonstrate their applicability to a variety of application and system tasks, gain popularity, and are absorbed into the operating system.

For example, the very first operating systems consisted of little more than collections of device management routines that supported input and output operations. Over time, creative programmers developed file management routines, and other programmers, recognizing the value of those routines, incorporated them into their own programs. Eventually, a set of standard file management routines emerged and joined the device management routines in the evolving operating system.

The evolutionary process continues today. Windows got its start as a shell that ran on top of MS-DOS, in effect as an application program. Today, the shell, Windows, has *become* the operating system, effectively absorbing MS-DOS. Similarly, Web browsers and communication support software started as application programs. Today the distinction between those routines and the operating system is hazy at best. Perhaps over the next several years, voice input will become commonplace. If that happens, voice recognition software is likely to migrate from application routine to operating system feature.

Assembling Systems

Breaking a given layer into sublayers helps to simplify system maintenance. Going the other way, plugging a given layer into higher-level layers is an excellent way to construct a complex system. For example, you have probably copied a spreadsheet into a slide presentation or copied a paragraph from an e-mail message into a word processing document. Such copy operations work because several application programs can run concurrently on the same operating system. Similarly, if you have ever exchanged e-mail messages or viewed a Web page, you know that your system can be plugged into other systems, literally worldwide. The layering concept is the key to understanding how systems are assembled and how they interact. Because each layer is functionally independent, stacking layers is like stacking building blocks. Understand layering and you understand the context in which the individual components and subassemblies operate.

Open Source and Proprietary Operating Systems

Throughout the balance of this book, you will study several different operating systems. Some, like UNIX and Linux, are **open source;** in other words, they are based on open, published source code that can be modified and improved by anyone. Many open source operating systems can run on virtually any computer. At the other extreme are **proprietary** operating systems such as the one that supports Apple's Macintosh computers. Proprietary operating systems are closed. For example, OS X is designed specifically to run on Macintosh computers and most of the underlying source code is accessible only to Apple's programmers.[1] Microsoft Windows is a bit of a hybrid; it runs on computers supplied by numerous vendors, but the operating system's source code is proprietary. The strengths and weaknesses of the open source and proprietary philosophies will be explored in subsequent chapters.

A Look Ahead

This book is divided into five parts. Part 1 (Chapters 2 through 4) covers a computer's basic hardware, software, and data resources, essentially exploring the contents of the application program and hardware layers. For

---

[1]OS X has one open source routine called darwin, but the rest of the operating system is proprietary.

some students, these three chapters will be largely review. Part 2 (Chapters 5 and 6) explains the essential functions performed by a modern operating system by exploding the operating system layer. Part 3 (Chapters 7 through 9) introduces the user interfaces and command languages for three well-known operating systems: MS-DOS, Windows XP, and UNIX/Linux. Part 4 (Chapters 10 through 15) explains how those three operating systems plus Macintosh OS X and IBM's traditional mainframe operating systems work internally. Finally, Part 5 (Chapters 16 through 21) investigates modern networks and intercomputer communication. Think of layering as the common thread that ties together all these topics.

◾ Summary

An operating system is a set of software routines that sits between the application program and the hardware and serves as a hardware/application software interface, acts as a repository for shared services, and defines a platform for constructing and executing application software. The operating system's environment can conveniently be viewed as a set of layers of abstraction, where each layer is an independent black box. A modern operating system incorporates a user interface or shell, file management routines (sometimes called the file system), device management routines, memory management routines, processor management routines, and communication services. Some operating systems are open source; others are proprietary; others are a hybrid of open source and proprietary.

◾ Key Words

abstraction	memory management
black box	open source
communication services	operating system
device management	platform
file management	processor or process management
file system	proprietary
independent	service
interface	shell
layering	user interface

Review Questions

1. Briefly, what is an operating system? What is an interface? Identify the operating system's interfaces.

2. What is a service?

3. The operating system is a convenient repository for common, shared routines. Why?

4. An operating system serves as a platform for constructing and running application programs. What does this mean and why is it important?

5. What is an abstraction? What is layering? How can viewing an information system as a set of layers of abstraction help you to better understand operating systems?

6. Describe Figure 1.1 as a set of independent layers of abstraction.

7. What is a black box? Relate the black box concept to the layering concept. Why is functional independence important?

8. List and briefly describe the primary services provided by a modern operating system.

9. What are communication services and why are they important?

10. Explain how a complex system can be constructed by plugging together a set of layers.

11. Distinguish between open source and proprietary.

Exercises

1. Identify the operating system that runs on your computer.

2. Study the application programs you use regularly and look for shared features. For example, it is likely that most if not all of the application programs that run on your system interpret such basic mouse operations as click, double click, and drag identically, include essentially the same set of commands on any of the drop down menus, and so on. Such common functions are likely to be performed by the operating system. Why does that make sense?

3. In your opinion, what multimedia applications or tasks, if any, might be candidates for inclusion in a near-future operating system?

4. Imagine that we really do learn how to inexpensively beam people and products from place to place as they do on Star Trek. How would that breakthrough affect the established transportation infrastructure? How would the resulting changes affect population patterns?

5. One factor that stands in the way of the widespread acceptance of such transportation alternatives as electric-powered automobiles is the established infrastructure for distributing gasoline. Explain why.

System Resources

This section overviews a computer's basic resources. Chapter 2 is an overview of a stand-alone computer's key hardware components, Chapter 3 discusses software and data, and Chapter 4 focuses on how those basic resources are linked. For some readers, at least of the material in Part 1 will be review. The intent of this section is to ensure that all readers begin with a strong technical foundation.

Hardware

When you finish reading this chapter you should be able to:

▶ Relate the terms bit, byte, and word.

▶ Explain how a computer's memory is addressed.

▶ Identify the key components of a processor.

▶ Explain what happens during a computer's basic machine cycle.

▶ Describe several common input and output devices and media.

▶ Briefly explain the process of reading data from or writing data to disk.

▶ Explain the purpose of a disk's directory.

▶ Distinguish between a simple microcomputer interface and the channels and control units used on mainframes.

▶ Explain the purpose of a buffer.

◾ Memory

This chapter focuses on key hardware layer components (Figure 2.1). We begin with memory.

A computer's **main memory** (henceforth, just **memory**) holds currently active programs and data. A program must be stored in memory before it can be executed. Data must be stored in memory before the computer can manipulate them, and all data input to and output from a computer must pass through memory.

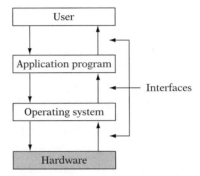

FIGURE 2.1

This chapter focuses on key hardware layer components.

Physical Memory Devices

A computer's memory holds binary digits, or **bits** (see Appendix A for a review of number system concepts). Almost any device that can assume either of two states (on, off) can serve as computer memory, but most computers use integrated circuit chips.

When you **read** memory, you extract the contents but you do not change them. When you **write** memory, in contrast, you record new values and thus destroy the old contents. Write is a "destructive" operation. Read is not destructive.

Most computer memory is random access memory (RAM). The programmer (through a program, of course) can read or write RAM; its contents are easy to change. Usually, this flexibility is an advantage. Sometimes, however, it makes sense to record key software or data in more permanent, read-only memory (ROM). As the name implies, ROM can be read, but not written.

Bytes and Words

A single bit can hold either a 0 or a 1. Generally, however, the contents of memory are envisioned as groups of bits called bytes and words. A **byte** contains enough bits (usually eight) to represent a single character. For example, the ASCII code for a capital A is 01000001. Within memory, the letter A would be stored by recording that bit pattern in a single byte (8 bits).

Bytes are fine for storing characters, but are too small to hold a meaningful number. Most computers are able to manipulate a group of bytes called a **word.** Some small computers have 8-bit words, but 16-bit (2-byte), 32-bit (4-byte), and even 64-bit word computers are more common.

Thus we have a memory hierarchy (Figure 2.2). The basic unit of storage is the bit. Bits are grouped to form bytes, which in turn are grouped to form words. In one application, a given word might hold a binary number. In another, that word's bytes might hold individual characters or a program instruction.

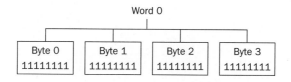

FIGURE 2.2

In a computer's memory, bits are grouped to form bytes, which in turn are grouped to form words.

Addressing Memory

Memory capacity is typically measured in megabytes (millions of bytes) or gigabytes (billions of bytes). To distinguish them, each byte (more generally, each physical storage unit) is assigned a unique **address.** On most computers, the bytes (or words) are numbered sequentially—0, 1, 2, and so on. The processor accesses a specific memory location by referencing its address.

For example, if the processor (the component that manipulates the data) needs the data stored in byte 1048, it asks memory for the contents of byte 1048. Since there is only one byte 1048, the processor gets the right data. Depending on the computer, bytes or words are the basic *addressable* units of memory. Data move between the processor and memory one byte or one word at a time.

Cache Memory

One way to increase processing speed is to move program instructions and data from memory to the processor more quickly. To help accomplish this objective, many computers contain a block of high-speed **cache** (pronounced "cash") **memory**. Think of cache as a staging area for the processor (Figure 2.3). The program is stored in standard RAM. As the program executes, the active instructions and the active data are transferred to high-speed cache memory. Subsequently, the individual instructions and the data referenced by those instructions move from cache to the processor. Thus, the processor waits for high-speed cache instead of slower RAM, and that increases processing speed.

If the relationship between main memory, cache, and the processor reminds you of layering, good.

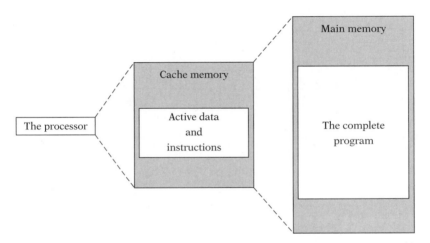

FIGURE 2.3

Think of cache memory as a staging area for the processor.

■ The Processor

The **processor,** often called the central processing unit (CPU) or main processor, is the component that manipulates data. A processor can do nothing without a program to provide control; whatever intelligence a computer has is derived from software, not hardware. The processor manipulates data stored in memory under the control of a program stored in memory (Figure 2.4).

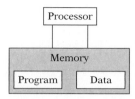

FIGURE 2.4

The processor manipulates data stored in memory under the control of a program stored in memory.

Program Instructions

A **program** is a series of **instructions** each of which tells the computer to perform one of its basic functions: add, subtract, multiply, divide, compare, copy, start input, or start output. Each instruction has an operation code and one or more operands (Figure 2.5). The operation code specifies the function to be performed, and the operands identify the memory locations or data that are to participate in the operation. For example, the instruction in Figure 2.5 tells the computer to add the contents of memory locations 1000 and 1004.

Operation code	Operands
ADD	*1000, 1004*

FIGURE 2.5

Each instruction has an operation code and one or more operands.

The Processor's Components

The processor contains four key components (Figure 2.6). The **instruction control unit** (ICU) fetches instructions from memory. The **arithmetic and logic unit** (ALU) holds or activates the computer's instruction set (the circuits that add, subtract, multiply, and so on) and executes instructions. **Registers** are temporary storage devices that hold control information, key data, and intermediate results. The **clock** (which typically occupies a separate chip of its own) generates precisely timed electronic pulses that synchronize the other components.

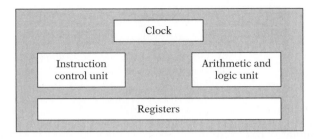

FIGURE 2.6
The processor contains four key components.

Machine Cycles

A good way to understand how a computer's internal components work together to execute instructions is to use a model of a simple computer system (Figure 2.7a) to illustrate a few **machine cycles.** Start with the processor. In addition to the clock, it contains an instruction control unit, an arithmetic and logic unit, and several registers, including an instruction counter, an instruction register, and a work register called the accumulator. The computer's other major component, memory, holds program instructions and data values. Note that each memory location is assigned an address.

The process starts when the clock generates a pulse of current that activates the instruction control unit (ICU). The ICU's job is to decide what the machine will do next. The computer is controlled by program instructions, which are stored in memory. The address of the next instruction to be executed is always found in the instruction counter (Figure 2.7a). (*Note:* The operating system places the address of a program's first instruction in the instruction counter when the program is launched or started.) The instruction control unit checks the instruction counter, finds the address, fetches the next instruction, and puts it into the instruction register (Figure 2.7b). Fetching an instruction from memory takes time, giving the instruction control unit an opportunity to increment the instruction counter to point to the next instruction (Figure 2.7b, again).

Once the fetch operation is complete, the instruction control unit activates the arithmetic and logic unit, which executes the instruction (in this case, a copy instruction) found in the instruction register (Figure 2.7c). Following execution of the instruction, a data value is copied from memory to the accumulator register.

Once again, the clock "ticks," activating the instruction control unit and starting the next machine cycle (Figure 2.7d). Referring to the instruction counter, the instruction control unit fetches the next instruction and copies it into the instruction register (Figure 2.7e). Once again, note that the instruction register now points to the *next* instruction.

The arithmetic and logic unit gets control and executes the instruction found in the instruction register (Figure 2.7f). As a result, a data value from memory is added to the accumulator. The next clock pulse once again activates the instruction control unit. As before, the instruction counter points to the next instruction. As before, this instruction is fetched into the instruction register. As before, the instruction control unit then activates the arithmetic and logic unit, which executes the instruction.

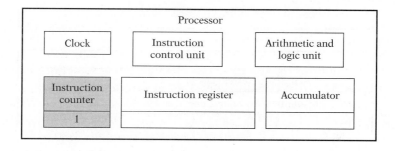

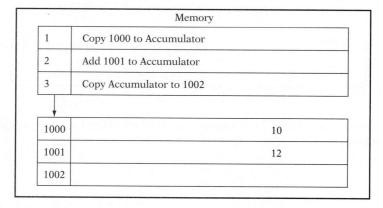

FIGURE 2.7

A computer executes instructions by following a basic machine cycle.

a. As the example begins, memory holds both program instructions and data. The instruction counter points to the first instruction to be executed.

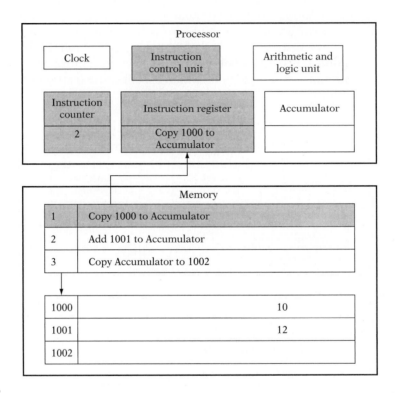

FIGURE 2.7

b. The first instruction is fetched from memory and stored in the instruction register. Note that the instruction counter points to the *next* instruction.

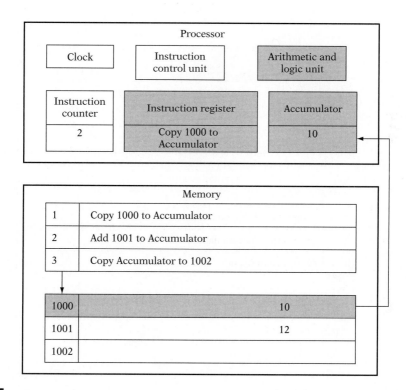

FIGURE 2.7

c. The arithmetic and logic unit executes the instruction in the instruction register.

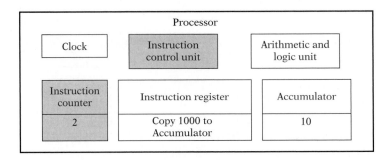

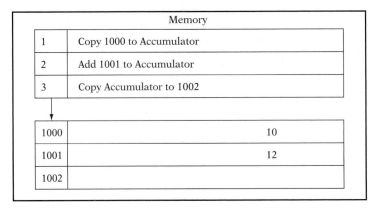

FIGURE 2.7

d. The instruction control unit once again looks to the instruction counter for the address of the next instruction.

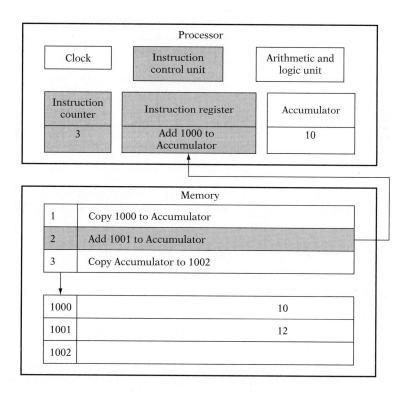

FIGURE 2.7

e. The next instruction is fetched into the instruction register. Note that the instruction counter points to the *next* instruction.

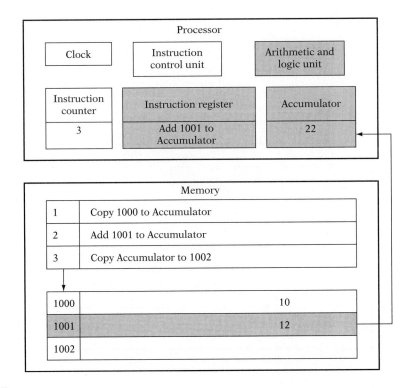

FIGURE 2.7

f. The arithmetic and logic unit executes the instruction in the instruction register.

An instruction is fetched by the instruction control unit during **I-time** or **instruction time** and executed by the arithmetic and logic unit during **E-time** or **execution time.** Together, both steps make up a single machine cycle (Figure 2.8). This process is repeated over and over again until the program is finished. The clock drives the process by generating pulses at precisely timed intervals. The rate at which those clock pulses are generated determines the computer's operating speed. Clock speed is typically expressed in megahertz (MHz) (millions of cycles per second) or gigahertz (GHz) (billions of instructions per second). For example, a 1.5 gigahertz processor is driven by a 1.5 gigahertz clock that "ticks" 1.5 billion times per second and thus is theoretically capable of executing 1.5 billion instructions per second. Actual processing speed is typically less than this theoretical limit, however, because many instructions need more than a single machine cycle to execute.

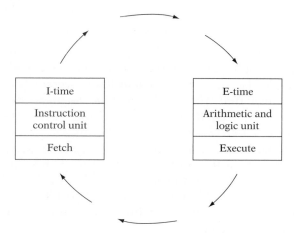

FIGURE 2.8

During a single machine cycle, an instruction is fetched by the instruction control unit during I-time and executed by the arithmetic and logic unit during E-time.

Coprocessors

Some computers contain more than one processor. A **coprocessor** is a special-purpose processor that assists the main processor on certain operations. For example, a math coprocessor performs floating-point computations, and a graphics coprocessor manipulates graphic images.

Moore's Law

In 1965, Gordon Moore, cofounder of Intel Corporation, observed that the number of transistors on an integrated circuit chip doubled roughly every eighteen months. Because the speed of a processor chip and the storage capacity of a memory chip are directly related to the number of transistors on the chip, his observation, which has become known as Moore's Law, suggested that both processing speed and memory capacity would double every eighteen months, and that's pretty much what happened. Most experts expect Moore's Law to hold true for at least the near future.

◼ Microcode

Computer hardware is typically designed as a set of interconnected layers. For example, on many computers a layer of **microcode,** sometimes called firmware, lies between memory and the processor (Figure 2.9). The arithmetic and logic unit works with machine-language instructions, which are subsequently translated into lower-level microinstructions before they are executed by the processor. Because the microcode insulates the software from the hardware, hardware changes can be accommodated without affecting the operating system or the application software. In some cases, key operating system routines are actually implemented in microcode to improve efficiency. Additionally, microcode is relatively difficult to "clone," and that can give a company with a successful architecture a significant competitive advantage.

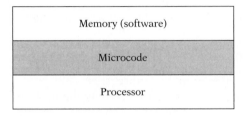

FIGURE 2.9
A layer of microcode lies between memory and the processor.

◼ Input and Output Devices

Input and output devices provide a means for people to access a computer. The basic **input** devices on most personal computer systems are a keyboard and a mouse. As characters are typed, they are stored in memory and then copied from memory to the basic **output** device, a display screen. In effect, the screen serves as a window on memory, allowing the user to view selected contents. Traditionally, display units have relied on cathode ray tube (CRT) technology, but flat-panel LCD (liquid crystal display) screens are becoming increasingly popular as they drop in price.

The image displayed on a screen is temporary; it fades as soon as the power is cut. By routing the output to a printer, a permanent copy (called a hard copy) is obtained. Computers are not limited to displaying characters, of course; graphic output is possible, too. Laser and ink jet printers are popular tools for generating hard copy text and graphic output in both color and black and white.

Several common input media rely on magnetic properties. For example, the characters on the bottom of most checks are printed with a type of magnetic ink called MICR (magnetic ink character recognition) that can be read electronically. On a magnetic strip card, the strip of magnetic tape holds such data as a customer's account number and credit limit, and is read much like sound recording tape. A smart card uses an embedded integrated circuit chip to hold data.

Other media are read optically. For example, consider standardized test forms. Students use a black pencil to mark their answers. The white paper reflects light; the black spots reflect much less; and variations in the intensity of the reflected light can be converted to an electronic pattern. OCR (optical character recognition) equipment uses the same principle to read typed or even handwritten material. Bar codes, such as the Universal Product Code (UPC) printed on most retail items, can be scanned at a checkout station. General-purpose scanners are used to convert a hard copy to a bit pattern that can be manipulated by a computer. Special software can be used to convert the bit patterns that represent a printed page into discrete characters.

Perhaps the most natural way of communicating with a computer is by voice. Voice response (output) is already common. Because of the tremendous variety of human speech patterns, voice recognition (input) is much more difficult to achieve, but increased processing speeds have already moved applications featuring limited voice recognition into the mainstream.

Many modern computer applications utilize multimedia, mixing text, graphics, sound, animations, and other elements to form an integrated, interactive environment. Not too many years ago, such processor- and memory-intensive applications would have been impossible, but increased processing speeds and memory capacities have made them common. Today, most computers are sold with sophisticated sound systems, advanced graphics features, and other multimedia tools, and electronic gamers often enhance their systems with special joysticks and even tactile feedback devices. In many ways, multimedia represent the state of the information technology art.

■ Secondary Storage

There are numerous problems with RAM. For one thing, although cost continues to decline, it is relatively expensive and the supply on most machines, though substantial, is limited. The big problem, however, is volatility; RAM loses its contents when the power is cut.

Secondary storage is a fast, accurate, inexpensive, high-capacity, non-volatile extension of main memory. Note, however, that a computer cannot execute a program on secondary storage unless it is first copied into memory, nor can it manipulate the data stored on a secondary medium until they have been copied into memory. Main memory holds the current program and the current data. Secondary storage is long-term storage. The input and output devices described earlier in this chapter provide human access to the computer system; taken together, they are sometimes called the computer's front end. Secondary storage is a machine-readable medium. Data are stored in a form convenient to the computer, and can be read and written only by the machine. Taken together, a computer's secondary storage devices form its back end. The only way people can access the data stored on secondary storage is by instructing the computer to read the data into memory and then write the data to the screen (or some other output device).

Magnetic Disk

Most computers incorporate a **disk,** or **hard disk,** for storing software and data. The storage capacity of a hard disk is typically measured in gigabytes (billions of bytes). The data on a disk are recorded on a series of concentric circles called tracks (Figure 2.10). The tracks are subdivided into sectors,

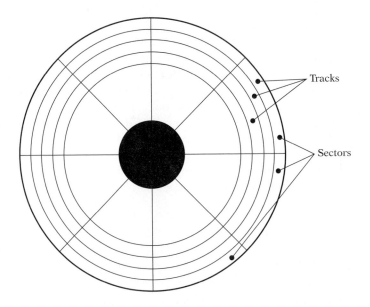

FIGURE 2.10

The data on a disk are recorded on a series of concentric circles called tracks. The tracks are subdivided into sectors.

and it is the contents of a sector that move between the disk's surface and memory. To distinguish the sectors, they are addressed by numbering them sequentially—0, 1, 2, and so on.

When a *read disk* instruction is executed, the processor sends a control signal to the drive. In response, the access mechanism is moved to the track that holds the desired data (Figure 2.11a). The time required to position the access mechanism is called seek time. Data are transferred between the diskette and memory a sector at a time, and the desired sector may be anywhere on the track. The time required for the sector to rotate to the access mechanism (Figure 2.11b) is called rotational delay. The time that elapses between the processor's initial request for data and the actual start of data transfer (in effect, the sum of seek time and rotational delay) is called latency.

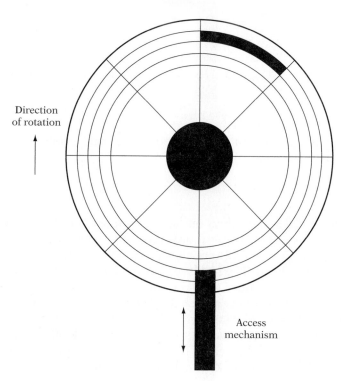

FIGURE 2.11

Reading a sector from disk.

a. During seek time the access mechanism is positioned over the track that holds the desired data.

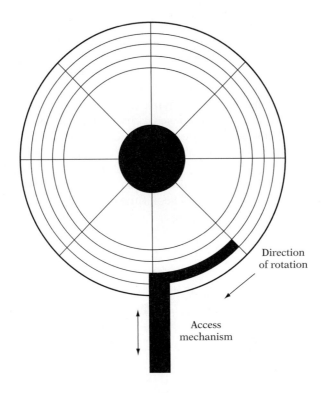

Direction
of rotation

Access
mechanism

FIGURE 2.11
b. The system waits while the sector rotates to the read/write head (rotational delay) and the data are transferred into memory.

Most hard disks store data on both the upper and lower surface, and disk packs consisting of two or more recording surfaces stacked on a common drive shaft (Figure 2.12) are also available. Typically, each surface has its own read/write head. The heads are arrayed on a single, comblike access mechanism, so they all move together. Imagine, for example, that the access mechanism is positioned over track 30. The top read/write head will access track 30 on surface 0. Moving down, surface by surface, the second head will be over track 30 on surface 1, the third over track 30 on surface 2, and so on. One position of the access mechanism corresponds to one track on each surface. This set of tracks is called a cylinder.

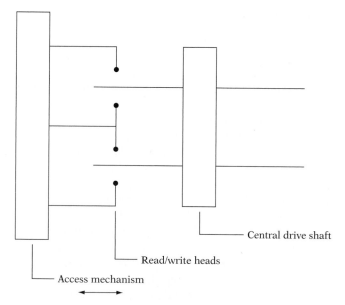

FIGURE 2.12

Each surface on a disk pack has its own read/write head.

Usually, the tracks are divided into fixed-length sectors. Data move between the disk's surface and the computer's memory a sector at a time. However, some hard disks, particularly on large mainframes, are track addressed, with tracks subdivided into physical records or blocks. A physical record can be any length, from a single byte to a full track; the physical record length (or block size) is chosen to fit the application. On such systems, data are transferred between secondary storage and memory a block at a time.

Backup

Given the tremendous capacity of a hard disk, losing one, through human error, fire, flood, or similar disaster, can destroy a great deal of important data. Consequently, it is crucial that the contents of a disk be regularly backed up, usually by copying them to some other secondary medium. Should a disk be lost, the **backup** copy is used to restore its contents.

Other Secondary Media

A **diskette** is a thin circular piece of flexible polyester coated with a magnetic material. Diskettes are typically used to store backup copies of files and to transfer data and software from one computer to another. A double density diskette holds 720 KB of data; a high-density diskette holds 1.44 MB. These capacities are fine for text files, but modern multimedia (particularly graphics and sound) applications generate very large files that may not fit on a diskette. Consequently, high-capacity alternatives to standard diskettes, such as CD-ROM (Compact Disk, Read-Only Memory), CD-R (CD-Read), CD-RW (CD-Read/Write), and DVD (Digital Video Disk) disks, are gaining popularity. Jaz disks and zip disks are removable, diskette-like media with considerably greater storage capacities. Except for CD-ROM,which is a read-only medium, all these media can be used for backup and to transfer data and software between computers.

Magnetic tape (similar to reel-to-reel or cassette recording tape) is a common backup medium. Accessed through high-speed drives, tape is fast, with data transfer rates comparable to disk. Its storage capacity is quite high, and a reel of tape is inexpensive. Unfortunately, data can be read or written only in a fixed sequence, which limits tape to a few applications.

Longevity

Sumerian cuneiform and Egyptian hieroglyphics have existed in readable form for millennia. The Gutenberg Bible was printed in the mid-1400s, and readable copies still exist over five hundred years later. Unfortunately, not all electronic storage media have exhibited such longevity.

In the early 1980s, a mere two decades ago, 5.25-inch floppy disks were the de facto personal computer secondary storage standard. As we enter the twenty-first century, try finding a computer that can read, much less interpret the contents of, a 5.25-inch floppy disk. Floppy disks were replaced by 3.5-inch diskettes, but not all computers can read a 3.5-inch diskette anymore. Today's personal computers store information on CD-ROM, CD-R, CD-RW, and DVD. How confident are you that you will be able to read those media twenty years from now?

The Directory

Because of its storage capacity, a typical hard disk holds thousands of programs and/or the data for hundreds of different applications. If you are a computer user, however, you want a particular program, and you want to access a particular data file. How does the computer find the right program or the right data?

Start by reviewing how data are stored on disk. The surface is divided into tracks, which in turn are divided into sectors or blocks. The tracks are numbered sequentially. The outer track is 0. Moving toward the disk's center, the next track is 1, then 2, and so on. The sectors (or blocks) on a track are also numbered sequentially starting with 0. Track 5, sector 8 is a particular sector; track 5, sector 9 is a different sector; and track 6, sector 8 is yet another one. Each sector has a unique track/sector address.

Depending on the operating system, when a file is stored on disk it is either recorded in consecutive sectors (or blocks) or its sectors are in some way linked sequentially. Consequently, if the computer can find the file's first sector, it can find the entire file. To record the starting address of each of its files, a portion of the disk's first track is set aside to hold a **directory** (Figure 2.13). When the file is first written to disk, it is assigned a name. The file's name is then recorded in the directory, along with the track and sector (or track and block) address where it begins. Later, to retrieve the file, a user enters the file's name. Given a name, the computer reads the directory, searches the directory for the file name, extracts the file's start address, and reads the file.

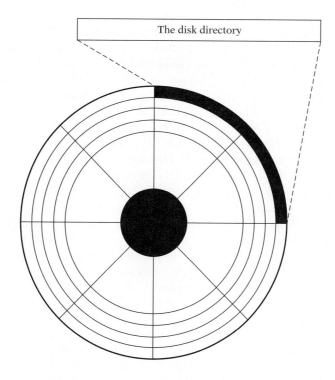

FIGURE 2.13

The programs and data files stored on a disk are listed in the disk's directory.

◨ Communication Hardware

Given the emergence of e-mail, Web browsing, and other online activities, most modern computers come equipped with communication hardware. Perhaps the most familiar device is a **modem** that allows the computer to communicate over standard telephone lines. Access to high-speed communication lines (such as cable) often calls for a **cable modem** or a network interface card (NIC). Typically, a modem, cable modem, or NIC is the computer's point of access to a network such as the Internet. You will examine networks and the Internet in depth in Part 5 of this text.

◨ Linking the Components

Data are stored in memory as patterns of bits. Within a given machine, the patterns are consistent; for example, if the code for the letter A is 01000001, this pattern, and only this pattern, will be used to represent an A.

The rule does not apply to input, output, or secondary storage devices, however. On a keyboard, each key generates one character. A laser printer represents characters as patterns of dots. An optical device reads light intensity, while a disk drive records and reads magnetized spots. Each peripheral device represents or interprets data in its own unique way, and the signals used by a device may or may not match the signals stored inside the computer. If these dissimilar devices are to communicate, translation is necessary. That is the function of an **interface** board.

Consider, for example, a keyboard. When a key is pressed, an electronic signal is sent to the keyboard's interface. In response, the interface generates the code that represents the character inside the computer, and transfers the coded data into memory (Figure 2.14a). Change the device to a printer (Figure 2.14b). As output begins, the data are stored in memory as binary-coded characters. Assume the printer requires a dot pattern. The coded characters are sent to the printer's interface, which translates the computer's binary codes to printer form.

The printer and the keyboard are different; the signals that physically control them and the electronic patterns they use to represent data are device-dependent. However, because the device-dependent tasks are assigned to the respective interface boards, both can be attached to the same computer. On input, an interface translates external signals into a

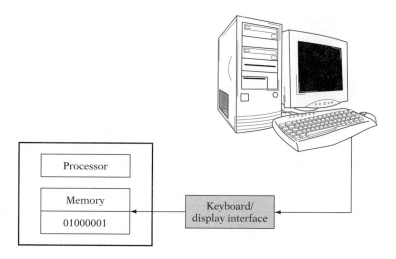

FIGURE 2.14

The functions of an interface board.

a. Input from the keyboard is converted to the computer's internal form by the keyboard/display interface.

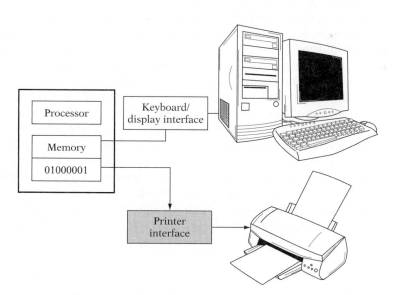

b. Data stored in memory are sent to the printer interface, converted to printer form, and output.

form acceptable to the computer. Output signals are electronically converted from the computer's internal code to a form acceptable to the peripheral device. Because they are electronically different, a printer and a keyboard require different interface boards.

Secondary storage devices are linked to the system through interfaces, too. The interface physically controls the disk drive, accepting seek, read, and write commands from the processor, positioning the access mechanism, and managing the flow of data between the disk surface and memory. Because the disk drives attached to a given computer are virtually identical, a single interface often controls two or more drives.

Many interfaces contain buffers. A **buffer** is temporary memory or storage used to adjust for the speed differential between adjacent devices. For example, if you have ever waited for a lengthy paper to print, you know that a printer is much slower than a computer. If waiting for the printer is a problem, add a buffer to your printer interface. Then, instead of the computer sending the contents of memory directly to the printer, it can send the information to the buffer at computer speed. Subsequently, as the characters are dumped from the buffer to the printer at printer speed, you can use the computer for some other task.

Assigning one interface to each device is reasonable on a microcomputer system. However, on a large system with hundreds of peripherals, this approach is simply unworkable. Instead, input and output devices are linked to a large computer system through channels and control units.

Certain functions (for example, deciding where the next byte can be found or stored in memory and counting the characters transferred to or from an external device) are common to almost all types of input and output. On a microcomputer, they are performed by each interface; in effect, they are duplicated for each device on the system. On larger machines, these common functions are assigned to data **channels** (Figure 2.15).

Note that a channel handles device-independent functions. What about such device-dependent functions as interpreting magnetic patterns or moving a disk's access mechanism? They are implemented through **I/O control units** or interface units. Each physical device has its own control unit. The channel communicates with the computer in the computer's language; the control unit communicates with the external device on the device's terms; the channel and the control unit, working together, translate.

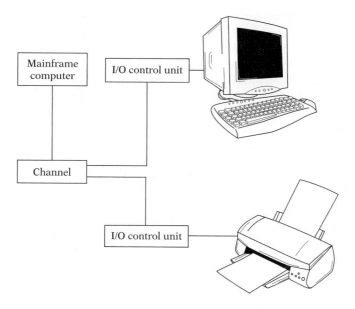

FIGURE 2.15

On a mainframe, peripheral devices are linked to the system through a channel and an I/O control unit.

▇ Summary

A computer's memory holds active programs and data. Memory is grouped into bytes, or words, or both, and each basic storage unit is assigned an address. Using this address, the processor can read or write selected bytes or words. High-speed cache memory serves as a staging area for the processor.

The processor consists of a clock, an instruction control unit, an arithmetic and logic unit, and registers. During I-time, the instruction control unit fetches an instruction from memory; during E-time, the arithmetic and logic unit executes that instruction. Precisely timed electronic pulses generated by the clock drive this basic machine cycle. Some computers contain coprocessors.

People access a computer through its input and output devices. The chapter briefly reviewed several common input and output devices and media.

Data are stored on a disk's surface on a series of concentric circles called tracks. The tracks are subdivided into sectors. On input, the contents of one sector are copied from disk to memory; on output, one sector is copied from memory to the disk's surface. To access disk, it is first necessary to move the access mechanism over the track containing the desired data (seek time). Additional time is lost waiting for the desired sector to rotate to the read/write head (rotational delay). Often, several surfaces are stacked on a single drive shaft to form a disk pack.

Because data are so valuable, disks are normally backed up. Diskettes, CD-R, CD-RW, and DVD disks are used to store backup copies of files and to transfer data and software from one computer to another. Magnetic tape is a common backup medium. A single disk can contain numerous programs and data files. The disk's directory identifies the programs and data files and indicates the disk address where each one begins. Most modern computers incorporate such communication devices as a modem, a cable modem, or a network interface card.

Each peripheral device is electronically different, but internally the computer always deals with a common code. An interface serves to bridge this gap. A buffer can help to adjust for the speed differential between adjacent devices. On larger computers, each peripheral device is linked to a control unit, the control units are plugged into channels, and the channels are connected to the computer.

▌ Key Words

address	instruction
arithmetic and logic unit	instruction control unit
backup	interface
bit	I-time (instruction time)
buffer	machine cycle
byte	main memory
cable modem	memory
cache memory	microcode
channel	modem
clock	output
control unit (I/O)	processor
coprocessor	program
directory	read (memory)
disk	register
diskette	secondary storage
E-time (execution time)	word
hard disk	write (memory)
input	

▌ Review Questions

1. Distinguish between reading and writing memory. Distinguish between ROM and RAM.
2. Distinguish between physical memory and its contents.
3. Distinguish bits, bytes, and words.
4. How is a computer's memory addressed? Why is addressing memory important?
5. What is cache memory? Why is cache memory used?
6. Explain what happens during a computer's basic machine cycle.
7. What is a coprocessor? Why are coprocessors needed?
8. What is microcode?
9. How are input/output and secondary storage devices similar? How are they different?
10. Why is secondary storage necessary?
11. Distinguish cylinders, tracks, and sectors.
12. Briefly explain the process of reading data from or writing data to disk.
13. Why is it so important to back up the contents of a disk?
14. Identify several secondary storage media other than hard disk.
15. What is the purpose of a disk's directory? Why is it needed?
16. What is the purpose of an interface? Why are interfaces needed?
17. What is a buffer? Why are buffers used?
18. Distinguish between a microcomputer interface and the channel/control unit architecture used on mainframes. How are they similar? How are they different?
19. Why do computer manufacturers use channels and control units instead of simple interface boards on large computer systems?

▌ Exercises

1. Draw a sketch showing the key components of a processor. Add blocks representing memory, a program, and data.
2. Open a computer and investigate its internal contents. Compare your observations to the sketch you drew in Exercise 1.
3. Exercise 1 asked you to sketch a computer's internal components. Add channels, control units, I/O devices, and secondary storage devices to your sketch.
4. Compile a list of the I/O devices, secondary storage devices, and other peripherals on your computer.
5. A computer is a binary machine. What does that statement mean?
6. Investigate how typical processor speeds have changed over the past decade. Do your results confirm or conflict with Moore's Law?

7. Relate microcode to the layering concept.

8. Why do you suppose that modern secondary storage media have such a short shelf life? Can you think of strategies you might try to overcome that problem?

9. If you have access to a computer running Microsoft Windows, double-click the *My Computer* icon and view the contents of selected folders. Where do you suppose the computer finds the information it displays?

10. There are 35 key words at the end of Chapter 2, and you will find subsequent chapters to be equally rich in terminology. If you are tempted to look up the definitions of each of those key words and memorize all those definitions, you will quickly exceed the capacity of your short-term memory. A better strategy is to visualize the terms in the context of a two-dimensional model; for this chapter, Figure 2.7a is a good candidate. Once you have selected a diagram, go through the list of key terms and write each one where it best fits. Skip unfamiliar terms on the first pass. Then go back for a second pass; you'll be surprised how many of the remaining terms seem to fall into place, effectively defined by related terms. If a term is still unfamiliar, reread the relevant text discussion. When you finish, your diagram will give you a context for understanding the technology. Use the same strategy to structure the key terms at the end of subsequent chapters.

CHAPTER 3

Application Software and Data

When you finish reading this chapter you should be able to:

▶ Explain how an assembler, a compiler, an interpreter, and a nonprocedural language differ and how they are similar.

▶ Distinguish between traditional structured software and object-oriented software.

▶ Define the terms object, method, encapsulation, signal, and operation.

▶ Define the terms source code, object module, and load module.

▶ Explain the purpose of an application programming interface (API).

▶ Define data element and data structure. Identify a list, a linked list, a stack, and a queue.

▶ Relate characters, fields, records, and files.

▶ Explain the relative record concept.

▶ Distinguish between sequential and direct (or random) access.

▶ Discuss the advantages derived from using a database.

◼ Hardware, Software, and Data

A computer is a machine (hardware) that processes data under control of a stored program (software). All three elements—hardware, data, and software—must be present or the system cannot function. This chapter focuses on application software and the data processed by that software within the application program layer (Figure 3.1). Hardware (Chapter 2) is physical. Software and data, in contrast, are logical; they consist of nothing more substantial than electronic patterns stored on the hardware in binary form. One pattern of bits might represent a machine-level instruction (software). Another might hold an ASCII coded character, a binary integer, or a floating-point number (data). Thus, it makes sense to group software and data together.

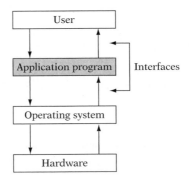

FIGURE 3.1
This chapter focuses on the application program layer.

◼ Software

A **program** is a series of instructions that guides a computer through a process. Each **instruction** tells the machine to perform one of its basic functions: add, subtract, multiply, divide, compare, copy, request input, or request output. The processor fetches and executes a single instruction during each machine cycle. A typical instruction (Figure 3.2) contains an operation code that specifies the function to be performed and one or more operands that specify the memory locations or registers that hold the data to be manipulated. For example, the instruction

AR 3,4

tells a hypothetical computer to add the contents of registers 3 and 4.

Operation code	Operands
AR	3,4

FIGURE 3.2

A typical instruction contains an operation code and one or more operands.

Because a computer's instruction set is so limited, even simple logical operations call for multiple instructions. For example, imagine two data values stored in memory. To add them on many computers, both values are first loaded (or copied) into registers, the registers are added, and then the answer is stored (or copied) back into memory. That's four instructions: LOAD, LOAD, ADD, and STORE. If four instructions are needed to perform a simple add operation, imagine the number of instruction in a complex program.

A computer runs under the control of a program stored in its own memory. Because memory stores bits, it follows that a program stored in memory must be in binary form. Figure 3.3 shows the binary, machine-level instructions needed to load two numbers into registers, add them, and store the answer in memory. If programmers had to write in **machine language** there would be very few programmers.

```
0101100000110000
1100000000000000
0101100001000000
1100000000000100
0001101000110100
0101000000110000
1100000000001000
```

FIGURE 3.3

The binary, machine-level instructions needed to add two numbers.

Absolute and Relative Addressing

A computer's memory is addressed by numbering the bytes sequentially—0, 1, 2, and so on up to the total number of bytes in memory. Hardware works with these **absolute addresses,** fetching and storing the contents of individual bytes by referencing their byte numbers.

Absolute addresses are not convenient for software, however. A program that references absolute addresses must be loaded in exactly the same place in memory every time it runs. Additionally, absolute addresses tend to be lengthy. For example, a 32-bit word computer might use 32-bit addresses. A typical instruction contains an operation code plus two addresses (for example, the locations of the two data values to be added), and if those addresses are expressed in absolute terms, a single instruction on a 32-bit word computer would be over 64 bits long. Such lengthy instructions tend to produce huge programs.

An alternative is to use relative addresses. A **relative address** is an address expressed relative to some base location. For example, a program routine might be written as though its first byte (usually, its entry point) is address 0, with every other location in the routine expressed as an offset or **displacement** from that starting point. When the routine is subsequently loaded into memory, the absolute address of its entry point is stored in a register, thus establishing a **base address** for the routine. Before a given instruction is executed, hardware (during the I-time portion of each machine cycle) adds each relative address (the displacement) to the base address (which is stored in a register) to get the equivalent absolute address. The process of converting a relative address to an absolute address is called **dynamic address translation.**

Relative addressing achieves two objectives. First, it allows a routine to be relocated in memory—in other words, to be loaded into a different location in memory each time it runs. Because every location in the routine is expressed relative to the entry point and the actual entry point address is stored in a base register, it is always possible to compute a given byte's absolute address by adding the entry point address to the displacement. Second, because only the displacement portion of the address must be stored in the instruction, fewer bits are required to hold each address, yielding smaller instructions and, hence, smaller programs.

Programming Languages

One option to writing programs in machine language is to use an **assembler language**. For example, Figure 3.4 shows how two numbers might be added using an IBM mainframe assembler language. The programmer writes one mnemonic (memory aiding) instruction for each machine-level instruction. AR (for add registers) is much easier to remember than the equivalent binary operation code: 00011010. L (for load) is much easier to remember than 01011000. The operands use labels (such as A, B, and C) instead of numbers to represent *symbolic* memory addresses, and that simplifies the code, too. The assembler program assigns numeric relative addresses to the labels as part of the assembly process.

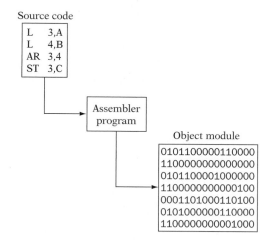

FIGURE 3.4

An assembler converts each source statement to a single machine-level instruction.

There are no computers that can directly execute assembler language instructions. Writing mnemonic codes may simplify the programmer's job, but computers are still binary machines and require binary instructions. Thus, translation is necessary. An assembler program (Figure 3.4) reads a programmer's **source code,** translates the source statements to binary, and produces an **object module.** Because the object module is a machine-level version of the programmer's code, it can be loaded into memory and executed.

An assembler language programmer writes one mnemonic instruction for each machine-level instruction. Because of this one-to-one relationship between the source code and the object code, assemblers are machine dependent, and a program written for one type of computer will not run on another. On a given machine, assembler language generates the most efficient programs possible, and thus an assembler often used to write operating systems and other system software routines. However, when it comes to application programs, machine dependency is a high price to pay for efficiency, so application programs are rarely written in assembler.

A computer needs four machine-level instructions to add two numbers because that's the way a computer works. Human beings should not have to think like computers. Why not simply allow the programmer to indicate addition and assume the other instructions? For example, one way to view addition is as an algebraic expression:

$$C = A + B$$

Why not allow a programmer to write statements in a form similar to algebraic expressions, read those source statements into a program, and let the program generate the necessary machine-level code (Figure 3.5)? That's exactly what happens with a **compiler.** Compare the binary instructions in Figures 3.4 and 3.5. They are identical.

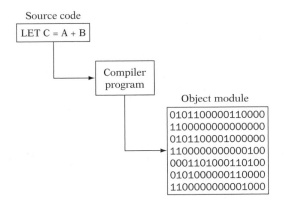

FIGURE 3.5

A compiler converts each source statement to one or more machine-level instructions.

Many compiler languages are algebraically based. In contrast, COBOL (Common Business Oriented Language) statements resemble brief English-language sentences. Note, however, that no matter what language is used, the objective is the same. The programmer writes source code. The assembler or compiler reads the source code and generates a machine-level object module.

With an assembler, each source statement is converted to a single machine-level instruction. With a compiler, a given source statement may be converted to any number of machine-level instructions. Note, however, that both assemblers and compilers read a complete source program and generate a complete object module. An **interpreter,** in contrast, works with one source statement at a time, reading it, translating it to machine-level, executing the resulting binary instructions, and then moving on to the next source statement. Each language has its own syntax, punctuation, and spelling rules, so a C source program is meaningless to a COBOL compiler or a BASIC interpreter. However, no matter what language is used, the objective is the same: defining a series of steps to guide the computer through a process.

With assemblers, compilers, and interpreters, the programmer defines a "procedure" that tells the computer exactly how to solve a problem.

However, with a nonprocedural language (sometimes called a fourth-generation or declarative language), the programmer simply defines the logical structure of the problem and lets the language translator figure out how to solve it. Examples include Prolog, Focus, Excel, and many others.

Layers of Abstraction

A machine language programmer writes binary object code, so the object code itself is the only possible source of application layer errors. In contrast, the compilation process adds at least two new layers of abstraction to the process of creating object code (Figure 3.6). Think of each of those layers as a possible source of error. In a compiled application, a programmer error might add a bug to the source code, the compiler might introduce an error by misinterpreting a source statement, and an electronic error of some kind might change a few object code bits.

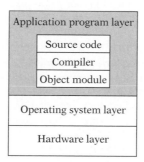

FIGURE 3.6

The compilation process adds two layers of abstraction to the application program layer.

If the source code and the compiler are potential sources of error, why not code in machine language? To answer that question, look back at Figure 3.5 and compare the source code to the string of binary digits that represent the equivalent object code. Then grab a sheet of paper and copy the bits. Are you really sure you got every bit right? Get one bit wrong and the program fails, so precision is crucial. The point is that writing binary machine language code is extremely difficult, very time consuming, and highly error prone.

Programmers find it much easier to write source statements such as LET C = A + B than the equivalent bit strings. As a result, they write their programs much more quickly and are much less likely to introduce errors into the source code. Ironically, in spite of the extra layers of abstraction, compiled object code almost always contains fewer bugs than the equivalent code written directly in machine language. Add significant productivity gains to improved quality and you can clearly see why most programs are written at the source code level.

Layers and Vulnerability

Imagine you are using an application program when an error occurs. Your first impulse is probably to assume that you did something wrong. Perhaps you selected the wrong option. Maybe you forgot to click the appropriate icon. Often, if you undo the operation and try it again you get the correct result.

Blaming yourself is a good strategy because it usually works, but what if redoing the task doesn't help? What if you are absolutely certain you did everything correctly but you still get that same error? Where else might the problem lie? To answer that question, just look at the layers summarized in Figure 3.6. The programmer might have overlooked a bug in the source code. If the source code is correct, an error could have been inserted into the object code by the compiler or by a hacker. The program might harbor a bad macro. There could be a bug in the operating system. Although they are extremely rare, errors are even possible down in the hardware layer.

Implementing software as a set of independent layers simplifies the task of correcting errors within a given layer. In fact, the ability to isolate errors to a single module or object is properly cited as a major advantage of layered approaches to program development. On the other hand, however, layering can significantly complicate the task of finding and correcting an error when the responsible layer is unknown, and the hidden nature of those "other" layers makes a computer system more vulnerable to attack because it gives the attacker places to hide. For example, the most destructive viruses tend to enter a system through the macro layer or the operating system layer, in part because the typical user is essentially unaware of what happens in those layers.

Structured Software

A **structured program** consists of a series of logical modules linked by a control structure (Figure 3.7). The idea is to achieve module independence by:

1. designing each module to perform a single, cohesive function,
2. assigning each module its own local data (data values known only within the module), and
3. linking the modules by passing between them the minimum number of global data elements (data known to all modules) necessary.

The existence of a pool of shared, global data serves to limit module independence, however, because an error that affects a global data value can ripple though numerous modules.

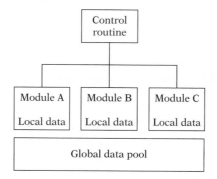

FIGURE 3.7
A structured program.

Object-Oriented Software

The basic idea of the **object-oriented** approach to software development is to design and write the software as a set of independent objects linked by signals. Many modern operating systems are object-oriented. Common object-oriented programming languages include C++, Java, and many others.

An **object** is a thing about which data are stored and manipulated. An object contains both data and **methods** (Figure 3.8). A method is a process that accesses and manipulates the object's data. The data form the core of the object. The only way other objects can access the object's data is through one of its methods. That makes the object highly independent. Hiding implementation details in this way is called encapsulation.

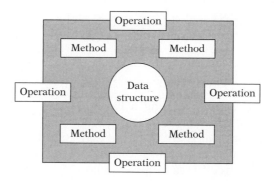

FIGURE 3.8
An object contains both data and methods.

Objects communicate by transmitting and responding to **messages,** where a message might contain a **signal** (information about an event or occurrence) or data. The messages are sent and received by entities called **operations.** An operation is an external view of the object that can be accessed by other objects. The methods hidden inside the object are private. Operations, in contrast, are public methods. Think of the object as a black box and the operation as a point of interface with other objects.

The objected-oriented approach tends to produce higher quality software because it reduces the risk of errors propagated throughout a program by erroneous global data. However, the object-oriented metaphor adds yet another layer of abstraction between the source code and the compiler (Figure 3.9).

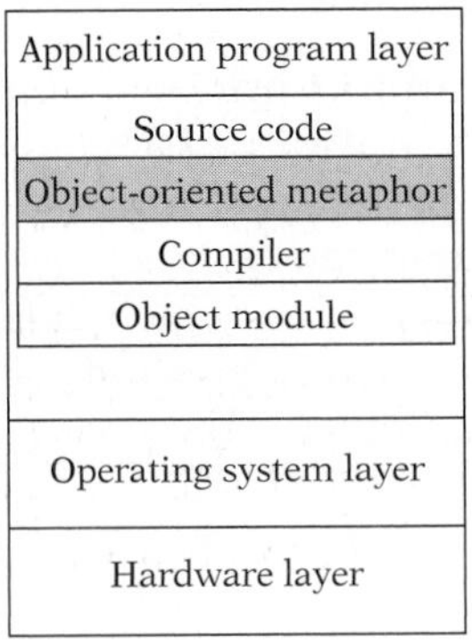

```
┌─────────────────────────────────┐
│ Application program layer       │
│  ┌───────────────────────────┐  │
│  │       Source code         │  │
│  ├───────────────────────────┤  │
│  │ Object-oriented metaphor   │  │
│  ├───────────────────────────┤  │
│  │        Compiler           │  │
│  ├───────────────────────────┤  │
│  │      Object module        │  │
│  └───────────────────────────┘  │
│                                 │
├─────────────────────────────────┤
│ Operating system layer          │
├─────────────────────────────────┤
│ Hardware layer                  │
└─────────────────────────────────┘
```

FIGURE 3.9

The object-oriented metaphor adds another layer of abstraction.

Libraries

Picture a programmer writing a large routine. As source statements are entered, they are manipulated by an editor program and stored on disk. Because large programs are rarely written in a single session, the programmer will eventually stop working and close the source file. Later, when work resumes, the source file is reopened and new source statements are added to the old ones. That same disk might hold other source programs and even routines written by other programmers. It's a good example of a source statement **library** (Figure 3.10).

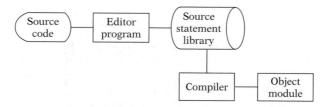

FIGURE 3.10
Source code is stored on a source statement library.

Eventually, the source program is completed and compiled. The result-ing object module might be loaded directly into memory, but more often, it is stored on an object module library (Figure 3.11). Because object modules are binary, machine-level routines, there is no inherent difference between one produced by an assembler, one produced by a COBOL compiler, and one produced by a C++ compiler, so object modules generated by different source languages can be stored on the same library.

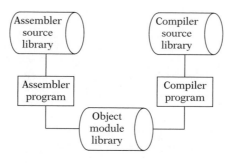

FIGURE 3.11
Object modules are stored on an object module library.

Some object modules can be loaded into memory and executed. Others, however, include references to subroutines that are not part of the object module. For example, imagine a program that simulates a game of cards. If, some time ago, another programmer wrote an excellent subroutine to deal cards, it would make sense to reuse that logic.

Picture the new program after it has been written, compiled, and stored on the object module library (Figure 3.12). The subroutine that deals cards is stored on the same library. Before the program is loaded, the two routines must be combined to form a **load module** (Figure 3.13). An object module is a machine-language translation of a source module that may include references to other (external) subroutines that are not part of the object module. A load module is a complete, ready to execute program with all subroutines in place. Combining object modules to form a load module is the job of the **linkage editor** (Figure 3.14). A linkage editor prepares a complete load module and copies it to a load module library for immediate or eventual loading and execution.

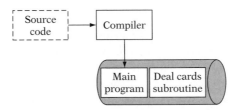

FIGURE 3.12
Object modules can contain references to external subroutines.

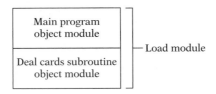

FIGURE 3.13
Before a program can be executed, the object modules for the main program and any external subroutines must be combined to form a load module.

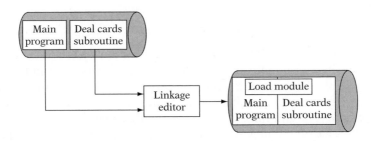

FIGURE 3.14
The linkage editor combines object modules to form a load module.

Reentrant Code

Many programs modify themselves as they run, changing key data values and even executable instructions. Imagine two users concurrently accessing the same program. Any attempt to share the code would be doomed because changes made by one user could have unforeseen consequences for the other. If the program can modify itself, there must be one copy in memory for each concurrent user.

A **reentrant** program or program module does *not* modify itself. Consequently, since the code does not change, two or more users can share the same logic. Often, the secret to creating reentrant code is breaking the program into two components: a logic segment and a data segment (Figure 3.15). The data segment belongs to an individual user, and can be modified as the program runs. The logic segment, on the other hand, consists of reentrant program instructions that cannot be changed. Given such segmentation, it is possible to assign each of several users their own data segments and allow them to share a single logic segment. Avoiding duplication of program logic can save a great deal of memory space.

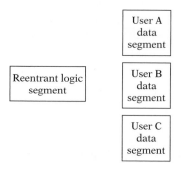

FIGURE 3.15

Using reentrant code, it is possible for several users to share the same logic segment.

An operating system is composed of system software modules that support application programs. On a large system, several applications might execute concurrently. It makes little sense to include multiple copies of the same support logic, so (almost by definition) an operating system contains a great deal of shared, reentrant code.

An Application Program's Interfaces

An application program sits between the user and the operating system (Figure 3.16). It communicates with the user through a user interface. For example, a word processing program's user interface allows you to enter data and manipulate icons, menus, and windows to request such services as open, create, edit, save, and print. The application program also communicates with the operating system through an operating system interface. In between the two interfaces is an application logic layer, sometimes called the business logic layer.

Almost by definition, you cannot effectively use an application program unless you are familiar with its user interface layer; in fact, learning a new application essentially means learning the program's user interface. The business logic and operating system interface layers are hidden, however, responding transparently, black box-like, to commands and data entered through the user interface.

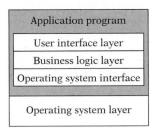

FIGURE 3.16
An application program's interfaces.

The Application Programming Interface (API)

An application program's user interface and application (or business) logic lie outside the scope of this book, but the program's interface with the operating system does not. Often, the interface with the operating system is implemented through an **application programming interface** or **API** (Figure 3.17). An API is a set of source-level functions and calling conventions. When the source code is compiled, each API reference is translated into a call to the appropriate operating system service. The API allows the programmer to view the various operating system services as black boxes and essentially ignore the details of how the service is performed, which simplifies programming and enhances **portability,** the ability to run the application program on multiple platforms.

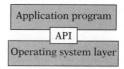

FIGURE 3.17
The application programming interface (API).

◼ Data

Like software, data are stored on hardware as patterns of bits. Simply storing the data is not enough, however. A typical computer system, even a small one, can have multiple disks each holding data for dozens of different applications, and for any given application, one and only one set of data will do. Additionally, data are often processed selectively, a few elements at a time, so it must be possible to distinguish the individual data elements, too. These are the primary concerns of data management.

Data Elements

A **data element** is a single, meaningful unit of data, such as a name, a social security number, or a temperature reading. Most computers can store and manipulate pure binary integers, floating-point numbers, decimal numbers, and character or string data. See Appendix A for a review of these data types.

Data Structures

The key to retrieving data is remembering where they are stored. If the data elements are stored according to a consistent and well understood structure, it is possible to retrieve them by remembering that data structure. The most basic **data structure** is a list (Figure 3.18). Each entry in the list is called a node, and each node holds a single data element. Lists are frequently used by operating systems.

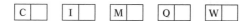

FIGURE 3.18
The most basic data structure is a list.

In a **linked list** (Figure 3.19), each node contains data plus a pointer to the next node. Note that the data items need not be stored in adjacent memory locations because the pointers define the list's logical order. To insert a node into a linked list, locate the prior node, change its pointer to the new node, and set the new node's pointer to the next node (Figure 3.20). To delete a node from a linked list, change the appropriate pointer to "jump over" the deleted node (Figure 3.21).

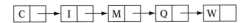

FIGURE 3.19

A linked list.

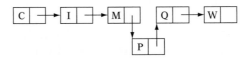

FIGURE 3.20

Inserting a node into a linked list.

FIGURE 3.21

Deleting a node from a linked list.

A **stack** (Figure 3.22) is a type of linked list in which all insertions and deletions occur at the top. Access to the stack is controlled by a single pointer. Because insertions and deletions occur only at the top, the last item added to the stack is the first item removed from the stack (last in, first out).

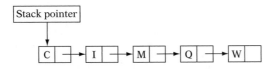

FIGURE 3.22

A stack is a type of linked list in which all insertions and deletions occur at the top.

A **queue** is a type of linked list in which insertions occur at the rear and deletions occur at the front. Access to a queue is controlled by two pointers (Figure 3.23), and the first item added to a queue is the first item removed (first in, first out).

Most programming languages support a more complex, spreadsheet-like data structure called an array. Each array element holds one data value. Each element is assigned a unique identifying number (or numbers), and individual data elements can be inserted, extracted, or manipulated by referencing those numbers.

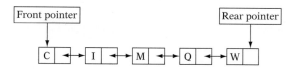

FIGURE 3.23

A queue is a type of linked list in which insertions occur at the rear and deletions occur at the front.

Data Files

Consider a program that generates name and address labels. Each label requires a name, a street address, a city, a state, and a zip code. A list structure might be adequate for a few labels, but separating the elements would soon become tedious. An option is setting up an array of names and addresses, with each row holding the data for a single label. The only problem is that the entire array must be in memory before the individual elements can be accessed, and memory space is limited.

A better solution is to organize the data as a **file** (Figure 3.24), perhaps the most familiar type of data structure. On a file, the data elements are called fields, a group of related fields forms a record, and the file is a set of related records. For example, in a name and address file, an individual's name is a field, each record holds a complete set of data for a single individual (a name, a street address, and so on), and the file consists of all the records.

The data in a file are typically processed record by record. Normally, the file is stored on a secondary medium such as disk. Programs are written to read a record, process its fields, generate the appropriate output, and then read and process another record. Because only one record is in memory at a time, relatively little memory is needed. Because many records can be stored on a single disk, a great deal of data can be processed in this limited space.

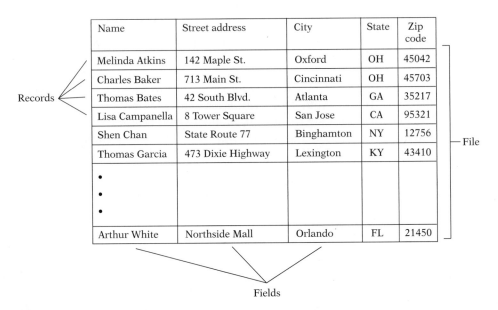

FIGURE 3.24
Fields are grouped to form records. A file is a set of related records.

Multimedia Files

Not all files are broken into records and fields. For example, multimedia files (sounds, pictures, graphic images) often contain a single logical entity such as a photograph or a sound track; see Appendix A for a list of common multimedia file formats. When an image file or an MP3 file is loaded from disk into memory, the entire file is transferred. In effect, the image or the sound track can be viewed as the file's only record.

The Relative Record Concept

Normally, however, the contents of a traditional data file are processed one record at a time. Often, the key to finding the correct record is the **relative record number.** Imagine a string of 100 records. Number the first one 0, the second 1, the third 2, and so on. The numbers indicate a given record's position relative to the first record in the file. The file's first record (relative record 0) is at "start of file plus 0," its second record is at "start of file plus 1," and so on.

Now, store the records on disk (Figure 3.25), one per sector. Number the sectors relative to the start of the file—0, 1, 2, and so on. Note that the relative record number (a logical concept) and the relative sector number (a physical location) are identical. Given a relative record number, it is possible to compute a relative sector number. Given a relative sector number, it is possible to compute a physical disk address.

Relative record 0	Relative record 1	Relative record 2	Relative record 3	Relative record 4

Relative sector   0   1   2   3   4

FIGURE 3.25

A relative record number indicates a record's position relative to the first record in the file.

Assume a file begins at track 30, sector 1, and that one logical record is stored in each sector. As Figure 3.26 shows, relative record 0 is stored at track 30, sector 1, relative record 1 is at track 30, sector 2, and so on. Note that the relative record number indicates how many sectors away from the beginning of the file the record is stored. The file starts at track 30, sector 1. Relative record 10 is stored 10 sectors away at track 30, sector 11. The one record per sector assumption is not realistic, but even with multiple records per sector it is possible to develop a simple algorithm to compute a record's physical location given its relative record number.

Relative record number	Actual disk address	
	Track	Sector
0	30	1
1	30	2
2	30	3
3	30	4
4	30	5
5	30	6
6	30	7
7	30	8
... and so on		

FIGURE 3.26

Given the start of file address and a relative record number, a physical disk address can be computed.

Not all data access techniques rely on relative record numbers; in fact, some computer experts consider the very concept of a record an unnecessary anachronism left over from punched card days. On many modern operating systems, most notably UNIX, there are no records. Instead, data stored on disk are treated as a simple strings of bytes, and no other structure is imposed. On such systems, programmers address data by relative byte number, the same way they address memory.

Access Techniques

Imagine preparing meeting announcements for a club. You need a set of mailing labels, and each member's name and address is recorded on an index card. Probably the easiest way to generate the labels is to pick up the first card and copy the data, turn to the second card and copy its data, and so on, processing the records sequentially, from the beginning of the file to the end.

Magazine publishers face the same problem with each new issue, but need mailing labels for tens of thousands of subscribers. Rather than using index cards, they store customer data on a secondary storage medium, one record per subscriber. The easiest way to ensure that all the labels are generated is to process the records in the order in which they are stored, proceeding sequentially from the first record in the file to the last. To simplify handling, the records might be presorted (by zip code or a mailing zone, for example), but the basic idea of processing the data in physical order still holds. A relative record number indicates a record's position relative to the start of the file. With **sequential access,** processing begins with relative record 0, then moves to relative record 1, 2, and so on. In other words, accessing data sequentially involves little more than counting.

Processing records in sequence is not always acceptable. For example, when a subscriber moves, his or her address must be changed. Searching for that subscriber's record sequentially is like looking for a telephone number by reading the telephone book line by line. That is not how you use a telephone book. Instead, knowing that the records are stored in alphabetical order, you use the index at the top of the page to quickly narrow your search to a portion of a single page and then begin reading the entries, ignoring the bulk of the data. The way you use a telephone book is a good example of **direct,** or **random, access.**

A disk drive reads or writes one sector at a time. To randomly access a specific record, all the programmer must do is remember the address of the sector that holds the record, and ask for it. The problem is remembering all those disk addresses. One solution is maintaining an index of the records. As a file is created, records are written to disk one at a time in relative record number order. Additionally, as each record is written, the record's key (a field that uniquely identifies the record) and the associated relative record number are recorded in an array or index (Figure 3.27). After the last record has been written to disk and its position recorded on the index, the index is itself stored on disk.

Key	Relative record
Melinda Atkins	0
Charles Baker	1
Thomas Bates	2
Lisa Campanella	3
Shen Chan	4
Thomas Garcia	5
•	
•	
•	

FIGURE 3.27

An index can be used to convert a logical key to a relative record number.

Once the index has been created, it can be used to find individual records. Imagine, for example, that Sarah Smith has changed her address. Assuming that the customer name has been used as a key, a program could change her address on the file by:

1. reading the file index into memory,
2. searching the index for her name,
3. finding her relative record number,
4. computing the disk address and reading her record,
5. changing her address, and
6. rewriting the record to the same place on disk.

Note that only Sarah Smith's record is accessed, and that no other records in the file are involved.

The basic idea of direct access is assigning each record an easy-to-remember, logical key, and then converting that key to a relative record number. Given this relative location, a physical address can be computed and the record accessed. Using an index is one technique for converting keys to physical addresses. Another option is passing a numeric key to a hashing algorithm and computing a relative record number.

Data Redundancy

Not too long ago, one of this book's authors received a telephone call from a former student. The young woman expressed regret at having missed an on-campus seminar she'd wanted to attend because, even though she'd graduated more than a decade earlier, her invitation had been sent to her parent's old address and by the time the letter found its way to her, the seminar date had passed. In contrast, the alumni office always seemed to know exactly where she lived no matter how often she moved. How, she wondered, was that possible?

The answer, most likely, was data redundancy. Simply put, her former academic department and the alumni office kept track of her name and address independently, and they did not share their information. While she was in school, her department maintained current information about all its majors, including her. When she graduated, however, the department stopped updating information about her because it had no reason to do so. That's why the department office sent the seminar announcement to the wrong address. When she graduated she became an alumnus. Fund raising is a major part of the alumni association's job, so they have a reason to keep alumni mailing addresses current, and that is why she consistently received her annual contribution request. Any time there are two (or more) values for the same data element (or elements), at least one of those values must be wrong. A central database can help by eliminating redundant data and allowing everyone to share the most current information available.

Database Management

There are problems with traditional data management. Many result from viewing applications independently. For example, consider payroll. Most organizations prepare their payrolls by computer because using a machine instead of a small army of clerks saves money. Thus, the firm develops a payroll program to process the data on the payroll file. Inventory, accounts receivable, accounts payable, and general ledger are similar applications, so the firm develops an inventory program to process the data in an inventory file, an accounts receivable program to process the data in an accounts receivable file, and so on. Each program is independent, and each processes its own independent data file.

The problem is that different applications often need the same data elements. For example, schools generate both bills and student grade reports. View the applications independently. The billing program reads a file of billing data and the grade report program reads an independent file of grade data. The outputs of both programs are mailed to the students' homes, so student names and addresses must be redundantly recorded on both files.

What happens when a student moves? Unless both files are updated, at least one will be wrong. Redundant data are difficult to maintain.

Data dependency is a more subtle problem. There are many different file organizations, each has its own rules for storing and retrieving data, and certain "tricks of the trade" can significantly improve the efficiency of a given program. If the programmer takes advantage of these efficiencies, the program's logic can become dependent upon the physical structure of the data. When a program's logic is tied to its physical data structure, changing that structure will almost certainly require changing the program. As a result, programs using traditional access methods can be difficult to maintain.

The solution to both problems is organizing the data as a single, integrated **database.** The task of controlling access to all the data can then be concentrated in a centralized database management system (Figure 3.28). On a centralized database, all data are collected and stored in a single place, so there is one and only one copy of any given data element. When a new value for a data element such as an address is received, the change is noted on the database. Subsequently, any program requiring access to this data element gets the same value, because there is only one value. Additionally, since the responsibility for accessing the physical data rests with the database management system, the programmer can ignore the physical data structure, so programs tend to be much less dependent upon their data and are generally easier to maintain. Note, however, that a database management system adds another layer of abstraction to the process of manipulating data.

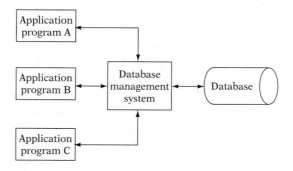

FIGURE 3.28

Many of the problems associated with traditional data access techniques can be solved by using a database.

▌Summary

A program is a series of instructions that guides a computer through a process. An assembler translates each mnemonic instruction into a single machine-level instruction. Hardware works with absolute addresses. Software generally references addresses that are expressed relative to a base location. A compiler reads source statements, translates each one into one or more machine-level instructions, and combines them to form an object module. An interpreter reads and executes one source statement at a time. Using a compiler adds two layers of abstraction to the process of creating a program.

A structured program consists of a series of logical modules linked by a control structure. The basic idea of the object-oriented approach is to design and write the software as a set of independent objects linked by signals. An object contains both data and methods. Objects communicate by transmitting and responding to signals that are sent and received by entities called operations. Hiding implementation details in this way is called encapsulation.

Source code is stored on a source statement library; an object module is stored on an object module library. A linkage editor or loader combines object modules to form a load module. A reentrant program does *not* modify itself. An application program incorporates a user interface and an interface with the operating system. An application programming interface is a set of source-level functions and calling conventions that are compiled to operating system calls.

A data element is a single, meaningful unit of data. The simplest data structure is a list. In a linked list, each node contains data plus a pointer to the next node. A stack is a type of linked list in which all insertions and deletions occur at the top. A queue is a type of linked list in which insertions occur at the rear and deletions occur at the front.

In a file, individual characters are grouped to form fields, fields are grouped to form records, and a set of related records forms the file. Many multimedia files contain only a single record. Accessing the data on a file involves reading and writing individual records. Often, the key to finding a specific record is its relative record number or relative byte number. With sequential access, data are stored and retrieved in a fixed order. With direct or random access, individual records can be retrieved without regard for their positions on the physical file.

Traditional data files often exhibit data redundancy and data dependency. With a database, there is only one copy of each data element, so the data redundancy problem is minimized. Because every program must access data through a database management system, programs are insulated from the physical data structure, thus reducing data dependency.

◼ Key Words

absolute address	machine language
application programming	message
interface (API)	method
assembler language	object
base address	object module
compiler	object-oriented
database	operation
data element	portability
data structure	program
direct access	queue
displacement	random access
dynamic address translation	reentrant
file	relative address
instruction	relative record number
interpreter	sequential access
library	signal
linkage editor	source code
linked list	stack
load module	structured program

◼ Review Questions

1. Identify the components of a machine language instruction.
2. Distinguish between an absolute address and a relative address.
3. What is dynamic address translation?
4. How do an assembler, a compiler, an interpreter, and a nonprocedural language differ? What do they have in common?
5. Using a compiler adds two layers of abstraction to the process of creating an application program. What does that mean? If the statement is true, why do programmers use compilers?
6. Distinguish between traditional structured software and object-oriented software.
7. Define the terms object, method, encapsulation, message, and operation.
8. What is a library? Why are libraries useful?
9. Distinguish among source code, an object module, and a load module.
10. What does a linkage editor do?
11. What is reentrant code? Why is reentrant code important?
12. Identify an application program's interfaces.
13. What is an application programming interface (API)?
14. What is a data element? Describe several different types of data elements.

15. What is a data structure? Why are data structures important?

16. Describe a list, a linked list, a stack, and a queue.

17. Relate the terms character, field, record, and file. Distinguish between a traditional data file and a multimedia file.

18. Explain the relative record concept.

19. Distinguish between sequential and direct (or random) access. Relate both techniques to the relative record concept.

20. What is a database? Why are databases useful?

◼ Exercises

1. Without a program to provide control, a computer is little more than an expensive calculator. Do you agree? Why, or why not?

2. Relate the idea of an instruction to a computer's basic machine cycle from Chapter 2.

3. Why are programming languages necessary?

4. Manually copy the bit string pictured in Figure 3.3 to a sheet of paper. Check the accuracy of your copy and correct any errors you might have made. Then copy the equivalent BASIC instruction, LET A = B + C, to the same sheet of paper. When you finish, write a few paragraphs comparing your impressions of the relative coding efficiency and accuracy of machine-level programming and compiler-level programming.

5. Explain how software layering can make a system more vulnerable to attack.

6. Students who change their address with the university often find that correspondence is sent to their old address long after they report the change. Why do you suppose that happens?

7. If a student changes his or her address during an academic term, that term's grade report is often sent to the old address, but the next term's bill is almost always sent to the correct address. How do you explain that?

8. Some modern operating systems do not recognize records, treating data stored on disk as simple strings of bytes. What advantages might you expect from such an approach? What disadvantages?

9. Figures 3.6 and 3.18 are useful templates for organizing many of this chapter's key terms, although traditional file and database terms do not fit either model very well.

CHAPTER 4

Linking the Hardware Components

When you finish reading this chapter you should be able to:

▶ Identify several common bus types.

▶ Relate a computer's word size to its processing speed, memory capacity, precision, and instruction set size.

▶ Illustrate how a computer's internal components interact by outlining the steps in a complete machine cycle.

▶ Explain how a single-bus architecture computer's internal components are physically linked.

▶ Distinguish between single-bus architecture and multiple-bus architecture.

▶ Explain how channels and control units are used to link peripheral devices to a multiple-bus architecture computer.

▶ Define primitive operation.

▶ Explain what happens when a file is opened.

▶ Distinguish between logical I/O and physical I/O.

▶ Distinguish between an access method and a device driver.

▪ Linking Hardware

This chapter focuses on how the hardware layer components are physically connected to each other and how the operating system layer communicates with the hardware layer (Figure 4.1). We begin with the hardware layer.

The Bus

A computer's internal components are physically linked by a **bus,** a ribbon-like set of electrical lines (or wires) that carries several bits at a time, in parallel. Some of those lines transmit power. Others carry instructions, data, addresses, or commands.

Modern computers incorporate different types of buses to perform different functions. A processor bus delivers information to and from the processor, while a memory bus carries information between memory and the processor, and a cache bus, sometimes called a backside bus, links the system cache and the processor. On many computers, a single system bus combines the functions of both the processor bus and the memory bus. The local I/O bus links high-speed peripherals, such as a disk, to the system, while slower devices such as the keyboard and the mouse are linked through a standard I/O bus. For example, many personal computers feature a local I/O bus that follows the **PCI (Peripheral Component Interconnect)** standard and a slower **ISA (Industry Standard Architecture)** bus.

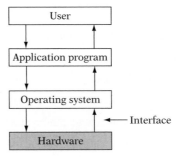

FIGURE 4.1

This chapter focuses on how the hardware layer components are physically connected and how the operating system layer communicates with the hardware layer.

Word Size

Communication between components is greatly simplified if they are electronically similar. Thus, on most systems the internal components are designed around a common **word** size. For example, on a 32-bit computer, the processor manipulates 32-bit numbers, memory and the registers store 32-bit words, and data and instructions move over a 32-bit bus.

A computer's word size affects its processing speed, memory capacity, precision, instruction set size, and cost. Consider speed first. A 32-bit bus contains 32 parallel lines that can carry 32 bits at a time. A 16-bit bus has only 16 parallel lines and thus can carry only 16. Because the wider bus moves twice as much data in the same amount of time, the 32-bit machine is clearly faster. Generally, the bigger the word size, the faster the computer.

Memory capacity is also a function of word size. To access memory, the processor must transmit over a bus the address of a desired instruction or data element. On a 32-bit machine, a 32-bit address can be transmitted. The biggest 32-bit number is roughly 4 billion in decimal terms, so the processor can access as many as 4 billion different memory locations. A 16-bit computer, in contrast, transmits a 16-bit address, limiting it to roughly 64,000 memory locations. Generally, the bigger its word size, the more memory a computer can address.

There are 16-bit microcomputers that access considerably more than 64 K bytes of memory. How is that possible? A 16-bit machine can access more than 64 KB if addresses are broken into two or more parts and transmitted during successive machine cycles. Each machine cycle takes time, however, so memory capacity is gained at the expense of processing speed.

Next, consider precision, the number of significant digits a machine can manipulate. Registers generally hold one word, and the processor's internal circuitry is usually most efficient when manipulating words. A 64-bit processor adds 64-bit numbers; a 32-bit processor adds 32-bit numbers; clearly, the machine with the bigger word size is more precise. While the 32-bit machine may be able to add two 64-bit numbers, it will need several machine cycles to do so, sacrificing speed for precision.

Like data, instructions move from memory to the processor over a bus, and a 32-bit bus can carry a bigger instruction than a 16-bit bus. The bigger instruction size means more bits are available for the operation code, and that means (potentially) a bigger instruction set.

Word size also influences a system's cost because a larger word size complicates production. Generally, a bigger word size means a faster, more precise machine with greater memory capacity, a larger, more varied instruction set, and a higher price tag.

Obsolescence

The very first personal computers were built around 8-bit processor chips. By the early 1980s, the standard word size was 16 bits. Today, 32-bit machines are the norm and 64-bit processors are common.

As word size increases, we tend to assume that older, obsolete processors fade quietly into oblivion, but that is simply not the case. In fact, the number of 8-bit (and even 4-bit) processors currently in use is staggering. Where do you find such "obsolete" electronic components? Inside virtually any consumer electronics product you can imagine, including cameras, receivers, cell phones, pagers, watches, automobiles, calculators, CD players, camcorders, and on and on. Why? Because those so-called "obsolete" processors are perfectly adequate for such applications and they are very inexpensive.

Machine Cycles

Perhaps the easiest way to envision how the various components of a computer are linked is to follow the steps in a typical **machine cycle.** Consider the computer pictured in Figure 4.2a. Memory holds a program and some data. In the processor, some of the registers hold key control information and other work registers are used by the programmer for computations or addressing. A single bus links the processor, the registers, and memory.

During instruction time or I-time, the instruction control unit fetches the next instruction from memory. The address of the next instruction is found in the instruction counter. The instruction control unit extracts this address and sends it (as part of a fetch command) over the bus to the memory controller (Figure 4.2a). The memory controller accepts the command, reads the requested memory location, and copies its contents onto the bus (Figure 4.2b). This takes time, giving the instruction control unit an opportunity to increment the instruction counter to point to the next instruction. Meanwhile, the current instruction moves over the bus and into the instruction register (Figure 4.2c).

During execution time or E-time, the instruction control unit activates the arithmetic and logic unit, which executes the instruction in the instruction register (Figure 4.2d). Assume the instruction calls for loading the contents of a word stored in memory into a work register. In response, the arithmetic and logic unit issues, again over the bus, a command to fetch the contents of the specified memory location (Figure 4.2e). As before, the memory controller reads the requested word and copies the contents onto the bus. Once on the bus, the data flows to a work register (Figure 4.2f).

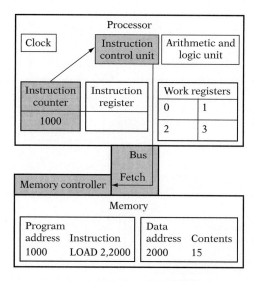

FIGURE 4.2

A machine cycle. **a.** The instruction control unit sends a fetch command to memory.

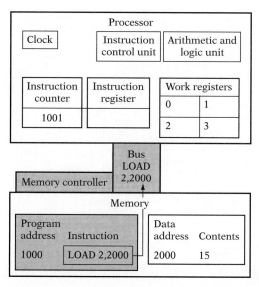

b. The memory controller copies the contents of the requested memory location onto the bus.

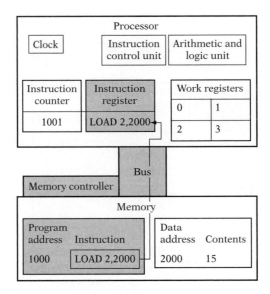

FIGURE 4.2

c. The instruction moves over the bus and into the instruction register.

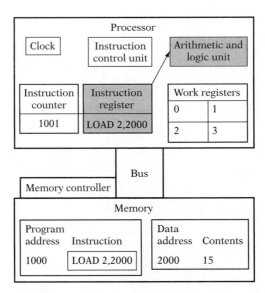

d. The arithmetic and logic unit executes the instruction in the instruction register.

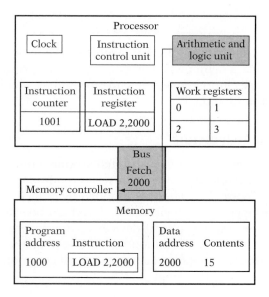

FIGURE 4.2

e. The arithmetic and logic unit sends a fetch command to memory.

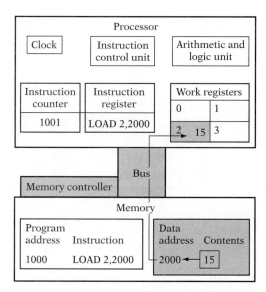

f. The memory controller copies the contents of the requested memory location onto the bus and the data value flows into a work register.

◼ Architectures

Computer scientists use the term **architecture** to describe the interconnections that link a computer's components. As you read the next several topics, note how computer architecture resembles the layering concept you read about in Chapter 1.

Single-Bus Architecture

Most microcomputers are constructed around a **motherboard** (Figure 4.3), a metal framework that contains a series of **slots** linked through a bus to a processor (Figure 4.4). Memory is added by plugging a memory board into one of the open slots (Figure 4.5). Interface boards are used to connect external buses and peripheral devices to the system. Because all the components are linked to a common bus, this arrangement is called **single-bus architecture** (Figure 4.6). At some point, all communication between components flows over this single bus.

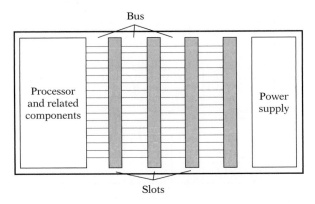

FIGURE 4.3

Most microcomputers are constructed around a motherboard.

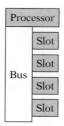

FIGURE 4.4

A schematic drawing of a motherboard highlighting the slots.

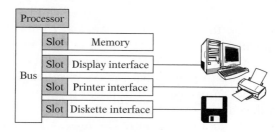

FIGURE 4.5

Memory, peripherals, and secondary storage devices are added to the system by plugging the appropriate board into an open slot.

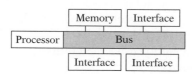

FIGURE 4.6

With single-bus architecture all the components are linked by a common bus.

Interfaces

Because the electronic signals controlling a keyboard, a display, a printer, and a disk drive are different, each peripheral device must have its own. One side of the **interface** communicates with the computer and uses internal codes (Figure 4.7). The other side is device-dependent and communicates with the external device in the peripheral's external form. The interface translates.

For example, outside the computer the letter A is represented physically both as a key on a keyboard and as a dot pattern on a laser printer. When a user types the letter A, an electronic pulse enters the keyboard interface where it is translated to the binary code that represents A inside the computer. Later, on output, this same code is sent to a printer interface where it is translated to the electronic signals needed to form the proper dot pattern. Note that the computer always uses the same binary code no matter what peripheral device is involved. To the processor all peripherals look the same.

If you turn to the back of a personal computer, you will see several **device ports** for plugging peripheral devices into the system. Your keyboard and your mouse typically use **serial ports** that transmit one bit at a time. A printer is usually plugged into a **parallel port** that transmits several bits in parallel. Your display unit might plug into either a serial or a parallel port, depending on its specifications. A peripheral is plugged into its interface through a device port. The interface, in turn, plugs directly into the bus. Thus, there is an unbroken path leading from the peripheral device, through a cable, to a **port**, to an interface, to the bus, to the processor and memory.

Controllers

The act of transferring data from a bus to a peripheral device or from a peripheral device to a bus involves such logical tasks as counting and synchronization. The necessary intelligence is provided by a **controller,** a chip mounted on the interface board that controls the transfer process. Obviously, a controller chip must be compatible with the underlying bus and the peripheral device.

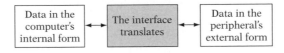

FIGURE 4.7

An interface translates between internal and external data forms.

Earlier in this chapter, in the narrative that accompanied the multiple steps in Figure 4.2, you read about a memory controller. Much as an interface controller controls the transfer of data between a peripheral device and a bus, the memory controller provides the intelligence needed to transfer information from memory to the system bus and from the system bus into memory.

External Buses

On a single-bus architecture system, the number of available slots limits the number of peripheral devices that can be connected to the system. One solution to this limitation is to use an **external bus** to connect several peripheral devices through a single port. For example, it is possible to plug a printer, a scanner, a mouse, a modem, and other serial devices into a **USB (Universal Serial Bus)** hub and then plug the USB hub into a single USB port that connects all those devices to the system. On some systems, printers, external disk drives, and similar parallel devices are connected to the system through a **SCSI (Small Computer System Interface)** bus that plugs into a SCSI (pronounced "skuzzy") port. USB and SCSI connections are beginning to replace traditional serial and parallel ports. Incidentally, a port is typically used to connect one device or one external bus to the system, while a bus can (potentially) link numerous devices.

Channels and Control Units

Microcomputers are designed for a few users, so single-bus architecture is reasonable. A mainframe is much more powerful and expensive, however, so mainframes generally support multiple concurrent users. A mainframe's processor still fetches and executes one instruction at a time, however. How is it possible to support multiple concurrent users when the processor executes only one instruction at a time?

One key is freeing the main processor from responsibility for input and output. Controlling input and output involves such logical functions as selecting the path over which the data are to flow, counting characters, and computing memory addresses. Because the main processor is the only source of logic on a microcomputer system, it must perform these common tasks for every input or output operation. While it is controlling input and output, the processor is not available to execute application program instructions, but given the nature of a microcomputer system, the resulting inefficiency is a minor problem.

Most mainframes assign the task of controlling input and output to **channels** (Figure 4.8). A channel is an independent, special-purpose computer with its own processor, so it can perform logical functions in parallel with the mainframe's main processor. That frees the main processor to do other things.

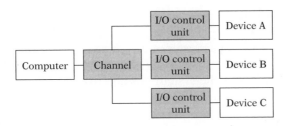

FIGURE 4.8
On a mainframe, device-independent functions are assigned to a channel and device-dependent functions are assigned to an I/O control unit.

Some input and output functions are device-dependent; for example, controlling the movement of an access arm is a disk problem, while a laser printer requires that characters be converted to a dot pattern. Other tasks, such as selecting a data path, counting characters, and computing memory addresses, are common to all input and output operations no matter what peripheral device is involved. The channel handles these device-independent functions. The device-dependent functions are assigned to an input/output **control unit.** Each physical device has its own control unit.

Multiple-Bus Architecture

Single-bus architecture creates a number of problems on a multiple-user system. Channel communication is one of the easiest to visualize. A channel moves data between memory and a peripheral device. The computer's processor manipulates data in memory. Allowing a channel and a processor to simultaneously access memory will not work on a microcomputer system because the single-bus architecture provides only one physical data path. Simultaneous access requires independent data paths, so most mainframes use **multiple-bus architecture** (Figure 4.9).

Start with a channel. Typically, two buses link it to the computer (Figure 4.9a)—one for commands and one for data. As an input or output operation begins, the main processor sends a *start I/O* command over the command bus to the channel's processor. In response, the channel assumes responsibility for the I/O operation, establishing a link with the external device and controlling the transfer of data into memory over the data bus (Figure 4.9b). Note that the *channel's* memory serves as a buffer between the peripheral device and the computer's memory. Because the channel manages the I/O operation, the main processor can turn its attention to another program.

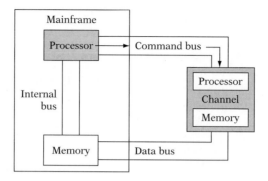

FIGURE 4.9

Most mainframes use multiple-bus architecture.

a. The main processor starts an I/O operation by sending a signal to the channel.

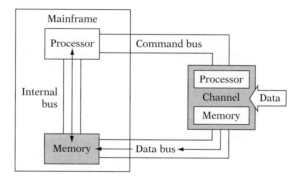

b. The channel assumes responsibility for the I/O operation and the processor turns its attention to another program.

The channel is an independent, asynchronous computer with its own processor and memory. It controls the I/O operation. Because the channel and the computer are independent, the main processor has no way of knowing when the I/O operation is complete unless the channel tells it. Thus as the last character of data flows across the channel, the channel processor sends the main processor an electronic signal called an interrupt (Figure 4.9c). When it receives the **interrupt,** the main processor knows the requested I/O operation has been completed and the program that requested that operation can resume processing. The interrupt process will be discussed in detail in later chapters.

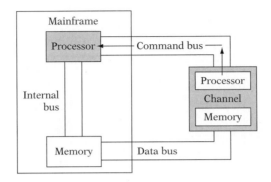

FIGURE 4.9

c. The channel sends an interrupt to the processor to signal the end of the I/O operation.

▌ The Hardware/Software Interface

Application programs perform I/O operations by sending a logical request to an operating system service. The operating system responds by converting that logical I/O request to the appropriate physical I/O commands and communicating those commands from the operating system to the hardware through a hardware/software interface.

For example, picture a sequential file on disk and imagine a program designed to process the file's records. Whenever a READ statement is executed, the programmer expects the next record to be copied from disk into memory. Think about that for a minute. The "next" record is a logical concept. In effect, the programmer is saying, "Get me the next record in sequence, and I don't care what physical steps are involved." It's not that easy.

Primitives

The interface (or control unit) that controls a peripheral device is limited to a few **primitive** operations. For example, a disk interface (more accurately, a disk controller) can send the disk drive one of the following three commands:

1. move the access mechanism to a specific track (seek),
2. read a specific sector, or
3. write a specific sector.

Because printers, disk drives, and display screens are so different, they are controlled by different sets of primitive operations and thus by different interfaces. Interfaces and control units execute special programs that consist of primitive commands.

Open

Because computers and their peripherals are physically independent, their electronic signals must be carefully synchronized before they can begin communicating. Often, an initial electronic link is established by exchanging a set of prearranged signals at **open** time. An operating system service initiates and interprets those signals. After a device is officially opened, the operating system knows it exists and knows how to communicate with it.

The open operation might involve more than simply establishing communication with a peripheral device, however. For example, a single disk can hold hundreds of programs and data files. For a given application, only one program and only one set of data will do. How does the system select the right program or the right data file?

The files stored on a disk are identified by name in the disk's directory (see Chapter 2). On a given system, the directory is always stored in the same place (for example, track 0 sector 2). Once initial contact with the disk drive has been established, the open logic (an operating system service) can issue the primitive commands to read the directory (seek track 0, read sector 2). Once the directory is in memory, the open logic can search it for the file's name. Recorded along with the file name is the disk address of the file's first sector. Given the address of a file's first sector, the location of its other sectors can be computed.

Logical and Physical I/O

A disk's interface or control unit is (essentially) limited to three primitive functions:

1. seek to a track,
2. read a sector, or
3. write a sector.

The concept of the "next" record is meaningless at this level. To find data physically on disk, you must specify a track and issue a seek command and then, subsequently, specify a sector and issue a read command. The programmer is concerned with **logical I/O.** The act of physically transferring a unit of data between memory and a peripheral device is called **physical I/O.** Note that logical I/O is performed by software and physical I/O is performed by hardware.

The process of bridging this gap begins when the application program issues a logical I/O request. The problem is converting this logical request into a series of primitive physical I/O operations. Often, the key is the relative record number.

A relative record number indicates a record's position relative to the beginning of a file. How does the system know where the file begins? One function of the open logic is reading the disk's directory, searching it for the file's name, and extracting the file's start address. In general, once a file is opened, its start address is known and the location of any record on that file can be computed by using the appropriate relative record number.

Imagine a program that reads data sequentially. When the file is opened, the disk address of its first record is known. The file's first record is relative record 0; its second record is relative record 1, and so on, so accessing individual records involves little more than counting them. For example, imagine that relative record 5 has just been read. Clearly, the "next" record is relative record 6. Where is it physically located? Given the start of file address (from open), and knowing that the desired record is at "start of file plus 6," its disk address can be computed and the necessary primitive commands issued.

Now, picture a direct access application. A program needs data for student number 123456. In some way, that student number must be converted to a relative record number. One option is using a hashing algorithm. Another is reading an index of student numbers and their associated relative record numbers and doing a table look-up. The start of file address is known from open, so once the student number has been converted to a relative record number, the process of computing its disk address is easy. Given the disk address, the necessary primitive commands can be issued.

Most students are surprised to learn that a task as apparently simple as reading data from disk can be so complex. In fact, the complexity associated with physical I/O is one of the major reasons why operating systems and systems software came into being. Even today, input/output control services form the core of most modern operating systems.

Access Methods

Few programmers communicate directly with peripheral devices at a primitive level. Generally, the responsibility for translating a programmer's logical I/O requests to physical commands is assigned to an operating system service (Figure 4.10). Because there are so many data access techniques available, some mainframe computers assign application-dependent portions of this translation process to special subroutines called **access methods** (Figure 4.11), keeping only application-independent logic in the operating system. The linkage editor adds the access method to the load module at load time (Figure 4.12), so application-dependent I/O logic occupies memory only when the application program occupies memory. Another option is assigning responsibility for all database access to a database management system.

FIGURE 4.10

A programmer's logical I/O request is converted to the appropriate physical I/O operations by the operating system.

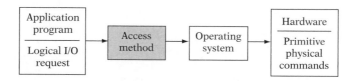

FIGURE 4.11

Some mainframes assign application-dependent portions of the logical-to-physical translation process to access methods.

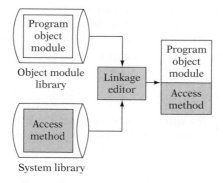

FIGURE 4.12

The access method is added to the load module at load time.

Once a record's physical location has been determined, the process of communicating with the peripheral device can begin (Figure 4.13). Typically, the access method identifies the necessary primitive commands, sets up a channel program, and calls the operating system. The operating system then sends a *start I/O* signal to the channel. The channel,

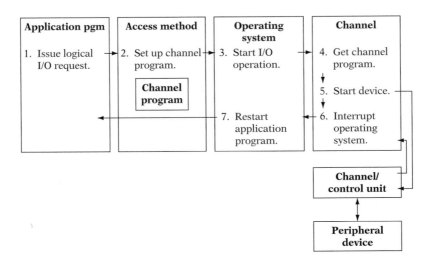

FIGURE 4.13

The process of converting a logical I/O request to primitive physical commands on a mainframe.

subsequently, accesses memory, finds the channel program, and transfers it to the I/O control unit. Once the data have been transferred, the channel notifies the operating system (through an interrupt) that the I/O operation is complete, and the program can resume processing.

Device Drivers

Microcomputers do not use channels and control units. With single-bus architecture, each peripheral device is plugged into an interface board, which in turn is plugged into the bus. It seems simple, but there are complications.

For example, imagine that your printer is attached to your computer by a cable that runs from the printer to the parallel port. What happens when you change printers? Assume, for example, that you want to take your black-and-white laser printer offline and hook up your color printer so you can print some color images. You should be able to unplug the parallel cable from the laser printer and plug it into the color printer with no problem because everything fits. But even though the physical connection remains intact, the color printer is unlikely to work unless you also make some logical (software) changes.

Although they can all be plugged into the parallel port, laser printers, ink jet printers, color printers, and even functionally similar printers manufactured by different companies are different. (The same problem occurs with other peripheral devices such as display units, scanners, and so on.) Providing a custom port and/or interface for each manufacturer's peripheral is not a reasonable solution to this problem. Instead, the responsibility for performing unique, device-specific tasks is assigned to a software routine called a **device driver.** Many common device drivers are preinstalled into the operating system. When you purchase a new peripheral, it typically comes with an installation disk. Among other things, the disk usually contains the latest device driver for the peripheral. During the installation process, the device driver is installed on the system's hard disk.

Assume the peripheral device is a printer and you have just clicked on an application program's *Print* icon. In response, the program passes a print request to the operating system (Figure 4.14). The operating system, in turn, finds the appropriate device driver on disk and launches it. The device driver communicates with the interface card, which passes the request to the printer. If a subsequent input or output operation calls for communicating with a different peripheral device, the operating system selects a different device driver appropriate for that peripheral. Note how Figure 4.14 reflects the layering concept.

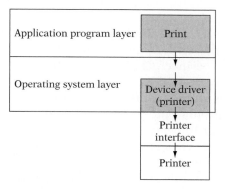

FIGURE 4.14

Microcomputers use device drivers as part of the logical-to-physical I/O conversion process.

Updating Device Drivers

If you purchase a new computer or install a new operating system, there is a very good chance that one or more previously working peripherals will no longer operate. Often, the problem is an incompatible device driver, and the solution is to install an updated device driver. A good starting point is the peripheral manufacturer's Web site; for example, if you have a Canon printer, go to *www.canon.com* and if you have a Hewlett-Packard printer go to *www.hp.com*. Once you reach the Web site, look for a link to *Downloads, Software,* or a similar term that seems to make sense or, if the site supports a search feature, search on *device drivers.* You'll probably need such information as the peripheral's make and model, the version of your operating system, and, perhaps, the manufacturer and model of your computer system, so be prepared. Other possible sources of downloadable device drivers include your operating system supplier, your computer's manufacturer, or any of a number of independent Web sites that specialize in software downloads and patches.

▌ Summary

A computer's internal components communicate over a bus. Modern computers incorporate different types of buses. On most computers, the internal components are designed around a common word size. The communication between internal components was illustrated by following a single machine cycle.

Computer scientists use the term architecture to describe the interconnections that link a computer's components. Typically, each peripheral device requires its own interface board. A peripheral is plugged into its interface via a device port, and a controller provides the interface's intelligence. Multiple peripherals can be attached to a system through a single port by using an external bus.

Mainframes often support multiple concurrent users and assign responsibility for controlling input and output to a channel and a control unit. When a channel completes an I/O operation, it notifies the main processor by sending it an electronic signal called an interrupt. Most mainframes use multiple-bus architecture.

An I/O control unit and an interface execute primitive commands to physically control a peripheral device. The first step in accessing a peripheral device is opening it. Few programmers actually deal with physical I/O operations. Instead, they assign responsibility for translating logical I/O requests to physical form to the operation system, an access method, or a database management system. On many single-bus architecture systems, the responsibility for performing unique, device-specific tasks is assigned to a software routine called a device driver.

▌ Key Words

access method	motherboard
architecture	multiple-bus architecture
bus	open
channel	parallel port
control unit (I/O)	PCI (Peripheral Component Interconnect)
controller	physical I/O
device driver	port
device port	primitive
external bus	SCSI (Small Computer System Interface)
interface	serial port
interrupt	single-bus architecture
ISA (Industry Standard	slot
Architecture)	USB (Universal Serial Bus)
logical I/O	word
machine cycle	

▌ Review Questions

1. Explain how a computer's internal components are physically linked.
2. What functions are performed by a processor bus, a memory bus, a local I/O bus, and a standard I/O bus? Distinguish between a PCI bus and an ISA bus.
3. Discuss the purpose of a processor bus, a memory bus, an I/O bus, and a standard bus.
4. On most computers, all internal components are designed around a common word size. Why?
5. Explain how a computer's word size affects its processing speed, memory capacity, precision, and instruction set size.
6. Illustrate how a computer's internal components interact by outlining the steps in a complete machine cycle.
7. What is meant by a computer's architecture?
8. Relate the terms motherboard, slot, and bus.
9. On a typical microcomputer system, each input, output, and secondary storage device has its own interface. Why?
10. What is a device port? Distinguish between a serial port and a parallel port.
11. What is the function of a controller?
12. What is the purpose of an external bus? Distinguish between a USB bus and an SCSI bus.
13. Trace the electronic path that links a peripheral device to a single-bus architecture computer's internal components.
14. Distinguish between single-bus architecture and multiple-bus architecture.

15. On a mainframe computer, peripheral devices are linked to the internal components through channels and control units instead of simple interfaces. How? Why?

16. What is a primitive operation?

17. Explain what happens when a file is opened.

18. Distinguish between logical I/O and physical I/O.

19. What is a device driver? Why are device drivers necessary?

20. Distinguish between an access method and a device driver.

▌ Exercises

1. Identify several current uses for apparently obsolete 8- and 16-bit processors.

2. Find a computer that is no longer in use. Remove the cover and identify the processor, memory, the bus, and the various interface boards. Prepare a sketch showing how the internal components are linked. Compare your sketch to the generic architecture diagrams in the book.

3. Disassemble the computer from Exercise 2 and study the components. Then reassemble the computer.

4. Relate the idea of a disk's directory to a library catalog.

5. Relate computer architecture to the layering concept.

6. Identify at least three potential sources for device drivers for each of the peripheral devices attached to your computer.

7. Figures 4.2, 4.6 and 4.13 are useful templates for organizing many of this chapter's key terms.

PART 2

Basic Operating System Concepts

Chapters 5 and 6 focus on essential operating system concepts and principles. If you understand these basic ideas, you will find it much easier to grasp the content of subsequent chapters.

CHAPTER 5

The User Interface, the File System, and the IOCS

When you finish reading this chapter you should be able to:

▶ Identify the basic functions performed by an operating system's user interface.

▶ Distinguish a command interface, a menu interface, a graphical user interface, a voice-actuated interface, and a Web-form interface.

▶ Identify the primary functions performed by the file system.

▶ Distinguish between logical I/O and physical I/O.

▶ Distinguish between directory management and disk space management.

▶ Identify the primary functions performed by the input/output control system.

▶ Distinguish between the input/output control system and the file system.

▶ Distinguish between a resident routine and a transient routine.

▶ Outline the boot process.

◼ An Operating System's Basic Functions

As you learned in Chapter 1, most modern operating systems incorporate the functions summarized in Figure 5.1. The user interface provides a mechanism for the system operator and the user to communicate with the operating system and request operating system services. The file system incorporates routines that allow the user or programmer to create, delete, modify, and manipulate files by name. The device management function is responsible for controlling communications with the system's peripheral devices. Processor management is concerned with efficiently managing the processor's time. Memory management is concerned with managing the system's memory resources, allocating space to applications as needed and ensuring that those applications do not interfere with each other. Finally, as the name implies, communication support makes it possible for one computer to communicate with another.

Memory management and processor management are largely transparent to the user. They will be covered in Chapter 6. Communication is the subject of Part V, Chapters 16-21. This chapter discusses the shell, the file system, and device management.

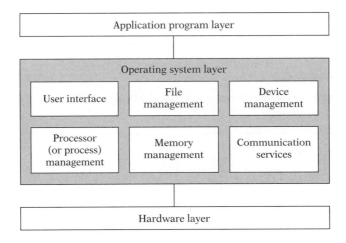

FIGURE 5.1

The components of a modern operating system.

The User Interface

Most of the time, a user communicates with a computer through an application program's user interface (Figure 5.2). The application program, in turn, transparently requests operating system services through an application programming interface (API).

Before a user can begin to access an application program's user interface, however, the operating system must first be told to launch the program. A system operator or a user identifies the program to be launched by issuing one or more **commands** directly to the operating system. The operating system's **user interface** accepts, interprets, and carries out the commands. Each command tells the operating system to perform a single service, such as log a user onto the system, start an application program, allocate a peripheral device, and so on. The user interface interprets each command and requests support from other operating system layers as appropriate.

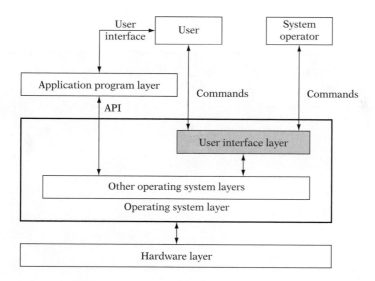

FIGURE 5.2

The user interface accepts, interprets, and carries out commands.

User Interfaces

A user communicates with a **command line interface** or **shell** by typing brief, cryptic commands, such as

COPY file-A file-B

MS-DOS line commands are a good example. Cryptic commands can save a sophisticated user a great deal of time, but command line interfaces require considerable user training.

A **menu interface** presents the user with a list of available options. The user selects the desired option by highlighting it and pressing enter, by typing the option's identifying letter or number, or by pointing to the option and clicking the mouse. Often, selecting one option leads to a second menu listing suboptions, so the user might have to work through a hierarchy of related menus. Compared to commands, menus are easier to use and easier to learn, but traversing multiple menus can be time consuming.

The Apple Macintosh and Microsoft Windows both feature a **graphical user interface** (GUI) that presents the user with a selection of windows, icons, and menus (Figure 5.3). The user points to the desired element and

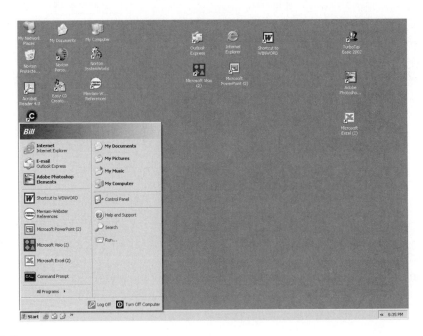

FIGURE 5.3

A graphical user interface.

clicks a mouse button to trigger the associated action. Graphical user interfaces are relatively easy to understand, learn, and use. Compared to commands and simple menus, however, they consume considerable processor time and memory. A graphical user interface is sometimes called an object-oriented interface or an icon-based interface.

A **voice-activated interface** utilizes such natural language processing elements as voice recognition, voice data entry, and voice response. Keyboards, pointing devices, and microphones are the primary input devices, and speakers provide audio output. Natural language processing requires a powerful computer with a great deal of memory and a fast processor. The current state of the art can be observed in sophisticated multimedia applications and online games.

A **Web-form interface** follows the metaphor established by the Internet and the World Wide Web. Because so many people use the Web, adopting Web rules to support a non-Web interface minimizes the need for additional training.

Because the user interface is implemented as an independent layer, its contents can be changed without affecting the other layers. As a result, several different user interfaces can coexist on the same computer. For example, imagine that your operating system supports a command line interface and a voice-activated interface in addition to the default graphical user interface (Figure 5.4). Normally you use the GUI, but the command line interface is convenient for certain file management tasks and the voice-activated interface is an excellent choice for certain computer games. Clearly, the rules the user must follow to communicate with the three interfaces are different, but as long as all three interfaces pass the same parameters down to lower operating system layers, those lower layers have no need to know how the user interface works.

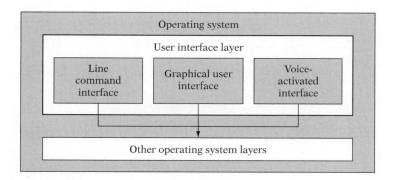

FIGURE 5.4

The user interface layer can support several different interfaces.

The Command Language

Although the rules for using different types of interfaces can vary considerably, they all do basically the same thing. The user interface allows the user to issue a command by typing it, selecting it, speaking it, or taking some other action. The command is then interpreted and passed on to another layer for processing.

Inside the user interface layer are links to a number of routines, each of which performs a single service (Figure 5.5). For example, one routine contains the instructions that guide the computer through the process of loading a program from disk into memory and launching it, while another contains the instructions to open a file, and so on. The user tells the user interface which service to perform by issuing a command such as *Open, Copy,* or *Save.* The user interface interprets the command and calls the appropriate service routine. The set of available commands and their syntax rules forms a **command language.**

For example, consider the task of launching a program. It is the user's responsibility to specify or otherwise select the program or routine to be executed by typing the program name, double-clicking on the program's icon, or selecting the program's name from a menu. In response to the user's action, the command flows into memory (Figure 5.6a). The user interface then interprets the command and calls the routine that loads the requested program (Figure 5.6b). Once the program is loaded into memory, the user interface starts it (Figure 5.6c).

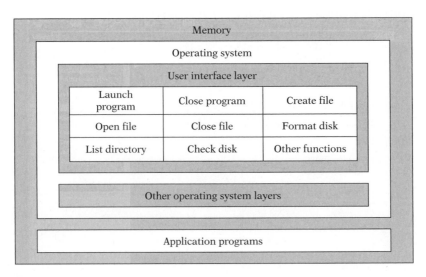

FIGURE 5.5

The user interface layer links to a number of routines, each of which performs a single service.

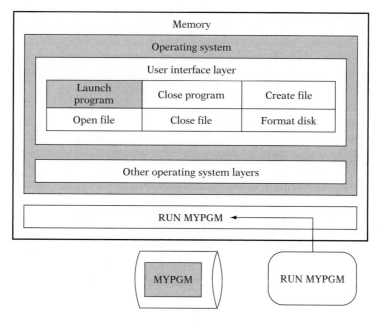

FIGURE 5.6

Launching an application program. **a.** The user selects the program.

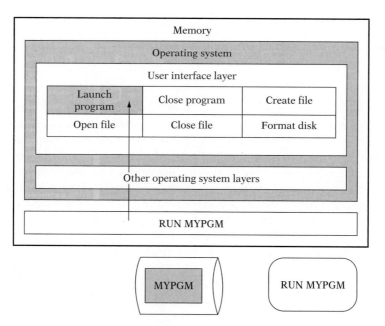

b. The user interface calls the *launch program* routine.

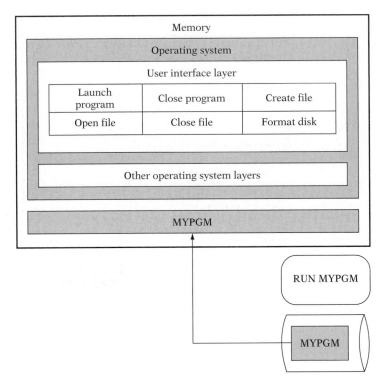

c. The application program is loaded into memory and started.

Peripheral device requirements are also specified through the user interface. Most interactive systems rely on default device assignments, and personal computers support a limited number of peripherals, so the end user rarely encounters a need to specify a peripheral device, but it does happen. In contrast to users, system operators and mainframe programmers specify peripheral devices on a regular basis. Typically, each program's peripheral device needs are identified in a series of commands. Given a list of device needs, the operating system can determine if the necessary resources are available before loading the program.

Other commands support run-time intervention. A simple example is rebooting a personal computer system. If a program stops functioning properly and locks up the system, the user can often terminate the program by simultaneously pressing *control, alt,* and *delete* (or some other combination of keys). Run-time intervention can be considerably more complex on a multiple user system.

Batch Commands

Imagine a payroll application in which input data are verified by a program named VERIFY, sorted (SORT), and processed (PAYCHECK) before the checks are printed (PAYPRINT). The commands to perform these functions might include:

> VERIFY TIMEDATA
> SORT TIMEDATA
> PAYCHECK
> PAYPRINT

Payroll is run weekly, so the same four commands must be typed (or selected) once a week.

Computers are much better than people at repetitive tasks, so most operating systems support **batch files.** To create a batch file, the programmer types a set of commands and saves them in a file. Given the batch file, the application can subsequently be run by typing (or selecting) the batch file name, for example,

> payroll

The command processor responds by searching the system disk for a batch file named *payroll,* reading the file, and then carrying out the commands stored in the file.

A Human Perspective

Sometimes a human perspective can help clarify a technical concept. For example, the evolution of the user interface can be explained (at least in part) by the amount of work a computer can perform in an "instant." An instant is a brief, almost imperceptible period of time. If something happens instantly, it happens immediately, and you, as a human being, are unaware that time has passed. Few people are capable of actually sensing anything that happens in less then 0.001 seconds, so let's use 0.001 seconds as a working definition of an instant. If a computer is to respond instantly, it must be capable of accepting all relevant input data, processing the data, and outputting the results within 0.001 seconds.

Back in the late 1970s and early 1980s the first personal computers were capable of processing about one line of data (80 characters) within 0.001 seconds. In those days, a line command could be executed "instantly," but processing more data (such as a full screen) took considerably longer, so line command interfaces made sense. By the middle 1980s, faster processors were able to "instantly" support monochrome screens (80 characters by 25 lines), making menu interfaces viable. A few years later, processors were capable of supporting low-resolution

The File System

The user interface allows the user to communicate with the operating system. The **file system** occupies a lower operating system layer (Figure 5.7) and helps keep track of the data and programs stored on disk and other secondary storage devices.

Directory Management

A disk can hold hundreds of different files and programs, but if you want to load a particular program, only that program will do, and if the program needs data from a particular file, only that file will do. As you learned in Chapter 2, the location (the start address) of every file stored on a disk can be found by searching the disk's directory (Figure 5.8). (*Note:* A program is a type of file.) The file system manages the directory.

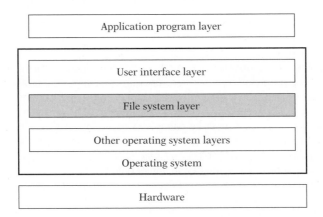

FIGURE 5.7

The file system layer.

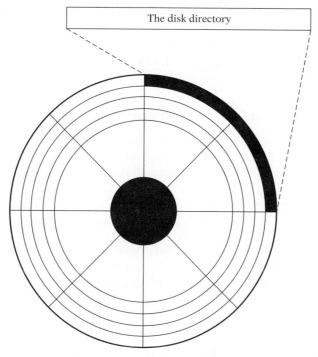

FIGURE 5.8

The location of every file stored on a disk can be found by searching the disk's directory.

For a given operating system the directory is always stored at the same location on every disk, so the file system can always find it. When a program is first installed or a data file is first created, its name and physical location are recorded in the directory by the file system. To retrieve the program or open the file, the file system reads the directory, searches it for the program or file name, and extracts the program or file's disk address. When a program or file is deleted, the file system removes its entry from the directory.

Launching a Program

For example, the process of launching a program begins when a user types a command such as SPACEWAR or clicks on the *Spacewar* icon. The user interface interprets the command and passes the program name to the file system, which reads the directory. Once the directory is in memory, the file system searches it. Each program is identified by name, and following the program's name is its physical location on disk—the track and sector address of its first instructions. The file system extracts the program's disk address and passes it to the device management layer, which physically loads a copy of the program into memory. Once the program is loaded, the file system notifies the user interface, which starts the program.

Opening and Closing Data Files

Programs are normally installed and launched in response to operator or user commands. Data files, on the other hand, are created and accessed through application programs. To create a new file, the user enters some data through an application routine and then saves the file. When a file is saved for the first time the file system creates a directory entry, allocates disk space to hold the file, and notes the file's start address in the directory.

To find an existing file, the user issues an **open** command. When a file is opened, the file system reads the directory, finds the file's directory entry, extracts the file's start address, and (sometimes) reads all or part of the file. Generally, when a program is finished processing a file, it closes the file. In response to a **close** command, the file system updates the directory to indicate such information as the file's length and ending address.

Logical I/O and Physical I/O

A similar process supports reading and writing data records from a file. The process begins after the file is opened. The program issues a **logical I/O** request such as "get the next record" or "get the record for student 123456." Note that the logical I/O request asks for a specific logical unit of data but does not indicate where (or how) the data are physically stored.

The act of physically transferring a unit of data between a peripheral device and memory is called **physical I/O.** Physical I/O is the responsibility of a lower operating system layer, the device management layer. The file system accepts the logical I/O request from the application program layer and converts it into a physical I/O request by reading the directory and finding the record's physical address. The file system then transfers the request to the device management layer which communicates with the physical device. Incidentally, the file system relies on the device management layer to physically read and write the directory.

Logical and Physical Records

A **physical record** is the unit of data (for example, a sector) that is transferred between a peripheral device and memory. A **logical record** is the unit of data processed by a single iteration of an application program. They are not necessarily the same, and that can complicate things.

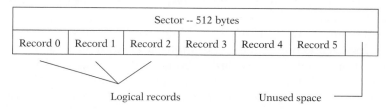

FIGURE 5.9
Blocking.

For example, imagine a program that processes a series of 80-byte (single line) logical records stored on disk. A disk, as you know, transfers one sector at a time into memory, so the physical record is a sector. Assume that each sector holds 512 bytes. Storing one 80-byte logical record in each 512-byte physical sector means wasting 432 bytes per sector, which is clearly unacceptable. One solution is to **block** the data, storing several logical records in each sector (Figure 5.9); for example, six 80-byte records can be stored in a single 512-byte sector leaving 32 bytes of unused space. Note that one physical record (one sector) holds six logical records.

Some applications involve lengthy records. For example, the academic history of a college senior might not fit in a single 512-byte sector (Figure 5.10), so the logical record (a single student's grade history), is bigger than the physical record (a single sector). Thus, assembling the data to support a single logical read calls for two or more physical input operations, while a single logical write implies two or more physical writes. A single logical record that extends over two or more physical records is called a **spanned record.**

Sector 0		
Personal data	Freshman year	Sophomore year

Sector 1		
Junior year	Senior year	

FIGURE 5.10
A single logical record that extends over two or more physical records is called a spanned record.

Hardware transfers a single physical record (a sector) between the disk's surface and memory. When an application program issues a logical read command, however, it needs a single logical record. Somewhere between the logical and physical I/O operations, a software routine must either select a portion of a physical record or combine the data from two or more physical records to form the logical record required by the application program. Depending on the system, that task might be performed by an access method, an application program routine, the file system, or a database management system.

Disk Space Management

The file system is also responsible for allocating space on disk. Ideally, when a file is created its data are stored in a series of consecutive sectors, but because many different files share the same disk, that is not always possible. For example, imagine that a file is created on Wednesday and updated on Thursday. Wednesday's data might occupy consecutive sectors, but data belonging to some other file might lie between Wednesday's data and Thursday's data. The file system bridges this gap.

Often, a linked list of sector numbers (or cluster numbers, where a cluster is a set of sectors) called a file allocation table is maintained on disk (Figure 5.11). When a file is created, the file system records the number of the file's first sector in the directory. When that first sector is filled, the file allocation table is searched and the next available free sector is allocated to the program. (In this example, free sectors are identified by a 0 table value.) Note that the next free sector might not be physically adjacent to the first one.

To link the sectors, the second sector's number is recorded in the first sector's file allocation table entry. Follow the chain of pointers (the linked list) in Figure 5.11. The directory indicates that file A starts in sector 6. The file allocation table entry for sector 6 points to sector 7, sector 7's entry points to sector 9, and sector 9's file allocation table entry points to sector 12. Because sector 12's file allocation table entry holds a sentinel value, it marks the end of the file. Of course, not all file systems use 0 to mark free sectors and -1 as a sentinel value, but this example gives you a sense of how disk allocation techniques work.

Directory Management and Disk Space Management

Note carefully the difference between the file system's directory management and disk space management functions. Directory management

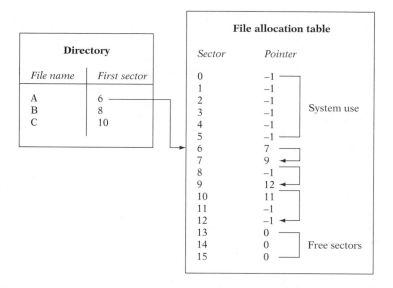

FIGURE 5.11

Many operating systems maintain a linked list of sectors to help manage disk space.

works with the directory. When a file is created, directory management establishes a directory entry. When a file is opened, directory management finds the file's physical address by reading and searching the directory. When a file is deleted, directory management deletes the associated directory entry.

Disk space management, in contrast, works with the file allocation table. When a file is created, the disk space management routine finds the first available free sector, marks it as no longer free, and passes the physical address of that sector back to the directory management routine, which notes it on the file's directory entry. As the file grows, the disk space management routine finds the necessary free space, assigns it to the file, and notes the assignment in the file allocation table. The directory and the file allocation table are tightly linked, with each directory entry pointing to the start of a linked list on the file allocation table. They are separate entities, however. Together, directory management and disk space management represent an interesting example of layering.

Early Operating Systems

The very first operating systems were developed back in the late 1950s and early 1960s primarily to support physical I/O. In those days, program instructions were prepared on a keypunch, one instruction per card, and the deck of cards was submitted to the computer operator for eventual processing. Standard input and output operations such as read a card or print a line appeared in virtually every program, so many computer centers prepared stacks of prepunched I/O routines for programmers to insert into their card decks. Eventually, someone came up with the idea of writing the I/O routines as a set of macros, storing them on disk, and allowing an assembler or a compiler to insert the code into the object module in response to a macro reference. Over time, those macros split into two components: a set of application-dependent routines called access methods and a smaller set of physical I/O routines. Those physical I/O routines evolved into a primitive IOCS that formed the core of many early operating systems.

The Input/Output Control System

As you learned in the previous section, following a logical I/O request from an application program, the file system searches the directory and finds the appropriate physical address. The file system then passes the physical address to the operating system's device management layer. On many operating systems, the device management routine that generates primitive physical I/O commands and communicates directly with the peripherals is called the **input/output control system** or **IOCS** (Figure 5.12).

Consider, for example, the process of reading a sector from disk. A disk drive is limited to a few primitive operations, including:

1. seek to a track,
2. read a sector from that track,
3. write a sector to that track.

The only way to read a program or a set of data from disk into memory is to send the drive a series of primitive commands asking it to seek and read the contents of one or more sectors. Note that the disk drive must be told exactly where to position the access mechanism and exactly which sectors to read. If your program needs the data stored on track 20, sectors 8 and 9, the IOCS would have to tell the hardware to:

SEEK 20
READ 8
SEEK 20
READ 9

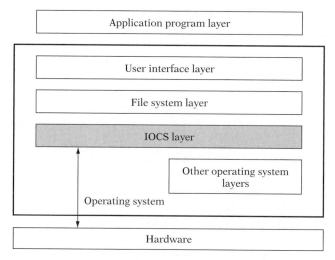

FIGURE 5.12

The IOCS generates the primitive commands that control a peripheral device.

All the application program wants, of course, is the data.

Quickly review the process. The input/output process starts when an application program passes a logical I/O request to the file system. The file responds by translating the logical I/O request into a physical I/O request, which it passes to the IOCS. The IOCS then generates the appropriate primitive commands that control the physical peripheral device. In other words, the application program performs logical I/O, the IOCS performs physical I/O, and the file system translates—another example of layering.

■ Resident and Transient Routines

In addition to its primary layers, most operating systems incorporate a set of **utility** routines such as linkage editors, loaders, line editors, disk formatting routines, sort routines, debugging features, library management routines, and so on. Other utilities designed to recover lost data, convert data from one format to another, optimize the way data are stored on a disk, make backup copies of files or disks, check a file for viruses, and perform similar support services can be purchased from independent sources. As such third-party utilities gain popularity their functions are often absorbed into a future release of the operating system.

Utilities are needed only occasionally, so most are treated as **transient** routines that are stored on disk and loaded into memory only when necessary.

In contrast, the file system and the IOCS support application programs in real time as they execute and thus must be **resident** in memory at all times.

The Boot

Because it performs essential support services, the operating system must be in memory before any application program can be executed. On some systems, the operating system resides in read-only memory. ROM is permanent. It keeps its contents even when power is lost, so a ROM-based operating system is always there. The main memory of most computers is composed of RAM, however. RAM is volatile; it loses its contents when power is cut. Consequently, the operating system must be loaded into memory each time the computer is restarted.

Typically, the operating system is stored on disk, and the program that loads the operating system into memory, the **boot,** is stored on the first sector (or two) of the same disk (Figure 5.13). Hardware is designed to read the boot automatically whenever the power is turned on or the system is restarted (Figure 5.13a), often by executing a small, ROM-based routine. The boot consists of only a few instructions, but they are sufficient to read the resident portion of the operating system into memory (Figure 5.13b); note how it is seemingly "pulled in by its own bootstraps." Once the operating system is in memory, a user can issue the commands to launch application programs.

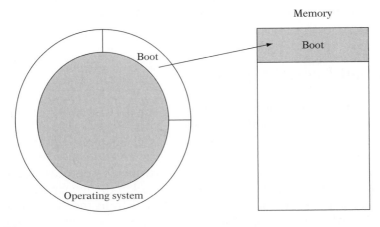

FIGURE 5.13

The boot.

a. Hardware automatically reads the boot when power is turned on.

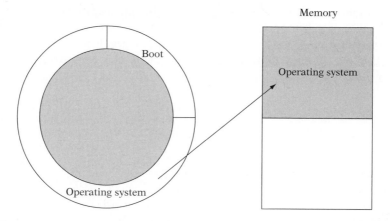

FIGURE 5.13

b. The boot reads the rest of the operating system into memory.

Loading the operating system from scratch is called a cold boot or cold start. If the computer is already running, it is often possible to warm boot or warm start the operating system by pressing a specific key combination such as *ctrl, alt,* and *delete.* Because key control information is already in place, a warm boot can bypass certain preliminary tasks, and that saves time. Note that on many modern operating systems, pressing *ctrl, alt,* and *delete* opens a window that gives you several options.

Summary

People communicate directly with the operating system through the user interface by issuing commands. There are several different types of user interfaces, including a command interface or shell, a menu interface, a graphical user interface or GUI, a voice-activated interface, and a Web-form interface. The set of available commands and their syntax rules forms a command language. Often, a batch file is used to simplify issuing repetitive commands.

Files and programs are accessed by name through the file system. Each file name is recorded in a disk directory. The file system manages the directory and also manages disk space. Programs are launched or closed in response to commands. Data files are opened and closed and data is read and written in response to program instructions. Blocking and spanned records complicate the task of reading and writing data. The input/output control system communicates with the physical devices. Most operating systems include utility routines. Resident routines are stored in memory. Transient routines are stored on disk and loaded into memory only when they are needed. The routine that loads the operating system is called a boot.

◙ Key Words

batch file	menu interface
block	open
boot	physical I/O
close	physical record
command	resident
command line interface	shell
command language	spanned record
file system	transient
graphical user interface	user interface
input/output control system	utility
(IOCS)	voice-activated interface
logical I/O	Web-form interface
logical record	

◙ Review Questions

1. Identify the basic functions performed by an operating system's user interface.
2. Distinguish a command interface or shell, a menu interface, a graphical user interface, a voice-activated interface, and a Web-form interface.
3. What is a command? What is a command language? How are commands used to communicate with the user interface?
4. What is a batch command file? Why are batch files used?
5. What functions are performed by the file system?
6. What happens when a program is launched?
7. What happens when a data file is opened? What happens when a data file is closed?
8. Distinguish between launching a program and opening a data file. How are these processes similar? How do they differ?
9. Distinguish between logical I/O and physical I/O.
10. Distinguish between a physical record and a logical record.
11. What is blocking? What is a spanned record?
12. Distinguish between directory management and disk space management.
13. Identify the primary functions performed by the input/output control system.

14. Distinguish between the input/output control system and the file system.

15. What is a utility?

16. Distinguish between a resident routine and a transient routine.

17. What is a boot? Why is a boot necessary? What happens during the boot process?

▊ Exercises

1. Explain the relationship between the evolution of the user interface and the amount of work a computer can perform within a single instant.

2. Do you think a voice-activated user interface will ever become the standard? Why, or why not?

3. Many old-time programmers are happy to talk about their experiences writing code back in the batch processing days before personal computers and interactive user interfaces became the norm. Many are retired or rapidly approaching retirement age, so you might not be able to talk to one of the old timers, but if you can, ask about what programming was like back in the (not so) good old days.

4. Why does it make sense to shift the details associated with opening and closing files, physical I/O, and disk space management down into the operating system? Can you think of any possible dangers that might arise from this approach?

5. Identify several utility programs that are marketed independently of the operating system.

6. Figure 5.12 is a useful template for organizing many of this chapter's key terms.

CHAPTER 6

Resource Management

When you finish reading this chapter you should be able to:

▶ Define several common measures of computer performance.

▶ Distinguish between resident and transient routines.

▶ Distinguish among fixed-partition memory management, dynamic memory management, segmentation, paging, and segmentation *and* paging.

▶ Explain dynamic address translation.

▶ Explain how virtual memory works.

▶ Discuss the role of control blocks and interrupts in the dispatching process.

▶ Explain how the queuing routine and the scheduler work together to load application programs.

▶ Distinguish between multiprogramming and time-sharing.

▶ Explain the virtual machine concept.

▶ Explain why deadlock is a problem.

◾ Measures of Effectiveness

On most modern computers, the operating system serves as the primary resource manager, allocating and managing processor time, memory space, peripheral devices, secondary storage space, and data and program libraries. A well-designed operating system attempts to optimize the utilization of all the system resources.

The first step in achieving optimization is to define precisely what you mean by optimum. Consider an analogy. What is the optimum automobile? Are you primarily interested in speed or safety? Do you prefer fuel efficiency or interior space and a comfortable ride? Are you interested in low cost transportation or high status? Until you define your criteria, you cannot *begin* to discuss the precise meaning of the word optimum because the criteria conflict. What is best for you is not necessarily *best* for me because best is a relative term.

Several criteria are commonly used to measure a computer system's performance (Figure 6.1). The perfect system would maximize throughput while minimizing both turnaround and response time. The system would be available on demand, and would be remarkably easy to use. Security would, of course, be absolute, system reliability would approach 100 percent, and the system would quickly recover on its own from the occasional error. All this would be accomplished at very low cost, of course. Unfortunately, such perfection is impossible to achieve because the measures of effectiveness conflict.

Resource management is a key operating system function. The operating system's job is to manage the computer system's resources as efficiently as possible, but the precise definition of efficiency depends on the computing environment. Your personal computer, a corporate mainframe, and a network computer that manages machine-to-machine communications perform very different functions and emphasize different criteria, so their operating systems will differ. Keep those differences in mind as you read this chapter and study the various operating systems discussed in the balance of this book.

◾ Memory Management

Chapter 5 discussed the shell, the file system, and the IOCS, three major operating system components that directly support an application program's input and output operations. This chapter focuses primarily on memory management and processor management. **Memory management** is concerned with managing the computer's available pool of memory, allocating space to application routines and making sure that they do not

Criterion	Meaning
Throughput	Generally, total execution time (for all programs) divided by total elapsed time, often expressed as a percentage. Higher is better.
Turnaround	The elapsed time between job submission and job completion. Shorter is better.
Response time	The elapsed time between a request for the computer's attention and the computer's response. Shorter is better.
Availability	A measure of a user's ability to gain access to a computer system. Expressed variously as the ration of free time to elapsed time (higher is better), the ratio of unavailable time to elapsed time (lower is better), or wait time to gain access (lower is better). Availability is concerned with getting on the system in the first place. Throughput, turnaround, and response time are relevant only after access is gained.
Security	A measure of a system's ability to avoid being compromised. Difficult to measure precisely. See Chapter 18.
Reliability	The probability that a system will perform as expected for a specified period of time. Higher is better.
Robustness	The ability of the system to recover quickly from errors or unusual circumstances.
Cost	The system's cost. Lower is better.
Ease of use	A subjective measure, sometimes expressed negatively as the time required to learn how to use a system. Quicker is better.

FIGURE 6.1

Some commonly used measures of computer system effectiveness.

interfere with each other. **Processor management** is concerned with managing the processor's time. Unlike the topics of Chapter 5, these resource management tasks are largely hidden from the user's view.

We begin with memory management.

Resident and Transient Routines

The operating system is a collection of software routines. Some routines, such as the ones that control physical I/O, directly support application programs as they run and thus must be **resident.** Others, such as the routine that formats diskettes, are used only occasionally. These **transient** routines are stored on disk and read into memory only when needed.

Generally, the operating system occupies low memory beginning with address 0 (Figure 6.2). System control information comes first, followed by the various resident operating system routines. The remaining memory, called the **transient area,** is where application programs and transient operating system routines are loaded.

Concurrency

Given the speed disparity between a computer and its peripherals, input and output operations significantly impact efficiency. For example, picture a computer with a single program in memory. The program cannot process data it does not yet have, and success cannot be assumed until an output operation is finished, so the program waits for input or output. Since the program controls the computer, the computer waits, too. Typically, given the speed disparity between the processor and its peripheral devices, a program spends far more time waiting for I/O than processing data.

Why not put two programs in memory and allow them to execute concurrently? Then, when program A is waiting for data, the processor can turn its attention to program B. And why stop at two programs? With three concurrent programs, even more otherwise wasted time is utilized (Figure 6.3). Generally, the more programs in memory, the greater the utilization of the processor.

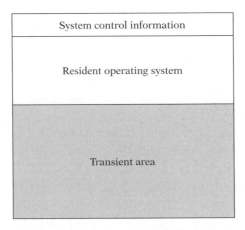

FIGURE 6.2

The operating system occupies low memory. Application programs and transient operating system routines are loaded into the transient area.

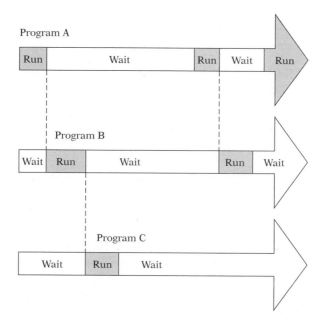

FIGURE 6.3

Multiple programs can be loaded into memory and executed concurrently.

Partitions and Regions

The simplest approach to managing memory for multiple, concurrent programs, **fixed-partition memory management** (Figure 6.4), divides the available space into fixed-length **partitions** each of which holds one program. Partition sizes are generally set when the system is initially started, so the memory allocation decision is made before the actual amount of space needed by a given program is known. Because the size of a partition must be big enough to hold the largest program that is likely to be loaded,

Concurrent and Simultaneous

The processor fetches and executes a single instruction during each machine cycle. Clearly, if the processor can execute only one *instruction* at a time, it cannot possibly execute two or more programs at a time. Thus, although multiple programs can share memory, only one can be active at any given time. Simultaneous means "at the same instant." No single processor can execute two or more *programs* simultaneously. Concurrent means "over the same time period." A processor can certainly execute two or more programs concurrently.

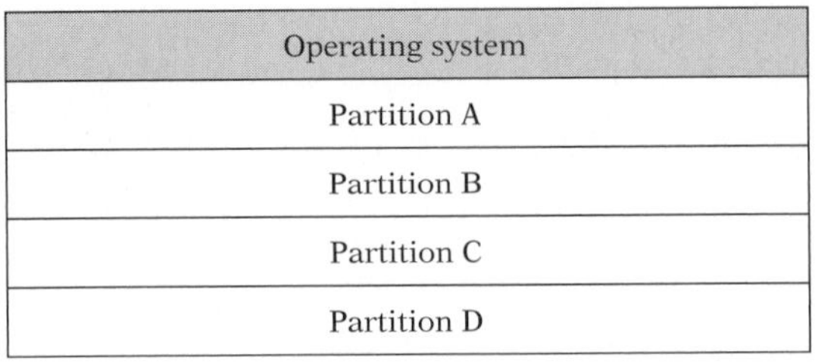

Operating system
Partition A
Partition B
Partition C
Partition D

FIGURE 6.4

Fixed-partition memory management divides the available space into fixed-length partitions.

fixed partition memory management tends to waste space. Its major advantage is simplicity.

Under **dynamic memory management,** the transient area is treated as a pool of unstructured free space. When the system decides to load a particular program, a **region** of memory just sufficient to hold the program is allocated from the pool. Because a program gets only the space it needs, relatively little is wasted.

Dynamic memory management does not completely solve the wasted space problem, however. Assume, for example, that a 64MB program has just finished executing (Figure 6.5). If there are no 64MB programs available, the system might load a 25MB program and a 30MB program, but note that 9MB remains unallocated. If no 9MB or smaller programs are available, the space will simply not be used. Over time, little chunks of unused space will be spread throughout memory, creating a **fragmentation** problem.

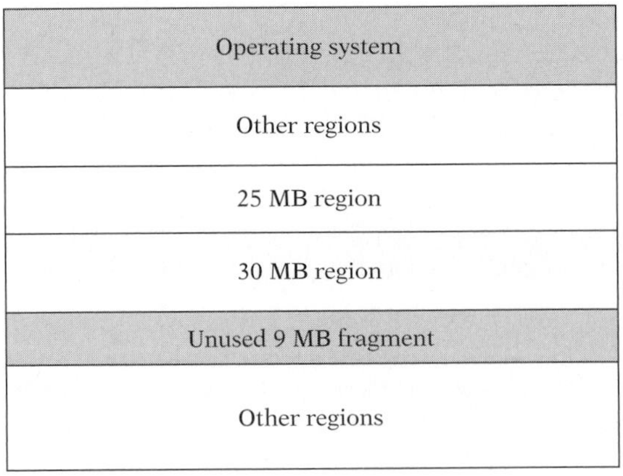

Operating system
Other regions
25 MB region
30 MB region
Unused 9 MB fragment
Other regions

FIGURE 6.5

Under dynamic memory management, the transient area is treated as a pool of unstructured free space. Fragmentation is a possible problem.

Segmentation

One reason for the fragmentation problem is that both fixed-partition and dynamic memory management assume that a given program must be loaded into *contiguous* memory. With **segmentation,** programs are divided into independently addressed segments and stored in *noncontiguous* memory (Figure 6.6).

Segmentation requires adding a step to the address translation process. When a program is loaded into memory, the operating system builds a segment table listing the (absolute) entry point address of each of the program's segments (Figure 6.7). (Note that there is one segment table for each active program.) Later, when the operating system starts a given program, it loads the address of that program's segment table into a special register.

As the program runs, addresses must be translated from relative to absolute form because programmers still write the same code and compilers still generate base-plus-displacement addresses. After fetching an instruction, the instruction control unit expands each operand address by adding the base register and the displacement. Traditionally, the expanded address was an absolute address. On a segmented system, however, the expanded address consists of two parts: a segment number and a displacement (Figure 6.7).

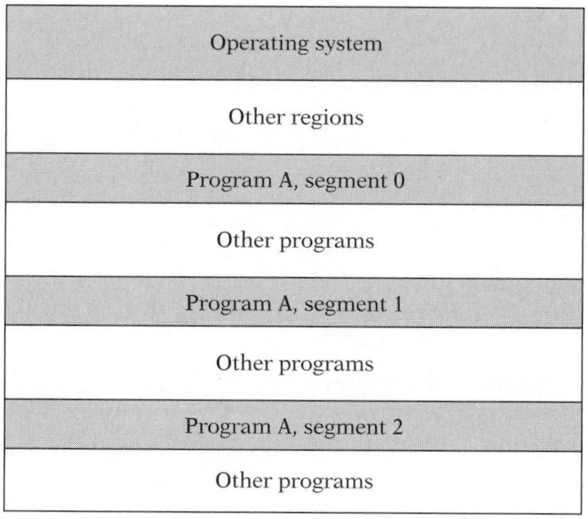

Operating system
Other regions
Program A, segment 0
Other programs
Program A, segment 1
Other programs
Program A, segment 2
Other programs

FIGURE 6.6

With segmentation, independently addressed segments are stored in noncontiguous memory.

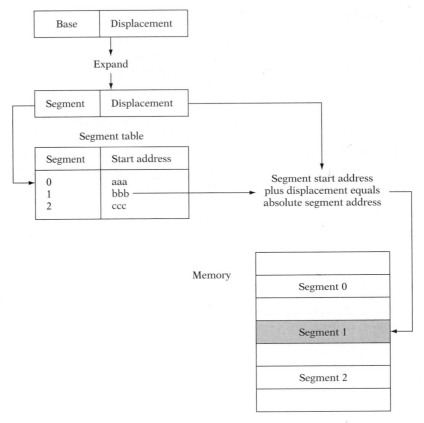

FIGURE 6.7
Dynamic address translation of a segment address.

To convert the segment/displacement address to an absolute address, hardware:

1. checks the special register to find the program's segment table,
2. extracts the segment number from the expanded address,
3. uses the segment number to search the program's segment table,
4. finds the segment's absolute entry point address,
5. adds the displacement to the entry point address to get an absolute address.

The process outlined in Figure 6.7 is called **dynamic address translation.**

Paging

A program's segments can vary in length. Under **paging,** in contrast, a program is broken into *fixed-length* pages. Page size is generally small and chosen with hardware efficiency in mind.

Like segments, a program's pages are loaded into noncontiguous memory. Addresses consist of two parts (Figure 6.8), a page number in the high-order positions and a displacement in the low-order bits. Addresses are dynamically translated as the program runs. When an instruction is fetched, its base-plus-displacement addresses are expanded to absolute addresses by hardware. Then the page's base address is looked up in a program page table (like the segment table, maintained by the operating system) and added to the displacement.

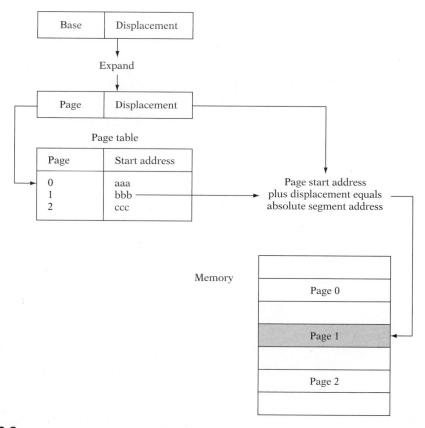

FIGURE 6.8

Dynamic address translation of a page address.

Segmentation *and* Paging

With **segmentation *and* paging,** addresses are divided into a segment number, a page number within that segment, and a displacement within that page (Figure 6.9). After the instruction control unit expands the relative address, dynamic address translation begins. First, the program's seg-

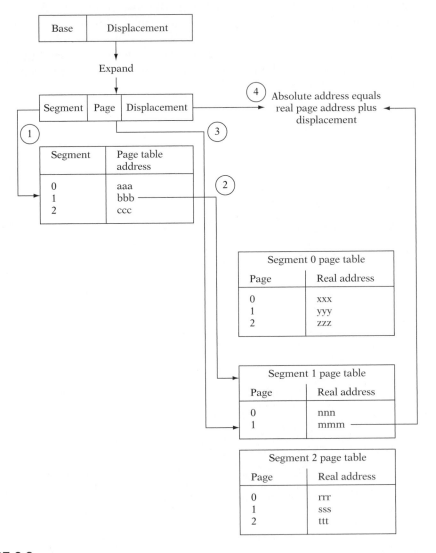

FIGURE 6.9

Under segmentation *and* paging, addresses are divided into three parts: a segment, a page, and a displacement.

ment table is searched for the segment number, which yields the address of the segment's page table. The page table is then searched for the *page's* base address, which is added to the displacement to get an absolute address.

Memory Protection

The contents of RAM are easily changed. With multiple programs sharing memory, it is possible for one program to destroy the contents of memory space belonging to another, so the active programs must be protected from each other. Generally, the operating system keeps track of the space assigned to each program. If a program attempts to modify (or, sometimes, even to read) the contents of memory locations that do not belong to it, the operating system's **memory protection** routine intervenes and (usually) terminates the program.

▉ Virtual Memory

If a processor can execute only one instruction at a time, why is it necessary for *every* instruction in a program to be in memory before that program can begin executing? It isn't. Loading only currently active pages is the underlying principle behind modern **virtual memory** systems.

Overlay Structures

The computers of the 1950s and early 1960s contained relatively little main memory. For example, imagine a second generation programmer faced with the problem of running a 32K program on a 16KB (yes, kilobyte) machine. One solution was to use overlay structures.

The idea was to break the program into logically independent modules. For example, imagine a program with four 8K modules (Figure 6.10a). Module 1 holds the main control logic and key data common to the entire program. Module 2 processes valid input data. Occasionally, errors or unusual data values call for the logic in module 3. Module 4 generates end-of-program statistics, so it is needed only when the program terminates.

Clearly, module 1 must remain in memory at all times. If no errors are encountered, there is no need for module 3. On the other hand, if an error occurs, module 3's logic must be executed, but modules 2 and 4 are superfluous. Thus, the program begins with modules 1 and 2 in memory (Figure 6.10b). When an error occurs, module 3 overlays module 2 (Figure 6.10c) and stays in memory until the next valid set of data is read, at which time module 2 replaces it. Finally, just before the program ends, module 4 overlays 2 or 3 (Figure 6.10d) and generates its statistics.

Module 1: Main control and key data
Module 2: Normal data processing logic
Module 3: Error processing
Module 4: End-of-job summary computations

FIGURE 6.10

With overlay structures, only the active portions of a program are loaded into memory.

a. The complete program consists of four modules.

Module 1: Main control and key data
Module 2: Normal data processing logic

b. Under normal conditions, only modules 1 and 2 are in memory.

Module 1: Main control and key data
Module 3: Error processing

c. When errors occur, module 3 overlays module 2.

Module 1: Main control and key data
Module 4: End-of-job summary computations

d. At end-of-job, only modules 1 and 4 are needed.

Modern computers have much more memory than their second generation ancestors, but overlay structures are still used. More significantly, the idea of loading only a program's active modules into memory lives today in modern virtual memory systems.

Implementing Virtual Memory

Figure 6.11 illustrates a common approach to implementing virtual memory. It shows three levels of storage—virtual memory, the **external paging device,** and **real memory.** Real memory is good, old-fashioned main memory, directly addressable by the processor. The external paging device is usually disk. Virtual memory is a model that simplifies address translation. It "contains" the operating system and all the application programs, but it does not physically exist anywhere. Instead, its contents are physically stored in real memory and on the external paging device.

Virtual memory is divided into two components. The first part is exactly equal to the amount of real memory on the system and is physically stored in real memory. It holds the resident operating system and the transient program area (called the page pool). The second component of virtual memory consists of space over and above real memory's capacity. It is physically stored on the external paging device and holds application programs and transient operating system routines. The resident operating system is loaded into real memory. Application programs and transients are loaded onto the external paging device. Selected pages are then swapped between the real memory page pool and the external paging device (Figure 6.12).

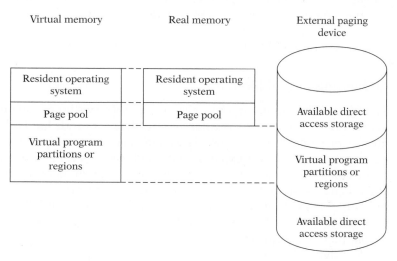

FIGURE 6.11

Virtual memory.

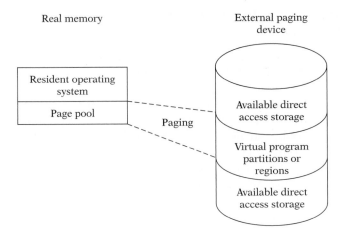

FIGURE 6.12
Pages are swapped between the external paging device and the real-memory page pool.

Traditionally, the operating system's memory management routine was concerned with allocating real memory space. On a virtual memory system, an equivalent module allocates space on the external paging device. Space on the external paging device can be divided into fixed-length partitions, variable-length regions, segments, pages, or any other convenient unit. Swapping pages between the external paging device and real memory is a system function and thus is transparent to the user.

Addressing Virtual Memory

The instructions that run on a virtual memory system are identical to the instructions that run on a regular system. The operands hold relative (base-plus-displacement) addresses. As is the case on non-virtual systems, the instruction control unit expands each address by adding the displacement to the contents of a base register immediately after an instruction is fetched. On a regular system, the base register holds the program's load point in real memory. On a virtual system, however, the base register holds the program's load point in *virtual* memory, so the computed address reflects the page's *virtual* memory location.

The dynamic address translation process (which resembles segmentation *and* paging addressing; see Figure 6.9) starts when the program is loaded into virtual memory. The operating system allocates space on the external paging device and notes the virtual addresses of the program's segments and pages in the program's segment and page tables. Later, when a given page is swapped into real memory, the page's *real* address is noted in the page table.

Note that a page must be in real memory for the processor to execute its instructions. When an instruction executes, the instruction control unit (in its usual way) adds the base register and the displacement to get an address in virtual memory. To convert a virtual address to a real address, hardware then:

1. accesses the program's segment table using the high-order bits of the virtual address as a key,
2. locates the program's page table using the pointer in the segment table,
3. accesses the page table to find the page's *real* base address using the middle bits in the virtual address as a key,
4. adds the displacement found in the low-order bits of the virtual address to the page's real memory base address.

On most systems, the process is streamlined through the use of special registers and other hardware.

Page Faults

When a virtual address points to a page that is not in real memory, a **page fault** is recognized and a page-in (or swap-in) operation begins. If no real memory is available for the new page, some other page must be swapped out. Often the "least currently accessed" or "least currently used" page (the page that has gone the longest time without being referenced) is selected.

Bringing pages into memory only when they are referenced is called **demand paging.** An option called **pre-paging** involves predicting the demand for a new page and swapping it into memory before it is actually needed. Many pre-paging algorithms assume that segments hold logically related code, so if the instructions on page 1 are currently executing the chances are that the instructions on page 2 will be executed next. While far from perfect, such techniques can significantly speed up program execution.

Thrashing

When real memory is full, a demand for a new page means that another page must be swapped out. If this happens frequently, the system can find itself spending so much time swapping pages into and out from memory that little time is left for useful work.

This problem is called **thrashing,** and it can seriously degrade system performance. The short-term solution is removing a program or two from real memory until the system settles down. The long-term solution is to improve the real-to-virtual ratio, usually by adding more real memory.

Memory Mapping

Memory mapping is a technique for minimizing the number of physical I/O operations. The idea is to map an image of the target file into the program's virtual memory address space, in effect storing the file in virtual memory. Once a file is mapped, data can be transferred between memory and disk by taking advantage of the system's paging mechanism, which is considerably more efficient than physical I/O.

◼ Multiprogramming

Multiprogramming is a common approach to processor management when two or more programs occupy memory and execute concurrently. Originally developed to support batch-processing applications, multiprogramming takes advantage of the extreme speed disparity between a computer and its peripheral devices. Traditionally, the key measures of multiprogramming effectiveness are throughput (run time divided by elapsed time) and turnaround (the time between job submission and job completion).

The Serial Batch Era

Back in the 1950s and early 1960s, most computers operated in serial batch mode. Programs were submitted, usually in punched card form, to a human operator who scheduled the computer. When the time came to run a given program, the operator cleared the computer of all residual settings from the last program; set up the new job by loading the necessary disk packs, tape volumes, special printer forms, and other media; and started the program. As it ran, the program had exclusive use of all the computer's resources. Only when the program finished processing was the next program set up and run.

As you might imagine, the serial batch process resulted in lengthy wait times, and 24-hour turnaround (the elapsed time between submitting a job and getting the results) was considered normal. By the mid-1960s, multiprogramming, with its ability to concurrently support several application programs, had significantly reduced average turnaround time to a matter of hours. Today, we consider a delay of more than a few seconds to be intolerably long. It is interesting to note how our perspective of time has changed over the years.

The Dispatcher

Imagine two programs concurrently occupying memory. Some time ago, program A requested data from disk (Figure 6.13). Because program A was unable to continue until the input operation was completed, it dropped into a **wait state** and the processor turned to program B.

Assume program A's input operation has just been completed. Both programs are now in a **ready state;** in other words, both are ready to resume processing. Which one goes first? Computers are so fast that a human operator cannot effectively make such real-time choices. Instead, the decision is made by a processor management routine called the **dispatcher.**

Consider a system with two partitions: foreground and background. The dispatcher typically checks the program in the foreground partition first. If the program is ready, the dispatcher restarts it. Only if the foreground program is still in a wait state does the dispatcher check the background partition. The foreground has high priority; the background has low priority.

This idea can be extended to larger systems with multiple concurrent programs in memory. The dispatcher checks partitions in a fixed order until a ready state program is found. The first partition checked has highest priority; the last has lowest priority. The only way the low-priority program can execute is if all the higher-priority partitions are in a wait state.

Control Blocks

There are several control fields that must be maintained in support of each active program. On many systems, a **control block** is created to hold a partition's key control flags, constants, and variables (Figure 6.14). The control blocks (one per partition) form a linked list. The dispatcher typically determines which program to start next by following the chain of pointers from control block to control block. A given control block's relative position in the linked list might be determined by its priority or computed dynamically, perhaps taking into account such factors as program size, time in memory, peripheral device requirements, and other measures of the program's impact on system resources.

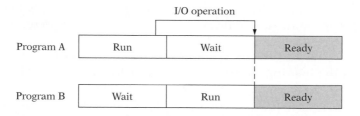

FIGURE 6.13

When two or more programs are in a ready state, the dispatcher decides which one executes first.

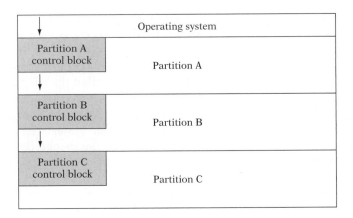

FIGURE 6.14
The dispatcher determines which program to start next by following a linked list of control blocks.

Interrupts

A program normally surrenders control of the processor when it requests an I/O operation and is eligible to continue processing when that I/O operation is completed. Consequently, the key to multiprogramming is recognizing when input or output operations begin or end. The operating system knows when these events occur because they are marked by **interrupts.**

An interrupt is an electronic signal. Hardware senses the signal, saves key control information for the currently executing program, and starts the operating system's **interrupt handler** routine. At that instant, the interrupt ends. The operating system then processes the interrupt and calls the dispatcher, which starts an application program. Eventually, the program that was executing at the time of the interrupt resumes processing.

Interrupts can originate with either hardware or software. A program issues an interrupt to request the operating system's support (for example, to start an I/O operation). Hardware issues an interrupt to notify the processor that an asynchronous event (such as the completion of an I/O operation or a hardware failure) has occurred. Other types of interrupts might signal an illegal operation (a zero divide) or the expiration of a preset time interval.

For example, follow the steps in Figure 6.15. When an application program needs data, it issues an interrupt (Figure 6.15a). In response, hardware starts the interrupt handler routine, which saves key control information, drops the application program into a wait state (Figure 6.15b), and calls the input/output control system to start the I/O operation. Finally, control flows to the dispatcher, which starts a different program (Figure 6.15c).

Later, when the I/O operation is finished, the channel issues an interrupt (Figure 6.15d). Once again the interrupt handler routine begins executing (Figure 6.15e). After verifying that the I/O operation was successfully completed, it resets the program that initially requested the data (program A) to a ready state. Then it calls the dispatcher, which starts the highest priority "ready" application program (Figure 6.15f). In this example, note that program A, the higher priority program, goes next even though program B was running at the time the interrupt occurred.

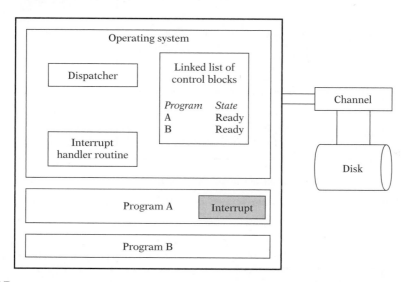

FIGURE 6.15

The dispatching process.

a. The program issues an interrupt.

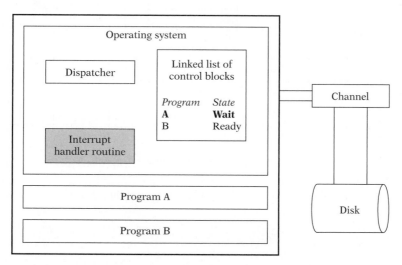

b. The interrupt handler routine sets the program to a wait state.

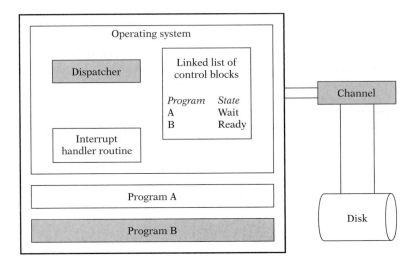

c. The dispatcher starts another application program.

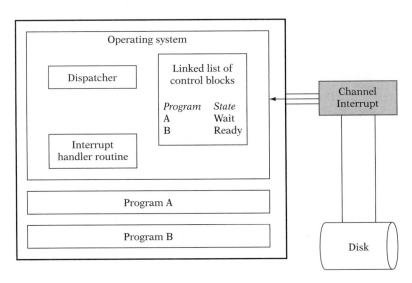

d. The channel signals the end of the I/O operation by sending the processor an interrupt.

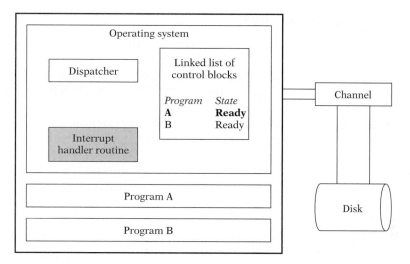

e. The interrupt handler routine resets program A to a ready state.

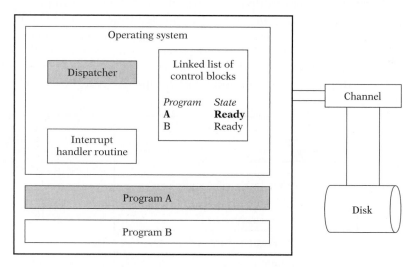

f. The dispatcher selects an application program and starts it.

Queuing and Scheduling

Processor management is concerned with the *internal* priorities of programs already in memory. A program's *external* priority is a different issue. As one program finishes processing and space becomes available, which program is loaded into memory next? This decision typically involves two separate modules, a **queuing routine** and a **scheduler.** As programs enter the system, they are placed on a queue by the queuing routine (Figure 6.16). When space becomes available, the scheduler selects a program from the queue and loads it into memory.

Clearly distinguish between a program's internal and external priorities. Once a program is in memory, the dispatcher uses its *internal* priority to determine its right to access the processor. In contrast, the program's *external* priority has to do with loading it into memory in the first place. Until the program is in memory, it has no internal priority. Once in memory, its external priority is no longer relevant.

◾ Time-Sharing

Time-sharing is a more interactive approach to processor and memory management for multiple concurrent users. The most important measure of effectiveness is response time, the elapsed time between entering a transaction and seeing the system's response appear on the screen. Note, however, that time-sharing and multiprogramming are not mutually exclusive. In fact, it is not uncommon for an interactive, time-sharing system to run in the high priority partition on a large, multiprogramming mainframe.

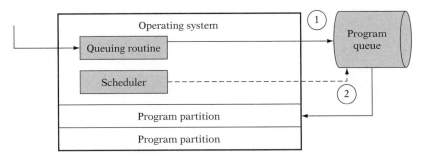

FIGURE 6.16
Queuing and scheduling.

Roll-In/Roll-Out

Picture a typical time-sharing application. A series of brief transactions (single program statements, single lines of input data, single commands) are typed through a keyboard. In most cases, very little actual processing is required to support each transaction. Typing is (relatively speaking) slow, perhaps two transactions per minute.

To the computer, each user represents a string of brief, widely spaced processing demands. Consequently, as a given transaction is processed, the system knows that considerable time will pass before that user's next transaction arrives, so the workspace can be rolled out to secondary storage, making room for another application in memory. Later, when the first user's next transaction arrives, his or her workspace is rolled back in. Most time-sharing systems use such **roll-in/roll-out** techniques to manage memory space.

Time-Slicing

Imagine that you have just spent twenty minutes typing the data for a statistical analysis program. Each line of data was one brief transaction; your work to this point is a typical time-sharing application. Your last transaction is different, however. It is a command that tells the system to process the data, and that command initiates a computational routine that can easily run for several minutes. While your transaction is being processed, the other users on the system will have to wait, and given the objective of maintaining good response time, that is unacceptable.

The solution is **time-slicing.** Each program is restricted to a maximum "slice" of time, perhaps 0.001 second. Once a program begins executing, it runs until one of two things happens. If the program requires input or output before exhausting its time slice, it calls the operating system and "voluntarily" drops into a wait state, much like a multiprogramming application. If, however, the program uses up its entire time slice, a timer interrupt transfers control to the operating system and the time-sharing dispatcher starts the next program.

Polling

Often, a time-shared system uses a **polling** algorithm to determine which program to start next. Imagine a table of program control blocks (Figure 6.17). Starting at the top of the table, the dispatcher checks program 1's status. If program 1 is ready, the dispatcher starts it. If not, program 2's status is checked. Assume that program 2 is ready and the dispatcher starts it.

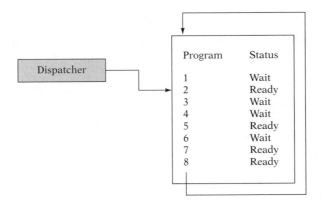

FIGURE 6.17
Some time-sharing dispatchers rely on a polling algorithm.

One time slice later, program 2 is forced to surrender control of the processor. Because the last program executed was number 2, the dispatcher resumes polling with the *third* table entry; note that program 2 is now at the end of the line. Eventually, the dispatcher works its way through the entire table, returns to the top, and repeats the process. Program 2 will get another shot only after every other program has a chance.

There are alternatives to simple round robin polling. Two (or even more) tables can be maintained, with high priority programs on the first one and background or low priority routines on the second. Another option is to place multiple references to a crucial program on the table, thus giving it several shots at the processor on each polling cycle. Some systems use a priority scheme and recompute priorities every second or two. A common priority algorithm is dividing actual run time by elapsed residency time. The limit of this computation is 1, which is considered low priority. The more processor time a program uses, the worse its priority becomes, so compute-bound tasks tend to drop to the end of the line.

The Virtual Machine Concept

Start with a full-featured mainframe. Share its resources among several concurrent users. If those users occupy partitions, regions, or workspaces, you have a traditional multiprogramming or time-sharing system.

Now take the idea a step further. Instead of simply allocating each application routine some memory and running it directly under the operating system, simulate several imaginary computers on that **real computer** (Figure 6.18). Assign each **virtual machine** its own virtual operating system and its own virtual peripherals. Traditionally, multiprogramming and time-sharing imply running several *application routines* concurrently. The virtual machine concept calls for multiprogramming or time-sharing at the *operating system* level.

Each virtual machine has its own virtual operating system, its own virtual memory, and its own virtual peripherals. Because all the virtual machines run on the same real computer, their access to facilities is limited only by the facilities of the real machine. Thus, each virtual machine has access to gigabytes of storage and scores of peripherals, and can execute billions of instructions per second. Because they share a single real computer, program development can take place on one virtual machine in interactive mode, while production applications run on another virtual machine under a traditional multiprogramming operating system.

To the user, the virtual machine is *the* computer. The details associated with the real machine are transparent, hidden by the facilities of the "real" operating system. Thus, much as a time-sharing user can ignore other, concurrent users and imagine that he or she directly controls the computer, a virtual machine user can ignore other virtual machines.

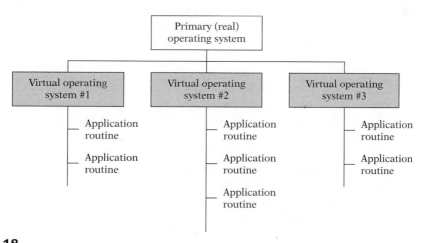

FIGURE 6.18

The virtual machine concept implies multiprogramming at the operating system level.

◼ Peripheral Device Management

In addition to memory and the processor, most computer systems also have numerous peripheral devices, and only a few of those peripherals can be shared by multiple concurrent users. For example, consider a printer. Once you start a print operation, you expect the entire document or report to print contiguously as a single entity, and if output data from some other program is interspersed with your data, the printout is useless. The operating system incorporates routines that manage peripheral device allocation and ensure that device assignments to multiple concurrent applications do not conflict.

Spooling

Imagine a program that generates payroll for 10,000 employees. Printing 10,000 checks takes several minutes. Why not write the checks to disk and print them later, in the background? That way, the memory allocated to the payroll program is freed for another program much more quickly.

That is the essential idea behind **spooling.** Even with multiprogramming, it is common for all application programs to be waiting for I/O. During these idle periods, the operating system's spooling module reads data from such slow devices as terminal keyboards and stores them on a high-speed medium such as disk. Later, when the program is loaded, its input data can be read from high-speed disk. On output, data are spooled to disk and later dumped to the printer during idle periods. Because the application program deals only with high-speed I/O, it finishes processing and thus frees space for another program much more quickly. Because output is spooled before it is printed, the various programs' printouts are kept separate.

Deadlock

Deadlock is one possible consequence of poor resource management. Imagine, for example, that two programs need data from the same disk. Program A issues a seek command and drops into a wait state. Subsequently, program B begins executing and issues its own seek command. Eventually, the first seek operation is completed and the dispatcher starts program A, which issues a read command. Unfortunately, the second seek command has moved the access mechanism, so A must reissue the seek command and once again drop into a wait state. Soon B issues its read command, discovers that the access mechanism is in the wrong place, and reissues its own seek command.

Consider the outcome of this nightmare. Program A positions the access mechanism. Program B moves it. Program A repositions it; program B repositions it again. Picture the access mechanism moving rapidly back and forth across the disk's surface. No data are read or written. Neither program can proceed. The result is deadlock.

Deadlock is not limited to peripheral devices. It happens when two (or more) programs each control any resource needed by the other. Neither program can continue until the other program releases its resource. If neither program is willing to give in, the system, almost literally, "spins its wheels." At best, that leads to inefficiency. At worst, it can bring the entire system to a halt. One solution is prevention; some operating systems will not load a program unless all its resource needs can be guaranteed. Other operating systems allow some deadlocks to occur, sense them, and take corrective action.

▮ Summary

The chapter opened with a brief discussion of various measures of computer system effectiveness. Memory management is concerned with managing the computer's available pool of memory. Some operating system routines directly support application programs as they run and thus must be resident. Other transient routines are stored on disk and read into memory only when needed.

Many modern operating systems support multiple concurrent programs. Fixed-partition memory management divides memory into fixed-length partitions. Greater efficiency can be achieved by using dynamic memory management. Under segmentation, a program is broken into variable-length segments that are independently loaded into noncontiguous memory. Segmented addresses are converted to absolute form through a process called dynamic address translation. Paging is similar to segmentation except that pages are fixed in length. With segmentation *and* paging, programs are broken into logical segments and the segments subdivided into pages. Most operating systems incorporate memory protection features.

With overlay structures, a program is broken into logically independent modules, and only those modules that are actually active are loaded into memory. On a virtual memory system, programs are loaded on the external paging device and individual pages are paged-in to real memory as needed. Virtual memory is a logical model that supports dynamic address translation. If a referenced page is not in real memory, a page fault is recognized and the needed page is swapped in. Excessive paging can lead to thrashing, which degrades system performance.

Multiprogramming is a processor management technique that relies on the speed disparity between a computer and its peripherals. Typically, interrupts mark the beginning and end of each input and output operation. Following an interrupt, the dispatcher finds the highest priority ready state program on a linked list of control blocks and starts it.   When a program first enters a system, it might be stored on a queue by a queuing routine. Later, when space becomes available, a scheduler selects the next program from the queue and loads it into memory. Time-sharing supports multiple concurrent interactive applications using roll-in/roll-out techniques for memory management and time-slicing for processor management. Often, the dispatcher follows a polling algorithm to determine which program to start next. The virtual machine concept calls for multiprogramming or time-sharing at the operating system level.

The operating system incorporates routines that manage peripheral device allocation. With spooling, slow output operations are shifted to the background. Deadlock occurs when two programs each control a resource needed by the other but neither is willing to give up its resource.

◗ Key Words

control block	processor management
deadlock	queuing routine
demand paging	ready state
dispatcher	real computer
dynamic address translation	real memory
dynamic memory management	region
external paging device	resident
fixed-partition memory	roll-in/roll-out
management	scheduler
fragmentation	segmentation
interrupt	segmentation *and* paging
interrupt handler	spooling
memory management	thrashing
memory mapping	time-sharing
memory protection	time-slicing
multiprogramming	transient
page fault	transient area
paging	virtual machine
partition	virtual memory
polling	wait state
pre-paging	

◗ Review Questions

1. Define throughput, turnaround, response time, availability security, reliability, and robustness. Explain why these measures of effectiveness conflict.

2. Distinguish between resident and transient routines. What is the transient area?

3. Distinguish between fixed-partition memory management and dynamic memory management.

4. Segmentation and/or paging can help to minimize fragmentation because programs are loaded into noncontiguous memory. Briefly explain what that means.

5. Distinguish between segmentation and paging. Explain segmentation *and* paging.

6. Explain dynamic address translation.

7. Why is memory protection necessary?

8. What is an overlay structure? Why are overlay structures used?

9. How does a virtual memory system work? Distinguish between virtual memory, the external paging device, and real memory.

10. What is a page fault? Distinguish between demand paging and pre-paging. Explain thrashing.

11. What is multiprogramming?

12. What are control blocks and why are they necessary?

13. What is an interrupt? What is the interrupt handler routine?

14. Explain how a multiprogramming system's dispatcher relies on control blocks and interrupts to manage the processor.

15. Explain how the queuing routine and the scheduler work together to load application programs. Distinguish between a program's internal and external priorities.

16. Distinguish between multiprogramming and time-sharing. Explain roll-in/roll out, time-slicing, and polling.

17. Explain the virtual machine concept.

18. What is spooling? Why is spooling used?

19. What is deadlock? Why is deadlock a problem?

◼ Exercises

1. Why do you suppose there are so many different operating systems?

2. Distinguish between concurrent and simultaneous. A single processor can execute two or more programs concurrently but not simultaneously. Why?

3. A student can concurrently study and watch television, but he or she cannot simultaneously study and watch television. Explain.

4. Overlay structures can be viewed as precursors to modern virtual memory systems. Explain why.

5. During the serial batch era, 24 hours was considered a normal turnaround time. In contrast, modern microcomputer users expect the computer to respond almost instantaneously. Would you consider using a computer if you had to wait 24 hours for feedback? Why, or why not?

6. Most personal computer systems spool printed output. Consequently, you can usually perform other work while your document prints. Explain how spooling makes that possible.

7. Identify several noncomputer examples of the deadlock principle. For example, imagine that you have a CD player, your friend has a favorite CD, and neither one of you is willing to give up your resource. How would you solve that deadlock?

8. Figures 6.9, 6.11, and 6.15a are useful templates for organizing many of this chapter's key terms.

Communicating with the Operating System

This section focuses on the user interfaces for three popular operating systems: MS-DOS (Chapter 7), Windows XP (Chapter 8), and UNIX/Linux (Chapter 9). The material is presented from a user's perspective. Think of the user or the application program as one layer and the operating system as the next lower layer. The interface between them defines the rules for layer-to-layer communication.

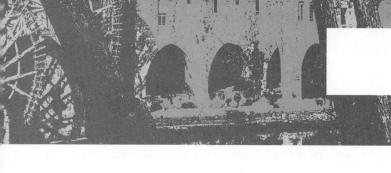

CHAPTER 7

MS-DOS Commands

When you finish reading this chapter you should be able to:

▶ Describe the structure of an MS-DOS command.

▶ Set the default drive and format a diskette.

▶ Define a valid MS-DOS file name, including an extension.

▶ Describe the MS-DOS hierarchical directory structure and define a path name.

▶ Use a directory command to view the contents of a directory.

▶ Create a directory.

▶ Distinguish between the root directory and the current working directory, and use a change directory command to change the working directory.

▶ Use copy commands to create a file from the console and to copy an existing file.

▶ Use wild card characters to copy several files with a single operation.

▶ Explain redirection, filters, and pipes.

◢ MS-DOS

Given the availability of Windows and other more intuitive interfaces, **MS-DOS** is rarely used today, so why bother to learn about MS-DOS? Basically, there are two reasons:

1. Windows and other, more sophisticated operating systems sometimes do a bit too much for the user, effectively hiding what is really happening inside the computer. MS-DOS is much more basic and direct. Consequently, if you can understand what is happening in MS-DOS, you may find it easier to understand what is happening in Windows.
2. Should your computer fail or become infected with a virus, many utility and virus protection programs include a special recovery diskette. Often, the recovery diskette uses MS-DOS commands to support the recovery process.

MS-DOS Commands

Typically, a user accesses a computer through an application program's interface and the program communicates with the operating system through an application programming interface (Figure 7.1). At times, however, the user must communicate directly with the operating system to perform such functions as launching a program. This chapter focuses on the MS-DOS user interface.

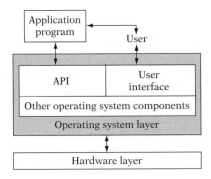

FIGURE 7.1

A user communicates with the operating system through a user interface.

MS-DOS and Microsoft

When IBM entered the personal computer marketplace in the fall of 1981, responsibility for creating an operating system was subcontracted to a company named Microsoft recently formed by two young men named Bill Gates and Paul Allen. The result, originally called PC-DOS, was a command-driven operating system that allowed users to issue cryptic, single-line commands through a command interface. Rechristened MS-DOS, Gates and Allen's operating system quickly became an industry standard and established a stable platform that served as a launching pad for the personal computer industry. MS-DOS also laid the financial base on which the founders built today's Microsoft.

Under MS-DOS, a user communicates with the operating system by issuing **commands.** The general form of an MS-DOS command is shown in Figure 7.2. The **default drive** and the system **prompt** are displayed by the operating system. The user responds to an active prompt by typing a command name followed by any necessary **parameters.** A **delimiter,** usually a space, separates the command from the parameters and (if there are several) the parameters from each other.

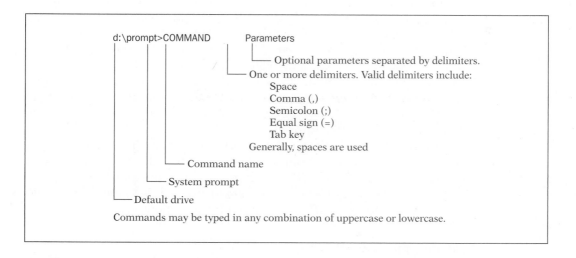

FIGURE 7.2

The general form of an MS-DOS command.

The Chapter Tutorial

This introduction to MS-DOS is presented as a tutorial. Do not simply read it. Instead, find a personal computer that runs Microsoft Windows, open your book, and follow along. As you read about a command, enter it and see for yourself how the computer responds. You will need a blank diskette. Later, you may find Appendix B a useful reference.

MS-DOS error messages tend to be rather cryptic and (often) not very useful. Common mistakes include misspelling a command or file name, failing to type a space between a command and its parameters (or between parameters), and adding extra, unnecessary parameters. If you type a command, press enter, and see an error message, simply retype the command after the next MS-DOS prompt.

▪ Getting Started

The easiest (and safest) way to access MS-DOS through Microsoft Windows is to select the *MS-DOS Prompt* from the *All Programs* or *Programs* menu. Click on the *Start* button. If you are using Windows XP, move the mouse pointer to *All Programs*, then *Accessories*. On the *Accessories* menu, you should find an entry labeled *Command Prompt* (Figure 7.3). On some earlier versions of Windows, the *Accessories* menu entry might read *MS-DOS Prompt,* and you might find the *MS-DOS Prompt* or *Command Prompt* entry on the *All Programs* menu rather than on the *Accessories* sub-menu.

In any event, click on *Command Prompt* or *MS-DOS Prompt* and the initial MS-DOS screen (or window) will appear (Figure 7.4). If you are using Windows XP, the system prompt should read *C:\Documents and Settings\default>*. On earlier versions of Windows, the prompt is likely to read *C:\>* or *C:\Windows>*. The precise wording of the prompt is not significant to the rest of this tutorial.

For future reference, there are at least two other ways to access MS-DOS. One is to boot the system from an MS-DOS system diskette. Alternatively, when you shut down a pre-XP version of Windows, one option on the shut down menu is *Restart,* or *Restart the computer* in MS-DOS mode. Stay with the *Command Prompt* or *MS-DOS Prompt* for now, however.

Selecting the Default Drive

The last line on the screen (Figure 7.4) holds the MS-DOS prompt

```
C:\Documents and Settings\default>
```

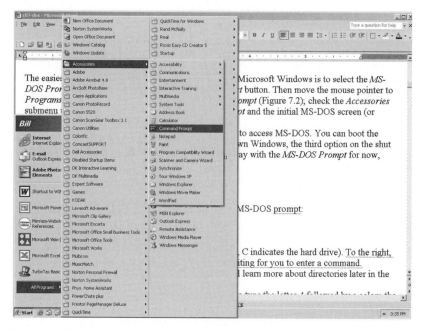

FIGURE 7.3

Accessing the command prompt through the Windows *Start* menu.

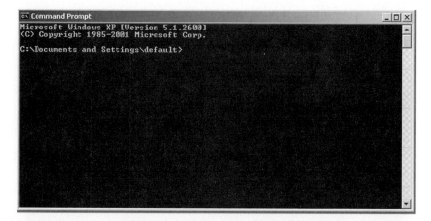

FIGURE 7.4

The initial MS-DOS prompt.

The C: indicates that C is the current default drive. (On most systems, C indicates the hard drive.) *Documents and Settings**default>* (or *Windows>*) is the name of the current directory; you will learn more about directories later in this chapter. The greater than (>) symbol indicates that MS-DOS is waiting for you to enter a command.

Insert a blank diskette into the diskette drive. Then type the letter A followed by a colon (:); the prompt line should read

C:\Documents and Settings\default>A:

In this tutorial, sample commands will be typed uppercase, but you can type commands in uppercase, lowercase, or mixed case because MS-DOS is not case sensitive. After you press enter, a new prompt will appear (Figure 7.5)

A:\>

Drive A (the diskette drive) is now the default.

Experiment a bit. Type the letter C followed by a colon and the initial C prompt will reappear. Type A: and you'll return to the A:\> prompt.

FIGURE 7.5
Changing the default drive to A.

Generally, type any drive letter followed by a colon and that drive becomes your default drive.

Make sure the prompt reads A:\> before you move on to the next step.

Formatting a Diskette

Later in the chapter you will need a work diskette. Before a diskette can be used, it must be formatted. The formatting process writes a pattern of sectors on the disk surface, records a copy of the boot routine on the first sector, and initializes control information.

The **FORMAT command** (Figure 7.6) is used to format a disk[1]. The simplest form of the command consists of a single word: FORMAT. If you issue such a command, MS-DOS will format the disk in the default drive to that drive's default density (for a diskette, usually 1.44 MB or high density). Several optional parameters are summarized in Figure 7.6. If you type more than one parameter, insert spaces to separate them.

A note of caution: *be careful*. FORMAT is a destructive command. When you format a disk, you erase whatever data might be stored on it. *If your default drive is a hard drive (for example, drive C), do not under any circumstances format that disk.* You could destroy your system.

Before you move on to the next step in this tutorial, make sure your default drive is your diskette drive (usually, drive A). If not, type A: and press the enter key.

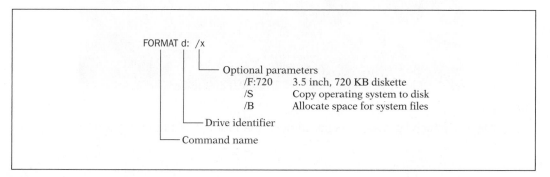

FIGURE 7.6

The FORMAT command.

---

[1]Most diskettes are purchased pre-formatted, so it may be unnecessary to format a new diskette. Using a FORMAT command to re-format a previously used diskette is common, however.

Even with the default drive set correctly, it is a good idea to specify the target drive as part of your command. For example, type the command

FORMAT A:

(Figure 7.7). The A: parameter identifies drive A as the target drive. A message will tell you to insert the diskette to be formatted into drive A and press the enter key[2]. After you press enter, a series of messages will track the format routine's progress as it formats the diskette. In response to the *Volume label* prompt you can optionally specify an identifying label that will be

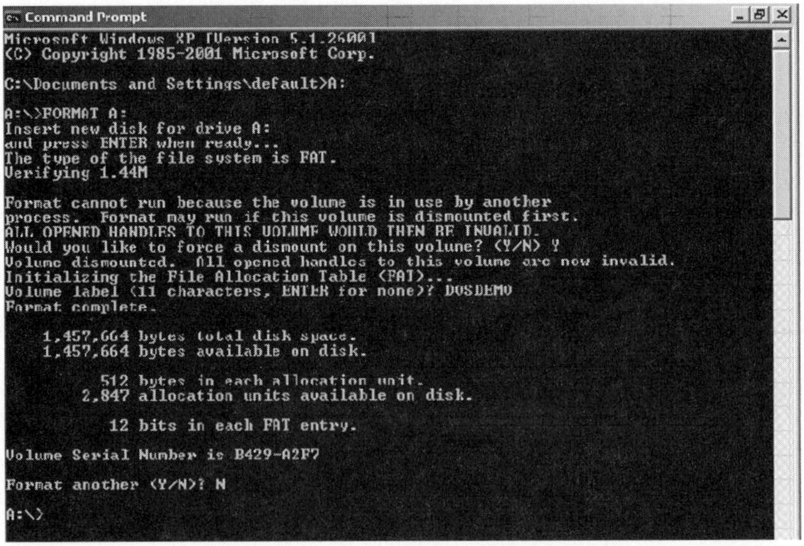

FIGURE 7.7
The FORMAT command guides the user through the process of formatting a diskette.

[2]Windows XP users might get a *Format cannot run …* message, as shown in Figure 7.7. If the message appears, type *Y* and press enter in response to the *… force a dismount …* query. Users of other versions of Windows should not get this message.

stored electronically on the disk. Type DOSDEMO. The format routine then summarizes the space available on the diskette, assigns a volume serial number, and asks if you would like to format another diskette. Type N (for no) and press the enter key.

◼ The File System

The MS-DOS **file system** allows a user to identify, save, and retrieve files by name. Note that a program is a type of file.

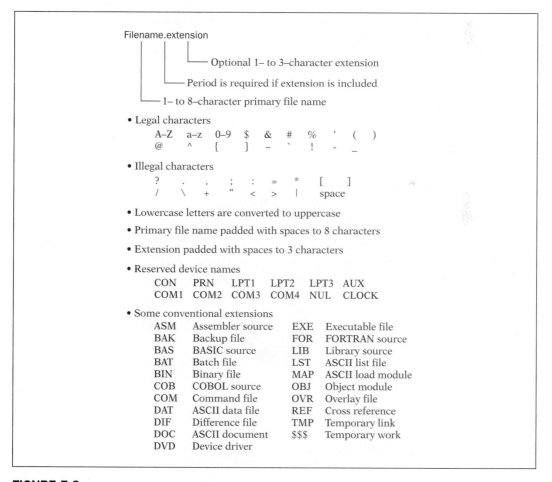

Filename.extension

└──── Optional 1– to 3–character extension

└──── Period is required if extension is included

└──── 1– to 8–character primary file name

- Legal characters

  A–Z a–z 0–9 $ & # % ' ( )
  @ ^ [ ] ~ ` ! - _

- Illegal characters

  ? . , ; : = * [ ]
  / \ + " < > | space

- Lowercase letters are converted to uppercase

- Primary file name padded with spaces to 8 characters

- Extension padded with spaces to 3 characters

- Reserved device names

  CON PRN LPT1 LPT2 LPT3 AUX
  COM1 COM2 COM3 COM4 NUL CLOCK

- Some conventional extensions

ASM	Assembler source	EXE	Executable file
BAK	Backup file	FOR	FORTRAN source
BAS	BASIC source	LIB	Library source
BAT	Batch file	LST	ASCII list file
BIN	Binary file	MAP	ASCII load module
COB	COBOL source	OBJ	Object module
COM	Command file	OVR	Overlay file
DAT	ASCII data file	REF	Cross reference
DIF	Difference file	TMP	Temporary link
DOC	ASCII document	$$$	Temporary work
DVD	Device driver		

FIGURE 7.8

The rules for defining a file name.

File Names

A **file name** (Figure 7.8) is composed of the name itself and an optional **extension.** The name consists of from 1 to 8 characters. A few file names are reserved by the system, and delimiter characters may not be used in a file name. Otherwise, just about any combination of characters you can type is legal. Incidentally, most Windows users can issue line commands that reference long file names (Chapter 8), but the traditional MS-DOS 8-character limit featured throughout this chapter is valid no matter what version you might be using.

The file name is separated from its optional, 1- to 3-character extension by a period. Some extensions have special meaning to the operating system; they are summarized near the end of Figure 7.8. The extension is sometimes used to identify a version of a program or data file; for example, VITA.1, VITA.2, and so on.

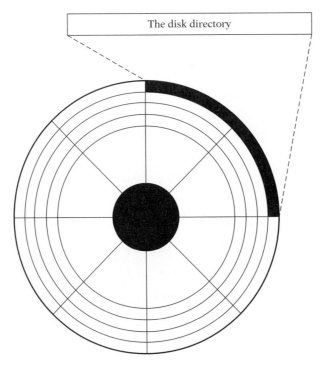

FIGURE 7.9

A file's name and starting address are recorded in the disk directory.

Directories

Directory management is a key MS-DOS file system function. The first time a file is written to disk, its name, disk address, creation date, and other information are recorded in the disk's **directory** (Figure 7.9). Later, when the file is retrieved, the operating system reads the directory and searches it for the file name. When a file is modified, the file system updates its directory entry. When the file is deleted, its directory entry is marked as deleted.

Subdirectories

When a disk is first formatted, a single **root directory** is created by the format routine. Using a single directory is fine for a few files, but as the number of files increases, distinguishing them becomes increasingly difficult.

For example, imagine a work disk that holds several different types of files. To simplify keeping track of the files, MS-DOS allows the user to create special files called **subdirectories.** For example, Figure 7.10 shows the root directory and three subdirectories. LETTERS holds letters and other correspondence. A book's chapters are stored under subdirectory BOOK. Finally spreadsheets are grouped in subdirectory WS. Think of a subdirectory as a file folder that allows you to group related files and thus organize the disk.

Path Names

When subdirectories are used, you need more than a simple file name to find a file. For example, it is possible to have files named PAY stored in two different subdirectories. A reference to PAY would thus be ambiguous— which PAY do you mean?

To fully identify a file you need a complete **path name** (Figure 7.11). For example,

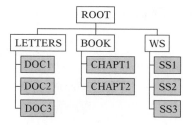

FIGURE 7.10

Subdirectories help to organize the data stored on a disk.

\LETTERS\PAY

and

\WS\PAY

are two different files. The first one is stored in subdirectory LETTERS. The second one is stored in subdirectory WS.

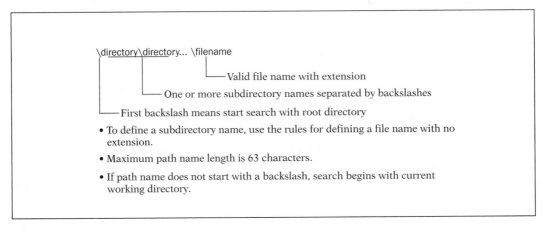

FIGURE 7.11

The rules for defining a path name.

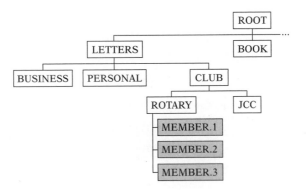

FIGURE 7.12

Directories can be subdivided into lower-level subdirectories.

Study the first path names listed above. The first backslash references the root directory. The second backslash separates the subdirectory name from the file name. The first path name shown above tells MS-DOS to start with the root directory, find a subdirectory named LETTERS, and search the subdirectory for a file named PAY. The second path name tells MS-DOS to start with the root directory, find a subdirectory named WS, and search the subdirectory for a file named PAY.

It is possible to divide a subdirectory into lower-level subdirectories. For example, Figure 7.12 shows LETTERS broken into three subdirectories. One, CLUB, is further subdivided into ROTARY and JCC. To retrieve a document named MEMBER.3 from the ROTARY subdirectory, the path name would be

\LETTERS\CLUB\ROTARY\MEMBER.3

Note how the path name leads from directory to directory until you reach the desired file.

At first glance, subdirectories may seem to complicate rather than simplify the task of accessing files. In practice, however, people rarely use such lengthy path names. Instead, they select a working directory and allow the operating system to keep track of the subdirectories needed to complete a path name. Later in the chapter you will learn how to select a working directory.

The Backslash

Why did Microsoft decide to use a backslash (\) as a separator in an MS-DOS path name? A good way to answer that question is with another question: When is the last time you typed a backslash other than in a path name? Simply put, the backslash character is almost never used, so adopting it as a path name field separator was unlikely to create confusion.

Viewing a Directory

Before you begin creating and manipulating directories, it might be wise to look through an existing one. Following the A-prompt, type

C:

and press the enter key. The new prompt (Figure 7.13) should read

FIGURE 7.13
Make the C drive your default drive.

C:\Documents and Settings\default>

or

C:\Windows>

It tells you that drive C is your default drive and it identifies the **current directory.**

No matter what the default directory, all versions of Windows contain a directory named *Windows* that holds numerous system files. To list the contents of the *Windows* directory, type a **directory (DIR) command** (Figure 7.14).

DIR \WINDOWS

Figure 7.13 shows the command as typed. DIR is the command name and \WINDOWS (note the initial backslash) is the path name of the *Windows* directory. Press the enter key, and a list of file names and other information will scroll rapidly across your screen[3]. Figure 7.15 shows the last screen followed by a new prompt.

---

[3]If necessary, ask your instructor to help you find the WINDOWS directory on your system.

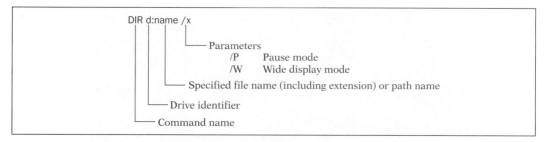

FIGURE 7.14

The directory (DIR) command displays a directory's contents.

As entered, the directory command was not very useful because the list of files in directory Windows is much too big to fit on a single screen. Try adding a pause parameter. Type the command

DIR \WINDOWS /P

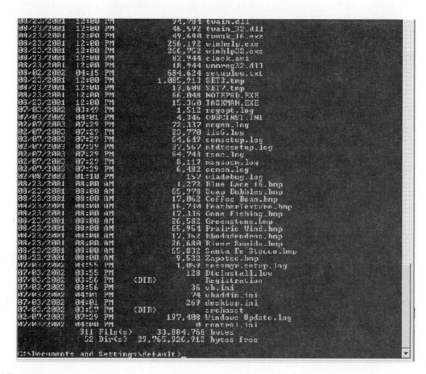

FIGURE 7.15

The last page of a directory list.

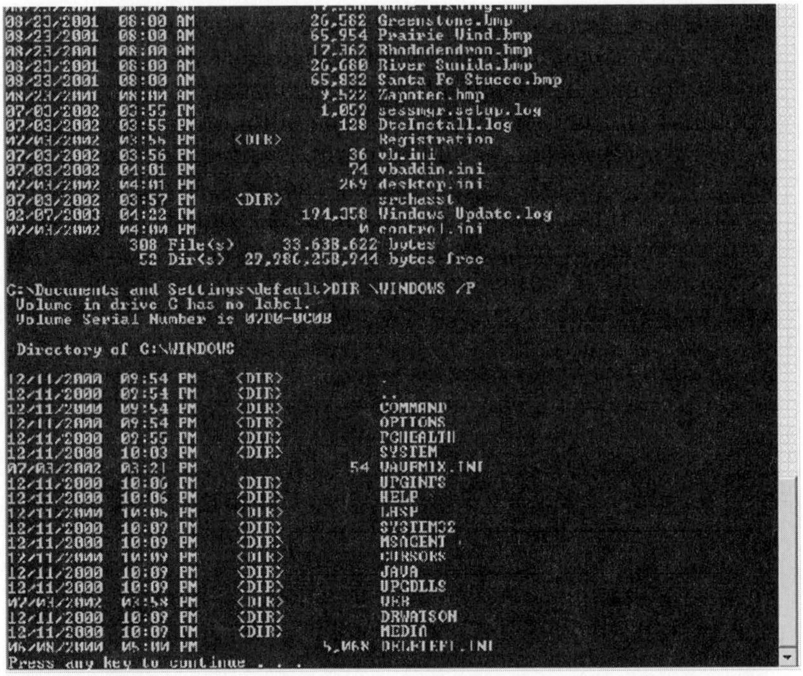

FIGURE 7.16
A directory command with a pause option.

A space separates the command from the parameter, and the slash is a regular slash, not a backslash. Press the enter key, and a single page of information will appear on your screen (Figure 7.16). Reading from left to right, each Windows XP line displays a file's creation date and time, either <DIR> (for a directory) or the file length, and the file name. On non-XP versions of Windows, the file name comes first.

The last line on Figure 7.16 reads *Press any key to continue*. Press the space bar, and a new screen of file names will appear. Continue pressing the space bar to step through the directory one screen at a time.

The wide mode display is another useful option. When the next prompt appears, type the command

```
DIR \WINDOWS /W
```

FIGURE 7.17
A wide mode directory list.

and press enter. The resulting screen (Figure 7.17) lists only file names, two across on Windows XP and between two and five across on earlier versions of Windows. The *Windows* directory contains so many files that not even a wide mode list will fit on a single screen.

Creating Directories

Before you move on to the next task, make sure the diskette you formatted is in the drive. Then change your default drive back to the diskette drive by typing

A:

and pressing enter. You are about to create three new directories and several files on your diskette.

Use the **make directory (MKDIR, or MD) command** (Figure 7.18) to create a directory. For example, type the command

MKDIR \LETTERS

(Figure 7.19) and press enter. The backslash indicates that LETTERS is a subdirectory of the root directory. Use similar MKDIR commands to create

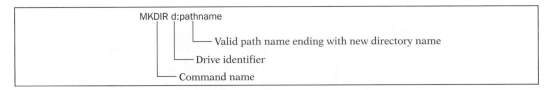

FIGURE 7.18

The make directory (MKDIR) command creates a new directory.

two more directories: BOOK and WS. When you finish creating the directories, type a DIR command with no parameters. A DIR command with no parameters will list the contents of the current directory, which is your diskette's root directory. As Figure 7.19 shows, three subdirectories have been added to the diskette's root directory.

A MKDIR command is used to create a subdirectory. To remove or delete a directory, issue a remove directory (RMDIR, or RD) command.

Creating Files

Most files are created by application programs such as a word processor, a spreadsheet, a database manager, and so on, but you can also copy an existing file. When MS-DOS carries out a **COPY command** (Figure 7.20), it reads the file specified in the first parameter (the source file) and copies it to the file specified in the second parameter (the destination file).

A simple way to create a short file is to copy it from the console (your system's keyboard and display). For example, type the command

```
Command Prompt                                          _ □ ×

C:\Documents and Settings\default>A:

A:\>MKDIR LETTERS

A:\>MKDIR BOOK

A:\>MKDIR WS

A:\>DIR
 Volume in drive A is DOSDEMO
 Volume Serial Number is 7C50-C9BD

 Directory of A:\

02/07/2003  04:37 PM    <DIR>          LETTERS
02/07/2003  04:37 PM    <DIR>          BOOK
02/07/2003  04:37 PM    <DIR>          WS
               0 File(s)              0 bytes
               3 Dir(s)       1,456,128 bytes free

A:\>_
```

FIGURE 7.19

The commands to create and list three subdirectories.

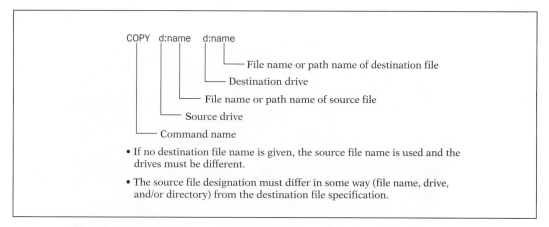

- If no destination file name is given, the source file name is used and the drives must be different.

- The source file designation must differ in some way (file name, drive, and/or directory) from the destination file specification.

FIGURE 7.20

The COPY command copies one or more files from a source to a destination.

COPY CON A:\LETTERS\JIM

(Figure 7.21). The first (source) file name, CON, stands for the console. The second (destination) file name specifies a path name. (Read the command from left to right.) The destination file will be stored on drive A, subdirectory LETTERS and assigned the file name JIM.

If you haven't already done so, press enter to issue the COPY command. The cursor will appear directly under the command line (you will see no prompt). At this point you can type whatever you want. (If you'd like your file's

```
A:\>COPY CON A:\LETTERS\JIM
Looking forward to spring break!
Will I see you in Florida?
^Z
        1 file(s) copied.

A:\>COPY CON A:\LETTERS\SALLY
Sorry, Jim.
I'm going skiing in Utah!
^Z
        1 file(s) copied.

A:\>COPY CON A:\LETTERS\TOM
Note:
Math assignment.
Chapter 8, problems 10-14.
^Z
        1 file(s) copied.

A:\>
```

FIGURE 7.21

Copy these three files from the console to directory LETTERS.

FIGURE 7.22
Copy this pretend spreadsheet to WS and this opening sentence to BOOK.

contents to match subsequent examples, refer to Figure 7.21 and type what you see.) When you reach the end of a line, press the enter key. When you have typed all your lines, press function key F6 or simultaneously press *ctrl-Z* (either generates the COPY command's sentinel value) and then press enter.

Copy the three files you see in Figure 7.21 (or substitute your own content) to directory LETTERS. Then refer to Figure 7.22, copy a line that represents a pretend spreadsheet to directory WS, and copy the first line of Chapter 1 to directory BOOK.

Changing Directories

Now that your diskette holds some directories and files, investigate it. Start by typing the command

DIR A:

and pressing enter. Only the three directories (the contents of the root directory) are listed (Figure 7.23). To view the contents of the LETTERS directory, type

DIR A:\LETTERS

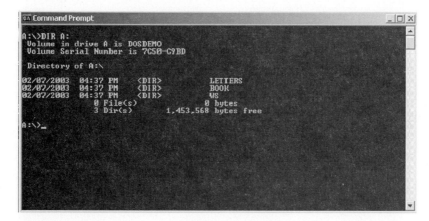

FIGURE 7.23
Your diskette's root directory.

and press enter. Note that the three files you just created are listed (Figure 7.24).

Look carefully at Figure 7.24. Directory LETTERS contains two unusual files: (**.**) and (**z**). The single dot refers to the directory itself. The double dot is a reference to its parent, in this case, the root directory.

The root directory is the current **working directory.** To shift to a different working directory, type a **change directory (CHDIR,** or **CD) command** (Figure 7.25)

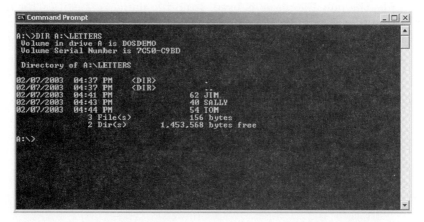

FIGURE 7.24
The contents of subdirectory LETTERS.

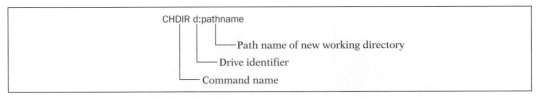

CHDIR d:pathname
Path name of new working directory
Drive identifier
Command name

FIGURE 7.25
Use a change directory command to change the working directory.

CHDIR A:\LETTERS

and press enter. Then type the command

DIR A:

with no parameters and press enter again. The output should match Figure 7.24. If no directory is specified, MS-DOS assumes the current working directory. The change directory command allows you to specify a new working directory.

Manipulating Files

Earlier, you copied some text from the console to create a file on diskette. More generally, any existing file can be copied. The COPY command's first parameter specifies a source file and its second parameter specifies a destination file. If drive designators are prefixed to a parameter, a file on one disk can be copied to another. If a file name is specified for the destination file, the new file name is used. If no file name is specified for the destination file, the source file name is used.

For example, make sure your diskette is in the drive and type the command

COPY A:\LETTERS\TOM A:\LETTERS\TAMMY

(Figure 7.26). Note that a space separates the two parameters. Press the enter key. MS-DOS will read the file named TOM from the LETTERS directory on drive A, make a copy, and store the new copy on the LETTERS directory.

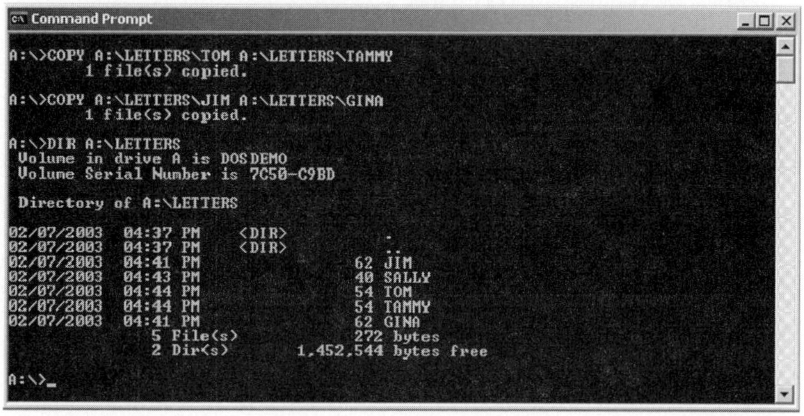

FIGURE 7.26
Some copy commands.

Wild Card Characters

Consider a few generic examples before you resume the tutorial. Special **wild card** characters allow a user to generalize the parameters. A question mark (?) represents any single character; for example, the file name

TERM.?

identifies TERM.1, TERM.2, TERM.C, and any other file named TERM with a 1-character extension. An asterisk (*) represents multiple characters; for example,

TERM.*

stands for every file named TERM with a 1-, 2-, or 3-character extension, including TERM.1, TERM.V6, and TERM.ABC.

Imagine you have been working on a BASIC program named MYPGM. By convention, your source module uses the extension BAS and your object module uses the extension OBJ. You want to copy both. You can, of course, issue two COPY commands, but you can copy both with a single command if you reference MYPGM.* or MYPGM.??? as your source file. Seeing the wild card characters, MS-DOS will look for all files that fit, so the single COPY command

COPY MYPGM.* A:\PROGRAMS

(which you should not issue) will copy both **MYPGM.BAS** and **MYPGM.OBJ** to a subdirectory named **PROGRAMS** on the A drive using the source file names.

Consider one more example before you resume the tutorial. Wild card characters are particularly useful for making backup copies of selected files or an entire disk. For example, the command

COPY C:\PAYROLL*.* A:

(which you should not issue) copies all the files from a directory named PAYROLL on the C drive to the diskette in the A drive. Similarly, the command

COPY C:\PROGRAMS*.BAS A:

(which you should not issue) copies all the files with the extension **BAS** from a directory named **PROGRAMS** on the C drive to the diskette in the A drive.

Now, back to the tutorial. Type the command

COPY A:\LETTERS\JIM A:\LETTERS\GINA

(Figure 7.26) and press enter. MS-DOS will retrieve a copy of the file named JIM from subdirectory LETTERS, rename it GINA, and store the copy on subdirectory LETTERS. To verify the copy operation, type the directory command

DIR A:\LETTERS

and press enter. Note the file named GINA on Figure 7.26. (You created the file named TAMMY earlier.)

Next, type the command

COPY A:\LETTERS\T* A:\WS

and press enter. It copies every file on subdirectory LETTERS that begins with the letter T to the directory named WS. To verify the copy operation, type the directory command

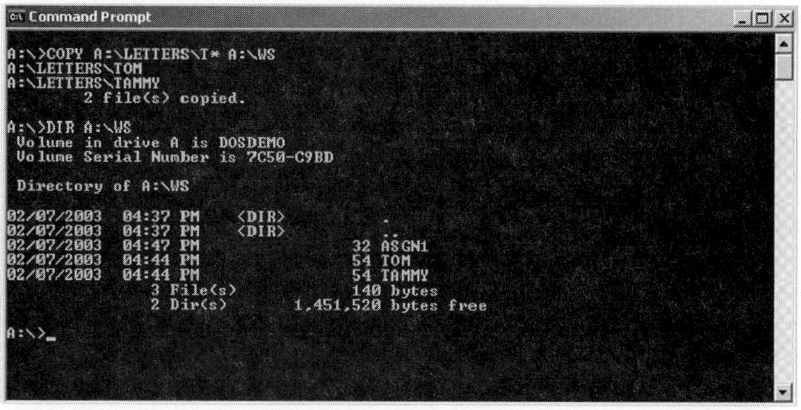

FIGURE 7.27
This copy command uses wild card characters.

DIR A:\WS

and press enter. As you can see in Figure 7.27, files named TOM and
TAMMY have been stored on subdirectory WS.

Incidentally, many people who learned MS-DOS in the pre-Windows era
still switch to the command prompt to take advantage of wild card characters for certain file manipulation tasks. Wild cards are very useful.

Batch Files

A **batch file** is a file of precoded MS-DOS commands. You can assign any
file name to a batch file, but the extension must be .BAT. If you type the
batch file's name and press enter, MS-DOS will execute the commands in
sequence. For example, if it exists, a file named AUTOEXEC.BAT is automatically executed each time the system is booted.

Program Files

A program is a special type of file. By convention, executable programs are
assigned the extension COM or EXE. To load and execute a program, simply type its file name (with or without its extension) as though it was a command. If no extension is given, MS-DOS will look for a command with the

specified file name and a .COM extension, then search for a .EXE file, and finally for a .BAT file.

◾ Pipes, Filters, and Redirection

Many MS-DOS commands assume a standard input or output device; for example, by default the directory command sends its output to the screen. By using **redirection** parameters (Figure 7.28) the user can change those defaults. For example, the command

DIR > PRN

sends the output directory listing to the printer instead of to the display screen.

Parameter	Meaning	Example
<	Change source to a specified device or file	<MYFILE.DAT
>	Change destination to a specified device or file	>PRN
>>	Change destination (usually) to an existing file and append output to it.	>>HOLD.DAT
|	Pipe standard output to another command or to a filter	DIR | MORE

FIGURE 7.28
Many MS-DOS commands and filters utilize the standard input and output devices. Redirection parameters allow a user to change to a specified file or device.

A **filter** is a special type of command. It accepts input from the standard input device, modifies (or filters) the data in some way, and sends the results to the standard output device. For example, the SORT filter, (Figure 7.29) accepts data from the keyboard, sorts the data into alphabetical or numerical sequence, and outputs the sorted data to the screen. You can add

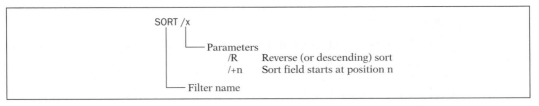

FIGURE 7.29
The SORT filter.

redirection parameters to override or change the standard input device, output device, or both.

For example, consider the command

SORT <A:\LETTERS\JIM

Because of the redirection parameter (<), this **SORT** filter accepts its input from the file named JIM. The output, the lines of text that you typed when you created JIM sorted into alphabetical order, should appear on your screen[4]. For future reference, to sort and store the output on a different file, code something like

SORT <MYFILE >RESULT

Note that both source and destination redirection parameters are included.

MORE is another useful filter (Figure 7.30). It sends output to the terminal one screen at a time. MORE is often used with pipes. A **pipe** causes one command's standard output to be used as the standard input to another command. Pipes are designated by a vertical line (|); you will find this character on the right of most alphanumeric keyboards, often just below the *Backspace* key.

For example, type

C:

and press enter to make drive C your default drive. Then type

DIR /WINDOWS

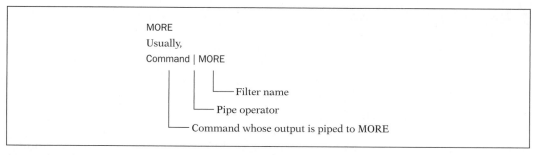

FIGURE 7.30
The MORE filter.

---

[4]The SORT filter may not be supported by all versions of Windows

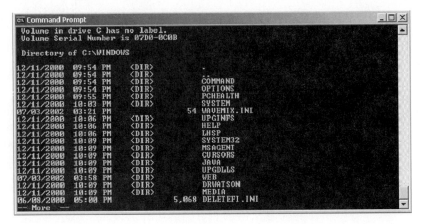

FIGURE 7.31
The MORE filter displays data one screen at a time.

Press enter and watch the file names scroll by too quickly to read. Now type the command

DIR /WINDOWS | MORE

The directory command's standard output will be routed to the MORE filter rather than directly to the screen. The filter will display one screen and then wait until you press the enter key before it displays the next screen (Figure 7.31).

Returning to Windows

That completes the chapter tutorial. To return to Windows, type the command

EXIT

and press the enter key.

MS-DOS is a powerful operating system and you have barely scratched the surface of its command language. However, given a clear understanding of the commands in this brief tutorial, you should be able to read a reference manual and determine how to use additional commands on your own.

◼ Summary

MS-DOS is a command-driven operating system that allows users to issue cryptic, single-line commands through a command interface. The default drive and the system prompt are displayed by the operating system. The user types a command name followed by necessary parameters.

You can access MS-DOS or the command prompt through Microsoft Windows. The FORMAT command is used to format a disk. The MS-DOS file system allows a user to identify, save, and retrieve files by name. Directory management is a key function of the MS-DOS file system. When a disk is first formatted, a single root directory is created by the format routine. When subdirectories are used, you need a complete path name to fully identify a file.

The system prompt identifies the default drive and the current working directory. To list the contents of a directory, type a directory (DIR) command. Use the make directory (MKDIR, MD) command to create a directory. To shift to a different working directory, type a change directory (CHDIR, CD) command.

Use a COPY command to copy an existing file. When you issue a COPY command, special wild card characters allow a user to generalize the parameters and copy several files with a single operation. A batch file is a file of precoded MS-DOS commands. A program is a special type of file.

Many MS-DOS commands assume a standard input or output device. By using redirection parameters the user can change those defaults. A filter accepts input from the standard input device, modifies (or filters) the data in some way, and sends the results to the standard output device. A pipe causes one command's standard output to be used as the standard input to another command. To return to Windows from the MS-DOS prompt, type the command EXIT.

◼ Key Words

batch file
change directory (CHDIR, CD)
    command
command
COPY command
current directory
default drive
delimiter
directory
directory (DIR) command
extension
file name
file system
filter

FORMAT command
make directory (MKDIR, MD) command
MS-DOS
parameters
path name
pipe
prompt
redirection
root directory
subdirectory
wild card
working directory

◼ Review Questions

1. Given that Microsoft Windows has largely supplanted MS-DOS, why is it still useful to learn about MS-DOS commands?

2. Describe the general structure of an MS-DOS command. What are parameters? What are delimiters?

3. What is the significance of the default drive? How do you set the default drive?

4. Why must a disk be formatted before use?

5. Briefly describe the rules for defining a file name. What is the significance of the file name extension?

6. Briefly describe a hierarchical directory structure. What advantages does a hierarchical directory structure offer over using a single directory to hold all files?

7. Distinguish between a path name and a file name.

8. What is the purpose of a directory command?

9. Distinguish between a directory and a file. How are they similar? How are they different?

10. Briefly explain how to use a copy command to create a file and enter the data from the keyboard.

11. Distinguish between the root directory and the current working directory.

12. What are wild card characters? Why are they useful? Why can they not be part of a file's legal name?

13. What is a batch file? Why are batch files useful?

14. Explain redirection.

15. What are filters? What are pipes? Explain how they work together.

◼ Exercises

1. If you have not already done so, work through the chapter tutorial.

2. Create a set of directories to help keep track of your data files or programs. Add your existing files to the new directory structure by copying them.

3. MS-DOS established Microsoft as an industry leader, and Windows solidified the company's status as the owner of the de facto personal computer operating system standard. In your opinion, was that a good thing or a bad thing?

4. Do some research into the origin of MS-DOS and write a paper based on your results. You'll find appropriate material in numerous sources.

5. The most effective way to learn this chapter's key terms is to complete the chapter tutorial.

The Microsoft Windows User Interface

When you finish reading this chapter you should be able to:

▶ Describe the standard Windows desktop.

▶ Identify two ways to execute a program under Windows and explain how to switch between active programs.

▶ Maximize, minimize, and restore a window to its original size.

▶ Exit a program and shut down Windows.

▶ Describe the functions performed by the Windows file system.

▶ Distinguish between a regular file name and a long file name.

▶ Distinguish between the *My Computer* and *Explorer* views.

▶ Copy and rename a file. Copy multiple files. Copy an entire folder.

▶ Search for a file by name, by type, or by contents.

▶ Explain how the recycle bin allows you to recover a file you deleted by accident.

◼ Windows XP

Typically, a user accesses a computer through an application program and the application logic communicates with the operating system through an application programming interface. At times, however, it is necessary to communicate directly with the operating system to perform such functions as launching a program. This chapter presents an overview of the Microsoft **Windows XP** graphical user interface (GUI) (Figure 8.1). The Windows XP GUI incorporates a command line shell comparable to the MS-DOS user interface (Chapter 7).

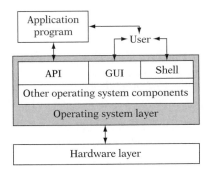

FIGURE 8.1

The standard Windows XP user interface is a GUI.

The Graphical User Interface

By most accounts, the first operational graphical user interface (GUI) was developed at Xerox Corporation's Palo Alto Research Center (PARC) in the 1970s, but Xerox was unable to convert the research into a marketable product. The first widely available computer that featured a GUI was Apple's Lisa, which reached the marketplace in 1983. Lisa faded quickly, but Apple's Macintosh platform proved a breakout product, effectively defining the look and feel of a modern GUI. Perhaps you have seen the company's famous "Big Brother" advertisement that was featured during the 1984 Super Bowl. Microsoft responded with its own GUI, Windows 1.0, a shell that ran as a separate layer on top of MS-DOS, but Windows didn't really catch on until Release 3.1 hit the market in 1992. Today, Windows is by far the dominant personal computer operating system. Apple's OS X is a significant competitor, but the Macintosh is a proprietary platform, which limits its potential market.

If possible, read this material while sitting in front of a computer and following along with the chapter tutorial. The screen captures were created using Windows XP Professional version running on an HP Pavilion computer, so your screens might not precisely match the text figures even if you are using XP. Although the screens will look different, you should be able to complete much of the tutorial using Windows 95, 98, ME, or 2000.

The User Interface

The standard Windows user interface is called the **desktop** (Figure 8.2). A single *Recycle Bin* **icon** that represents a subdirectory or folder that holds deleted files is displayed at the bottom right of the default desktop. However, users typically customize their desktops by adding icons for programs and files they access frequently. For example, the icons at the top left of Figure 8.2 represent *Internet Explorer*, a browser program, and the *Hummingbird Neighborhood*, a network frequently accessed by one of the authors.

Three key elements are found at the bottom of the desktop: the Start button, the taskbar, and the notification area. The ***Start* button** allows you to access a series of menus that lead to your system's application programs, key data folders, and numerous support functions. The **taskbar** holds a button for each currently active program. The **notification area** displays

Start button   Taskbar   Notification area

FIGURE 8.2
The desktop interface.

important information such as the current time. When an event such as the arrival of an e-mail message occurs, Windows notifies you by placing the appropriate icon in notification area.

The desktop is manipulated by using a mouse. Moving the mouse pointer (typically an arrow) to touch an icon or button is called pointing. If you point to an item and click the left mouse button you select that item; for example, if you click on *Start*, the *Start* menu appears (Figure 8.3). On the *Start* menu, frequently used programs are listed on the left side and frequently used folders (such as *My Documents*) are listed on the right side. Near the bottom of the right column are a Hewlett-Packard logo and a brief message asking the user to *Keep in touch with HP*. If you are not running an HP computer, you might see a different computer manufacture's logo or nothing at all in that space.

Launching or Starting a Program

Perhaps the easiest way to launch or start a program whose icon appears on the desktop is to double click the icon (point to the icon and rapidly click the left mouse button twice). For example, if the *Internet Explorer* icon appears on your desktop, double click it[1]. If you are not connected to the Internet, you might get a warning that the Web page is unavailable while offline. Respond by clicking *Stay Offline*.

Another way to start a program is from the Start menu (Figure 8.3). For example, if the *Internet Explorer* icon is not on your desktop look for *Internet Explorer* near the top left of the Start menu and click on it. More generally, to launch any program from the *Start* menu, click *All Programs* (lower left) and then select the program from the *All Programs* **menu** (Figure 8.4). The *All Programs* menu is organized hierarchically, so the program you need might be hidden within a submenu. Look for an arrow to the right of an All Programs menu item, point to that item, and the submenu will open. For example, *Notepad*, a text editor, is listed in a submenu of *Accessories*. To start *Notepad*, click the sequence *Start/All Programs/Accessories/Notepad*. Try it.

---

[1] If the icon is not on your desktop, you'll learn how to launch Internet Explorer in the next paragraph.

Later in this chapter, you will learn that you can also start a program by clicking on its taskbar button, searching for it using *Explorer* or *My Computer,* or issuing a command in MS-DOS mode. Additionally, if you double click most data file icons, the appropriate program will open; for example, if you double click a Word document icon, Word will open. Although some methods are better suited for certain tasks, how you choose to launch your programs is largely up to you.

FIGURE 8.3
The *Start* menu.

FIGURE 8.4

The *Start/All Programs* menu.

Switching Between Active Programs

At this point you should have two active programs: *Internet Explorer* and *Notepad*. (If you don't, go back to the previous paragraph.) Note that icons for both programs appear on the taskbar. To switch between them, simply click the taskbar icon that represents the program you want to run. Since *Notepad* was the last program you launched, it is probably the one you see on your screen. To switch to *Internet Explorer,* click the *Internet Explorer* taskbar icon. Running two or more programs concurrently is called **multitasking**.

Maximizing and Minimizing a Window

Each active program runs in its own **window.** You can enlarge a window to occupy the entire screen by clicking on the *maximize* button (the middle or square button) at the window's upper right (Figure 8.5). Once a window is maximized, the *maximize* button is replaced by the *restore down* button (two overlapping squares). If you click on *restore down* the window will return to its original size. You can also minimize a window by clicking on the *minimize* button (the leftmost or -sign button). When you minimize a window, it disappears from the screen but its icon remains on the taskbar.

The Menu Bar

If you haven't already done so, minimize *Notepad* and maximize *Internet Explorer*. Note the **menu bar** at the top left of the window (Figure 8.6). To open any menu, click on the appropriate key word. For example, click on *File* and the *File* menu drops down. You have probably accessed similar menus in a word processing or spreadsheet program.

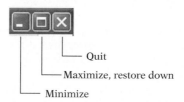

Quit
Maximize, restore down
Minimize

FIGURE 8.5

The maximize, minimize, and quit buttons.

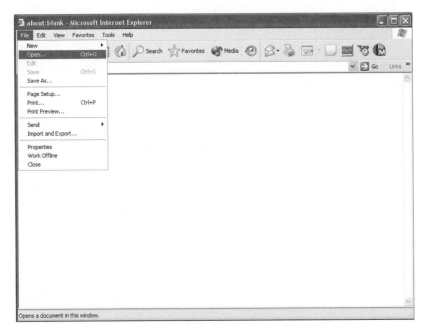

FIGURE 8.6
Selecting an entry on the menu bar pulls down a menu.

Quitting a Program

You can quit a program by opening the *File* menu and selecting *Exit* or by clicking on the *X* button (the rightmost button) at the window's upper right.

Look and Feel

You may have noticed that the drop down menus accessed from the menu bar in *Excel, Internet Explorer, Outlook, PowerPoint, Word,* and many other application programs are virtually identical. Such consistency is enabled by implementing the underlying menu functions in the Windows operating system rather than in the individual application programs. The result is a highly predictable interface in which the distinction between *Save* and *Save as* or *Cut* and *Copy* is clearly defined no matter what application program you might be using. Implementing common or shared functions in the operating system contributes to a consistent look and feel across applications. That consistency helps to reduce errors and simplifies the task of learning a new application.

For example, *Internet Explorer* should be the active program. (If not, click on its taskbar icon to activate it.) Close *Internet Explorer* by clicking on its close (X) button. Then activate *Notepad,* pull down its *File* menu, and click on *Exit* to close *Notepad*.

Shutting Down

When you are finished working on your computer, you normally shut it down[2]. Although you should not shut down now because the tutorial is just getting started, you might find it necessary to quit before you finish the chapter. For future reference, the process is simple. Click on *Start*. Then click *Turn off Computer*. A window should open listing your options. For now (if you already started the process) click the *Cancel* button at the lower right. Normally you click *Turn off*. You might be prompted to save your work in other active programs. Eventually, either your computer shuts down or a message appears informing you that you can safely exit the system.

◼ Working with the Windows File System

The Windows **file system** allows a user to identify, save, and retrieve files by name. (A program is a type of file). The file allocation table is a table maintained by Windows XP to identify the disk segments occupied by the various files. Windows XP supports three different file systems. FAT was the original MS-DOS file system and it works well for small disks up to 2GB in size. FAT32 is an enhancement of FAT that allocates the disk space in smaller units, creating a more efficient file system. NTFS not only manages files, handles large disk spaces, and so on, but also incorporates additional robustness features required by corporations and businesses.

At this point, you need not worry about which file system your computer uses because your operating system will automatically default to the correct one. You will learn more about FAT in Chapter 11 and FAT32 and NTFS in Chapter 12.

---

[2]*Note:* In many microcomputer labs, students never shut down the computer. Check with your instructor.

Formatting a Diskette

Later in the chapter you will need a work diskette, and before a diskette can be used, it must be formatted[3]. The formatting process writes a pattern of sectors on the diskette surface, may record a copy of the boot routine on the first sector, and initializes control information. A boot routine contains instructions that are read automatically on startup. Those instructions, in turn, read the rest of the operating system into memory.

Please be careful before you carry out the instructions in the next paragraph because the format operation is a destructive command; it erases all the data on the disk. In particular, make sure that you do *not* try to format your C drive.

To **format** a diskette, insert a blank diskette into the diskette drive (usually drive A). Click *Start/My Computer*. Right click (click the *right* mouse button) on the *3 1/2 Floppy* (A:) icon and then click *Format* (Figure 8.7). A

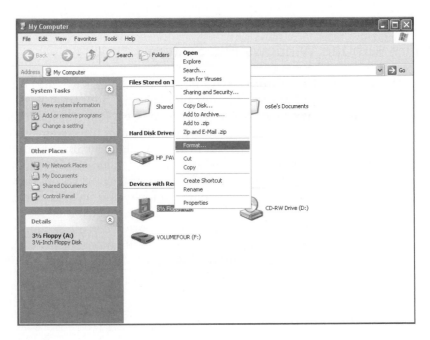

FIGURE 8.7

Using *My Computer* to format a diskette.

---

[3]Most diskettes are purchased preformatted, but reformatting does not hurt anything. The formatting process is useful for reinitializing a previously used diskette.

window will open (Figure 8.8). Type a *volume label* (such as the word CLASS) in the Volume label subwindow and click on Start. The system will respond by formatting your diskette to the drive's default capacity at 512 bytes per sector. (You might have to say *OK* if the diskette was previously formatted.)

After your diskette is formatted, a format results window is displayed. Click OK to close this window. Then click *Close* to close the formatting window.

File Names

As the term implies, a **file name** is the name you assign to a file. A file name is composed of the name itself and an optional extension. The FAT file system supports file names up to eight characters long with a 1- to 3-character

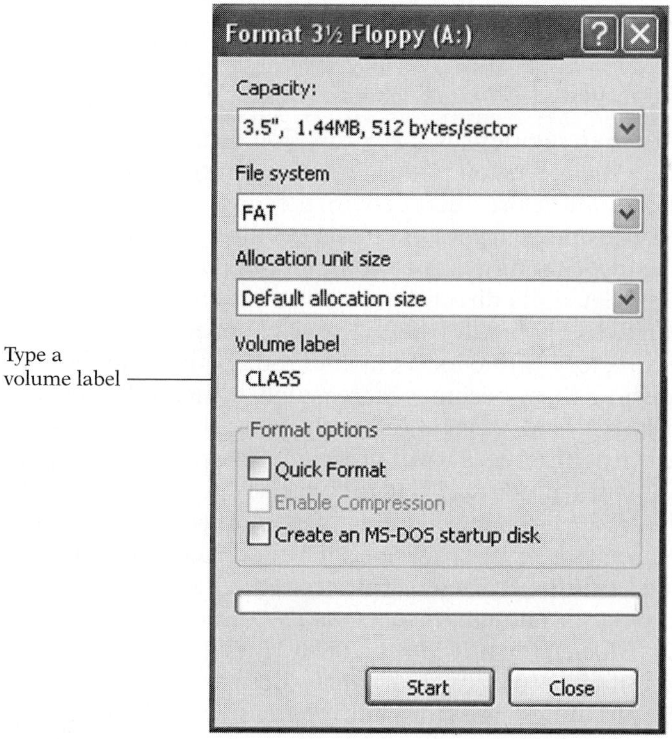

Type a
volume label ——

FIGURE 8.8
The format window.

extension (see MS-DOS file names in Chapter 7). The file name is separated from its extension by a period.

Windows XP supports FAT file names but also allows long file names. **Long file names** can be up to 255 characters long but cannot contain any of the following characters:

$$/ : * ? " < > | \setminus$$

Windows XP automatically translates the long file names to FAT file names for Windows 3.1 and DOS users. The extension in a long file name is used to identify an associated program that can open the file. For example, in a file named *resume.doc,* the extension *(.doc)* is used to associate the file with *Microsoft Word.* When a user double clicks on a file name with the extension *.doc,* the file is opened using Word.

Note that Windows is *not* case sensitive, so you can type a file name all lowercase, all uppercase, or mixed case. For example, *myfile, MYFILE,* and *MyFile* are all legal versions of the same file name.

Directories or Folders

Directory management is a key function of the Windows file system. The first time a file is written to disk, its name, disk address, creation date, and other information are recorded in the directory. Later, when the file is retrieved, the operating system reads the directory and searches it by name. When the file is modified, the file system updates the directory entry. When the file is deleted, its directory entry is marked as deleted.

When a disk is first formatted, a single **root directory** is created. Using a single directory is fine for a few files, but as the number of files increases, distinguishing them becomes increasingly difficult. For example, imagine a work disk that holds several different types of files. Letters and correspondence are generated by a word processor. Chapters for a book are output by the same word processor, but they clearly represent a separate group of files. Finally, images and pictures form another group of files.

To simplify keeping track of such file groups, the user creates special files called **subdirectories** or **folders.** For example, Figure 8.9 shows that the subdirectory named *My Documents* contains two lower-level subdirectories: *My Music* and *My Pictures.* (The *My Documents* subdirectory on your computer might contain additional subdirectories.) As the subdirectory names imply, images are stored in *My Pictures,* and music files are stored in *My Music.* Think of a subdirectory as a folder that is used to group related files and thus organize a disk. Given the sheer number of files on a hard disk, it is essential to create subdirectories or folders to organize the files. Later in the chapter you will learn to create your own folders.

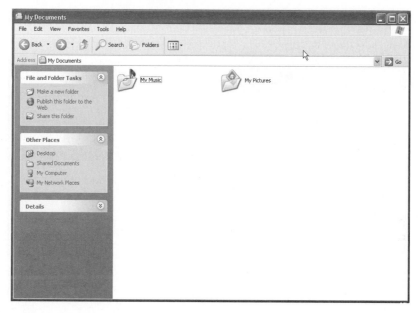

FIGURE 8.9

By default, *My Documents* contains two subdirectories or subfolders.

The Windows *Explorer*

Before you begin creating and manipulating directories, it might be wise to look through some existing examples. Windows ***Explorer*** provides a hierarchical view of the directories on your system. To access *Explorer* from Windows XP, click on *Start,* select *Programs,* select *Accessories,* and then click on *Windows Explorer.* To access *Explorer* from Windows 95, right click (using the right mouse button) the *Start* button and then select *Explore.*

The *Explorer* window (Figure 8.10) is organized into two panes. The left pane lists the folders on your C drive and, depending on your system settings, possibly your other drives. The right pane displays the contents of the selected folder, in this example the *My Documents* folder. Your screen might look different.

Any icon in the left pane with a + sign to its left contains subfolders. For, example, note in Figure 8.10 the + to the left of the *My Computer* folder. Click on the + next to *My Computer* to reveal your disk drives; note once again that your screen might look different. Next, click on the *3 1/2 Floppy(A:)* icon to view the contents of the diskette in drive A (Figure 8.11). You have not yet added any folders or files to the diskette you just formatted, so it should be empty.

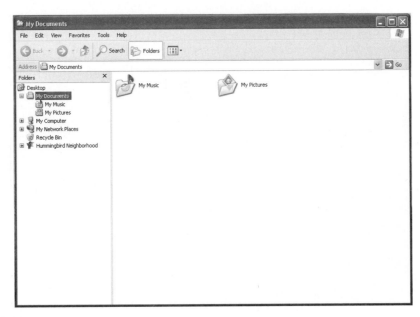

FIGURE 8.10

Explorer shows a hierarchical view of a system's directory structure.

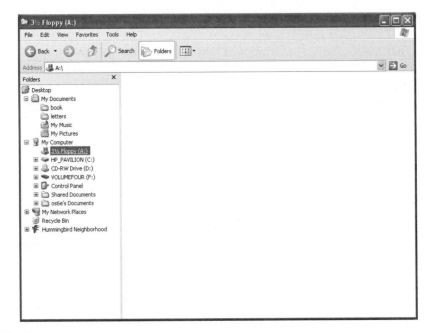

FIGURE 8.11

The diskette you just formatted should be empty.

Some of the disk drives shown under *My Computer* in Figure 8.11 are unique to the authors' installation; ignore them. Click on the C drive icon to view the contents of your local hard disk drive[4] (Figure 8.12). On the authors' system, the icon reads HP_PAVILION (C:) but your system's icon might read *Local Disk (C:)* or it might reference your computer's manufacturer. In any event, your C drive will contain numerous subdirectories. The contents of your C drive probably won't match Figure 8.12, but it will contain three key subdirectories—*Documents and Settings, Program Files,* and *Windows.* Respectively, they hold key documents, your computer's program files, and the system files required by Windows.

Click on the minus sign (-) to the left of the C drive icon to collapse the subdirectories. A plus sign (+) should appear to take its place. Clicking on a plus sign displays the list of subdirectories. Clicking on a minus sign collapses the list.

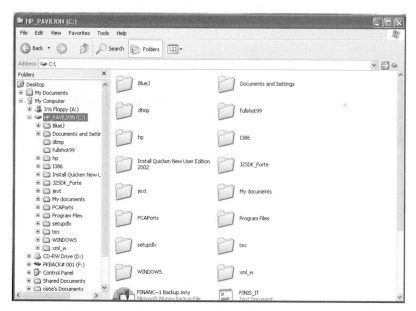

FIGURE 8.12

The C Drive.

---

[4]If the resulting screen reads *These files are hidden,* click on *Show the contents of this folder.*

Look down the list of folders under *My Computer* and click on the + sign to the left of *Control Panel* to reveal its subfolders. Click on *Fonts,* and you should see displayed in the right pane a set of icons for the type fonts that are installed on your computer (Figure 8.13). Move the mouse pointer to the menu bar, pull down the *View* menu, and click on *Details* to switch from icons to a list view that shows such details as file name, size, date last modified and so on (Figure 8.14). Click *View/List* to get a list of file names without the details. Then click *View/Icons* to go back to the icons. Once again, click the negative sign (–) icon on *Control Panel* to collapse or hide the subfolders.

My Computer

Close *Explorer* by clicking the X box at the window's upper right. Then click *Start* and select *My Computer* from the *Start* menu's left pane to open a different view of your computer's peripherals and subfolders (Figure 8.15). You may recognize the **My Computer** view from Figure 8.7 where you accessed it to format a diskette, but you can also use it to view the contents of any single device or folder. For example, look under *Other Places* on the left pane and click on *Control Panel* to view the control panel's contents. Click the *Back* button to return to the original *My Computer* view, and then double click the C drive icon on the right panel to view the contents of your local drive.

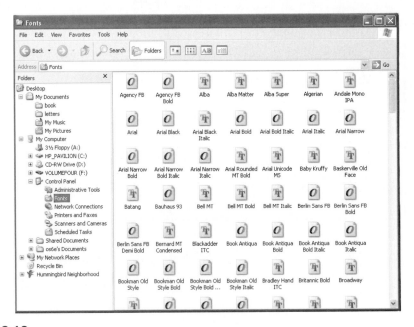

FIGURE 8.13

The Control Panel.

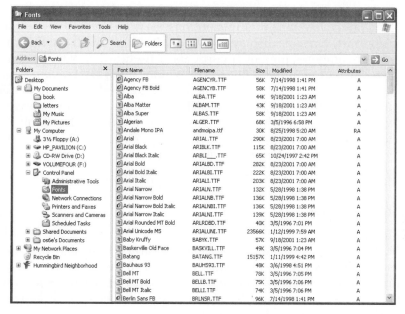

FIGURE 8.14

The *View* menu allows you to control the appearance of the right pane.

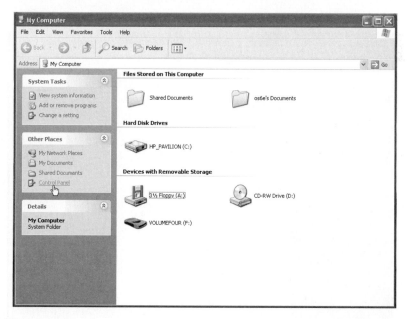

FIGURE 8.15

The *My Computer* View.

The *My Computer* view focuses on one device or folder at a time and offers on the left pane multiple options for working with the selected entity. In contrast, *Explorer* displays a hierarchical view of all the files and folders on your computer, making it particularly useful when you are working concurrently with multiple folders. On Windows XP, *My Computer* appears on the *Start* menu's right panel while launching *Explorer* requires negotiating submenus, so *My Computer* is clearly the default view. If you prefer to make the *Explorer* view your (permanent or temporary) default, open *My Computer*, pull down the View menu, select *Explorer Bar*, and select *Folders*. To return to the *My Computer* view, click on *View/Explorer Bar* and uncheck the *Folders* option.

Creating Folders

The next step in the tutorial calls for you to create a few subdirectories. Make sure the diskette you formatted earlier is in drive A. Your screen should display the *My Computer* view shown in Figure 8.15. (If it doesn't, return to the previous section and follow the instructions to return to *My Computer*.) Click on the *3 1/2 Floppy (A:)* icon to view the diskette's contents. At this point, it should be empty.

To create a new folder, look under *File and Folder Tasks* on the left pane and click on *Make a new Folder* (Figure 8.16). A new folder icon with its

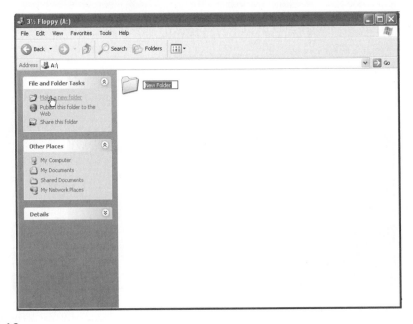

FIGURE 8.16

Creating a new folder.

default name highlighted will appear in the right pane. Type *Letters* to replace the default name and press enter. Then repeat the process to create two more folders named *Books* and *My Pictures* (Figure 8.17).

Creating Files

Most files are created by compilers, interpreters, word processors, spreadsheet programs, database managers, and other application routines. Because the *Notepad* editor is available on virtually all versions of Windows, use *Notepad* to create a few files.

Click on *Start,* point to *All Programs,* and then select *Accessories.* Select *Notepad* from the *Accessories* menu to start the *Notepad* editor. Position the cursor within the *Notepad* window and type the following:

Looking forward to spring break!
See you in Florida!

Pull down the *File* menu and click on *Save.* Because the file was just created, the *Save as* window will open (Figure 8.18). Click on the downward pointing arrow to the right of the *Save in* line near the top of the window and choose the A drive and the folder *Letters* from the drop down menu. Then move down to the *File name* line near the bottom of the window, name your file *Jim,* and click the *Save* button. When you finish, click on the *X* box at the upper right of the window to close *Notepad.*

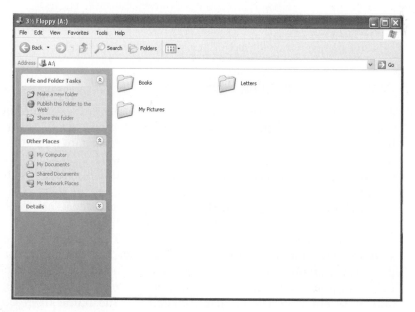

FIGURE 8.17
The diskette now holds three folders.

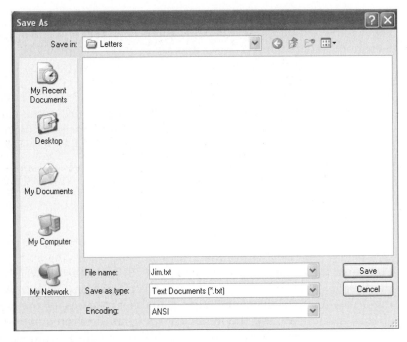

FIGURE 8.18
Saving a *Notepad* file.

Copying and Renaming Files

Another option for creating a file is to copy an existing file. At this point, your screen should resemble Figure 8.17. (If you closed *My Computer* before you opened Notepad, reopen *My Computer* and double click the A drive icon.) Switch to *Explorer* view *(View/Explorer Bar/Folders),* click on the + sign to the left of *3 1/2 Floppy (A:),* and select subdirectory *Letters* (Figure 8.19).

Click on *Jim* to highlight the file you just created. Then pull down the *Edit* menu and select *Copy* to store a copy of the file in memory. Next, click on *Edit* and then *Paste* to paste a copy of the file from memory back into the same folder. An icon for a file named *Copy of Jim* will appear on the right pane. Click on *Copy of Jim* to select the file. Then right click (click the *right* mouse button) the highlighted icon, choose *Rename* (Figure 8.20), type *Sally* and press enter. You have just changed the file name from *Copy of Jim* to *Sally*.

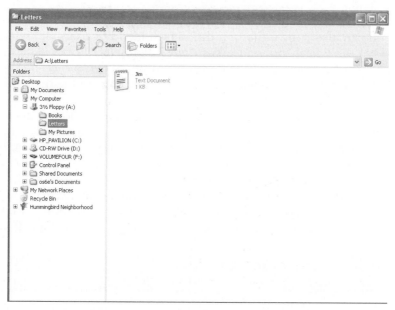

FIGURE 8.19

Selecting a subfolder.

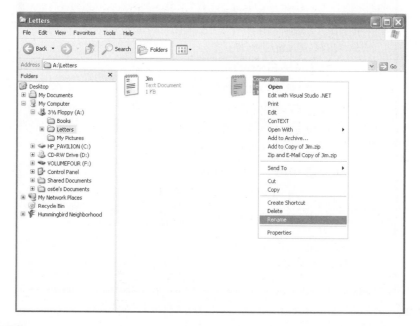

FIGURE 8.20

Renaming a file.

Copying to a Different Folder

You can also copy a file to a different folder. For example, select *Jim,* pull down the *Edit* menu, and select *Copy.* Then select *Books* from the left pane under *3 1/2 Floppy* and the currently empty folder named *Books* will open. Pull down the *Edit* menu, select *Paste,* and a copy of the file named *Jim* will appear in the *Books* folder.

There is a new option in Windows XP and Windows 2000 called the *Copy to Folder*[5] that is particularly valuable if you are unsure of the target folder's name. Reselect the folder *Letters* under *3 1/2 Floppy (A:)* on the left pane. Select *Jim,* pull down the *Edit* menu, and select *Copy to Folder.* A new window will open that allows you to browse for the target folder. Click on + to the left of *My Computer* to display the available drives (Figure 8.21). Click on + to the left of the A drive and then click on the *Books* folder. Finally, click on the *Copy* button to select *Books* and make the copy. If you already

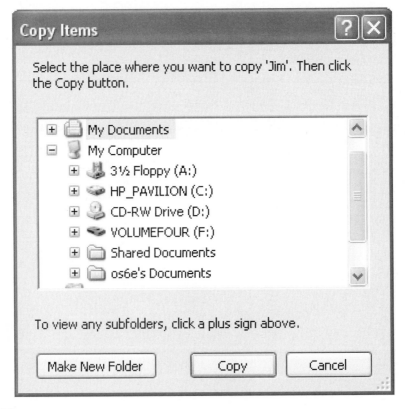

FIGURE 8.21

Browsing for a folder using the *Copy to Folder* option.

---

[5]This option is not available under Windows 95/98.

copied the file to the *Books* folder using the previous paragraph's technique, click on the *Yes* prompt to replace the file.

Copying Multiple Files

To copy multiple files, select the first file name or icon in the usual way. Then hold down the control *(Ctrl)* key while you select additional files. Once you have selected all the desired files, you can do an *Edit/Copy* to copy them into memory and a subsequent *Edit/Paste* to paste them into the target folder.

Make sure you are in the *Letters* folder by clicking on *Letters* in the left pane of the *Explorer* view. Click on *Jim* to select the file. Hold the control key and click on *Sally*, and both files will be highlighted. To create copies of both files, click on *Edit/Copy*. Then click on *Edit/Paste* to make copies of both files in the same folder. When you finish, four files will appear in the Letters folder: *Jim, Copy of Jim, Sally,* and *Copy of Sally.*

Copying Entire Subfolders

You can use *Explorer* (or *My Computer*) to copy an entire subfolder by highlighting the subfolder, performing an *Edit/Copy,* and then performing an *Edit/Paste* at the new location. Click on the A drive icon in the left pane to display the three folders in the right pane (Figure 8.22). Click on *Letters* to highlight the folder, pull down the *Edit* menu, and click on *Copy*. Then go

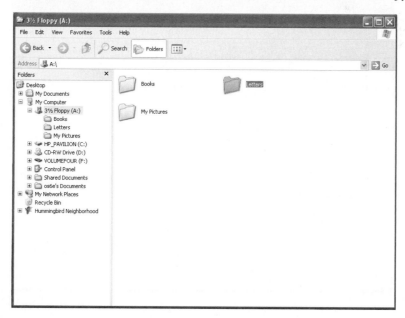

FIGURE 8.22

Copying an entire subfolder.

back to the left pane, click on *Books,* pull down the *Edit* menu, and click on *Paste*. The entire *Letters* folder will be copied to the *Books* folder. Note on the left pane that the *Books* folder now has a + to its left to indicate that it contains a subfolder.

Manipulating Files

Notepad creates simple text files with a .txt extension. *WordPad,* another standard Windows accessory, creates rich text format *(.rtf)* files in XP and WINDOWS 2000, and *.doc* files in earlier versions of Windows. To illustrate how Windows can distinguish different types of files, use *WordPad* to create a simple file with a different extension.

    Launch *WordPad* by clicking *Start/All/Programs/Accessories/WordPad* and enter the following data as your first *WordPad* document:

Sorry Jim.
I am going skiing.

Save the file as *tom* in the *A:\Letters* subfolder and close *WordPad*. Copy and paste the file named *tom* to create another file named *Copy of tom* in the *Letters* folder and then rename the file *bob*. Your *Explorer* view of the *Letters* subfolder in the A drive should resemble Figure 8.23. Note that the first four

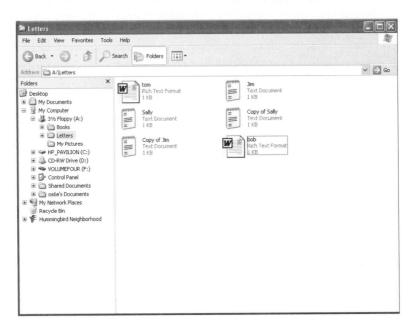

FIGURE 8.23
The *a:\letters* folder.

files you created are simple text documents, but *tom* and *bob* are rich text (or *.doc*) format documents.

Searching for Files

You can use either the *Explorer* view or the *My Computer* view to select just the *Notepad* files or just the *WordPad* files from subfolder *Letters* because their extensions, *.rtf* and *.txt,* provide a basis for distinguishing them. If you have been following along with the tutorial, your screen should resemble Figure 8.23 with the *Explorer* view active. Just for variety, return to the *My Computer* view by closing *Explorer* and clicking on *Start/My Computer*. Then click on the *Search* icon on the toolbar and the *Search Companion* will appear in the left pane (Figure 8.24).

Choose *All files and folders* from the *Search Companion* and a search criteria window will open (Figure 8.25). Assuming you are using Windows XP or Windows 2000, enter **.rtf*[6] in the text box labeled *All or part of the file*

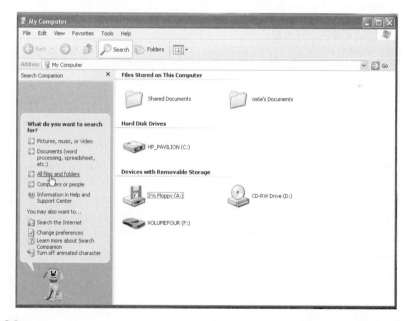

FIGURE 8.24

Search companion.

---

[6]Substitute *.doc* if you are using an earlier version of Windows.

name:. The asterisk (*) is a wild card character that represents one or more file name characters. The *rtf* indicates that the extension must be *rtf*. In this example, the * is the lone file name character, so this search criterion will match *bob.rtf, tom.rtf,* and any other *rtf* file name (of any length) in the target folder or folders. If you refine the search to *b*.rtf,* however, only file names that start with the letter *b* followed by any character or characters will match, so *bob* will be selected from the *Letters* subfolder but *tom* will not.

You can also use a question mark (?) as a wild card character to represent any single character. For example, the search criterion *bo?* identifies all file names that start with *bo* and contain exactly one additional character, such as *bob, boy, boa,* and so on. The wild card characters can be used anywhere in the name, including the extension. For example, the search criterion *bob.** would find *bob.txt, bob.rtf,* and *bob.doc.*

Use the downward pointing arrow to the right of the *Look in* box to select the A drive from a pull down menu (Figure 8.25). Then click on the *Search* button at the bottom right of the *Search Companion* to find all the *WordPad* files (more generally, the *rtf* files) on the A drive. When the search is finished, all the files that match the search criterion will be listed on the right pane (Figure 8.26).

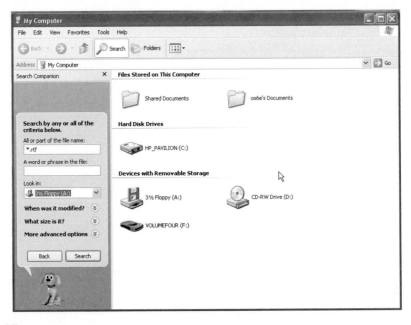

FIGURE 8.25
Search for files.

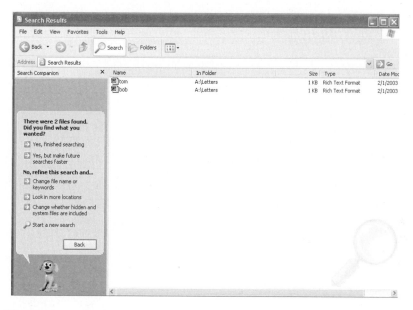

FIGURE 8.26
Search results.

In addition to the files themselves, you can also search for a string of text contained in one or more files. For example, click the *X* box just to the right of *Search Companion* to close the current *search*. Then start a new search by clicking the *Search* icon on the toolbar. Enter the word *Florida* in the text box labeled *A word or phrase in the file* and choose the A drive for *Look in*. Click on the *Search* button. The search results should list *Jim, Sally,* and all copies of the *Jim* and *Sally* files.

Sorting Files

In either the *My Computer* view or the *Explorer* view you can sort the file names shown on the right pane based on a variety of attributes. Close *Search Companion*. Then display the contents of the A drive's *Letters* sub-folder on the right pane. Pull down the *View* menu and choose *Details*. Then click on *View/Arrange Icons* to sort the files based on name, date, size, or type. For example, if you click on *name,* the entries will rearrange themselves into alphabetical order by file name. You can also click on *View/Choose Details* to select the columns (or attributes) you want to see in

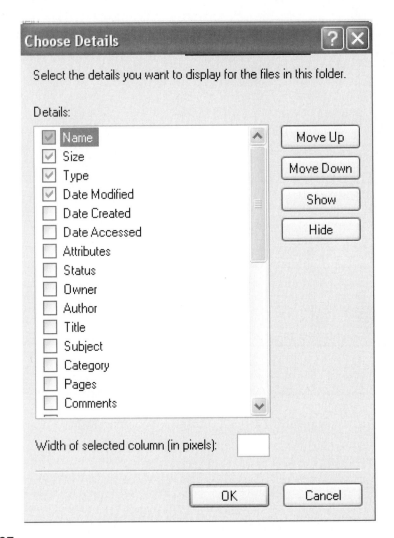

FIGURE 8.27

Column Settings control file details.

a detail view (Figure 8.27). A checkmark in a checkbox indicates that the selected attribute will be displayed in the right pane whenever *Details* is selected.

Shortcuts to Files

It is often useful to create **shortcuts** to files that you access frequently. A shortcut is a link to the file's original location, not a copy of the file. If you delete the shortcut, you delete only the link and not the file.

Try creating a shortcut on your diskette. Start *My Computer* (either view) and display the *A:\Letters* subdirectory. Select the file *tom* and right click the mouse. Choose *Create Shortcut,* (Figure 8.28) to create a shortcut to the file. Highlight the shortcut and click *Edit/Copy*. Then return to the diskette's root directory (click the *Back* button in *My Computer* view or click *3 1/2 Floppy (A:)* on the left pane in *Explorer* view) and click *Edit/Paste*. The shortcut will appear on the diskette's root directory. Normally, shortcuts are created for frequently used programs and files stored on your system's C drive. The shortcuts are then copied to the desktop to simplify the task of launching those frequently used programs. Basically, that is how you customize your desktop.

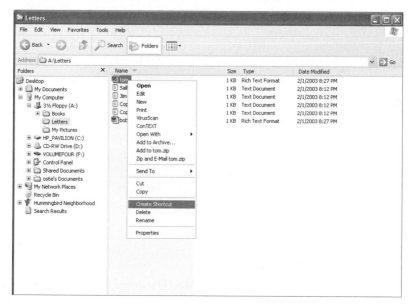

FIGURE 8.28
Creating a shortcut.

■ Other Features

That ends the chapter tutorial. You may shut down your system or follow the appropriate laboratory procedures for exiting now. The material that follows is not part of the tutorial but is intended for future reference.

The Recycle Bin

To delete a file or a folder, select the file in the *Explorer* or *My Computer* view and either select *File/Delete* from the menu bar or press the delete key. Deleted files or folders are not permanently removed from the computer, however. Instead, when you delete a file from the hard disk, its directory entry is transferred from its folder to the **recycle bin.** The file is permanently removed from the system only when you empty the recycle bin, so as long as the file name remains in the recycle bin, the file can be recovered. Note that files deleted from the A drive (more generally, any removable drive or network drive) are not sent to the recycle bin and thus cannot be recovered.

For future reference, to recover a file deleted from the C drive, click on the *Recycle Bin* desktop icon. Then select the file or files to be recovered from the recycle bin's right pane and click on the *Restore* option on the left pane. To permanently delete files from the recycle bin, click on *Empty the Recycle bin* on the left pane or pull down the *File* menu and click on *Empty the Recycle bin*.

The Command Line Interface

In addition to its graphical user interface, Windows XP also supports a **command line** interface that provides access to most if not all the features of MS-DOS. Almost everything that can be done from the GUI can be done from the command line. Additionally, you can create and run batch files to automate repetitive tasks. See Chapter 7 for more information on the command line interface.

Windows Scripting Host

The **Windows Scripting Host (WSH)** allows users to launch scripts written in scripting languages such as JavaScript or VBScript. Such scripts exploit the functionality of a modern Windows operating system much more effectively than do command line batch files. Scripts can be run from the command prompt or launched directly from the desktop by clicking on a script file icon. In addition to running repetitive tasks like batch files, the Windows Scripting Host lets you access and control applications such as Word and Excel, allowing you to write a single script that integrates features from diverse applications.

Multimedia Support

The switch from Windows 2000 to Windows XP brought a number of enhancements to Microsoft's multimedia support. For example, XP makes it easy to write to a CD, in effect treating a CD drive much like a hard disk drive. Additionally, the option to write to a CD is now associated with the *My Pictures* and *My Music* folders. XP also allows you to download images from a digital camera via a USB port, do some simple image editing, publish an image on the Web, or write an image to a CD. The Windows media player can play audio, video, and movies. The media player also supports ripping audio files and writing them to CD, but it does not support the popular *mp3* format. A video software moviemaker allows for simple video tape capture, edit, and write back. Microsoft also sells a modified version of Windows XP Professional called Windows XP Media Center Edition that lets you seamlessly capture, organize, and play back TV shows, DVD movies, music, photos, and other types of digital content.

▣ The Macintosh User Interface

The Apple Macintosh was the first commercially successful graphical user interface, and the authors seriously considered adding a chapter on the Macintosh interface. Although there are important differences between the Macintosh and Windows platforms, their GUIs are similar, and a separate chapter on the Mac interface is difficult to justify given the nature of this book. The internal differences are more dramatic, however, so Part Four features independent chapters on Windows XP internals (Chapter 12) and Macintosh OS X internals (Chapter 14).

▣ Summary

The desktop is the standard Windows user interface. To start a program, you double click its icon or select it from the *Start/All Programs* menu. Each program runs in its own window. You switch between active programs by clicking on the taskbar icon that represents the program you want to run. To enlarge a window, you maximize it. When you minimize a window, it disappears from the screen but its icon remains on the taskbar. To quit a program, open the *File* men and select *Exit* or click on the *X* button at the upper right of the window.

The file system allows a user to identify, save, and retrieve files by name. A file name is composed of the name itself and an optional extension. Windows XP supports both FAT file names and long file names up to 255 characters long. Directory management is a key function of the Windows file system. To simplify keeping track of multiple files, the user creates special files called subdirectories or folders. Both Windows *Explorer* and *My Computer* are used to view and manipulate folders and files. You can copy a file to the same folder or to a different folder, copy multiple files, and copy the contents of a complete folder. The *Search* feature allows you to search for files by file name, by partial file name using wild card characters, or by file contents.

Deleted files or folders are stored in the recycle bin. A file is permanently removed from the system when you empty the recycle bin. Windows XP provides a command line interface that allows the user to access all the features of MS-DOS. The Windows Scripting Host (WSH) allows users to launch scripts written in such scripting languages such as JavaScript or VBScript. Windows XP incorporates enhanced multimedia support.

▌ Key Words

command line	multitasking
desktop	*My Computer*
directory management	notification area
Explorer	recycle bin
file name	root directory
file system	shortcut
folder	*Start* button
format	subdirectory
icon	taskbar
long file name	window
menu	Windows XP
menu bar	Windows Scripting Host (WSH)

▌ Review Questions

1. Describe the standard Windows desktop and briefly explain how to manipulate the desktop.
2. Describe at least two different ways to execute a program under Windows. What is multitasking?
3. Explain how to switch between two active programs.
4. Explain how to maximize, minimize, and restore a window to its original size.
5. Explain how to exit a program. Explain how to shut down the system.
6. What does the file system do?
7. What does the formatting process do?
8. What is the difference between a regular file name and a long file name?

9. Briefly describe the Windows hierarchical directory structure. What is the root directory? What are subdirectories or folders?

10. Distinguish between the Windows *Explorer* and *My Computer* views.

11. How is *My Computer* used to create new folders?

12. Explain how to copy and rename a file. Explain how to copy a file from one folder to another, how to copy multiple files with a single command, and how to copy an entire folder.

13. Explain how the *Search* feature can be used to search for a file by name, by type, or by contents.

14. What is a shortcut? Why are shortcuts useful?

15. Explain how the recycle bin allows you to recover a file you deleted by accident.

16. Why is the command line interface useful?

17. What is the Windows Scripting Host?

18. Describe several enhancements to Microsoft's multimedia support that were implemented in Windows XP.

▌ Exercises

1. If you have not already done so, work through the chapter tutorial.

2. Use the Internet to find an archived copy of Apple's 1984 Super Bowl ad for the Macintosh and view it. From the perspective of two decades, describe your reaction.

3. Implementing common functions such as *Save* and *Save as* in Windows helps to promote a consistent look and feel from application to application. Explain this concept in terms of layering.

4. Create a set of directories to help keep track of your data files or programs. Add your existing files to the new directory structure by copying or renaming them.

5. What advantages does a hierarchical directory structure offer over using a single directory to hold all files?

6. Create a file on your C drive. Delete the file and then recover it from the recycle bin.

7. Why do you suppose Microsoft chose *not* to support the *mp3* file format on Windows XP?

8. Given a choice between a command line interface and a GUI, most people prefer the GUI. There are, however, people who prefer the command line interface. Why do you suppose anyone would prefer a command line interface?

9. The most effective way to learn this chapter's key terms is to complete the chapter tutorial.

CHAPTER 9

The UNIX/Linux User Interface

When you finish reading this chapter you should be able to:

▶ Describe the components of a UNIX/Linux path name.

▶ View a directory using both *Konqueror* and UNIX/Linux line commands.

▶ Create a directory using both *Konqueror* and UNIX/Linux line commands.

▶ Create a file using both KDE and UNIX/Linux line commands.

▶ List a file's contents using both *Konqueror* and UNIX/Linux line commands.

▶ Copy a file using both *Konqueror* and UNIX/Linux line commands.

▶ Search for a file using both KDE and UNIX/Linux line commands.

▶ Explain redirection, filters, and pipes.

■ UNIX

UNIX was developed at Bell Laboratories, a division of AT&T, in the 1970s. Largely the work of two individuals, Ken Thompson and Dennis Ritchie, the system's main thrust was providing a convenient working environment for writing programs. Almost from its inception, UNIX has been an open source operating system, a decision that in no small way has contributed to its development. Today, UNIX is an important standard that has influenced the design of many modern operating systems. Experienced programmers consider UNIX simple, elegant, and easy to learn. Beginners, on the other hand, sometimes find it terse and not very friendly.

Linux

In 1991, Linus Torvald, then a student at the University at Helsinki, created an open source version of UNIX called **Linux** designed to run on the Intel 386 chip, the precursor to today's Pentium family of chips. The complete source code is freely available on the Internet, and over the years Linux has been refined and modified to incorporate contributions from hundreds of software developers throughout the world. Today, versions of Linux are available for most platforms including most personal computers.

The **kernel** is the core of the operating system that communicates directly with the hardware. Applications such as the shell, utilities, compilers and other programs run on the kernel. Version 1.0, the initial stable version of the Linux kernel, was released in 1994. Subsequently, commercial vendors such as RedHat, Mandrake, and SuSe and open source distributions such as Debian and Gentoo have packaged the software for easy installation on a wide variety of personal computers and added enhancements that make Linux more useful. The sample screens in this chapter were created under Debian's stable woody version, which uses Linux kernel 2.4.18. Your screens will probably look a bit different.

The Hacker's Creed

In the late 1960 and early 1970s, the term hacker was used to describe a highly skilled programmer with a knack for writing tight, efficient, elegant code. Many of those early hackers shared a common set of values that were reflected in an often unpublished hacker's creed. Although there are many versions of the hacker's creed, most agree that a hacker should do no harm and should not benefit financially from his or her hacking. Another common principle was that information should be free, an idea consistent with open source software. The people who developed (and continue to develop) UNIX were hackers in the original sense of the word, and the hacker's creed still influences today's UNIX and Linux operating systems.

The User Interface

Typically, a user accesses a computer through an application program's interface and the application logic communicates with UNIX through an application programming interface such as **POSIX,** Portable Operating System Interface for UNIX. At times, however, it is necessary to communicate directly with the operating system to perform such functions as launching a program.

UNIX line commands are processed by a command processor or **shell** that lies between the user and the kernel (Figure 9.1). The shell is not really part of the operating system so it can be changed; in fact, the idea of implementing the command processor in its own independent layer was an important UNIX innovation. In UNIX terminology, the shell is the command line interface, but the term shell is sometimes used to refer more broadly to the user interface layer.

Beginners often find a command line interface a bit intimidating and prefer such alternatives as a menu interface, a graphical user interface, or voice commands. Many UNIX systems incorporate a standard graphical user interface called X-Windows. Most Linux systems provide either the **K-Desktop Environment (KDE)** or the GNOME interface, both of which are built on top of X-Windows and resemble the Windows interface (Chapter 8). KDE is the more popular of the two.

Because UNIX/Linux actively supports both line commands and a GUI, a key focus of this chapter is to compare and contrast these two types of interfaces. Much of the material is presented in the form of a tutorial. If possible, find a Linux or UNIX system and, as you read about a command, issue it and see for yourself how the computer responds. You will need a user name and a password; if necessary, see your instructor or your system's super user. Later, you may find Appendix C a useful reference.

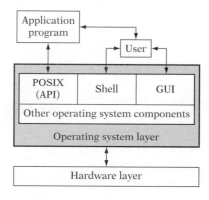

FIGURE 9.1

A UNIX user has several options for communicating with the operating system.

Logging On

Every UNIX session begins with a request for a **login name** and a **password.** If your system starts in command line mode, type your login name and press enter in response to the first prompt (Figure 9.2). Next, you'll be asked for your password. Type it and press enter. (For security reasons, passwords are never displayed.) If your system starts at the graphical user interface, the screen will look different but it should request the same information.

If you started with the graphical user interface, the KDE desktop should appear immediately after a successful login and you can simply read the rest of this paragraph. If you successfully logged in via the command line interface or shell, you will see on the last line a **prompt** consisting of your login name followed by a dollar sign ($), a percent sign (%), or a colon (:) (Figure 9.2). The precise format of the prompt depends on which UNIX shell is your system's default. At the prompt, type

startx

to start the KDE desktop.

The KDE Desktop

Like Windows (Chapter 8), the standard KDE 3.1 interface features a **desktop** metaphor (Figure 9.3); if you are following along on your own computer, your desktop might look different. On the left side of the desktop is a set of icons that represent programs or files. For example, the *Home* icon near the top left of Figure 9.3 represents a program named ***Konqueror,*** the KDE file manager. If you click the *Home* icon, *Konqueror* displays the contents of your home folder or directory.

```
Debian GNU/Linux 3.0 os6 tty3
os6 login: rajkumar
Password:
Last login: Sun Feb 9 21:00:55 2003 on tty3
Linux os6 2.4.18–bf2.4 #1 Sun Apr 14 09:53:28 EST 2002
i686 unknown

rajkumar@os6:~$ startx
```

FIGURE 9.2

A log on sequence.

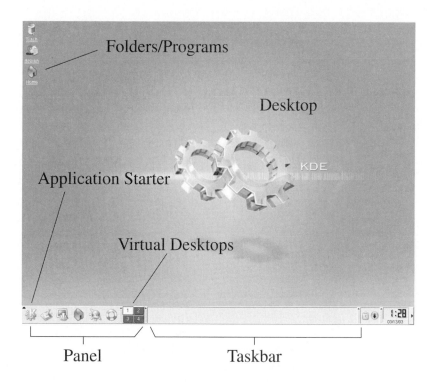

FIGURE 9.3

The KDE user interface.

The KDE desktop's **panel** is found at the bottom left. The first (or left-most) panel entry, an iconic *K*, represents the ***Application Starter***. Click on the *Application Starter* and a set of menu options for launching programs appears (Figure 9.4). Click any spot outside the application menu to return to the desktop (Figure 9.3). KDE supports multiple concurrent desktops called **virtual desktops.** You can select the active desktop by clicking on one of the numbered buttons to the right of the panel; for example, the current screen is virtual desktop number 1.

The **taskbar** lies to the right of the virtual desktop buttons. It displays an icon for each active program. To switch to a different program, simply click the new program's taskbar icon. The system date and time are displayed at the lower right, and the icon that resembles a clipboard with a lowercase k represents (as you might expect) the clipboard.

FIGURE 9.4

The KDE application menu.

Command Line Utilities

The third icon from the left on the panel resembles a shell; the program it represents is called **Konsole.** Click the *Konsole* icon to switch to the command line interface or **shell mode** (Figure 9.5). If a window displaying a *Konsole* tip pops up, click *Close.* At this point your screen should resemble Figure 9.5. Note that the shell runs in its own window and that an icon labeled *Shell—Konsole* appears on the taskbar. Note also that your prompt will start with your login name rather than *rajkumar.*

Figure 9.6 shows the format of a UNIX **line command.** Command names are generally terse (ed for editor, cp for copy a file), but meaningful. One or more spaces separate the command name from the options. If they are included, the options are usually preceded by a minus sign to

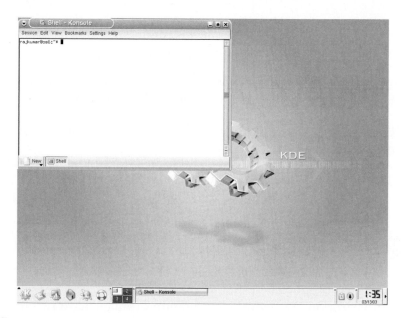

FIGURE 9.5

The command line shell.

distinguish them from the arguments. Most options are designated by a single lowercase letter, and multiple options can be coded. One or more spaces separate the options from the arguments, which usually consist of one or more file names.

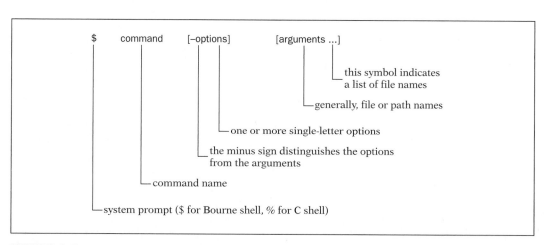

FIGURE 9.6

A UNIX line command.

Use the **passwd** utility to change your password. Type

passwd

The system will prompt for your current password and the new password; Figure 9.7 shows the contents of the shell window. Respond by typing the corresponding passwords into the system. After verifying the new password, UNIX will notify you that it has changed your password, but it will not display the new password.

Three more line commands are shown in Figure 9.8. The **date** utility displays the system date and time. Simply type

date

and press enter. Use the **who** utility to identify all the users who are currently logged onto your system by typing

who

A user working on more than one project might have two or more login names, and that can be confusing. The command

whoami

(no spaces) displays the user's current login name.

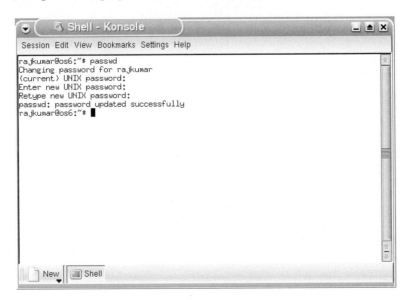

FIGURE 9.7

Use the passwd utility to change your password.

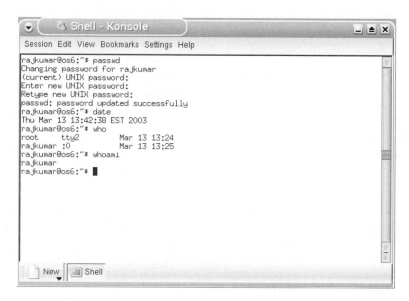

FIGURE 9.8

The date and who utilities.

Many other utilities are available. For example, the mail utility sends and receives e-mail, and most UNIX systems feature an on-line reference manual. To obtain a description of any utility, code man followed by the utility name. For example,

man who

displays a description of the who utility.

■ The File System

The **file system** is a key UNIX component that allows a user to identify, save, and retrieve files by name. (A program, remember, is a type of file.) Before you begin using the UNIX file system, however, you must first understand a few underlying concepts.

File Names

A UNIX **file name** (Figure 9.9) consists of from 1 to 255 characters. Do not use slashes (/), and avoid starting a file name with a minus sign or hyphen;

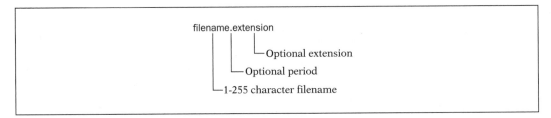

FIGURE 9.9
UNIX file names.

otherwise, virtually any combination of characters you can type is legal. Note that UNIX is case sensitive—it distinguishes between uppercase and lowercase, so A and a are different. If you include a period, the characters following the period are treated as the file name **extension.** The extension is significant to some compilers and to the linkage editor, but generally it is considered part of the file name.

Directories

Imagine a user who maintains several different types of files. Letters and other correspondence are generated by a text editor, chapters for a book are output by a word processor, and C programs form a third group. Dozens, perhaps even hundreds of different users will have similar needs. Keeping track of all those files in a single directory is virtually impossible. Instead, UNIX uses a flexible hierarchical **directory** structure (Figure 9.10).

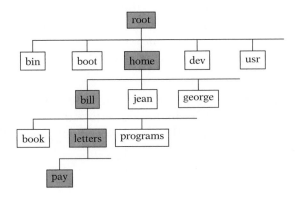

FIGURE 9.10
UNIX uses a hierarchical directory structure.

The structure begins with a **root directory**. Several "children" grow from the root. Some hold references to utilities and other system routines. One directory, *home*, holds all the user's directory names[1]. Note that *bill* is a child of *home* and a grandchild of the root directory. Under *bill* come subdirectories to hold letters, book chapters, and programs. Incidentally, a directory is a special type of file, so the rules for naming directories and files are identical.

Path Names

With all those directories, you need more than a simple name to find a file. For example, it is possible to have files named *pay* recorded under two different directories. A reference to *pay* would thus be ambiguous—which *pay* do you mean? To uniquely identify a file, you need a complete **path name** (Figure 9.11). For example,

/home/bill/letters/pay

defines the path to a file named pay on the *bill/letters* directory. Look at Figure 9.10, and follow the path name. The first slash[2] (/) indicates the root directory. Move down through the hierarchical directory structure to *home*, then *bill*, then *letters*, and finally to the file *pay*.

At first glance, subdirectories seem to complicate rather than simplify accessing files. In practice, however, you will rarely use such lengthy path names. Instead, when you log on, UNIX selects your **home directory** (its name usually matches your login name) as your initial **working directory**.

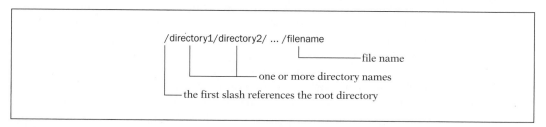

FIGURE 9.11
You must specify a complete path name to uniquely identify a file.

---

[1] Note that *home* is a generic directory name. The actual name of your home directory usually matches your login ID, which explains why the author's home directory is named *rajkumar*.

[2] Note: NOT a backslash (\). The backslash is an **MS-DOS** separator (Chapter 7).

Unless it is told otherwise, the operating system searches for files starting with your working directory. Thus, if bill is the working directory,

letters/pay

is all you need to find file *pay*. Later in the chapter, you'll see how to change working directories.

▣ Working with the File System

Both KDE and the shell allow a user to work with the UNIX file system. The material that follows switches back and forth between the two interfaces and asks you to perform essentially the same tasks under both, giving you an opportunity to compare and contrast a GUI and a line command interface.

Viewing a Directory

Konqueror is KDE's file manager. Like the Windows file manager (Chapter 8), *Konqueror* uses folders to represent directories. Your most recent commands were issued at the line command prompt (Figure 9.8) within the Konsole window, so click anywhere on the desktop to switch back to the KDE desktop (Figure 9.3).

There are two ways to open *Konqueror*. One is to click the *Home* icon at the KDE desktop's upper left. The second option is to click the application starter, an iconic *K* icon at the lower left, and then select *Home (Personal files)* from the program menu (Figure 9.12). Choose either option to start the file manager.

Konqueror displays two panels (Figure 9.13). (If you do not see two panels, click on *Window/Show Navigation Panel*.) The left panel, called the **navigation panel,** lists the folder's contents as a hierarchical directory structure. By default, *Konqueror* starts with your home directory; note that the path name of your home directory folder is displayed in the location toolbar just above the panels. The right panel displays the folders and files stored in the directory. Note that there are three folders and no files visible in the *Konqueror* window in Figure 9.13.

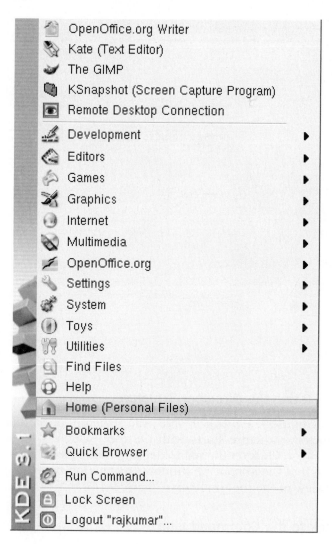

FIGURE 9.12

The *Konqueror* file manager.

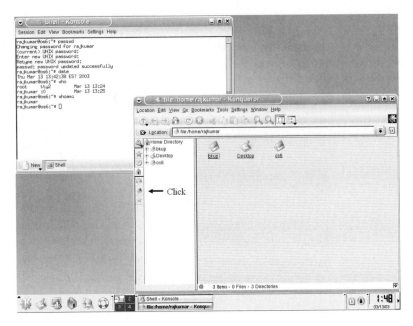

FIGURE 9.13

Konqueror panels.

Navigating the Directory Structure

You can use *Konqueror* to study the structure of the Linux file system. The directory structure starts with the root, which is identified by a / (slash) character. Click on the red folder icon, the second icon from the bottom to the left of the *Konqueror* window's navigation panel, to get a full hierarchical view of the root directory (Figure 9.14).

Back to the Command Line

Click on the Shell icon in the taskbar to switch back to the command line interface. Then clear the existing contents on the screen by typing the command

clear

and print or display your working directory by issuing the command

pwd

Your author's working directory appears on the second line of Figure 9.15. Your working directory's name will be different, of course. By default, it should be your home directory.

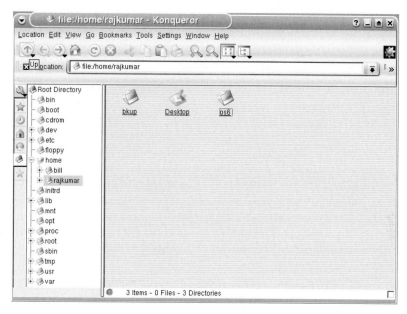

FIGURE 9.14
The directory structure.

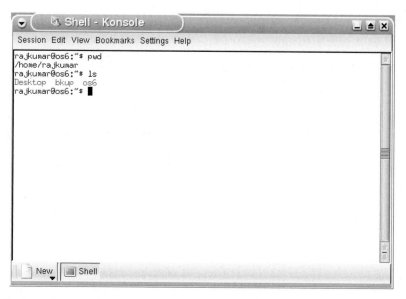

FIGURE 9.15
The pwd and ls line commands.

Even if this is the first time you have logged on, your home directory should contain a few files. To view their names, type an **ls** (list directory) command

ls

(Figure 9.15). As you can see, the author's working directory contains three files: *Desktop*, *bkup*, and *os6*. Your working directory will probably not include *bkup* or *os6*, but it should contain Desktop and perhaps some other files.

Before you move on, quickly compare Figures 9.14 and 9.15. In Figure 9.14, the right *Konqueror* panel shows icons for three files—*bkup, Desktop,* and *os6*. The same three file names appear just above the last prompt in Figure 9.15. In other words you just used two different interfaces, *Konqueror* and *Shell*, to display the same information. Under *Konqueror*, you clicked on your home directory name in the left panel. Under the *Shell*, you issued two line commands. But the results were identical.

Creating a Directory from *Konqueror*

The next step is to create a subdirectory under your home directory. Click the *Konqueror* icon on the taskbar to activate the KDE file manager. Click *Edit/New Directory*, enter *Books* for the directory name (Figure 9.16), and click on *OK* to create the folder *Books*. To open the new subdirectory *Books*, click on its icon in the left panel. To move back to your home directory, click on *Home Directory*.

Creating a Directory from the Command Line

Activate the shell by clicking on the *Shell* icon in the taskbar, issue a clear command to clear the previous topic, and then type the command

mkdir Letters

(Figure 9.17). From the command line, you use the **mkdir** (make directory) utility to create a directory and rmdir (remove directory) to remove or delete one.

To make the subdirectory *Letters* your working directory, issue a **cd** (change directory) command by typing

cd Letters

Type pwd to verify that the *Letters* subdirectory is your working directory, and then type

ls -a

to list the files (Figure 9.17).

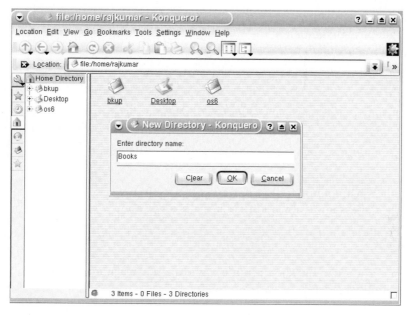

FIGURE 9.16

Creating a directory.

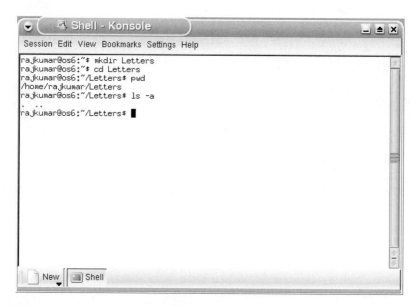

FIGURE 9.17

The mkdir utility and the cd line command.

Note the two files named (.) and (..) because they are significant. The single period stands for the working directory, and the double period is a synonym for its parent. They are useful shorthand for writing path names. Type

cd ..

to make the parent of *Letters* (your home directory) the working directory. Then try some other variations. For example, in the command

cd /

the slash identifies the root directory. Although UNIX displays no confirmation message, the root directory will be your new working directory. Now type

ls

and press enter. The output (on the author's system) appears in Figure 9.18. Finally, to return to your home directory, type

cd

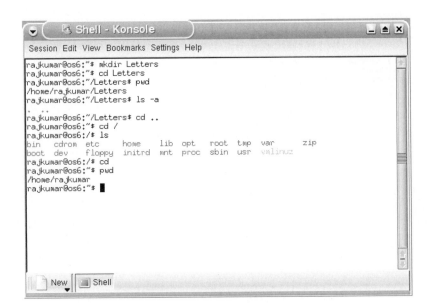

FIGURE 9.18

The contents of the author's root directory and home directory.

Then type

pwd

to verify that your home directory is your working directory.

Creating Files from the Command Line

Most user files are created by application programs such as editors, compilers, word processors, spreadsheet programs and database managers. Different systems feature different applications, but most UNIX systems incorporate a full screen visual editor called **vi** that you can use to create a few simple files.

First, however, change the working directory to *Letters*. *Letters* is a subdirectory of your home directory, which, if you've been following the tutorial, is your current working directory. Unless you specify otherwise, UNIX always assumes a file reference starts with the current working directory, so

cd Letters

changes the working directory to *Letters* (Figure 9.19).

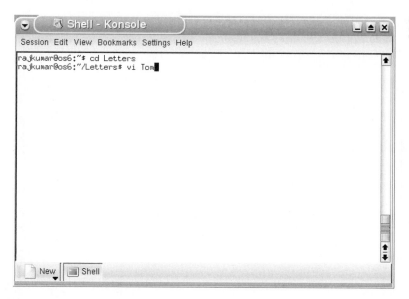

FIGURE 9.19
Starting the visual editor.

To launch the visual editor and use it to create (in the working directory) a file named *Tom,* issue the command

vi Tom

(Figure 9.19, second line). Except for a message at the bottom, the vi window should go blank. The visual editor has two operating modes: command and insert. As you begin, you are in command mode by default. To switch to insert mode, press *I.* You'll get no confirmation, but you should be able to begin entering text.

Type the following two lines:

Looking forward to spring break!
See you in Florida!

When you are finished, exit insert mode by pressing the escape key. (On some systems, you must press a function key—see your instructor.) Then type :wq, for write quit (Figure 9.20). (Some systems accept a pair of capital Zs as a command to exit vi.) You should see a system prompt indicating that you're back in the shell.

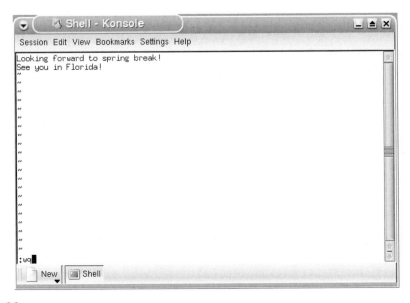

FIGURE 9.20
Exiting vi.

Type the command

ls –l

to verify that the file is on disk; the l option indicates long form. Then type a cd command to return to your home directory and issue another

ls –l

command to list the contents of your home directory in long form (Figure 9.21).

The first ten characters in a long form directory listing indicate the file type and its access permissions (Figure 9.22). The file can be an ordinary file (data or a program), a directory, or a special file that corresponds to an input or output device; note in Figure 9.21 that *Tom* is an ordinary file (type –) and the subdirectories on your home directory are all file type *d*. Three sets of permissions are included: one for the file's owner, a second for users in the owner's group, and a third for all other users. Based on the recorded values, a given user or group can be granted read *(r)*, write *(w)*, and/or execute *(x)* permission. A minus sign indicates no permission. Use the chmod utility to change a file's access permissions.

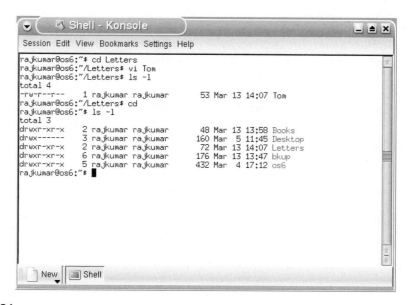

FIGURE 9.21

A long form directory listing.

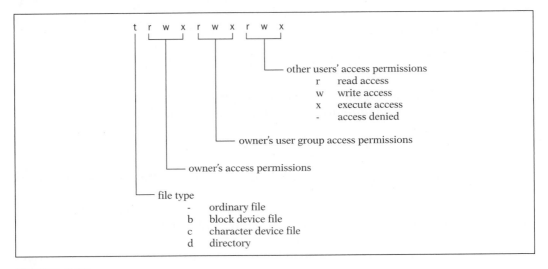

FIGURE 9.22

File type and access permissions.

Creating Files from KDE

Click on the *Konqueror* icon on the taskbar to activate the KDE file manager. One way to start a program from within KDE is to click on the *Application Starter* (the *K* icon) and then select the program you want to run from the menu (Figure 9.23). The menus are organized hierarchically and you might find the program you need in a subfolder; for example, *Kwrite*, a text editor, is in a subfolder called *Editors*. To start *Kwrite*, click the sequence *K/Editors/Kwrite*. (Check with your instructor if *Kwrite* is not in the *Editors* subfolder.) Then position the cursor within the *Kwrite* window's top right panel and type

Sorry Tom.
I am going skiing!

Click on *File/Save* to save the file (Figure 9.24). Choose the subdirectory *Letters*, give your file the name *Jim* and click *Save*. Then click on *File/Quit* to close *Kwrite*.

Note that the subdirectory *Letters* was created by a line command, but you just created a file under KDE and saved that file in *Letters*. The point is it doesn't matter whether you use the shell or the graphical user interface to create a subdirectory or a folder, because those two interfaces are simply different ways of doing essentially the same thing.

You can also use *Konqueror* to view the new file's permissions, much as you did with a long form list directory option in the previous section. Select the file *Jim* by holding down *Ctrl* and clicking the left mouse button. (Under KDE, just clicking on the file name opens the file.) Then right click on *Jim* and choose *Properties*. A new window will open. If necessary, click on the *Permissions* tab to access a set of check boxes that allow you to change the file's permission settings (Figure 9.25). For example, to allow everyone to modify the file Jim, give them Write permission by checking the *Write* box to the right of *Others*. For now, simply click on *Cancel* and return to *Konqueror*.

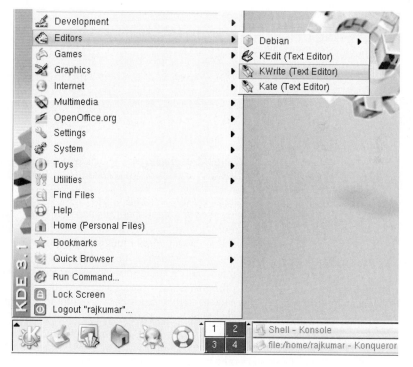

FIGURE 9.23

The Editor submenu.

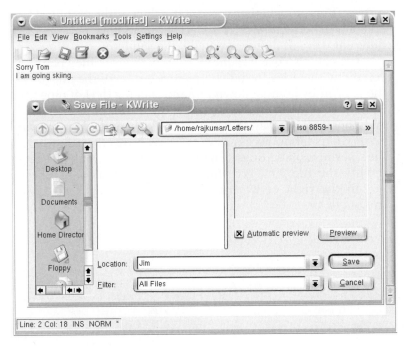

FIGURE 9.24

Saving a file.

The Ease-of-Use/Efficiency Tradeoff

A typical user begins a work session by logging on and launching an application program such as a word processor, a spreadsheet, or an e-mail program. Logging on and launching a program are operating system tasks, but once the application starts, subsequent communication with the operating system takes place indirectly (through the application program's interface) until the time comes to log off. The user might be an expert in manipulating the application interface, but the need to issue commands directly to the operating system is so rare that the efficiency of those interactions is irrelevant. Given the choice between a terse, non-intuitive line command interface and a relatively easy-to-use graphical user interface, most users prefer the GUI.

A system operator or sysop looks at the ease-of-use/efficiency tradeoff differently, however. The sysop works with the operating system, not with application programs. A GUI might be intuitive and easy to use, but working through a hierarchy of screens and menus is not very efficient when the process must be repeated frequently. To a sysop, those terse, nonintuitive line commands save time. Given a choice between navigating the multiple screens and menus of a graphical user interface and issuing relatively efficient line commands, most sysops prefer the line command interface.

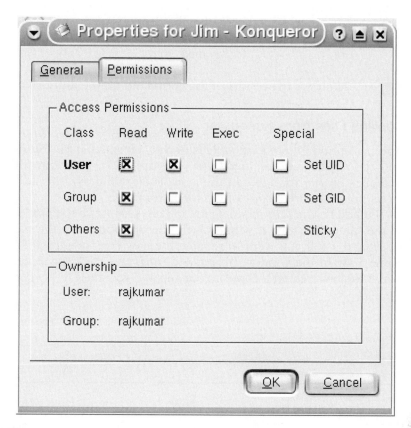

FIGURE 9.25
File properties.

Listing File Contents from Konqueror

Now that you've created some files, you can manipulate them. To display a file's contents from *Konqueror,* simply click on the file within *Konqueror.* For example, to view the contents of the file *Tom,* navigate to the *Letters* subdirectory and click on *Tom* to start the *Kwrite* editor. The contents of the file *Tom* will be displayed on screen and can be modified if desired. Click on *File/Quit* to close *Kwrite.*

Listing File Contents from the Command Line

Click on the *Shell Konsole* icon on the taskbar to activate the shell. Make sure that your current directory is *Letters* by typing

```
cd
cd Letters
pwd
```

Then use the *more* utility to display the contents of the file *Tom*. Type

more Tom

Figure 9.26 shows the results of the command on the author's system.

Copying Files from Konqueror

Another option for creating a file is to copy an existing file. Start *Konqueror* and choose the subdirectory *Letters* (Figure 9.27). Hold down the *ctrl* key and click on *Jim* to highlight the icon. Then pull down the *Edit* menu and select *Copy* to store a copy of the file in memory.

Pull down the *Edit* menu again and click on *Paste* to paste the file back to the same directory. A window will pop up to indicate the file name *Jim* exists and ask if you want to rename the new copy (Figure 9.28). Type the name *Sally* in the window (to replace *Jim*), and click the *Rename* button. You have just created a copy of your file and renamed it.

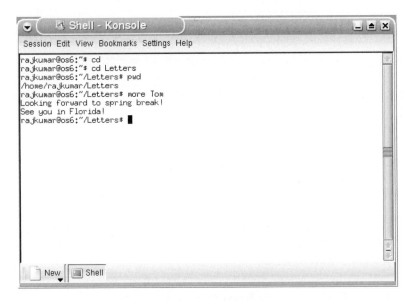

FIGURE 9.26

Viewing a file's contents with the more utility.

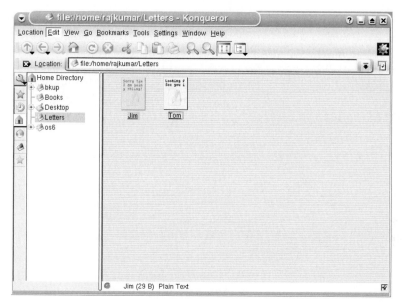

FIGURE 9.27
Copying a file.

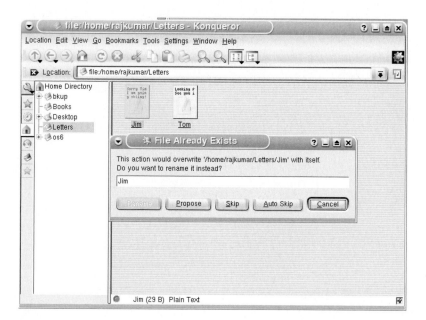

FIGURE 9.28
Rename on paste.

You can also copy a file to a different folder. Hold down *Ctrl* and click the file *Jim* to select it. Then simply drag its icon to the folder *Books* on the left pane. When you release the mouse button, *Konqueror* displays a menu (Figure 9.29). Choose *Copy Here,* and the file named *Jim* is copied into the *Books* folder. There are three other options listed in the pop-up window in Figure 9.29. *Move Here* copies the file to the new folder and deletes it from the original folder. *Link Here* neither copies nor moves the file. Instead it creates a reference to the file in the new directory. *Cancel,* of course, cancels the operation.

Copying Files from the Command Line

You can use the copy (**cp**) utility to copy a file from the command line. For example, click the *Shell* icon to switch to the line interface and make sure your home directory is the working directory (Figure 9.30). Then issue the command

cp Letters/Tom Books/Tom

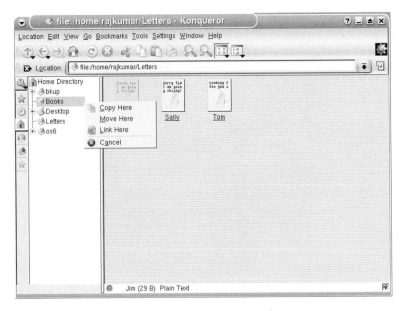

FIGURE 9.29

Copying to a different folder.

followed by

ls Books

to verify that the copy took place. Next, use the ln command to create a link
by typing

ln -s Letters/Sally Books
ls -l Books

You can see the results in Figure 9.30. Note that *Sally,* the second entry in
directory list, is file type *l,* for link.

Searching for Files from KDE

Kfind is a KDE utility that helps find a file when you know either a part of
its file name or a specific string of text within the file. Switch to KDE and
start *Kfind* by choosing *K(Application Starter)/Find Files.*

Assume you know you have a file whose name starts with *Sa* (note the
uppercase S), but you do not remember the full file name. Enter *Sa** in the

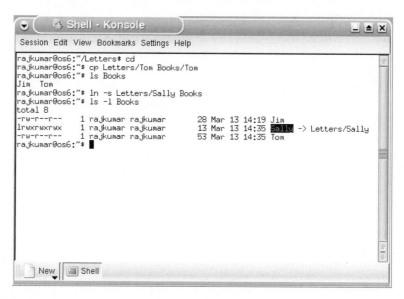

FIGURE 9.30

Copying and linking files at the command line.

Named box (Figure 9.31). The * (asterisk) is a **wild card** character that represents one or more characters in the file name. Since the search string you entered starts with Sa*, it will match *Sally, Saturday, Sam*, and any other file name that starts with Sa. After you enter *Sa** in the location box, click on *Find* and *Kfind* will return the *Sally* files in both the *Books* and *Letters* folders.

In addition to the * character, you can also use a question mark (?) as a wild card character. A question mark represents a single character; for example, the file name *Sa?* matches *Sam, Sat, Say*, and any other file name that starts with Sa and ends with any other single character. The wild card characters can be used anywhere in the search name.

Searching for Files from the Command Line

Use the *find* utility (Figure 9.32) to find files from the command line. Activate the shell by clicking on the *shell* icon on the taskbar. To search for files starting with Sa*, type

find . -name "Sa*"

and press enter. The single period (.) tells find to start the search from the current directory and its subdirectories, and the operator -name followed by the option "Sa*" identifies the search string. Figure 9.33 displays the results of a command line find command.

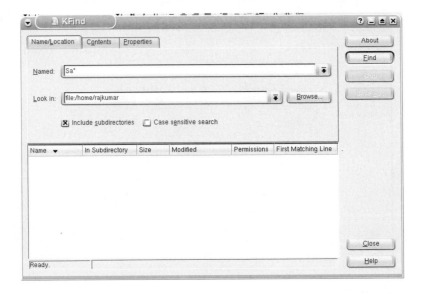

FIGURE 9.31

Finding files based on name.

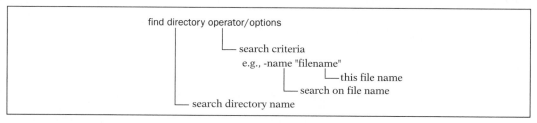

FIGURE 9.32
The find utility.

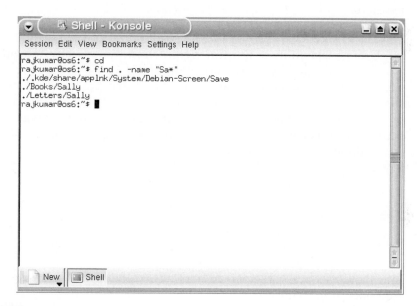

FIGURE 9.33
Using find.

Pipes, Filters, and Redirection

Many UNIX utilities and commands assume a standard input or output device; for example, find sends its output to the screen, while vi gets its input from the keyboard. By using **redirection** operators (Figure 9.34), a user can instruct the shell to change those defaults.

Operator	Meaning	Example
<	change source to a specified device or file	<myfile
>	change destination to a specified device or file	>tempfile
>>	change destination to an existing file and append new data	>>master.pay
|	pipe standard output to another command or to a filter	cat file1 | sort

FIGURE 9.34

Redirection operators.

Use the find utility to illustrate redirection. You already know that a find command followed by a directory name and a search string returns a list of file names that match the search string and that the ls command displays the contents of a file. Since no inputs or outputs are specified, the shell assumes the standard input and output devices (the keyboard and the screen). That is why the command results are displayed on the screen.

Redirect the output. Type

find . -name "Sa*" >Letters/findSally.txt

Then list your directory

ls -a Letters

You should see a new file named findSally.txt that contains the results of the find operation (Figure 9.35).

A **filter** accepts input from the standard input device, modifies (or filters) the data in some way, and sends the results to the standard output device. For example, the **sort** utility (Figure 9.36) reads input from the specified file or files (or the standard input device), sorts them into alphabetical or numerical sequence, and outputs the sorted data to the screen.

A **pipe** causes one utility's standard output to be used as another utility's standard input. Pipes are designated by a vertical line (|). For example, earlier in the chapter, you issued the command

find . -name "Sa*"

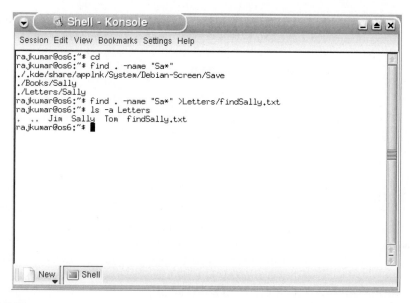

FIGURE 9.35

Redirecting output.

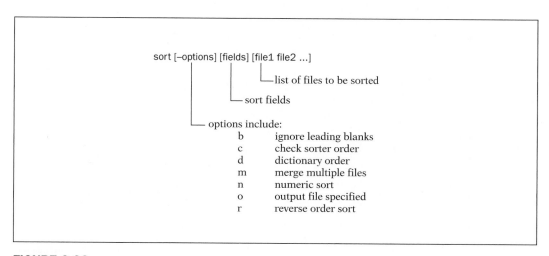

FIGURE 9.36

The sort utility.

Retype that command, but do not press enter. Instead, add a pipe operator to pipe the output to sort

find . -name "Sa*" | sort -r

and then press enter. As Figure 9.37 shows, the output has been routed through sort and, because of the r option the file names are now displayed in reverse alphabetical order.

Shell Scripts

Many computer applications are run daily, weekly, or at other regular intervals. Others, such as a program test, are repeated numerous times. Each time such applications are run, a set of commands must be issued, and retyping the same commands over and over again is annoying and error prone. An option is to write a **shell script.**

A shell script is a file that consists of a series of commands. (It resembles an MS-DOS BAT file—see Chapter 7.) The shell is actually a highly

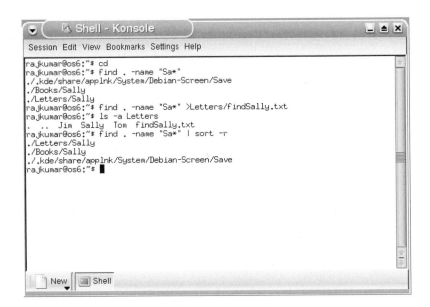

FIGURE 9.37

Using a pipe.

sophisticated, interpretive programming language with its own variables, expressions, sequence, decision, and repetitive structures. Writing shell scripts is beyond the scope of this book, but it is a powerful UNIX feature that you will eventually want to learn more about.

UNIX utilities, filters, and shell scripts are powerful command line features. View them as tools. Each one performs a single function. Instead of writing a massive program to perform a series of functions, it makes sense to use the existing tools and link them with pipes, filters, and redirection operators. As you become more experienced with UNIX, you will find many uses for them.

This marks the end of the chapter tutorial. To log off the system from *Konqueror,* click on *K/Logout*. To log off the system from the command line, type logout and press enter.

■ The Command Line and GUI Layers

Throughout this chapter, you used both the shell and KDE to communicate with UNIX. One way to grasp the differences between these two interfaces is to view them as layers (Figure 9.38). When you issue a line command, you communicate *directly* with the operating system; in other words, each command activates a specific operating system routine that carries out the requested operation. When you work through a graphical user interface, however, you communicate with a GUI interface such as the KDE desktop metaphor. Your mouse clicks and menu selections are essentially interpreted by the GUI to obtain the functional equivalent of line commands, and those command equivalents are, in turn, passed down to UNIX. The GUI is easier to use because it presents a visual picture of the available options, but communicating through a GUI is relatively inefficient because the commands must be processed by an extra layer. Typing line commands can seem intimidating to a beginner, but they are more efficient because they reduce the number of layers separating the user from the operating system.

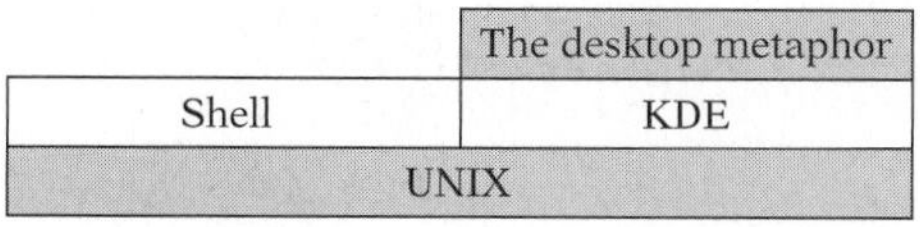

	The desktop metaphor
Shell	KDE
UNIX	

FIGURE 9.38

View the shell and a GUI as layers.

▣ Summary

Linux is an open source version of UNIX. The user of a modern Linux system can often choose between the traditional line command interface or shell and a graphical user interface such as KDE. The UNIX file system allows a user to store, retrieve, and manipulate files by name. The KDE file manager is called *Konqueror*. Because UNIX uses a hierarchical directory structure, a path name must be specified to completely identify a file.

The chapter tutorial switched back and forth between KDE and the command line shell. In the context of that tutorial, you viewed the contents of a directory, created a directory, created some files, displayed the contents of those files, copied files, and searched for files by file name.

Many UNIX utilities and commands assume the standard input or output device. Redirection tells the shell to change the defaults. A filter accepts data from the standard input device, modifies them in some way, and sends the results to the standard output device. Pipes allow a user to link utilities and other programs, treating the standard output generated by one as the standard input for another. A shell script is a file that consists of a series of commands. A graphical user interface is more user friendly but less efficient than a command line interface.

▣ Key Words

Application Starter	panel
cd	passwd
cp	password
date	path name
desktop	pipe
directory	POSIX
extension	prompt
file name	redirection
file system	root directory
filter	shell
home directory	shell mode
KDE (K-Desktop Environment)	shell script
kernel	sort
Konqueror	taskbar
Konsole	UNIX
line command	vi
Linux	virtual desktop
login name	who
ls	wild card
mkdir	working directory
navigation panel	

◗ Review Questions

1. Discuss the origins of UNIX and Linux.
2. Describe the KDE desktop interface.
3. Describe the general form of a UNIX line command.
4. Distinguish between the root directory, your home directory, and your working directory.
5. Describe the components of a UNIX path name, including any intermediate directories and the file name.
6. View the contents of a directory using *Konqueror*.
7. View the contents of a directory using UNIX line commands.
8. Explain the significance of the (.) and (..) file names. What do they mean? Why are they useful?
9. Create a directory using *Konqueror*.
10. Create a directory using UNIX line commands.
11. Create a file using KDE.
12. Create a file using UNIX line commands.
13. View the contents of a file using *Konqueror*.
14. View the contents of a file using UNIX line commands.
15. Copy a file using *Konqueror*.
16. Copy a file using UNIX line commands.
17. Search for a file using KDE.
18. Search for a file using UNIX line commands.
19. Explain how wild card characters can enhance the search process.
20. Explain redirection, filters, and pipes.
21. What is a shell script? Why are shell scripts useful?
22. Compare and contrast a graphical user interface and a line command interface. What are the strengths and weaknesses of each?

◗ Exercises

1. If you haven't already done so, work through the chapter tutorial.
2. Relate the UNIX shell and the KDE graphical user interface to the command processor introduced in Chapter 5.
3. Go online, find a version of the hacker's creed, and read it. Do you agree or disagree with the principles stated in that creed? Why?
4. Briefly describe a hierarchical directory structure. What advantages does it offer over a simple linear directory structure?

5. When you log on, your home directory is your working directory. Why would you want to change that?

6. Why is it that some people prefer the UNIX line command interface and other people prefer a graphical user interface such as KDE?

7. Relate pipes, filters, and redirection to the layering concept.

8. Compare a UNIX shell script to an MS-DOS batch file (Chapter 7).

9. Figures 9.1 and/or 9.38 are useful templates for organizing many of this chapter's key terms, but the most effective way to learn the key terms is to complete the chapter tutorial.

Operating System Internals

This section drops inside the operating system, discusses the Intel architecture (Chapter 10), and explains how several popular operating systems, including MS-DOS (Chapter 11), Windows XP (Chapter 12), Macintosh OS X (Chapter 13), UNIX/Linux (Chapter 14), and IBM's traditional mainframe operating system (Chapter 15), work internally. In Part 5, the stand alone systems discussed in this section will be treated as layers that can be plugged together to form complex distributed systems.

CHAPTER 10

The Intel Architecture

When you finish reading this chapter you should be able to:

▶ Explain how the Intel Pentium family of processors fetches and executes instructions.

▶ Describe the Intel architecture's execution environment.

▶ Distinguish between a logical address and a physical address.

▶ Distinguish between a flat memory model and a segmented memory model.

▶ Describe the process of translating a logical segment address into a physical address.

▶ Describe the components of an Intel task.

▶ Discuss the Intel architecture's memory protection features.

▶ Describe the Intel Pentium interrupt handling process.

▶ Explain pipelining.

▶ Distinguish between Intel's 32-bit architecture and Intel's 64-bit Itanium architecture.

◘ Introduction

Chapters 7, 8, and 9 focused on the operating system's user interface. This chapter is concerned with the Intel hardware environment and the operating system's hardware interface (Figure 10.1). Initially established with the release of the Intel 4004 in early 1971 and the Intel 8086 in the early 1980s, the Intel architecture (IA) remains the foundation of the processors that power most of the personal computers in operation today, including the Pentium family and the Celeron family. This chapter introduces the Intel architecture and its principles of operation. Chapters 11 and 12 describe two operating systems, MS-DOS and Windows XP, designed to work in the context of the Intel architecture.

◘ Intel Architecture Overview

A simplified block diagram of the Intel architecture that supports the Pentium family of processors is shown in Figure 10.2. The processor is responsible for fetching instructions and decoding those instructions into a series of micro-operations. The processor then executes the micro-operations.

Cache is an area of high-speed memory that sits between the processor and primary memory. Frequently accessed instructions and data are copied from memory to cache to speed up the processor because transfers from cache are faster than transfers from primary memory. The memory subsystem of the Pentium processor consists of primary memory and two integrated caches, a primary cache (L1) and a secondary cache (L2).

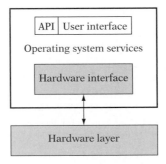

FIGURE 10.1

This chapter is concerned with the Intel hardware environment and the operating system's hardware interface.

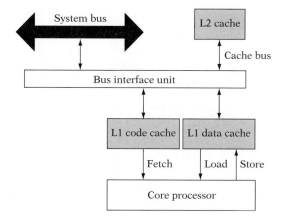

FIGURE 10.2

A simplified block diagram of the Pentium architecture.

Instructions are fetched into the L1 code cache. The L1 *data* cache holds frequently accessed data. A cache hit occurs when the processor requests data already present in the L1 data cache. A miss occurs when the data requested are not in the cache. In the event of a miss, the L1 data cache hands the operation off to the L2 cache, which requests the data from the system bus. In addition to distinguishing between the L1 and L2 caches, the Pentium processor also distinguishes between data and instruction (or code) caches. Consequently, the instruction fetch operation can proceed in parallel with the data access operation, which enhances cache read and write speed.

Intel Execution Environment

Inside an Intel architecture processor are eight 32-bit general-purpose registers, six 16-bit segment registers, and two status and control registers: EIP (the instruction pointer register), and EFLAGS (Figure 10.3). The general-purpose registers are used as storage areas for the results of arithmetic and logical operations, for address calculations, and for memory pointers. The six 16-bit segment registers—CS, DS, SS, ES, FS, and GS—hold pointers to segment locations in memory. The instruction pointer (EIP) register contains the offset (or displacement) in the current code segment for the next instruction to be executed. The EFLAGS register stores the status of most instructions. For example, several arithmetic status flags indicate the results (carry, parity, sign, overflow, and so on) of arithmetic instructions.

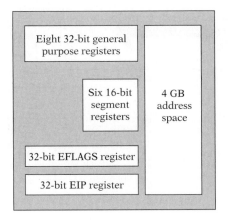

FIGURE 10.3

The Pentium's execution environment.

Architectures and Micro Architectures

When a company (such as Intel) designs a new processor, the engineers start by defining an architecture, defining a micro architecture, and selecting a clock speed. The architecture is intended to be stable for perhaps ten to twenty-five years; Intel's 32-bit architecture is a good example. Micro architectures, in contrast, change every few years; for example, the Intel 32-bit architecture supports the 486, Pentium I, Pentium II, Pentium III, Pentium IV, and P6 processors, but each of those processors has a different micro architecture. Clock speed, of course, changes very frequently—perhaps as often as several times a year.

Intel has defined a new architecture to support the company's 64-bit Itanium processors. The Itanium is targeted for the lucrative, $25 billion a year server market currently dominated by IBM and Sun. Intel's interest in the 64-bit server market is understandable when you look at the revenue numbers. Although 64-bit machines account for only about five percent of the total server units sold worldwide, they account for roughly sixty five percent of worldwide server revenue[1].

[1]Kirkpatrick, David. February 17, 2003. "See This Chip?" *Fortune:* 78-88.

Execution Mode

The Intel architecture supports four modes of operation. **Real address mode** is for systems that still run older 8086 programs. In this mode the processor is treated as a high speed 8086. MS-DOS operates in real address mode. After reset or power up, the processor goes into the real mode before most operating systems (except MS-DOS) switch into **protected mode.**

Operating systems such as Windows XP and Linux run in protected mode. Protected mode provides the code and data protection that allows multiple programs to run concurrently without interfering with each other. **Virtual 8086 mode** runs under protected mode. Under virtual 8086 mode, an 8086 processor is simulated in a separate protected region of memory, thus allowing 8086 applications to execute while still enjoying the full benefits of the protection mechanism. The primary purpose of this mode is to provide compatibility with old MS-DOS programs while allowing the concurrent execution of Windows XP or Linux applications. When a user opens an MS-DOS window in Windows 95, Windows 98, or Windows 2000, the processor is running in virtual 8086 mode. Finally, **system management mode** is used primarily for system security and power management.

◼ Memory Addressing

In Intel usage, real memory is called physical memory and is organized as a sequence of bytes. Each byte is assigned a unique **physical address** by counting the bytes sequentially starting with zero (0). The processor can reference physical addresses from 0 to a maximum 4 GB, but a typical microcomputer system contains far less physical memory.

Program instructions (software) specify **logical addresses.** A logical address consists of a base address and an offset from the base address. Note that a logical address is *relative* to some reference location and need not be associated with a *specific* physical address. For example, a logical address can refer to a location in virtual memory, and the translation from a logical virtual address to a real physical address can be postponed until execution time.

Address Translation

In a **flat memory model,** (Figure 10.4) the program sees a single continuous, byte addressable address space called the **linear address space.** The addresses run from 0 to 4 GB, and the base address is always 0. Hence, the offset is the actual physical address and is called a **linear address.**

In a **segmented model,** memory is pictured not as a continuous address space but as a group of independent address spaces called segments. In a segmented logical address (Figure 10.5), the **segment selector** identifies the segment. The segment selector, in turn, points to the **segment descriptor** (Figure 10.6) which holds the segment's base address. The actual logical address is an offset within this segment. At execution time, the processor translates the logical address to a linear address by adding the offset to the segment's base address. The segment descriptors for all the segments are stored in a **descriptor table.**

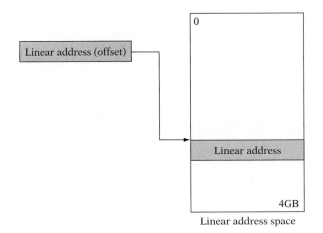

FIGURE 10.4

A flat memory model.

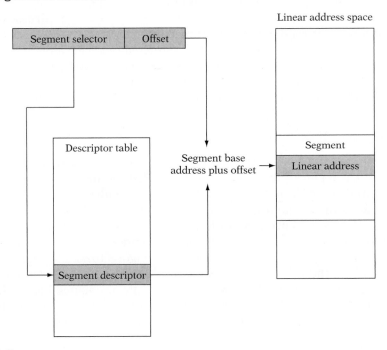

FIGURE 10.5

A logical, segmented address.

FIGURE 10.6

Segment address translation.

Paging

On a virtual memory system, the computed linear address refers to a location in virtual memory and not to a real physical address. Generally, virtual memory is divided into fixed length, 4 KB pages, and programs and data are swapped between virtual and real memory a page at a time. Consequently, additional address translation is required before the instruction can be executed.

On an Intel machine, when a program references a logical address, the processor's segmentation mechanism translates it into a physical address. First, the address is translated into a linear (virtual) address as described above. The linear address is then broken into three parts (Figure 10.7). The high-order bits (22 to 31) contain an offset to an entry in the **page directory** table. (The address of the page directory table is found in a system register.) The page directory entry points to a **page table** and bits 12 to 21 of the linear address contain an offset to an entry in the page table. The page table entry, in turn, points to a page, and bits 0 through 11 of the linear address contain an offset to the actual byte on this page. Since the page directory and page table offsets are 10 bits each, they can address 1024 times 1024 pages of 4 KB each, yielding a maximum address space of 4 GB.

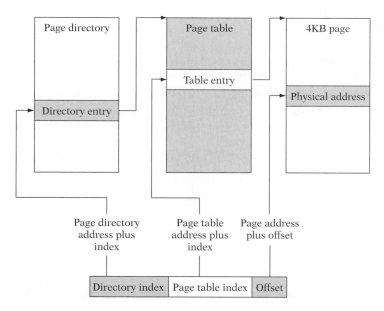

FIGURE 10.7

Linear-to-physical address translation.

Bit 0 of the page table or page directory entry contains the P or present flag. The P flag indicates if the page (or the page-table) pointed to by the entry is in physical memory. If the flag is 1, the page is already in physical memory and address translation is carried out. If the flag is zero (0), a page fault occurs and the referenced page is swapped into real memory. In order to speed up page translation, the processor stores the most recently accessed page directory and page table entries in the translation lookaside buffer (TLB).

◼ Task Management

A **task** is a unit of work that the processor can dispatch, execute, and suspend, such as a program, a process, an interrupt handler, or an operating system process. Under the Intel architecture, a task (Figure 10.8) consists of a **task execution space** and a **task state segment (TSS).** The task execution space holds the code, stack, and data segments. The task state segment points to the segments in the task execution space. It also provides a storage space for the processor's state information (such as the contents of the registers). When a user switches to a new task, the processor saves the state of the current task by storing all the registers in the task state segment before the new task starts executing.

◼ Memory Protection

Memory protection helps to prevent one task from accidentally or intentionally changing the contents of memory assigned to another task. Any vio-

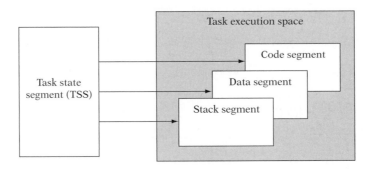

FIGURE 10.8
A task consists of a task execution space and a task state segment (TSS).

lation of a protection mechanism results in a general protection fault and, usually, the termination of the responsible task. Limit checking ensures that a given memory access is not beyond the segment's boundaries. For example, if a segment is defined to be 50 bytes long, the offset cannot not be greater than or equal to 50 because such an offset would result in a memory access beyond the segment's boundary. Type checking ensures that only code, data, or stack segment descriptors are used and that they are used as intended. The processor examines the segment descriptor to determine its type. It then ensures that the segment descriptor is used properly. For example, a code segment cannot be written into.

The processor's segment protection feature assigns one of four **privilege levels** (numbered 0 through 3) to each active task (Figure 10.9). Level 0 has the highest privilege and level 3 has the lowest privilege. A task executing at a lower privilege level cannot access a segment or page associated with a higher privilege task. Usually, the operating system runs at level 0 and applications run at level 3, which prevents applications from accessing operating system objects.

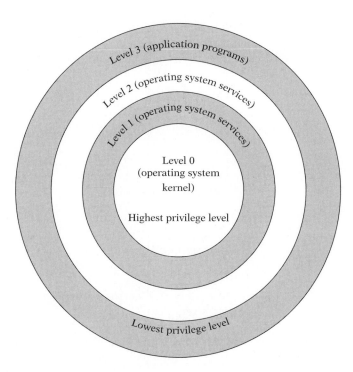

FIGURE 10.9
Segment protection privilege levels.

◼ Interrupt Handling

An interrupt is an electronic signal that results in the forced transfer of control to an interrupt handling routine. Interrupts can originate with either hardware or software. They are asynchronous; in other words, an interrupt can occur at any time and need not be timed to match the processor's clock pulses. In contrast, an **exception** is a synchronous event that is generated when the processor detects a predefined condition such as division by 0. Note that an exception occurs during the machine cycle when the predefined condition is detected. Because machine cycles are driven by the clock, exceptions occur in response to a clock pulse and thus are synchronized with the processor. The processor handles interrupts and exceptions similarly by halting execution of the current task and switching to an interrupt handling procedure. If possible, the interrupted program or task resumes processing upon completion of the interrupt handling procedure.

Associated with every interrupt (Figure 10.10) is an identification number (0 through 255) called a **vector.** The processor maintains an **interrupt descriptor table (IDT)** that associates each interrupt vector with an

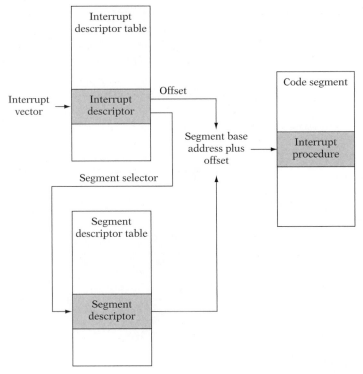

FIGURE 10.10

Interrupt procedure calls.

interrupt descriptor. (The address of the interrupt descriptor table is found in a system register.) The interrupt descriptor points to the base address of the executable code segment that holds the interrupt handling code. Adding the segment's base address and the offset (from the interrupt descriptor) yields the address of the first instruction in the interrupt handling procedure.

Improving the Performance of the Intel Architecture

Intel uses a variety of techniques to enhance processing speed and functionality with each processor chip upgrade.

Pipelining and Superpipelining

Pipelining is a technique that allows a single processor to simultaneously process multiple instructions. The underlying idea is to break the machine cycle into multiple stages, with each stage representing a portion of the cycle. For example, on many computers each machine cycle is broken into four discrete stages: fetch, decode, execute, and write-back. During fetch the instruction control unit retrieves the next instruction from memory (or cache) and moves it into the processor. During the decode stage, the processor translates the instruction into one or more simple instructions called micro-operations. During the execute stage, the micro-operations are dispatched and executed. Finally, the results are written back to memory.

A nonpipelined processor fetches a single instruction, decodes it, executes it, writes the results to memory, and then fetches the next instruction. A pipelined processor, in contrast, fetches the first instruction and then fetches the second instruction while the first instruction is being decoded. Thus, at any given time there are four instructions in the pipeline (Figure 10.11), with one instruction at each machine cycle phase. Pipelining increases the microprocessor's throughput.

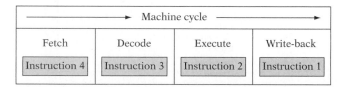

FIGURE 10.11

Pipelining.

The machine cycle on a **superpipelining** chip is broken into more than four stages, allowing a faster clock cycle than is possible with a normal pipelined processor. The Pentium II and Pentium Pro chips use a super-pipeline with twelve-stage instructions, and the Pentium IV chip features a twenty-stage machine cycle.

A **scalar** processor is a chip that uses a single pipeline. **Superscalar** chips use more than one pipeline and thus allow more than one instruction to be executed simultaneously. For example, the Pentium chip uses two integer pipelines and a floating-point pipeline and thus can execute as many as three instructions simultaneously.

Hyperthreading

The growing gap between processor speed and memory speed results in a latency problem as the processor waits for data to be transferred from memory. The result is processor underutilization. One solution is to utilize the idle latency time associated with a given task by performing computations related to a different task. Executing tasks (as opposed to instructions) in parallel is called **hyperthreading.**

Hyperthreading achieves thread-level parallelism by allowing the operating system to see two logical processors instead of just one. The system maintains copies of both logical processors' states (the contents of their general purpose registers and key control registers), and the logical processors share the remaining physical execution resources (Figure 10.12). From the real processor's perspective, instructions from the logical processors execute simultaneously on the shared execution resources, so the operating system can schedule tasks across the two logical processors. Intel has already implemented hyperthreading in their Pentium IV processors

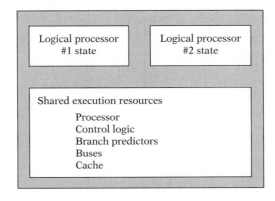

FIGURE 10.12

Hyperthreading presents the operating system with two logical processors.

operating at 3.06 GHz and above and estimates potential performance gains of as much as 25 percent. Those performance gains are far from guaranteed, however, because programs must be written specifically to take advantage of hyperthreading and few such programs exist today.

Out-of-Order Execution and Branch Prediction

Normally, the instructions in a program are executed sequentially, but if there are no dependencies among the instructions it is sometimes possible to execute them out of order. For example, consider the set of instructions outlined in Figure 10.13. Note that instruction B is dependent on instruction A because instruction B cannot be executed until the value of R1 is known. Consequently, instructions A and B must be executed in sequence. However, instructions C and D are independent of A and B and of each other, so they can be executed in any order.

If you assume that each instruction is executed in a single machine cycle and that the instructions are executed sequentially, the routine outlined in Figure 10.13 will finish processing in four machine cycles. However, if instructions A, C, and D are executed in parallel during a first clock cycle and B (which depends on A) is executed during a second clock cycle, the total time to execute the routine is cut in half. Note that the instructions are retired (written back to memory) in their original order to maintain data integrity.

A branch instruction is any instruction that causes a break in the sequential execution of instructions. Examples include branch, jump, procedure call, return, and interrupts. The Pentium processor attempts to identify the target instruction for the program's next jump, pre-fetches the instruction, decodes it, and speculatively executes it. If the prediction is correct, processor throughput is increased. If the prediction is incorrect, the processor must flush the speculative execution, fetch the correct instruction, and execute it instead. The Pentium chip tries to predict up to the next branch. The P6 chip goes a step further and predicts multiple branches and returns. The Pentium IV generates fewer incorrect branch predictions than the P6 by keeping a detailed history of its past branches in a buffer and using an improved branch prediction algorithm.

A	R1 = Mem(x)
B	R2 = R1 − R3
C	R4 = 100
D	R5 = R5 − 10

FIGURE 10.13

Out-of-order instruction execution.

MMX Technology

MMX (Multimedia Extensions) **technology** is a set of extensions built on top of the Intel architecture that enhance the performance of multimedia applications such as video, audio, and 3D graphics. The extensions include new registers, data types, and additional instructions to support multimedia.

With a normal instruction, the processor works on one piece of data at a time. In contrast, with the new MMX instructions the processor simultaneously manipulates many data values in parallel. For example, multiplying all the elements in an array by a constant is a common operation in image processing and graphical analysis. On a non-MMX processor, the multiplication is performed repetitively on every element in the array. With MMX, new data types are supported for these applications and all the multiplication is done in parallel, which enhances processor speed.

The L2 cache (Figure 10.2) is useful only if the data are reused frequently by the processor. However, when you play back a streaming video (such as an MPEG file or an MP3 audio file), you process the data only once. The new MMX instructions remove the L2 cache from the data transfer path, writing and reading directly from memory instead. The result is better multimedia performance.

The PowerPC

The PowerPC is the processor that drives Apple's Macintosh computers and runs in 64-bit mode on the Nintendo and Sony PlayStation 2. The Apple G4 uses the PowerPC 7450 and 7455 processors, both of which deliver good performance relative to comparable Pentium processors. Much like an MMX-enhanced Pentium processor, the PowerPC supports single instruction multiple data (SIMD) processing which enables the acceleration of multimedia operations. The SIMD instructions are executed in a separate functional unit within the processor, allowing the system to crunch data while simultaneously performing extensive multimedia operations. The PowerPC instruction set is not compatible with the Intel platform, however, which helps to explain the difference between Intel and Apple multimedia data formatting standards.

◼ Intel's 64-Bit Itanium Architecture

The Intel 64-bit **Itanium** architecture is a radical departure from the Intel 32-bit Pentium architecture, although the Itanium chip is designed to run existing Pentium code by emulating Intel's 32-bit architecture in hardware.

The Itanium chip can address up to 16 exabytes (10^{18} bytes) of logical memory and 8 exabytes of physical memory and has 128 general purpose registers, 128 floating-point registers, 64 predicate registers, and 8 branch registers. Additionally, because a 64-bit processor runs significantly faster than a 32-bit processor, the Itanium architecture enables an order of magnitude improvement in application performance. Today, 64-bit chips based on the IBM Power chip are an evolving standard in the highly demanding electronic game industry, where they power the Nintendo 64 and the Sony PlayStation 2.

There are two ways to increase a chip's throughput. One is to do things more quickly by, for example, increasing clock speed. Intel achieves this objective by implementing enhanced out-of-order execution and branch prediction capabilities in the Itanium chip.

A second option is to make the chip do more things in parallel. Intel increases parallelism by incorporating a technique called explicitly parallel instructional computing (EPIC) in its new Itanium architecture. The key to this technique is to bundle instructions. The Itanium fetches a 128-bit (2-word) instruction bundle that contains up to three 41-bit instructions and a 5-bit template that tells the processor how to handle the instructions (Figure 10.14). Sometimes the instructions must be executed in sequence, so the bundle holds only one instruction. In other cases, however, two or even all three instructions can be executed in parallel, so the bundle holds two or three instructions. With Intel's Itanium architecture, the compiler explicitly determines which instructions should share a bundle, an approach that distinguishes the Itanium architecture from other bundling systems such as Transmeta.

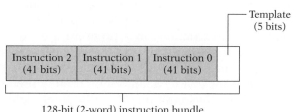

FIGURE 10.14
An Itanium instruction bundle.

▉ Summary

The processor is responsible for fetching instructions and decoding those instructions into a series of micro-operations. The Intel architecture relies on a set of caches to streamline the data and instruction fetch processes. The processor runs in one of four modes: real address mode, protected mode, virtual 8086 mode, or system management mode.

Each byte of physical memory is assigned a unique physical address. A logical address is made up of a base address and an offset from the base address. In a flat memory model, the program sees a single continuous address space called the linear address space. In the segmented model, the program sees memory as a group of independent address spaces called segments. When a program or task references a logical address, the processor's segmentation mechanism translates it to a physical address. First, the logical address is converted to a linear address. Then the linear address is broken into three parts: an index to a page directory, an index to a page table, and an offset on the page.

A task is a unit of work that the processor can dispatch, execute, and suspend. An Intel architecture task consists of a task execution space and a task state segment. The task execution space holds the code, stack, and data segments. Memory protection helps to prevent one task from changing the contents of memory assigned to another task. The processor assigns each task one of four privilege levels to support memory protection.

The processor handles interrupts and exceptions similarly by halting execution of the current task and switching to an interrupt handling procedure. Associated with every interrupt is an identification number called a vector. The processor maintains an interrupt descriptor table (IDT) that associates each interrupt vector with an interrupt descriptor that is used to service the interrupt.

Pipelining allows multiple instructions to be processed simultaneously, thus enhancing processor throughput. A superpipelining chip uses more than four stages to complete an instruction. Superscalar chips use more than one pipeline and thus allow more than one instruction to be executed simultaneously. Executing tasks in parallel is called hyperthreading. Normally, the instructions in a program are executed sequentially, in the order they are received, but if there are no dependencies among the instructions it is sometimes possible to execute them out of order. Additional throughput gains can be achieved by branch prediction. MMX technology is a set of extensions built on top of the Intel architecture that enhance the performance of multimedia applications. The Intel 64-bit Itanium architecture is a radical departure from Intel's 32-bit Pentium architecture.

▌Key Words

cache	privilege level
descriptor table	protected mode
exception	real address mode
flat memory model	scalar
hyperthreading	segment descriptor
interrupt descriptor table (IDT)	segment selector
Itanium	segmented model
linear address	superpipelining
linear address space	superscalar
logical address	system management mode
memory protection	task
MMX technology	task execution space
page directory	task state segment (TSS)
page table	vector
physical address	virtual 8086 mode
pipelining	

▌Review Questions

1. Explain how the Intel Pentium family of processors fetches and executes instructions.

2. Describe the Intel architecture's execution environment.

3. Identify an Intel processor's four operating modes.

4. Distinguish between a logical address and a physical address.

5. Distinguish between a flat memory model and a segmented memory model.

6. Distinguish between a segment selector and a segment descriptor.

7. Describe the process of translating a logical segment address into a physical address.

8. Identify the components of an Intel architecture task.

9. Explain how a Pentium system switches to a new task.

10. Explain how limit checking, type checking, and privilege levels support memory protection.

11. Distinguish between an interrupt and an exception.

12. Explain how a Pentium system processes an interrupt.

13. Explain pipelining. Distinguish between pipelining and superpipelining.

14. Distinguish between a scalar processor and a superscalar processor.

15. What is hyperthreading? How does Intel implement hyperthreading?

16. Explain how a processor can execute instructions out of sequence.
17. Explain how branch prediction can help to enhance processor throughput.
18. What are some advantages of MMX technology?
19. Distinguish between Intel's 32-bit architecture and Intel's 64-bit Itanium architecture.

▌ Exercises

1. Identify the processor that powers your computer.
2. Read an advertisement for a state-of-the art personal computer system and interpret the specifications.
3. Why do you suppose companies like Intel distinguish between an architecture and a micro architecture?
4. Why is memory protection necessary?
5. Distinguish between the standard PC platform and the computer gaming platform operating environments.
6. Figures 10.2, 10.7, and 10.8 are useful templates for organizing many of this chapter's key terms.

CHAPTER 11

MS-DOS Internals

When you finish reading this chapter you should be able to:

▶ Distinguish between resident and transient modules.

▶ Relate the functions of COMMAND.COM to the general functions of a command processor or shell as described in Chapter 5.

▶ Identify the functions performed by IO.SYS and MSDOS.SYS and explain why it makes sense to split these sets of functions.

▶ Relate the functions performed by IO.SYS and MSDOS.SYS to the basic concepts of logical and physical I/O.

▶ Sketch the contents of an MS-DOS disk.

▶ Explain how a disk file's clusters are linked through the file allocation table.

▶ Explain how MS-DOS processes interrupts.

▶ Sketch the contents of memory immediately after MS-DOS has been booted.

◼ MS-DOS

MS-DOS was once the world's most commonly used microcomputer operating system. In fact, the earliest versions of Windows ran on top of MS-DOS, much like an application program. By the late 1990s, however, Windows had become an operating system in its own right and MS-DOS was relegated to the Windows *Accessories* submenu. Today, MS-DOS has essentially disappeared inside Windows, but you can still execute MS-DOS line commands from the Windows XP command line.

This chapter discusses the internal structure of MS-DOS before its functions were absorbed into Windows.

Resident and Transient Routines

Every operating system contains a set of **resident** routines that must be in memory at all times. Sometimes called the **nucleus,** the **kernel,** or the **supervisor,** the resident core typically contains an **input/output control system** or **IOCS,** a **file system,** various interrupt handling routines, and resource management routines (Figure 11.1). The **command processor** or **shell** is not generally considered part of the kernel, but it too must be resident. Also resident are a number of system constants, parameters, and

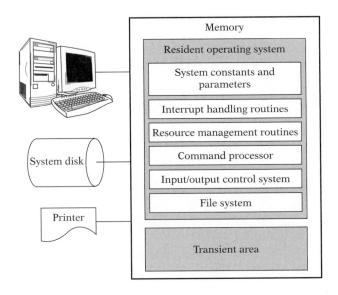

FIGURE 11.1

The components of a typical operating system.

control fields. These routines and parameters reside in memory and provide real-time support to active application and system programs.

Not all operating routines must be resident, however. Consider, for example, formatting a disk. Because the routine that performs this task is needed only when a disk is actually being formatted, it resides on disk and is loaded into memory on demand. The free area or **transient area** of memory (Figure 11.1), which contains all the space not allocated to the resident operating system, holds these **transient** modules and active application programs.

The Shell

MS-DOS is a command-driven operating system; you studied its command language in Chapter 7. Users request operating system services by typing commands in response to a system prompt. When the enter key is pressed, an operating system component called **COMMAND.COM** (the shell) interprets the command and calls the appropriate lower level routine or program. COMMAND.COM consists of a command interpreter and a number of resident operating system routines that remain in memory at all times (Figure 11.2). Other COMMAND.COM routines are transient and are read into memory on demand. Generally, the resident routines support active programs as they run.

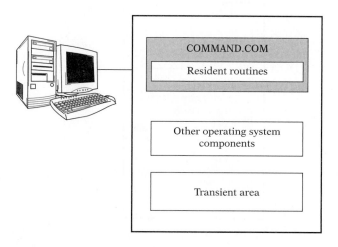

FIGURE 11.2

The MS-DOS command processor is called COMMAND.COM.

Accessing Peripherals

The task of accessing peripheral devices is divided between two operating system components: IO.SYS and MSDOS.SYS (Figure 11.3). **IO.SYS** is a hardware dependent module that issues *physical* data transfer commands. IO.SYS interacts with the basic input/output system (BIOS), which is usually implemented in read-only memory. Logical I/O is supported by a hardware *independent* module called **MSDOS.SYS.** MSDOS.SYS accepts logical I/O requests from application programs or other operating system modules, translates them into physical I/O commands, and passes the physical commands to IO.SYS. Note that only IO.SYS, the machine *dependent* module, communicates *directly* with peripheral devices. A version of MS-DOS written for a COMPAQ computer and one written for a Dell computer will differ only in their IO.SYS; other operating system modules should be the same.

Each physical device attached to the computer is described in a special file called a **device driver** (Figure 11.4). Character drivers control such devices as the keyboard, the screen, and the printer. Block drivers control disk and similar block-oriented devices and transfer data in 512-byte blocks. The device driver is used by MSDOS.SYS to translate logical I/O requests to physical form. Certain standard device drivers, such as COM1 (the first serial printer or modem), CON (the console), and PRN (the first parallel printer) are built into the operating system. Additional devices can be defined by adding a description to a special file called CONFIG.SYS.

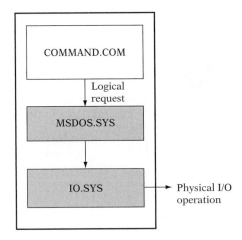

FIGURE 11.3

IO.SYS and MSDOS.SYS share responsibility for communicating with peripheral devices.

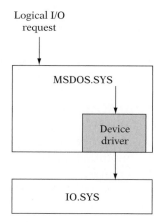

FIGURE 11.4

MSDOS.SYS uses a device driver to translate logical I/O requests to physical form.

Layering

If you look carefully at Figure 11.3, you'll see an excellent example of the layering concept introduced in Chapter 1. COMMAND.COM initiates an I/O operation (often in response to an application program request), MSDOS.SYS performs the necessary logical I/O functions, IO.SYS takes care of physical I/O, and those three modules communicate by passing parameters back and forth. Because the responsibility for I/O is divided among three independent routines, it is possible to enhance any one of those routines without affecting the others. Perhaps the most dramatic example of functional independence affected COMMAND.COM. The first releases of Microsoft Windows essentially replaced the traditional command processor with a GUI that passed commands down to the same MSDOS.SYS and IO.SYS routines that COMMAND.COM once called. Today's Windows incorporates enhanced logical and physical I/O support, but the modular design of MS-DOS allowed Microsoft to get a head start on the transition from command lines to a GUI.

The File System

MSDOS.SYS is the MS-DOS file system. In addition to translating logical I/O requests to physical form, it is also responsible for directory management. Chapter 7 introduced the MS-DOS directory structure; if you completed the chapter tutorial, you know how to create and delete directories with operating system commands. For example, when a make directory command, such as

MKDIR LETTERS

is accepted by COMMAND.COM, the shell calls MSDOS.SYS (Figure 11.5a), which, in turn, calls IO.SYS to read the directory (Figure 11.5b). MSDOS.SYS then inserts the new directory entry (Figure 11.5c), and calls IO.SYS to rewrite the modified directory back to disk (Figure 11.5d). Generally, MSDOS.SYS creates, deletes, and modifies directory entries in response to requests from COMMAND.COM (or an application routine), and relies on IO.SYS to perform the actual data transfer operations.

MSDOS.SYS also supports application program I/O. When a disk file is first opened, MSDOS.SYS calls IO.SYS to read the directory. MSDOS.SYS then extracts the location of an existing file or creates a directory entry for a new one and, if necessary, calls IO.SYS to rewrite the directory. As the program runs, each logical input and output operation implies a transfer of control to MSDOS.SYS. Using the start of file address from open, the operating system computes the physical address of the data and then passes the address to IO.SYS.

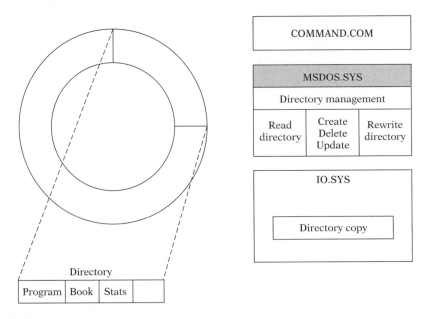

FIGURE 11.5

MSDOS.SYS is responsible for directory management.

a. Following a MKDIR command, COMMAND.COM calls MSDOS.SYS.

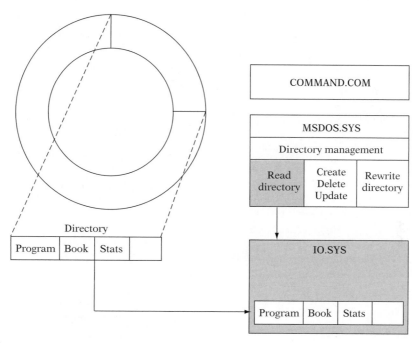

b. MSDOS.SYS calls IO.SYS to read the directory.

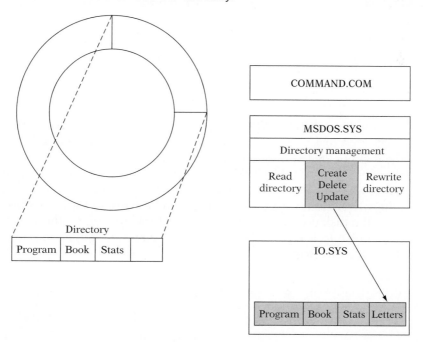

c. MSDOS.SYS adds a new directory entry.

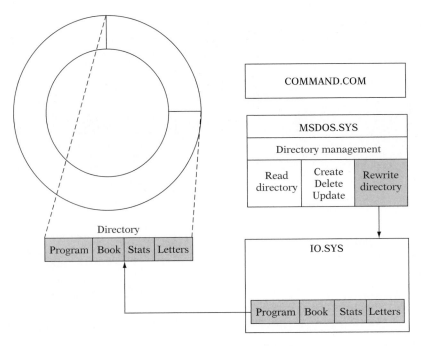

d. MSDOS.SYS calls IO.SYS to rewrite the directory to disk.

Another MSDOS.SYS responsibility is allocating space on disk. Quickly overview a disk's format (Figure 11.6). Track 0, sector 0 (the first sector on the disk) holds the boot routine. Next, in sectors 1 and 2 are two copies of the file allocation table (FAT); more about it later. The root directory begins with track 0, sector 5. On system disks, the various components of the operating system follow the root directory and the rest of the disk is used to hold files. If a disk does not contain a copy of the system, all the space after the root directory is used to hold files. Note that a file might contain software, data, or a directory.

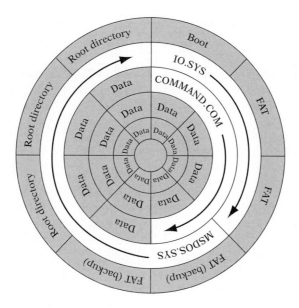

FIGURE 11.6
The format of a typical MS-DOS system disk.

The File Allocation Table (FAT)

Disk space is allocated in **clusters.** For example, on a diskette, each cluster holds 1024 bytes (two sectors) and the clusters are numbered sequentially starting with zero. The **file allocation table** contains an entry for each cluster on the disk.

When a file is created, the number of its first cluster is stored in the directory. As data are added to the file, the second cluster is assigned dynamically by recording its number in the first cluster's FAT entry; note that the first cluster points to the second one (Figure 11.7). As additional data are added, the third cluster's number is recorded in the second cluster's FAT entry, and so on. If you follow the chain of pointers from the directory, through the file allocation table, to the end of file marker, you step cluster by cluster through the file. Note that the clusters belonging to a file need not be contiguous.

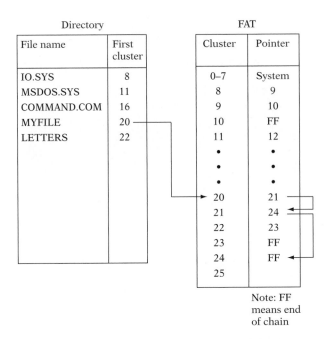

FIGURE 11.7
A file's clusters are linked by a chain of pointers in the file allocation table.

MS-DOS views the data stored in a disk file as a continuous stream of bytes. Logical I/O operations request data by relative *byte* (rather than by relative record or relative sector). A file's first cluster holds relative bytes 0 through 1023, its second cluster holds relative bytes 1024 through 2047, and so on. As part of its blocking and deblocking functions, MS-DOS.SYS calls IO.SYS to perform whatever physical I/O operations are necessary to access the requested string. Logically, data on disk are addressed just like data in memory.

Interrupt Processing

The Intel processor at the heart of most MS-DOS systems relies on **interrupts** to establish communication with its peripheral devices. As you may recall from Chapter 6, an interrupt is an electronic signal. Hardware senses the signal, saves key control information for the currently executing program, and starts the operating system's interrupt handling routine. At that instant, the interrupt ends. The operating system then processes the interrupt. Processing interrupts is an important MS-DOS function.

The key to MS-DOS interrupt processing is an **interrupt vector table** that occupies the first 1K bytes of memory. This table holds interrupt vectors, the addresses of up to 256 different interrupt processing routines, most of which are found in **MSDOS.SYS** or **IO.SYS**. Two special registers are also crucial. The instruction counter is found in the IP (instruction pointer) register, and another key register points to a memory stack.

The interrupt itself consists of an electronic pulse and the address of an interrupt vector. When an interrupt occurs, hardware immediately copies the contents of the IP register (along with a few other registers) to the stack (Figure 11.8a), and loads the specified interrupt vector into the IP register. (Figure 11.8b). With the next machine cycle, the first instruction in the interrupt processing routine is fetched (Figure 11.8c). Once the interrupt is processed, the contents of the stack are copied back into the IP register and the original program resumes processing (Figure 11.8d).

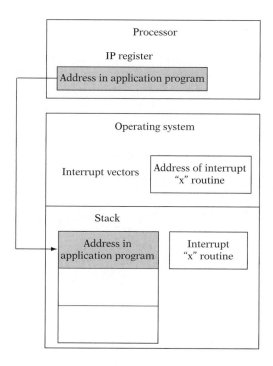

FIGURE 11.8

MS-DOS interrupt processing.

a. The contents of the instruction pointer (IP) register are copied to the stack.

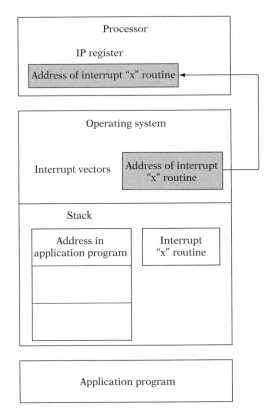

b. The specified interrupt vector is loaded into the instruction pointer.

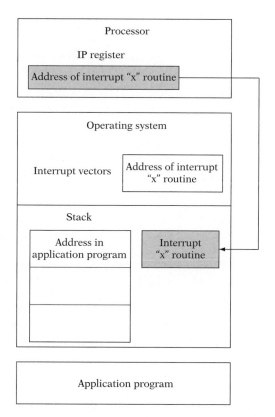

c. The first instruction in the interrupt processing routine is fetched.

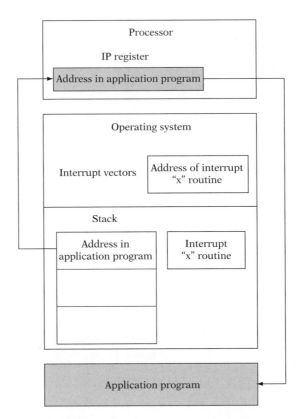

d. The contents of the stack are loaded back into the instruction pointer register and the application program resumes processing.

Interrupts are much more common than you might imagine. For example, an interrupt is generated each time you press a key on the keyboard. In response to the interrupt, the operating system copies a single character from the keyboard buffer into memory and then waits for the next interrupt to herald the arrival of the next character. A few keys, such as return and escape, signal the operating system to take a different action. Interrupts also allow the printer, a disk drive, and other peripherals to communicate with the processor.

Not all interrupts originate with hardware, however. Although it is legal for an application program to communicate directly with IO.SYS, most rely on MSDOS.SYS to translate their logical I/O requests to physical form. Branching to or calling an operating system module implies knowledge of MS-DOS internals that few people possess. Thus, by convention, an assembler language programmer who wants to perform I/O loads descriptive information into a few registers and then executes an interrupt instruction that references interrupt vector 33 (21 hex).

Hardware responds to a software generated interrupt exactly as if the source had been hardware, copying the IP register to the stack and loading the contents of the specified vector into the IP register. The address in vector 33 points to an MSDOS.SYS module that analyzes register contents and determines which I/O operation was requested. In compiler languages, the instructions to set registers and interrupt the operating system are generated for you.

Why Are Interrupts Necessary?

The telephone rings. How do you respond? Chances are, you stop what you're doing, pick up the telephone, and say "Hello." Think of the ring as an interrupt; note that it literally interrupts your train of thought. Think of "Hello" as the first step in processing the interrupt and you have a pretty good mental image of what an interrupt is.

But why are interrupts necessary? The answer, if you think about it, is pretty obvious—you had no idea someone was going to call you until the phone rang. You and your caller are independent. You function asynchronously. Unless you are incredibly psychic, you have no way of knowing precisely when someone might call, so you rely on the interrupt (in this case a ring, a buzz, or some other signal) to alert you when that asynchronous event occurs.

Inside a computer, such components as the processor, memory, and the bus are synchronized by the processor's clock, and intercomponent communication depends on precise timing. The peripheral devices in contrast operate asynchronously. For example, the processor has no way of predicting when you will press the next key on your keyboard. For all practical purposes, to the processor the timing of a keystroke is a random event comparable to the arrival of a telephone call.

When you press a key, the associated character is copied into a memory buffer and an interrupt is generated. In effect, the interrupt tells the system to "start accepting one character now." The process of transferring the character from the keyboard's memory buffer to the appropriate location in memory involves only internal components and thus can be synchronized by the processor's clock. In effect, the interrupt announces that a random event requiring processing has just occurred, giving the system a starting point for precisely timing its response to that event.

Much the same thing happens when an application program issues an interrupt to start an I/O operation. The processor and the peripheral are asynchronous. When the processor sends an interrupt to the peripheral, the electronic signal establishes a starting point for the two devices to synchronize their signals long enough to exchange the information the peripheral needs to carry out the operation. Simply put, interrupts are necessary because the computer and its peripherals are asynchronous and they must communicate with each other.

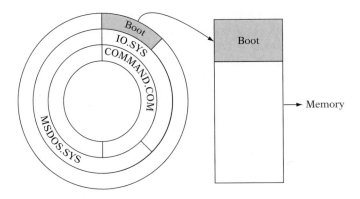

FIGURE 11.9

Hardware reads the boot routine from the first sector on the system disk.

Booting MS-DOS

Memory is volatile; it loses its contents when the computer loses power. Consequently, the operating system must be loaded into memory each time the computer is started. Under MS-DOS, the **boot** routine is stored on the first sector of each disk. Flipping the power switch (or simultaneously pressing *Ctrl*, *Alt*, and *Delete*) causes hardware to read into memory the first sector from the disk in the system drive (Figure 11.9). The boot then reads IO.SYS, which, in turn, initializes key system tables, reads MSDOS.SYS, and, finally, reads COMMAND.COM (Figure 11.10).

The COMMAND.COM modules that immediately follow MSDOS.SYS are resident. Other COMMAND.COM modules are stored at the high end of memory following the transient area. While technically resident, this second group of routines can be overlaid if necessary by a large application program. If they are overlaid, they must be restored after the program is finished.

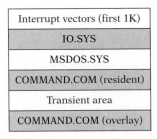

FIGURE 11.10

The contents of memory after MS-DOS is booted.

Running MS-DOS

Once the operating system is booted, MS-DOS controls literally everything that happens on the computer. First, COMMAND.COM is activated and, by calling IO.SYS, displays a system prompt on the screen. As the user types a command, each character generates an interrupt. Responding to the interrupt, the operating system reads the character, stores it in memory, and, again using IO.SYS, displays it on the screen.

Eventually, the user presses enter. Like any other key, the enter key generates an interrupt. The interrupt handling routine recognizes the enter key as a special case, however, and calls the COMMAND.COM module that interprets commands. This module, in turn, either displays an error message or takes whatever action is necessary to carry out the command.

For example, imagine the user has typed a resident command such as DIR. Since the appropriate routine is already in memory, COMMAND.COM simply calls it. When the resident routine finishes carrying out the command, it calls COMMAND.COM, which displays a prompt and waits for the next command.

What if the command refers to a transient module or to an application program? Because these routines are not yet in memory, they must be loaded before they can execute. Thus, COMMAND.COM calls MSDOS.SYS and passes it the requested routine's name. MSDOS.SYS, in turn, reads (by calling IO.SYS) the disk directory, searches it, finds the referenced routine, and instructs IO.SYS to load it into the transient area. Once the requested routine is in memory, control is returned to COMMAND.COM. At this point, with the transient module in memory, there is no real difference between calling it and calling a resident routine.

The basic workflow is simple. A prompt is displayed. The user types a command or a program name and MS-DOS calls the appropriate operating system module or application program. As the program runs, the operating system supports it by processing interrupts. Eventually, the program returns control to COMMAND.COM and the process is repeated, again and again until the machine is shut down. MS-DOS is command driven.

◪ Summary

The MS-DOS command processor is called COMMAND.COM. Physical I/O is controlled by IO.SYS. Logical I/O is the responsibility of MSDOS.SYS. The boot occupies the first sector of a disk. Next come two copies of the file allocation table, the root directory, the operating system (on a system disk), and, finally, file storage. Space on disk is allocated in clusters. The clusters are numbered sequentially, and an entry for each one is recorded in the file allocation table. The number of a file's first cluster is recorded in the directory. A file's clusters are linked by a series of pointers through the file allocation table.

The processor relies on interrupts to control communication with its peripherals, so interrupt processing is an important MS-DOS function. The first 1K bytes of memory hold up to 256 interrupt vectors. When an interrupt occurs, the contents of the instruction pointer are copied to the stack, the contents of the designated interrupt vector are loaded into the instruction pointer, and the interrupt processing routine begins running. After the interrupt is processed, the contents of the stack are loaded back into the instruction pointer and the original program resumes processing. Some interrupts originate with hardware; others originate with software.

The MS-DOS boot routine is stored on the first sector of each disk. When the computer is turned on, hardware reads the boot, which loads the rest of the operating system. The chapter's last section, *Running MS-DOS*, summarizes the operating system's primary features.

■ Key Words

boot	IO.SYS
cluster	kernel
command processor	MS-DOS
COMMAND.COM	MSDOS.SYS
device driver	nucleus
file allocation table (FAT)	resident
file system	shell
input/output control system	supervisor
(IOCS)	transient
interrupt	transient area
interrupt vector table	

■ Review Questions

1. Distinguish between resident and transient modules. Why does it make sense to have some modules transient? Why must other operating system modules be resident?

2. Relate the functions of COMMAND.COM to the general functions of a command processor or shell as described in Chapter 5.

3. The task of accessing physical devices is divided between IO.SYS and MSDOS.SYS. Briefly explain the functions performed by these two modules. Why does it make sense to split these sets of functions?

4. What is a device driver?

5. Relate the functions performed by IO.SYS and MSDOS.SYS to the basic concepts of logical and physical I/O.

6. Sketch the contents of an **MS-DOS** disk.

7. Explain how a disk file's clusters are linked through the file allocation table.

8. What is an interrupt? Explain how **MS-DOS** processes interrupts.

9. Why is a boot routine necessary?

10. Sketch the contents of memory immediately after **MS-DOS** has been booted.

▊ Exercises

1. Microcomputer operating systems generally contain a command processor, an input/output control system, and a file system;why *these* components?

2. Relate the modular design of **MS-DOS** to the layering concept you read about in Chapter 1.

3. Why are interrupts necessary?

4. Some interrupts originate with hardware. Others originate with software. Why?

5. Relate the process of communicating by telephone to the interrupt concept.

6. Figures 11.1 and 11.8a are useful templates for organizing many of this chapter's key terms.

CHAPTER 12

Windows XP Internals

When you finish reading this chapter you should be able to:

▶ Explain client/server mode.

▶ Discuss the relationship between the application program interface (API) and the dynamic link library (DLL).

▶ Identify the functions performed by the primary kernel mode components.

▶ Explain how the process manager creates a new process.

▶ Explain how the virtual memory manager implements paging.

▶ Describe the contents of a Windows XP 32-bit address and explain how a virtual address is translated into a physical (real) address.

▶ Discuss the organization of an NTFS disk.

▶ Explain how NTFS enables the smooth recovery of the file system following a system crash or disk failure.

▶ Explain how Windows XP uses caching.

▶ Explain the purpose of the registry.

◼ Windows XP

Windows XP is an update of Windows 2000, a multipurpose operating system that evolved from Windows NT and Windows 98. Windows NT was designed to run on several different types of processors and to support applications written for numerous environments such as MS-DOS, Windows, OS/2, and POSIX (a UNIX application programming interface), making it highly portable. Windows XP merges the best features of Windows 98 and Windows NT, but XP runs only on Intel architecture processors and no longer supports OS/2 or POSIX. Windows XP is available in 32-bit and 64-bit versions, and both home and professional versions are available. This chapter focuses on the 32-bit professional version's internal services that lie between the user interface and the hardware interface (Figure 12.1).

Client/Server Mode

In Windows usage, a module is a software component that provides a set of services to the rest of the system. Some Windows modules are configured in a hierarchical layered mode much like MS-DOS and UNIX. Other modules work in **client/server mode** (Figure 12.2). In client/server mode, each server module performs a single service such as a file service, a memory service, and so on. A client module requests a service by sending a message to the server module. The server module executes the request and sends the reply to the client module.

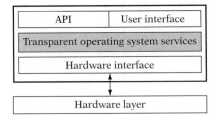

FIGURE 12.1

This chapter focuses on the 32-bit professional version's internal contents that lie between the user interface and the hardware interface.

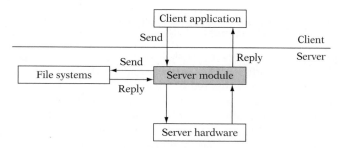

FIGURE 12.2
Client/server mode.

The client/server architecture offers several advantages over a hierarchy of layered modules[1]. It improves reliability because each service runs in its own process with its own memory that is protected from other processes. It provides a simple and uniform mechanism for processes to communicate with each other. Finally, it allows for new functionality to be added to the operating system by simply incorporating new service modules.

Reliability

Windows XP incorporates features that make it considerably more reliable than previous versions of Windows. For example, if you update a device driver and it does not function properly, XP allows you to roll back to a previous version. Additionally, the **system restore** feature allows you to roll back your entire system in the event of a problem. XP monitors changes to the system data and automatically creates system restore points at least daily. Restore points are also created whenever a device driver is updated or some other system change takes place. If a system failure occurs, the restore feature allows the system to be reset to the most recent restore point. Note that system restore does not monitor changes to your data, but Windows XP does include facilities that help to implement data monitoring.

---

[1]Note that it is still useful to view the client and the server as independent layers, but they are not linked to form a hierarchy.

> ### Robustness
>
> A system that recovers gracefully from errors is said to be robust. Earlier versions of Windows, particularly Windows 98 and Windows ME, were not known for their robustness because they tended to crash whenever an application misbehaved. In fact, system crashes were so common that the standard crash report, the so-called "Blue Screen of Death" or BSOD, has become a bit of a cliché. Windows XP evolved to a large degree from Windows NT, a much more stable operating system, and it is quite robust. For example, when your author was using Windows ME, his system typically crashed at least once a week. Since he upgraded to Windows XP, however, he has experienced zero (0) system crashes.

■ Windows XP Architecture

A simple block diagram of the Windows architecture is shown in Figure 12.3. The system operates in either **user mode** or **kernel mode.** User applications and a collection of subsystems run in user mode. The primary kernel mode modules include the hardware abstraction layer (HAL), the kernel, and executive services. In contrast to user mode, kernel mode processes have access to the entire system memory and all processor instructions and can bypass Windows security to access objects. As you learned in Chapter 10, the Pentium architecture defines four privilege levels to protect system code and data from being inadvertently overwritten. The kernel processes run at level 0, while user processes run at level 3.

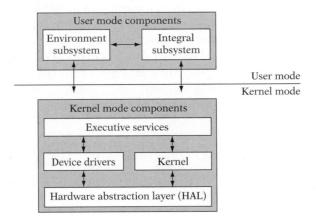

FIGURE 12.3

A block diagram of the Windows architecture.

User Mode

Application programs run in user mode within the **environment subsystem.** Because they are applications, they run at a lower priority than the kernel processes. Application programs are not allowed to directly access the hardware or the device drivers, so when a user issues a command (through the user interface) that requires operating system support, the program communicates with the kernel through an **application programming interface** or **API** (Figure 12.4). The API is a set of routines, protocols, and other tools that programmers, writing in a variety of languages, can use to build applications consistent with the underlying operating environment.

Rather than incorporating the API's routines and protocols into each application program, key functions and data are stored on the **dynamic link library (DLL).** From the programmer's perspective, the application program interface defines the rules for calling the dynamic link library's functions, and the DLL provides the necessary link with the operating system. Some DLL functions are written to support a specific application and are loaded statically when the program is launched. Most DLL functions are application independent, however. An application-independent function stored on the DLL can be accessed dynamically (as needed) and used simultaneously by numerous applications.

The 32-bit version of Windows XP is designed primarily to run 32-bit Windows (Win32) applications, but XP can also run MS-DOS applications and other 16-bit (Win16) applications (Figure 12.5), and you can optionally add the Interix subsystem to run UNIX applications. The Win32 subsystem is responsible for native Windows applications and screen-oriented I/O. Win16 and MS-DOS applications run on virtual DOS machines (VDMs) that understand the 16-bit calls.

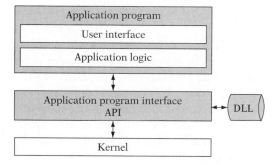

FIGURE 12.4

The application programming interface.

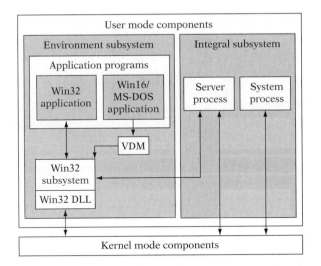

FIGURE 12.5
User mode components.

The other user mode component, the **integral subsystem,** is made up of server and system processes that provide protection and system services. A **service** is a program or process that performs a specific system function to support other programs. **Server processes** are Win32 services (such as event log, spooler, and so on) that are run automatically at startup. Server processes start up or shut down without user interaction, and many server processes are launched even before the user logs on. **System processes,** in contrast, do not run as services and require an interactive login. For example, the interactive login facility that accepts user logons and authenticates them is a system process.

Kernel Mode

One way to view the kernel mode processes is as a layered hierarchy (Figure 12.6). Starting at the bottom, the **Hardware Abstraction Layer (HAL)** hides the underlying hardware and provides a virtual machine interface to the other processes. Because such processor-specific functions as interrupt controllers and I/O interfaces are implemented in the hardware abstraction layer, the higher-level layers can be easily ported to different hardware environments.

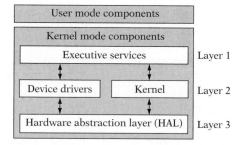

FIGURE 12.6
View the kernel mode processes as a layered hierarchy.

The second layer holds the device drivers and the kernel. The device drivers are responsible for translating logical I/O calls to specific physical I/O hardware primitives. The kernel (or microkernel) manages the microprocessor by coordinating dispatching and multiprocessor synchronization and handling asynchronous procedure calls such as interrupts, power notify, and power status functions (useful in laptops). Additionally, it provides the base kernel objects that are utilized by the executive.

The top layer consists of a set of modules collectively called the **executive** or **executive services** (Figure 12.7). Windows XP is an object-oriented system that uses objects for all its services and entities. Files, directories, processes, threads, and ports are all objects in Windows XP, and the **object manager,** pictured as the largest executive service, is responsible for creating, destroying, and granting access to an object's services or data. Access is provided to objects through a handle, a pointerlike reference to the object generated by the object manager.

Executive services							
Security manager	GDI	Window manager	P&P manager	Power manager	Process manager	Virtual memory manager	I/O manager
IPC manager	Object manager						File systems

FIGURE 12.7
The top layer in kernel mode is the executive.

Moving clockwise from the object manager (Figure 12.7), the inter-process communication (IPC) manager is responsible for client/server communication, including local procedure calls that link a server and a client on the same computer and remote procedure calls that link server and client modules on different computers. The security manager is responsible for the security of the local computer's objects. Security information is associated with an object via a security descriptor, and the security manager uses the security descriptor to support run-time object protection and auditing. The graphical device interface (GDI) supports the graphical user interface and incorporates functions for drawing and manipulating graphics. The window manager controls the creation, display, and destruction of windows and is also responsible for receiving input from the keyboard and the mouse and routing the data to the appropriate application. The plug and play (P&P) manager deals with plug and play devices, communicating with the device drivers to add and start the devices. The power manager manages power functions. The process manager, the virtual memory manager, the I/O manager, and the various file systems are discussed in detail in the balance of this chapter.

■ Process Management

A Windows XP **process** is an object that consists of an executable program. A program contains initial code and data, private memory address space, access to system resources (such as files, ports, and windows), and one or more threads. A **thread** is a unit of work that can execute sequentially and is interruptible.

The Windows XP **process manager** is responsible for providing services for creating and deleting processes and threads. For example, when a Windows application must create a process (Figure 12.8), it sends a message to the Win32 subsystem, which calls the process manager. The process manager in turn calls the object manager, which creates a process object and returns a handle to the process manager. The handle is then returned to the application.

Multithreading

A process contains one or more threads, and Windows XP can concurrently execute those threads using a technique called **multithreading.** Each thread has its own unique identifier, thread context (basically, its register contents), user mode and kernel mode stacks, and storage space for subsystems, dynamic link libraries, and run-time libraries. Additionally, the threads can exchange information via the common address space and other shared resources.

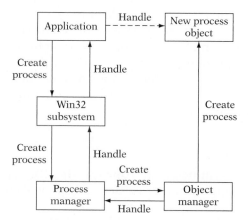

FIGURE 12.8

Process creation.

Multitasking

Windows XP also supports **multitasking,** the concurrent execution of two or more processes, which allows threads in different processes to execute concurrently. If the system has more than one processor, threads in the same process can run concurrently on different processors.

Multitasking is accomplished by **context switching.** With context switching a thread executes until it is interrupted by the operating system or must wait for resources (such as a file to be opened). When a thread is interrupted, the system saves the context of the thread (its register settings and so on), loads the context of another thread, and executes the new thread.

Windows XP is a **preemptive multitasking** operating system. Each thread or process is given a set amount of time called a quantum to access the processor. Once the quantum has expired, Windows XP interrupts the thread and starts another thread with the same priority. If a second thread with a higher priority is ready to execute, Windows XP interrupts the current thread to let the higher priority thread run.

Windows XP recognizes 32 different **priority** levels numbered 0 through 31. (Note that these priority levels are different from the Intel processor's privilege levels, which are concerned with memory protection.) Levels 16-31 are reserved for kernel processes and levels 0-15 are reserved for user processes.

Each user process has a base priority, but the priority of a given thread can be adjusted to help ensure quick response for interactive user threads without starving the background processes. For example, assume a process has a base priority of 8. A thread running within that process and waiting for user input might get a boost of 6, yielding a new thread priority of 14.

The kernel determines the magnitude of the priority boost dynamically; for example, a thread waiting for user input might get a priority boost of 6, while a thread waiting for a disk operation might have its priority boosted by only 1. To prevent compute-intensive threads from dominating, a thread's priority is adjusted for only a single quantum or time slice, and it falls by one priority level following each subsequent quantum until it reaches the process's base priority.

Multiprocessing

Windows XP is a **symmetric multiprocessing (SMP)** system. SMP systems run system and application processes on any available processor, ensuring that all available microprocessor resources are used efficiently. Windows XP combines **multiprocessing** and multitasking by dispatching a ready state thread to the next available microprocessor or (to take advantage of the memory caches from its previous execution) to the last microprocessor it ran on.

◼ Memory Management

Windows XP implements a flat linear 32-bit memory model. Addresses are 32 bits long, so the biggest possible address is 4 GB. Consequently, 4 GB of virtual address space is available to each process (Figure 12.9). Windows XP uses the top 2 GB for kernel mode threads and the bottom 2 GB for user mode threads.

Windows XP uses a **virtual memory manager (VMM)** to allocate and manage system memory. The VMM maintains a memory map table and is responsible for paging. When a process requests access to memory, it references an address in the process's virtual address space. The VMM translates the virtual address to the actual physical memory location and then transfers the data to the process.

FIGURE 12.9

Each process has up to 4 GB of virtual address space.

Paging

Paging is the process of swapping the contents of memory between physical (main) memory and disk. The virtual address space is made up of 4 KB pages that are designated as valid or invalid (Figure 12.10). A **valid page** resides in physical memory. An **invalid page** does not reside in physical memory because it has either been swapped out to disk or has not yet been loaded into memory.

When a process or thread references the contents of a virtual address on an invalid page, a **page fault** occurs. The system responds by reading (or swapping) the requested data (or code) from disk into the first available physical memory location. When physical memory is full and a thread subsequently references data or code not yet in memory, the VMM follows a first-in-first-out policy to clear space, swapping out to disk the page that was read into memory first. The code or data requested by the thread is then swapped into the freed memory. Swapping in response to a page fault is called demand paging.

The VMM combines demand paging with a technique called clustering. When a process reads in a specific page, it is likely that it will access adjacent pages in the near future. Thus, when a page fault occurs the VMM swaps in both the requested page and a few adjacent pages. Clustering tends to reduce the number of future page faults.

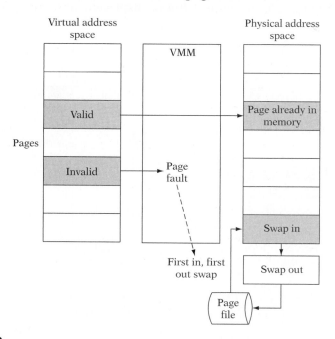

FIGURE 12.10

Valid and invalid pages.

Reserve and Commit

Every byte (real or virtual) in a process's address space exists in one of three states: free, reserved, or committed. Initially, the entire address space is free, or unallocated. When the program is launched, the virtual memory manager (VMM) **reserves** a range of virtual address space. Because no physical storage space is allocated either in memory or on the paging file, this task can be accomplished very quickly. The act of reserving virtual space before the space is actually needed is useful because a continuous range of addresses can be allocated to the process and, because a program typically executes sequentially, the virtual address space it occupies must be contiguous. The reserved memory does not count against the process's 2 GB limit until it is **committed** and actual physical pages are stored in memory and on the page file.

Address Translation

A 32-bit virtual address is split into three parts (Figure 12.11). The first 10 bits hold an index to the **page directory,** where a page directory entry (PDE) specifies the address of the appropriate page table. The second 10 bits hold an index to the **page table,** where a page table entry (PTE) points to the actual physical address of the page that holds the referenced code or data. The last 12 bits are the offset or displacement on the page.

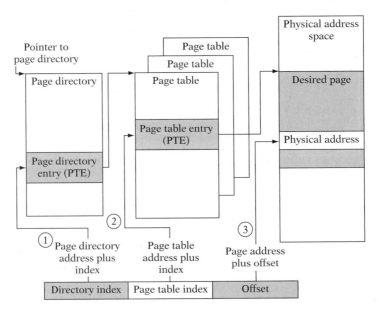

FIGURE 12.11

A 32-bit virtual address is split into three parts.

Disk Management

Windows XP incorporates several features that enhance disk management. For example, the **dynamic storage** feature allows a user to resize a disk without restarting Windows. A disk that is initialized for dynamic storage is called a dynamic disk. The dynamic storage feature creates a single partition that includes the entire disk.

You can divide a dynamic disk into volumes, where each volume consists of a portion or portions of one or more physical disks. The system's need for **fault tolerance** (the ability of the computer to recover data in case of errors) dictates the type of volume selected. A simple volume contains space from a single hard disk and is not fault tolerant. A spanned volume combines space from multiple hard drives. Data are written first to the first hard disk, then to the second hard disk, and so on. A spanned volume is not fault tolerant because if a hard disk fails, all data stored on it are lost. A mirrored volume contains disk space from two separate hard disks and keeps identical (duplicate) copies on both. A striped volume in contrast combines disk space from multiple hard drives into one logical volume and adds data to all the volumes at the same rate. A striped volume is not fault tolerant because the failure of a disk leads to a complete loss of information stored on the disk. A RAID-5 volume is a fault tolerant striped volume because a parity information stripe is added to each disk partition in the volume, and when a physical disk fails the parity information is used to reconstruct the data.

File Management

Windows XP supports FAT, FAT32, and its native NTFS file system. FAT, the MS-DOS file system, was discussed in Chapter 11. FAT32 is an enhanced version of FAT that allows long file names and supports access to larger disk drives. FAT and FAT32 do not offer many of the features supported by NTFS such as file- and folder-level security, encryption, enforcement of disk quotas for multiple users, and so on, so FAT and FAT32 should be avoided on a Windows XP system. Windows XP supports FAT32 on DVD-RAM devices such as CD, DVD, and rewriteable disks, but NTFS is the preferred file system.

NTFS

NTFS (the Windows NT file system) allocates a disk volume's space in **clusters,** where a cluster is one or more (generally, a power of 2) contiguous sectors. The cluster size is defined when the disk is formatted. NTFS uses logical cluster numbers as disk addresses. Multiplying the logical cluster number by the cluster size yields a physical disk (or volume) address.

Partition boot sector	Master file table	System files	File area

FIGURE 12.12

Each volume is organized into four regions.

Each volume is organized into four regions (Figure 12.12). The first few sectors contain the partition boot sector. Next comes the **master file table (MFT),** essentially the volume's master directory. Following the MFT is a system area that holds a partial copy of the MFT, log files to support recoverability, and other system information. The rest of the volume is the file area where larger files are stored.

The master file table, which is used by NTFS to access files, consists of an array of variable length records. The first 16 records describe the master file table (MFT) itself. Subsequent master file table records provide access to each file or directory on the volume. Small files (less than 1200 bytes) are written directly in the MFT. For larger files, the MFT entry contains index pointers to the clusters that hold the actual data.

Windows XP differs from MS-DOS (Chapter 11) and UNIX (Chapter 13) in the way it handles files. Both DOS and UNIX consider the file to be a string of bytes. In contrast, a Windows XP file is an object, and NTFS stores the file's attributes inside the object itself. Each file attribute is stored as a separate stream of bytes within the file.

A file's attributes are recorded in the master file table as an independent byte string that can be created, read, written, and deleted (Figure 12.13). As a minimum, certain standard information such as read-only, archive, time stamps, and so on must be associated with every file. The file name is the name associated with the file, and a file can have multiple names including an NTFS long file name and a short MS-DOS file name. The security descriptor specifies who owns the file and who can access the file; it

Standard information	File name or directory name	Security descriptor	Data or index to data	

FIGURE 12.13

Certain attributes are associated with every file.

protects the file from unauthorized access. The data or the index to the data tells Windows XP where to find the contents of the file.

Because files are objects, not all files must have the same attributes, and a user can design a file to meet his or her particular needs. For example, a Macintosh file can have attributes corresponding to its data fork and resource fork, and a multimedia file (such as an AVI file) can have separate audio and video streams.

A directory is a file of indexes to the other files within the directory (Figure 12.14). When a directory cannot fit in a master file table (MFT) record, its attributes are stored in a separate run of **virtual cluster numbers (VCNs).** These VCNs are mapped to their logical cluster numbers (LCNs) to identify the file on disk. For large directories, the file indexes are stored in index buffers that are organized as a B+ tree, where each entry points to a series of lower-level entries with lesser index values. For example, in Figure 12.14, the reference to file F4 points to an index buffer with file names less than itself. Conceptually, the files in this index buffer can point to another, still lower-level index buffer, and so on. With a B+ tree organization, the time to look up any particular file in the directory is fast and is the same for all files.

NTFS also has the capability to compress a file or a folder of files if necessary. If a compressed file is accessed by an application, NTFS decompresses the file before making it available. When the file is later saved by the application, NTFS converts it back to compressed form. Windows XP also supports file encryption.

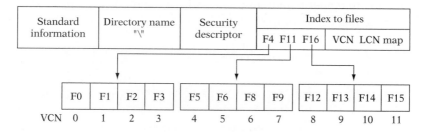

FIGURE 12.14

A directory is a file of indexes to the files stored or referenced in the directory.

File System Recovery

NTFS enables the smooth recovery of the file system following a system crash or disk failure. All changes to the master file table and file system structure are carried out using transactions. Before any changes are made, the change is written to a log. Subsequently, in the event of a system crash, the log can be used to undo partially completed transactions and redo (or recover) completed transactions. The key to file system recovery is a series of checkpoint records that are periodically (every 5 seconds) written to a log. Because earlier checkpoints are unneeded, all log entries prior to the checkpoint are discarded, which keeps the log file's size within reasonable bounds.

It should be noted that a transaction changes only the metadata (the data *about* the data), so although the file system can be recovered, NTFS does not guarantee the recovery of the file contents. In other words, you must still do your own backups.

Input Output Manager

The **input output manager or I/O manager** manages the system's device drivers, works with the virtual memory manager (VMM) to provide memory-mapped file I/O, and manages the file system buffers (Figure 12.15). Using buffers hides the speed disparity between the computer's internal components and slower I/O devices. Each request for service to the I/O manager is translated and formatted as a standard **I/O request packet (IRP),** and the IRP is forwarded to the appropriate device driver for processing. On completion of the request, the device driver sends a message to the I/O manager which, in turn, notifies the requesting process that that the service has been completed.

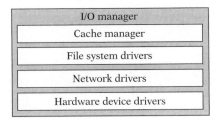

FIGURE 12.15

The I/O manager.

Device Drivers

A device driver is a software routine that allows the operating system to communicate with a specific piece of hardware. The Windows XP I/O manager supports four different types of drivers (Figure 12.15). All hardware devices (scanners, modems, printers, and so on) require hardware device drivers that manipulate the hardware to retrieve input from or write output to the physical device or network. File system drivers are device drivers that accept file-oriented I/O requests and translate them to the appropriate primitive I/O commands for the physical device. A network driver is a file system driver that redirects the I/O request to the appropriate machine on the network and receives data from the remote machine.

Windows XP device drivers meet a new standard called the Windows driver model (WDM) that enables Windows XP to share drivers with other Windows operating systems. WDM also incorporates features that enhance real time streaming media by processing the data in kernel mode rather than user mode.

Caching

Caching is a major I/O manager service that enhances performance by holding information in memory (rather than simply on disk) in case the information is needed again. File updates are written to the cache, not directly to disk. Later, when demand is low, the data are written to the disk by a background process. In most operating systems, caching is handled by the file system. In contrast, Windows XP implements caching as a centralized facility that provides service not only to the file system but also to all the components (such as the network components) under the control of the I/O manager. The size of the cache varies with the amount of free physical memory available in the system. Up to half the space in the system memory area (Figure 12.9) is allocated to cache by the virtual memory manager. The cache manager maps a file into this address space and uses the capabilities of the VMM to handle file I/O.

When a process requests an I/O service such as access to a file (Figure 12.16, step 1), the I/O manager passes an I/O request packet (IRP) to the cache manager (2). If the file is already in cache, the cache manager locates the information and copies it to the process's buffer via the virtual memory manager (3), which notifies the process that the requested I/O operation has been completed (4).

The process is a bit more complex if the file is not already in cache. As before, the process requests a service (Figure 12.17, step 1) and the I/O manager sends an IRP to the cache manager (2). Because the file is not in cache, the cache manager generates a page fault (3) and the virtual memory manager responds by sending a noncached service request back to the I/O

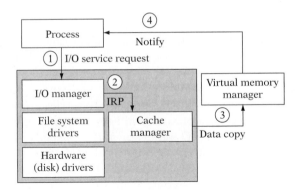

FIGURE 12.16

A cached I/O service request.

manager (4). The I/O manager then issues an IRP (5) to the file system driver. The file system driver, in turn, passes the IRP to the device driver (6) one or more times, depending on the size of the file. After the data (7) are read into the cache (8), the file is copied to the process's buffer (9) as if it had been in the cache when the initial I/O request was issued. The virtual memory manager then notifies the process that the I/O service request has been completed (10).

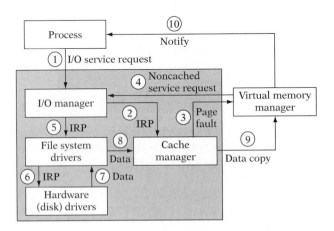

FIGURE 12.17

A non-cached I/O service request.

Whenever possible, Windows XP handles I/O requests in asynchronous mode. With asynchronous mode, the request is handed off to the I/O manager and the process or thread that made the request continues to execute while the I/O operation is being processed. Asynchronous mode execution helps to optimize application performance.

◼ The Registry

The **registry** is a hierarchical database that Windows XP uses to keep track of hardware and software settings within the computer. The registry holds information on the system's hardware (the processor, the bus type, the amount of system memory, and so on), its available device drivers, the network adapter (settings, network protocols), user and hardware profiles, and so on.

The registry is used by the kernel, administrative programs, the device drivers, and setup programs (Figure 12.18). On startup, the Windows XP bus driver (a software driver that services a bus controller) collects the list of installed hardware components and passes it to the kernel for inclusion in the registry. During the boot process, the kernel reads information about the devices and their load order from the registry, and starts the device drivers and services. The device drivers read from and write to the registry their configuration parameters. Application setup programs use the registry to determine whether the required components are already installed, and they add configuration information as necessary. When applications run, they use the registry to determine the system configuration. When multiple users use the system or when different hardware configurations exist on the computer, the appropriate data are stored in the registry.

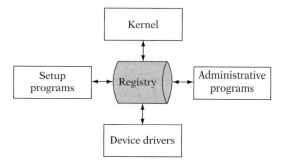

FIGURE 12.18

The registry.

Microsoft's Market Dominance

Imagine your software company is about to announce a major upgrade to your best-selling application program. Assuming the market responds positively, you plan to release versions for the Macintosh, UNIX, and Windows platforms, but which version should you release first? A rational decision maker would probably choose the version that has the greatest sales potential. By most accounts, Windows users represent at least 90 percent of the potential market, so the choice is obvious: you release the Windows version first. In fact, the decision to fully develop and release the Macintosh and UNIX versions will probably depend on how the marketplace responds to the Windows version.

Expand your viewpoint from a single company to the entire software industry and imagine numerous CEOs making equally rational decisions. That is why, with the exception of certain niche markets, the Windows version of a new software product or upgrade is almost always released first and versions for other platforms follow later, if at all. Walk into any retail software outlet and you will quickly discover that, except perhaps for games, Windows applications dominate the shelves, and a closer examination will probably reveal that many Windows titles are simply not available for other platforms. As a result, a Windows user can choose from more (and more recently updated) applications than can a Macintosh or a UNIX user. Although it may seem like circular reasoning, Microsoft's continuing market dominance is at least in part a function of Microsoft's continuing market dominance.

◼ Multimedia Support

Windows XP incorporates several useful multimedia features. For example, DirectX is an application programming interface (API) that supports the capture and playback of audio, full-color video, and 3-D graphics and such multimedia peripheral devices as a joystick. DirectX provides a hardware abstraction layer between the hardware and software, which enables device-independent applications to be developed. Windows XP also includes support for DVD playback using either hardware or software decoders. The kernel provides streaming drivers using the Windows driver model and also provides support for reading (but not for writing) the DVD universal disk format (UDF) file system. Also, you can write to DVD-RAM using the FAT32 file system.

Windows XP's Windows Media feature provides several special purpose audio and video codecs (compressor/decompressor routines) that achieve better compression ratios than MP3 and MPEG4, the industry's video standard. Windows XP also provides a media player for playback, media tools to develop content, a movie maker to transfer video into a computer, and services for distributing content. A Windows media file can be encrypted using Windows Media digital rights management to secure against unauthorized distribution.

Windows Media uses a content-independent container format called advanced streaming format (ASF) to store and distribute digital media (Figure 12.19). An ASF file begins with a header that describes the metadata (the data about the data) and defines the relationships between and configurations of the various data streams. The body of the container holds the interleaved data streams; for example, a multimedia file might consist of an audio stream, a video stream, and so on. The container ends with an optional index that holds pointers (such as frame numbers or time based coding) to the data to simplify retrieval.

▪ The 64-Bit Version

The 64-bit version of Windows XP runs on the Intel Itanium chip and supports up to 16 GB of physical memory and up to 16 TB (terabytes) of virtual memory. In contrast, the 32-bit version is limited to 4 GB and 16 GB respectively. The way the virtual address space is laid out is also different. As you learned earlier in the chapter, the 32-bit version allocates 2 GB for user space and 2 GB for system space, but the 64-bit version uses 7,152 GB (less than .00005 % of total available virtual memory) per user process and allocates the rest of the 16 TB to system processes and managing data. As a result, a 32-bit program running under the 64-bit version of Windows XP can exceed the old 2 GB memory limit, and applications with large data sets, such as computer-aided design and financial applications, can run faster.

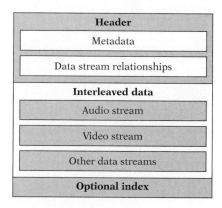

FIGURE 12.19

An ASF file container.

Thunking

Windows XP was designed for the IA64 Itanium chip and executes 64-bit applications in native mode. Running a 32-bit application on the IA64 architecture requires a **thunking**[2] layer (Figure 12.20) to convert the 32-bit calls into corresponding 64-bit calls; note how closely Figure 12.20 resembles Figure 12.5. The Windows on Windows (WOW64) subsystem provides this thunking layer and helps isolate the 64-bit applications from collisions with the 32-bit applications. Cut and paste and similar interoperability features can be used to pass information between 32- and 64-bit applications, however.

Disk Partitioning

The IA64 (Itanium) chip replaces the traditional BIOS firmware interface with the extensible firmware interface (EFI). EFI contains some platform specific information and provides consistent boot and run-time services across all platforms. The EFI specification also defines a new disk partitioning scheme called the Globally Unique Identifier Partition Table or GPT. GPT supports up to 128 primary partitions (up from 4) and very large disks with up to 18 exabytes of storage capacity, where one exabyte is 2^{60} bytes. GPT also enhances partition security and helps to ensure data integrity by using such measures as error checking and recording a redundant backup copy of partition information at the end of the disk. Windows XP supports the EFI interface in its 64-bit edition.

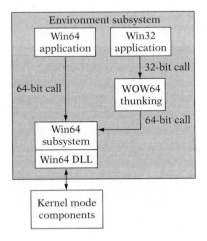

FIGURE 12.20

Thunking.

---

[2]According to the online *Jargon Dictionary,* a thunk is "a piece of coding which provides an address." See *http://info.astrian.net/jargon/terms/t.html#thunk*.

▌ Summary

Some Windows XP modules operate in hierarchical layered mode and others operate in client/server mode. The Windows XP system is divided into the user mode and the kernel mode. User applications and a collection of subsystems run in user mode. The user mode components include the environment subsystem and the integral subsystem. An application program communicates with the operating system by calling an application programming interface, which translates the call to kernel form by accessing the dynamic link library. Win32 applications communicate directly with the Win32 subsystem. Win16 and MS-DOS applications run on virtual DOS machines (VDMs). On the integral subsystem, server processes are run as services and system processes require an interactive logon.

One way to view the kernel mode processes is as a layered hierarchy that includes the hardware abstraction layer (HAL), the device drivers, the kernel, and the executive. The object manager is responsible for creating, destroying, and granting access to an object's services or data. The process manager creates and deletes processes and threads. Windows XP supports multithreading, preemptive multitasking, and symmetric multiprocessing.

Windows XP uses a virtual memory manager (VMM) to allocate memory to processes and to manage system memory. When a process or thread references a virtual address on an invalid page, a page fault occurs. The system responds by reading (or swapping) the requested data (or code) from disk into the first available physical memory location. Allocating memory in Windows is a two-step process: reserve and commit. A 32-bit virtual address is divided into three parts: an index to the page directory, an index to the page table, and the displacement on the page.

Dynamic storage is a feature that allows a user to resize a disk without restarting Windows XP. You can divide a dynamic disk into volumes. Fault tolerance is the ability of the computer to recover data in case of errors. Windows XP supports FAT, FAT 32, and its native NTFS file system. NTFS enables the smooth recovery of the file system in case of a system crash or disk failure.

The input output manager (I/O manager) manages cache and the file system, device, and network drivers. Each request to the I/O manager for service is translated and formatted to a standard I/O request packet (IRP). Caching increases performance by holding the information in memory in case the information is needed a second time. The registry is a hierarchical database used by Windows XP to keep track of hardware and software settings within the computer.

Windows XP incorporates several new multimedia features. The 64-bit version of Windows XP runs on the Intel Itanium chip and supports up to 16 GB of memory and 16 TB (terabytes) of virtual memory.

▌ Key Words

application programming
   interface (API)
caching
client/server mode
cluster
commit
context switching
dynamic link library (DDL)
dynamic storage
environment subsystem
executive, or executive services
fault tolerance
Hardware Abstraction Layer
   (HAL)
input output manager (I/O
   manager)
integral subsystem
invalid page
I/O request packet (IRP)
kernel mode
master file table (MFT)
multiprocessing
multitasking

multithreading
NTFS
object manager
page directory
page fault
page table
preemptive multitasking
priority
process
process manager
registry
reserve
server process
service
symmetric multiprocessing (SMP) system
system process
system restore
thread
thunk
user mode
valid page
virtual cluster number (VCN)
virtual memory manager (VMM)

▌ Review Questions

1. Explain client/server mode.
2. Distinguish between user mode and kernel mode.
3. Distinguish between user mode's environmental and integral subsystems.
4. What is an application program interface (API)? What is a dynamic link library (DLL)? How are an API and a DDL related?
5. Distinguish between server processes and system processes.
6. Identify the functions performed by the primary kernel mode components.
7. List the primary modules that make up executive services.
8. Define the terms module, process, and thread.
9. Explain how the process manager creates a new process.
10. Define multithreading, multitasking, and multiprocessing.

11. Explain how the virtual memory manager implements paging.

12. Distinguish between memory reserve and memory commit. Why is that distinction important?

13. Describe the contents of a Windows XP 32-bit address. Explain how a virtual address is translated into a physical (real) address.

14. What is dynamic storage and why is it considered important?

15. Why are mirrored and RAID-5 volumes considered fault tolerant while simple, spanned, and striped volumes are not?

16. Describe the organization of an NTFS disk.

17. Explain how Windows XP uses virtual cluster numbers to find files on disk.

18. How does NTFS enable the smooth recovery of the file system following a system crash or disk failure?

19. Explain how Windows XP uses caching.

20. What is the purpose of the Windows XP registry?

21. Identify several Windows XP multimedia support features.

22. Discuss several key differences between the 32-bit and 64-bit versions of Windows XP.

Exercises

1. According to your text, some Windows modules are configured in a hierarchical layered mode, but other modules work in client/server mode. However, a footnote in the same section stated that it is still useful to view the client and the server as independent layers. How do you explain that apparent contradiction?

2. Why is it so difficult to compete directly with a company like Microsoft that dominates its marketplace?

3. From the 1960s through most of the 1980s, IBM dominated the information technology marketplace. Although the company is still a major player, it is no longer the dominant player, however. Do a little research and see if you can find out why.

4. Why is robustness an important operating system criterion?

5. Relate fault tolerance to robustness.

6. If you are experienced with multimedia applications, review the new multimedia features bundled with XP and indicate why you might (or might not) find them useful.

7. Figures 12.3, 12.11, and 12.16 (without the numbers) are useful templates for organizing many of this chapter's key terms.

CHAPTER 13

UNIX and Linux Internals

When you finish reading this chapter you should be able to:

▶ Explain the significance of the UNIX kernel.

▶ Distinguish an image from a process.

▶ Differentiate a user's text, data, stack, and system data segments.

▶ Explain how processes are created under UNIX.

▶ Discuss UNIX dispatching.

▶ Explain how UNIX links a peripheral device and an application process.

▶ Sketch the contents of a UNIX disk.

▶ Explain how UNIX converts a file name to the file's location on disk.

▶ Explain how the buffer pool supports asynchronous I/O.

▶ Identify several unique features of Linux.

■ The UNIX System

A UNIX user communicates with the system indirectly through an application programming interface such as **POSIX** (Portable Operating System Interface for UNIX, a standard application programming interface) or directly through a shell or a graphical user interface (Figure 13.1). The shell and the GUI are treated much like application programs and are technically not part of the operating system, an important UNIX innovation that makes it relatively easy to replace the standard use interface with a custom user interface. For example, a professional programmer might consider the rather terse commands associated with the command line shell easy to use, while a nontechnical user might find the same commands intimidating and prefer a GUI.

Among its resident modules, the focus of this chapter, UNIX contains an input/output control system, a file system, and routines to swap segments, handle interrupts, schedule the processor's time, manage memory space, and allocate peripheral devices. Additionally, the operating system maintains several tables to track the system's status. Routines that communicate directly with the hardware are concentrated in a relatively small **kernel** (Figure 13.1). The kernel is (at least in part) hardware-dependent and varies significantly from system to system. However, the interface to the kernel is consistent across implementations.

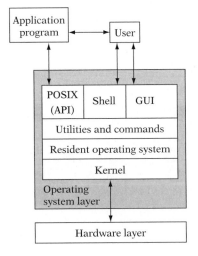

FIGURE 13.1

Hardware-dependent UNIX/Linux logic is concentrated in the kernel.

UNIX is a time-sharing system, with program segments swapped in and out of memory as required. To ensure reasonable response time, processor access is limited by time-slicing. Segmentation is the most common addressing scheme, and most UNIX systems implement virtual memory techniques.

Portability

Significant parts of most operating systems are written in assembler language and thus are limited to a single platform or a single architecture. In contrast, only a small portion of the UNIX kernel is written in assembler. The rest of the operating system is written primarily in a high-level language (C), making it highly portable. As a result, UNIX can run on virtually any platform, an extremely valuable attribute in today's distributed computing environment.

◼ Images and Processes

The pseudocomputer concept is an important UNIX innovation. A user's routine is viewed as an **image,** defined by Ritchie and Thompson as an "execution environment" that consists of program and data storage, the contents of general-purpose registers, the status of open files, the current directory, and other key elements. To the user, it *appears* that this image is executed on a private pseudocomputer under control of a command-driven operating system. In reality, UNIX is a multiple user, time-sharing system.

An image consists of three segments (Figure 13.2). Starting at virtual address 0 is a program **text segment** followed by a **data segment.** The image ends with a **stack segment.** Between the data and the stack segments is a free area. As the program runs, the data segment grows toward high memory (down in Figure 13.2), and the stack segment grows toward low memory.

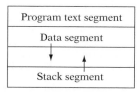

FIGURE 13.2

An image consists of a program text segment, a data segment, and a stack segment.

The execution of an image is called a **process.** As a process executes, the image's text, data, and stack segments must be in memory. (Note: they need not occupy contiguous memory.) Thus, the image is not *really* executed on a pseudocomputer. Instead, the image and the pseudocomputer serve as virtual models of the user's environment.

The program text segment is reentrant, and thus it can be shared. UNIX, remember, is a multiple user system. If two or more users access the same program, only one text segment is physically stored in memory. Both users have their independent images. Both *imagine* that they and they alone have access to their program code. Physically, however, they share a single text segment (Figure 13.3).

The data and stack segments, on the other hand, are private; for example, if two users are executing the same code, memory will hold one text segment, two data segments, and two stack segments. Additionally, each process has its own **system data segment** containing data needed by the operating system when the process is active. This system data segment is not part of the user's image, and the user cannot access it. When the user calls the operating system (for example, to request an input or output service), the process switches from a user state to a system state, making the system data segment available to UNIX.

Process Creation

A process is created when an executing process calls the ***fork*** routine (a system primitive). In response, UNIX duplicates the executing process, creating two identical copies. Because both copies contain the system data segment, they share open files and other key data. The operating system distinguishes between the parent and the child by giving them different return codes. Thus, although the parent and the child are identical, they can take different actions based on their return codes.

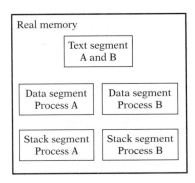

FIGURE 13.3
The text segment is reentrant. The data and stack segments are private.

The parent starts the process by calling *fork*. It is a system call, so a return address is stored in the process's system data area and UNIX gets control of the processor. After the duplicate process is created, UNIX returns control to the parent, which checks the return code. By convention, the parent gets the process number (called the **process id** or **pid**) of the child (a positive integer), while the child gets a return code of 0. (A negative return code indicates an error.) Because the return code is positive, the parent normally calls **wait,** and waits for the child to die[1] or finish processing (Figure 13.4a).

Eventually, the child is launched and begins to execute. Because it is a duplicate of the parent, the return address in its system data area points to the instruction immediately following *fork* (addresses are virtual). Thus, the child begins by checking the return code (Figure 13.4b). Because the return code is 0, the child calls another system primitive, **exec.** The *exec* routine responds by overlaying the child's text and data segments with the contents of a new file (Figure 13.4c). Technically, the resulting image is still the same process, but its contents are different. Later, when the child dies, the parent can resume processing (Figure 13.4d).

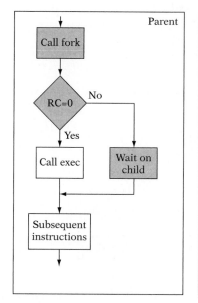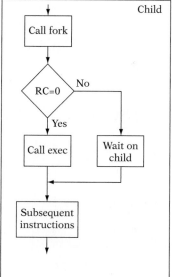

FIGURE 13.4

UNIX process creation.

a. The parent calls *fork* and drops into a wait state.

---

[1]UNIX terminology is sometimes a bit morbid.

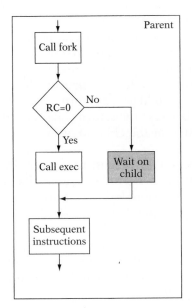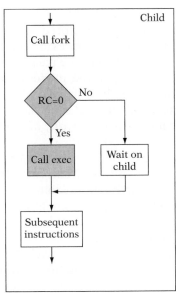

b. Because its return code is 0, the child calls *exec*.

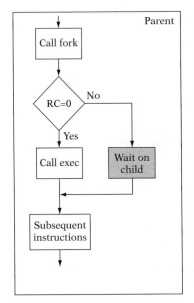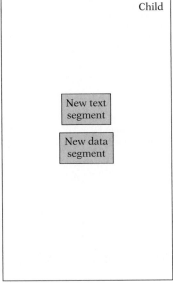

c. The exec routine overlays the child's text and data segments.

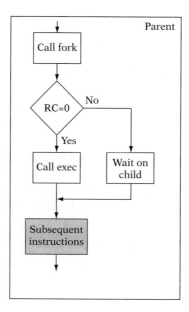

d. When the child dies, the parent resumes processing.

Briefly review the process creation sequence, because it is important. The parent calls *fork*. In response, UNIX duplicates the process, and returns control to the parent. Because the return code is a positive integer (the child's process number), the parent calls *wait*, and "goes to sleep" until the child dies.

Eventually, the child, a duplicate of the parent, is launched. When the parent called *fork*, the address of its next instruction was recorded in the system data area, so the child's system data area contains the same (virtual) return address. Thus, the instruction following *fork* is executed. Typically, this instruction checks the return code. Because the return code is 0, *exec* is called and a new program overlays the child. Following *exec*, the first instruction in this new program is executed. Eventually, the new program calls **exit** and the child dies. Consequently, the parent is awakened and, eventually, begins executing again.

Some applications call for parallel parent and child processes. As before, the child is created when the parent calls *fork*, but instead of calling *wait*, the parent executes regular instructions so both the parent and the child are active. With most operating systems, radically different commands or parameters are used to define parallel and serial processes. UNIX, in contrast, supports serial and parallel processes with remarkable consistency, one reason why professional programmers find it so elegant.

Initialization

When UNIX is booted, a process named ***init*** is activated. This "original ancestor" creates one logon process for each potential user; for example, if the system supports up to twenty concurrent users, twenty logon processes are created. A user logs on to one of these processes. The logon process then (normally) launches *(exec)* the shell, which overlays the logon process. Later, when the shell dies (in other words, when the user logs off), *init* creates a new logon process.

When a user logs on, the logon process scans a table of login names, identifies the user's default interface, and, typically, executes either a command line shell or a GUI. Because the shell is treated as a process, it's relatively easy to substitute a custom shell. Another option is no shell. In response to a particular login name, the logon process can start an *application* routine, effectively placing the user inside the shell and thus restricting that user to commands and responses appropriate to that application routine. The logon process overlays itself with the user's primary system interface. When that interface dies, *init* spawns another logon process, which waits for another user to log on.

The image described earlier allows a user to visualize a program. Real memory is a bit more complex, however. Imagine a UNIX system supporting four concurrent users (Figure 13.5). Three are active, so memory holds three shells. Running under each shell are user processes; note that two or more parallel processes can be associated with a single shell. A fourth potential user has not yet logged on, so the logon process is still active.

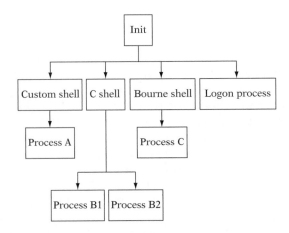

FIGURE 13.5

The possible contents of memory on a UNIX system supporting four concurrent users.

The user sees the image of a *single process* and can imagine that process running all by itself on a private pseudocomputer. The details associated with time-slicing, swapping, real memory allocation, and physical device access are buried in UNIX and thus are transparent to the user.

Process Management

UNIX is a multiple user operating system, with several concurrent programs occupying memory. It is inevitable that two or more programs will want to access the processor at the same time, so the operating system must carefully schedule them. The UNIX dispatcher is responsible for process scheduling.

The UNIX dispatcher relies on a **process table** that holds one entry for each process (Figure 13.6). The entry is allocated when the process is created *(fork)* and freed when the process dies. Each entry contains all the data needed by UNIX when the process is *not* active. Among other things, the process table entry indicates whether the process is ready (awake) or waiting (asleep).

For example, imagine the shell (the parent) has just received a command that requires a new process. The shell responds by calling *fork*. In response, the kernel creates the new process, assigns a process number (a positive integer), adds a new entry to the process table, and returns to the shell. The shell then (typically) calls *wait* and "goes to sleep" until the newly created child dies.

```
One entry per process.

Each entry contains:
        Process number
        Process state (ready, waiting)
        Process priority
        Event number process is waiting on
        Text table address
        Data segment address
        Stack segment address
        System data segment address
```

FIGURE 13.6

The process table contains one entry per process.

Meanwhile, the child is launched, calls *exec,* and carries out the command. Later, when it finishes processing, it calls exit and dies. The death of a process generates an **event** that produces a **signal.** The event is reported to the operating system's *event-wait* routine as a positive integer—the event number or process number. UNIX responds by searching the process table and waking (setting to a ready state) every process waiting for that event.

Each user process has a priority. Priorities are recomputed frequently by dividing execution time by elapsed real time (the smaller the number, the higher the priority). When an event signal is sensed, the operating system's *event-wait* routine is called. First, *event-wait* awakens all processes waiting for that event. Then, it searches the process table, selects the highest priority "ready" process, and starts it.

Events occupy no memory; they are represented by electronic signals. When a signal is sensed, *event-wait* scans the process table and awakens all processes waiting for the associated event. Then the system forgets that the event ever happened. What if time passes between the decision to wait and the implementation of the wait state? For example, imagine a process calls *fork,* performs some calculations, and *then* calls *wait.* What if, between *fork* and *wait,* the new process is launched and dies? By the time the parent calls *wait,* the event it plans to wait for has already happened. Because the child process has already died, it will not appear in the process table. When the UNIX *wait* routine gets control, it checks the process table and, if the calling routine has no children, returns an error code. A programmer should be prepared for this sequence of events any time parallel processes are activated.

▰ Getting Started

When *init* creates a logon process, it opens the standard input, output, and error files, thus allowing the logon process to accept user input from the terminal and display both normal output and error messages. When a user logs on, typically by entering a user ID and a password, a copy of the shell or a GUI is loaded into memory and overlays the logon process's text and data segments. The system data segment is not affected, however, so the standard input, output, and error files are still open. Consequently, the user can begin issuing commands without opening these standard files.

In response to a command, the shell sets up an *exec,* calls *fork,* and then waits for the child process to carry out the command. If the command is followed by an ampersand (&), the shell does not wait. Instead, it spawns a new process to carry out the command in parallel and immediately displays a prompt for the next command.

■ Time-Slicing and Interrupts

Under UNIX, the operating system schedules processes by responding to event signals. For example, an event occurs when a process dies. If the process is compute-bound, however, considerable time can pass between events, and that, in turn, can negatively impact response time. To minimize the risk that a single process will monopolize the system's time, time-slicing is imposed.

Programs are generally limited to a brief interval of processor time. If, during that time interval, the process voluntarily surrenders control, fine; normal dispatching rules are adequate. If, however, a process exceeds its allotted time interval, a special event (perhaps, a timer interrupt) is signaled and *event-wait* is called. After recomputing priorities (thus lowering the offending process's priority), *event-wait* searches the process table and selects the highest priority ready process.

Interrupt handling routines are located in the UNIX kernel. (Because UNIX is supported on a variety of computers, each of which might implement interrupts differently, the hardware details are not covered in this text.) When an interrupt occurs, control of the processor is transferred to the kernel. Once the interrupt is handled, *event-wait* awakens any processes waiting for the interrupt and then schedules the next process.

■ Memory Management

UNIX relies on virtual memory and segmentation techniques to manage memory space. The user's image is a virtual model of a pseudocomputer. The text, data, and stack segments that make up that image are independently loaded into real memory. As necessary, segments (and even complete images) are swapped out to secondary memory to free space for active processes.

Swapping (or Paging)

Consider swapping in more detail. When a process first enters real memory, the entire image is loaded. As the process grows, new primary memory is allocated, the process is copied to the new space, and the process table is updated. If sufficient memory is not available, the growing process is allocated space on secondary memory and swapped out. At this point, the process is ready to be swapped back in. Over time, several processes can reside on secondary memory.

The swapping process is part of the kernel (Figure 13.7) and thus can be activated each time UNIX gets control of the processor. It scans the process table looking for a ready process that has been swapped out. If it finds one, it allocates primary memory and swaps in the process. If sufficient memory space is not available, the swapping routine selects a process to be swapped out, copies the selected process to secondary storage, frees the memory space, and then swaps in the ready process.

The swap-in decision is based on secondary storage residency time—the longer a process resides on disk, the higher its priority. Generally, processes waiting for slow events are primary swap-out candidates. If there are several such processes, age in primary memory is a secondary criterion, and a slight penalty is imposed on large programs. To help minimize thrashing, processes do not become candidates for swapping out until they have achieved at least a minimum age in primary memory.

Early versions of UNIX swapped segments. Newer versions designed to run on page-oriented hardware subdivide segments into pages and swap pages.

Memory Space and Reentrant Code

Text segments contain reentrant code, and that has memory management implications. On the one hand, because several processes can physically share a single text segment the total amount of space that must be allocated to support all those processes is reduced. On the other hand, if several processes share the same text segment, that segment's space cannot be released until all the processes using it have died.

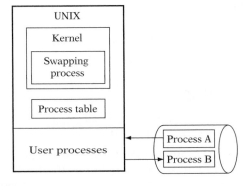

FIGURE 13.7
The swapping process is part of the kernel.

To keep track of active text segments, UNIX maintains a **text table** that lists each current text segment, its primary and secondary addresses, and a count of the number of processes sharing it (Figure 13.8). As a process dies, the count is decremented. Although the space associated with the data, stack, and system data segments can immediately be freed when a process dies, the text segment must remain in memory until its count reaches zero.

■ The File System

According to its designers, the **file system** is the key to UNIX. It offers compatible device, file, and interprocess I/O; in essence, the user simply sends and receives data. All data are treated as strings of bytes and no physical structure is imposed by the system. Instead, the user's program overlays its own data structure. The result is considerable freedom from any concern for physical I/O.

Block (structured) devices (normally, disk) hold files. A hierarchical directory structure maps the entire file system and allows the operating system to create, retrieve, and update data files by name. The information associated with a directory is itself kept in a file (another important UNIX innovation). Disk I/O will be discussed in some detail a bit later.

Character devices include printers and other nonblock peripherals. They operate through a simple queuing process. For example, to output data to a printer, UNIX places bytes, one by one, on the printer's output queue. The printer's controller subsequently retrieves them, one by one.

Character devices, block devices, and data files are all treated as files and are accessed by a common set of system calls (*open, read, write,* and so on). Data files are called **ordinary files.** Files that represent a block or character device are called **special files.** Once again, consistency makes the operating system easier to use.

> Each text table entry contains:
>   The text segment's identification
>   The text segment's primary memory address
>   The text segment's secondary memory address
>   A count of the number of processes using this text segment

FIGURE 13.8
UNIX maintains a text table to keep track of active segments.

Inside the operating system, each physical device is controlled by a **device driver** (Figure 13.9). All devices attached to the system are listed in a **configuration table** and identified by a major **device number** and a minor device number. When UNIX receives a request to start I/O, it uses the major device number to search the configuration table, finds the address of the appropriate device driver, and then activates the device driver. The minor device number is passed to the device driver. It might designate a specific disk drive on a multiple drive system, a specific peripheral on a channel, or, depending on the device, some other detail. As a system changes, device drivers and configuration table entries can be added or deleted, usually by the system's super user.

Accessing Disk Files

Disk is the standard block device. The disk surface is divided into four regions (Figure 13.10). The boot block, as the name implies, holds a boot routine. Next comes a **super block** that identifies the disk, defines the sizes of the disk's regions, and tracks free blocks. The third region holds the **i-list.** Each entry on the i-list is an **i-node,** a 64-byte file definition that lists the disk addresses of blocks associated with a single ordinary file. A special file describes a physical device, and a special file's i-node holds the device's major and minor device numbers. The i-nodes are numbered sequentially. An i-node's offset from the beginning of the i-list is its **i-number.** The

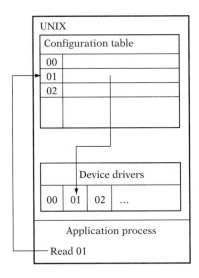

FIGURE 13.9

A configuration table lists all the device drivers.

combination of a device number and an i-number defines a specific file. Following the i-list, the remaining space on disk is divided into 1 KB blocks that hold data and/or directories.

A known i-node (often, i-number 2) points to the root directory. When a user logs on, UNIX reads the root directory, finds the user's home directory, and records the home directory's i-number in the process's system data area. In response to a change directory command, UNIX replaces the recorded i-number with the new directory's i-number.

When a program opens an ordinary file (Figure 13.11), UNIX uses the working directory's i-number to begin its search for the requested file. Each directory entry consists of a file name and an i-number. Once the file name is found in the directory, the associated i-number is extracted. The i-number points to the file's i-node. That i-node, in turn, holds the disk address of the file's first block and starts a chain of pointers that link all the file's blocks.

> - Boot block
> - Super block
>   - Region sizes
>   - Disk identification
>   - Free block list
> - i-list
>   - i-nodes (file definitions)
> - File and directory blocks

FIGURE 13.10

A UNIX disk is divided into four regions.

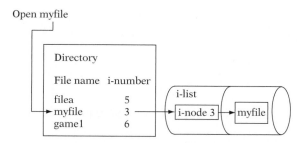

FIGURE 13.11

Associated with each file name on the directory is an i-number that points to a specific i-node.

UNIX, remember, is a multiple user system. Thus, at any given time, numerous devices and files will be open, and it is likely that two or more processes will try to concurrently access the same disk (or even the same file). To avoid conflicts, the operating system maintains a **system file table,** sometimes called the **i-node table** (Figure 13.12). When the file is opened, its i-node is copied into the system file table.

To the user's process, an open file is identified by a **file descriptor,** a small, nonnegative integer number. Within the process's system data area, the file is listed in a **process file table.** The process file table entry points, in turn, to an i-node in the system file table, so the process is only aware of its own open files. UNIX, on the other hand, can track every open file, no matter what process it might be associated with.

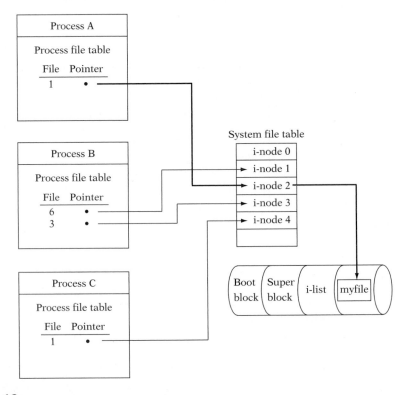

FIGURE 13.12

A process file table entry points to a system file table entry which, in turn, points to the file's location on disk.

Later, when the user process calls *read* or *write*, UNIX uses the *process* file table's pointer to locate the file's i-node in the *system* file table. That i-node, in turn, provides a start of file address. Because the file is viewed as a simple string of bytes, individual substrings can be accessed by using relative byte numbers. The UNIX file system assumes responsibility for converting relative byte addresses into physical disk addresses and reading or writing the appropriate block or blocks. The application program makes sense of the data by overlaying its own data structure.

Managing Disk Space

UNIX is also responsible for managing disk space. When a file is created or an existing file grows, the operating system scans the free block list in the super block and allocates space to the file. The free block list is a series of pointers that link unused disk blocks. After allocating space, UNIX updates the pointers.

Note that space is allocated dynamically. When a file is first created, it might be assigned several contiguous blocks, but subsequent requests for space are filled by allocating blocks located anywhere on the disk's surface. In addition to pointing to the start-of-file address, the i-node starts a list of pointers that link all a file's blocks, including the noncontiguous ones.

Buffering

All block I/O takes place through a buffer pool located in the operating system (no system buffers are found in the user's image). A *read* command implies a buffer search. If the requested block is already in memory, no physical input operation is needed. If physical I/O is necessary, the "least currently accessed" buffer is renamed and the block is read into it. Additionally, whenever UNIX must physically read a block, it automatically prereads the next one. Consequently, given the nature of most programs, the data are often already in memory when the next *read* command is issued.

Normally, when UNIX selects the least currently accessed buffer and renames it, the contents of that buffer are lost. To avoid destroying valid output data residing in a buffer, UNIX responds to a *write* command by marking the appropriate buffer **dirty** (basically, the operating system sets a switch). No physical output occurs at write time, however. Instead, when the buffer is later identified as least currently accessed, its contents are physically copied to disk before the buffer space is reassigned. Delaying the physical data transfer until a buffer is no longer active also tends to reduce physical I/O.

UNIX implements pipes by taking advantage of its buffering scheme. When data are sent to the standard output device, they are first copied to a buffer, and then output. Likewise, when data are read from the standard input device, they flow from the device into a buffer and are subsequently made available to the process. With pipes, the standard output is transferred to a buffer and simply held. The next process then gets its input directly from the first process's output buffer.

By reducing physical I/O operations, UNIX dramatically improves system efficiency. There are, however, disadvantages to the dynamic buffering approach. For one thing, although physical I/O may *appear* synchronous, it is really asynchronous (in other words, physical data transfers and logical read or write commands do not necessary occur in a predictable time sequence). This makes real-time error reporting or user error handling difficult to implement. Because of the delayed write described earlier, valid output data can be lost if UNIX crashes unexpectedly. Finally, the sequence of logical and physical I/O operations can differ, which can cause serious problems for applications that rely on data sequence. UNIX does allow a user to open a file in raw mode. Such files maintain a logical/physical correspondence. In spite of these problems, however, the UNIX I/O model has been adopted by a number of modern operating systems.

■ UNIX Internals

One of the best ways to get an overview of an operating system is to follow the pointers that link the system's components. Figure 13.13 summarizes the key UNIX tables. Start with the process table. For each process, the process table holds pointers to the process's data segment, stack segment, and system data segment. Additionally, the process table entry points to a text table entry which, in turn, points to the process's text segment. Thus, the process table and the text table link all the process's segments.

Each process has a system data segment. The i-number of the user's working directory is stored here. Physical devices are linked to the process through a list of open files. Each open file reference points to a configuration table entry which in turn points to a device driver. The files themselves are identified through pointers (in the process file table) to the system file table. Each system file table entry is an i-node that holds a file's disk address.

At first glance, Figure 13.13 appears complex, but compared to other operating systems, its use of tables and pointers to link a system's components is remarkably elegant, one reason why UNIX is so popular with computer professionals.

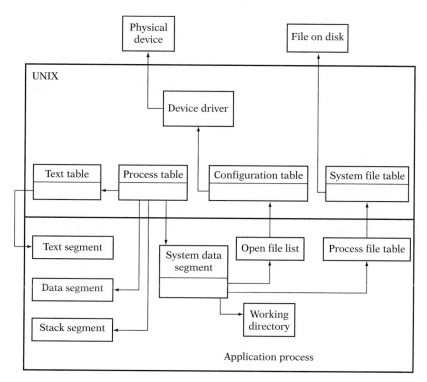

FIGURE 13.13

A summary of key UNIX system tables.

Linux

Linux is a POSIX-compliant clone of UNIX. This section notes some variations from standard UNIX and some unique features of Linux.

Linux Architecture

Linux features a layered architecture that resembles UNIX and Windows (Figure 13.14). While Linux is widely used on the Intel 32-bit architecture, it has been ported to many different hardware architectures including Intel's Itanium 64-bit architecture, the PowerPC, and the Alpha processor. Linux concentrates the architecture-dependent code at its lowest layer. Resting on the architecture-dependent layer is the kernel. The kernel processes are broadly classified as input/output-related (file systems, networking, and device drivers) and process-related (scheduling, memory management, and interprocess communication). On top of the process-related and input/output-related processes is the system call interface (the application program interface) that the kernel exposes to user processes. Even though user processes can make direct kernel calls using the system level interface, more often they do so using a user-level system library, such as *libc,* a standard C language application programming interface library. Referencing an intermediate system library simplifies the task of calling the kernel.

The architecture-independent services can be viewed as modules rather than layers. Each module, such as the scheduler, provides a core service. These modules can independently call each other, which is more efficient than calling a process in a higher or lower layer. For example, if the memory manager wants to swap the contents of a portion of memory to disk, it can call the file system directly.

The Linux kernel includes device drivers that communicate directly with the hardware layer's peripheral devices. Rather than including *all* the device drivers by default, Linux loads and unloads specific components (or modules) of kernel code as necessary, which allows the system to operate with a minimal kernel and frees up more memory for user programs.

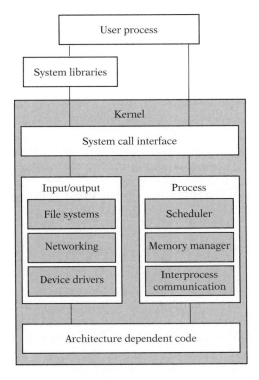

FIGURE 13.14

Linux system architecture.

The Profit Motive

One reason the Linux kernel is modular has to do with licensing. The Linux kernel is distributed under the Gnu license, which requires anyone who modifies the source code with the intent of selling or making money from their innovation to make the modified source code publicly available. Although making the source public was consistent with UNIX's open-source legacy, it discouraged business entities (who almost by definition are profit motivated) from contributing to the development of Linux. Linus Torvalds, the creator of the original open source Linux kernel, saw an elegant way out of this licensing straightjacket, providing hooks into the kernel and giving the kernel the ability to load and unload modules. Consequently, commercial enterprises were free to develop their own kernel-level enhancements without releasing their source code.

Linux Processes

The Linux process model closely resembles the UNIX process model, but it can call either a *fork* or a ***clone*** to create a process. The Unix/Linux *fork* routine calls *exec* to give the process its new context. In contrast, a clone gives the process a new identity but does not call *exec*. The clone can share both the text and data segments with the parent if needed. Associated with each Linux process is a property called a **personality identifier.** Personality allows Linux to emulate the behavior of other versions of UNIX (such as System V Release 4) and allows programs from these other versions to run under Linux without modification.

A Linux process can be divided into multiple threads, where a **thread** is a basic unit of work that can be executed and is interruptible. Linux uses *clone* primarily to create threads. Threads run concurrently within the associated process's memory space; in other words, all the threads within a process share the same memory space.

The Linux Task Scheduler

The Linux scheduler is thread based and distinguishes between normal threads and real-time threads. Each process is assigned a priority between +20 and -20. Associated with each thread in a process is a goodness value equal to the process's base priority for a normal thread and the base priority plus 1000 for a real-time thread. The scheduler schedules the next ready state thread with the highest goodness value, so real-time threads always run ahead of normal threads.

Real-time threads are further classified as first-in/first-out or round robin. A first-in/first out real-time thread either runs to completion or is unable to proceed because it is waiting for an I/O operation. A round robin real-time thread, in contrast, runs for a single time slice and then yields to the next ready state real-time thread.

A normal thread resembles a first-in/first-out real-time thread, but its goodness value is decremented by 1 following every quantum or time slice. The thread continues to run until its goodness value reaches 0, until the thread is unable to proceed because it is waiting for an I/O operation, or until a wait state thread with a higher goodness reverts to a ready state. When all ready-state threads have reached a goodness value of 0, the goodness values for all threads (both waiting and ready) are dynamically recalculated by the scheduler using the algorithm goodness/2 + priority. By setting the priority for background or compute-intensive process to low, Linux automatically gives higher priority to interactive or I/O bound processes for which a quick response is necessary.

Linux, like UNIX, can run on multiprocessor machines and supports symmetric multiprocessing (SMP). When the SMP version of Linux is used, the scheduler normally runs all threads that belong to the same process within the same processor. Under many UNIX and Linux systems, however, the administrator can assign a given process to a specific processor.

Linux Memory Management

Linux assigns every process 4 GB of virtual address space (Figure 13.15). The high order 1 GB is reserved for kernel space and can be addressed only in kernel mode. The remaining 3 GB is allocated to user space, which enables large programs to run.

Linux is designed to run on several different architectures, so it uses an architecture independent three-level set of page tables for translating virtual addresses to physical addresses (Figure 13.16). A linear (virtual) address contains a page directory index, a page middle directory index, a page table index, and an offset. The page directory index points to one of several page middle directories. Each entry in the page middle directory points to one of several page tables in the page table array. The page table entry, in turn, points to a specific page in physical memory. The page's entry point address is added to the page offset to calculate the actual physical address. In contrast, Windows uses a two-level addressing scheme (Figure 12.11) consistent with the Intel Architecture. When Linux runs on a 32-bit Intel architecture machine, the size of the page middle directory is set to one (1) by the memory manager, so the page middle directory essentially disappears.

Linux uses demand paging to load executable images into memory. When a user executes a command, the executable file is opened and its contents are mapped into the process's virtual memory address space. Pages belonging to other processes might be swapped out to create room for the new process. Linux uses a least recently used page aging technique to

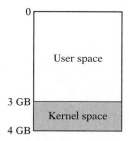

FIGURE 13.15

Linux virtual address space.

decide which pages to swap out. A page that was accessed recently is considered young. In contrast, a page that has not been accessed for some time is stale and is considered old. The oldest pages are swapped out first.

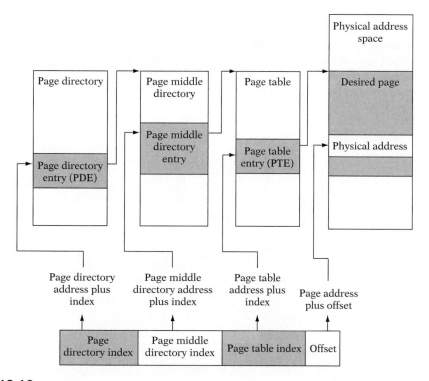

FIGURE 13.16

Linux supports three levels of page tables.

The Linux File System

The native Linux file system, **ext2fs,** resembles the standard UNIX model and can support additional file systems such as Fat32 (Windows) and HFS+ (Macintosh). The kernel maintains a layer called **virtual file system (VFS)** that allows processes to access all file systems uniformly (Figure 13.17). When a process accesses a file, the kernel directs the request to VFS, which calls the appropriate file system.

Like the standard UNIX file systems, ext2fs uses a block-based allocation mechanism. The file contains two logical units: a metadata block and the file's data. The metadata block keeps track of the i-node structure, i-node maps, free block allocation maps, and so on. When data are added to a file they are written in new blocks, so both the metadata and the data must be written to disk. The metadata are written asynchronously, so changes to the data might be written to disk before the metadata. If a system crashes before the metadata are written, the file system can become unstable and, because there is no redundant copy of the i-node table, the data loss can be substantial.

Journaling file systems use a log to keep track of changes to the metadata in an effort to compensate for such problems and provide improved consistency and recoverability. A copy of the metadata is written to the log when the metadata changes. If the system should crash before the metadata are written to disk, the log can be used to undo any partially completed task that would leave the system in any unstable state. ReiserFs, a journaling file system, comes standard with Linux. Other journaling file systems, such as XFS from Silicon Graphics and JFS from IBM, are also available.

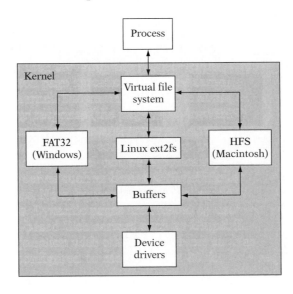

FIGURE 13.17

The virtual file system allows the various processes to access all file systems uniformly.

The Logical Volume Manager

Linux 2.4 incorporates a logical volume manager to support a layer of logical volumes between the physical peripherals and the kernel's I/O interfaces. The **logical volume manager** allows a user to combine two or more physical disks to create a volume group, a virtual disk that can be partitioned into logical volumes upon which file systems can be built. File systems are mounted on these logical volumes instead of on the physical disks.

For example, consider Figure 13.18. At the top are two physical disks, A and B. Disk A is divided into two physical partitions numbered 1 and 2, while disk B contains only partition 3. Using the logical volume manager, it is possible to logically reallocate those three physical partitions into two logical volume groups (Figure 13.18, middle layer). Logical volume group 1 encompasses disk A's physical partition 1 and disk B's physical partition 3. Logical volume group 2 corresponds to disk A's physical partition 2.

Once the logical volume groups are defined, it is possible to reallocate them into logical volumes (Figure 13.18, bottom layer). For example, logical volume group1 might be renamed logical volume 1, allowing the file system to reference the information on physical partitions 1 and 3 as though they occupied a single logical partition. At the same time, logical volume group 2, which holds only a single physical partition, might be divided into logical volume 2 and logical volume 3, effectively simulating a two-partition disk. Note that the physical volumes on which the data are actually stored and the logical volumes referenced by the file system can be quite different from each other.

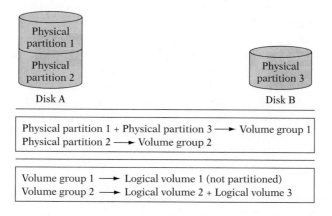

FIGURE 13.18

The logical volume manager allows a user to combine two or more physical disks to create a volume group that can be partitioned into logical volumes.

Multimedia Support

Linux supports many sound cards either directly (by the kernel) or by using technology such as Alsa (Advanced Linux Sound Architecture) that provides the appropriate drivers. On multiuser, multiprocess systems such as Linux, numerous application programs require access to the sound card, and sound servers such as aRts (analog real time synthesizer) fulfill this need. aRts is currently integrated into the KDE environment (Chapter 9) and is scheduled to be integrated into the Linux kernel. Support for video is also available within Linux, although it is less standardized than sound. Drivers for popular hardware acceleration cards are available and can be used effectively by X-Windows, the Linux window manager. Application software for playing back video is packaged with many Linux distributions and includes such software as *xine* and *mplayer* that can play back *mpeg* files, *avi* files, and so on.

Summary

Under UNIX, key resident operating system services are concentrated in a relatively small kernel. To a user, an executing program image appears to be running on a personal pseudocomputer. The image consists of a text segment, a data segment, and a stack segment. The execution of an image is called a process. Processes are created by the *fork* system primitive. The death of a process creates an event signal.

UNIX manages memory space by swapping or paging processes between primary and secondary memory. The process table contains pointers that link each process's segments. The text segment is reentrant, so text segments are tracked in a text table. UNIX supports both block and character devices. Files that represent devices are called special files, and data files are called ordinary files. A system's device drivers are listed in a configuration table. An I/O operation references a device number which is used to search the configuration table for the address of the appropriate device driver.

A UNIX disk is divided into four regions: a boot block, a super block, an i-list, and a data area. The i-list contains a series of i-nodes, each of which defines the disk address of a file. A given i-node's relative position on the i-list is its i-number. The combination of a device number and an i-number uniquely defines a file. A list of open file i-nodes called the system file table is maintained by the operating system. UNIX manages disk space by maintaining a list of free block pointers in the super block. The i-node starts a series of pointers that link a file's blocks, so the blocks need not be contiguous. Block I/O takes place through a system buffer pool. Logical and physical I/O operations are asynchronous. Figure 13.13 is a useful summary of UNIX tables and pointers.

Linux features a layered architecture that resembles UNIX and Windows. Linux can call either a *fork* or a *clone* to create a process. The Linux scheduler is thread based and distinguishes between normal threads and real-time threads. Linux assigns every process 4 GB of virtual address space. The Linux logical volume manager allows a user to combine two or more physical disks to create a volume group that can be partitioned into logical volumes. The native Linux file system, ext2fs, resembles the standard UNIX model and can support additional file systems. The kernel maintains a layer called virtual file system (VFS) that allows processes to access all file systems uniformly. Linux provides considerable multimedia support.

Key Words

clone	kernel
configuration table	logical volume manager
data segment	ordinary file
device driver	personality identifier
device number	POSIX
dirty	process
event	process file table
exec	process id (pid)
exit	process table
ext2fs	signal
file descriptor	special file
file system	stack segment
fork	super block
i-list	system data segment
image	system file table
init	text segment
i-node	text table
i-node table	thread
i-number	virtual file system (VFS)
journaling file system	*wait*

Review Questions

1. What is the UNIX kernel?
2. Briefly explain the pseudocomputer concept. Relate the pseudocomputer concept to the ease-of-use criterion.
3. Describe (or sketch) a UNIX user program image.
4. Distinguish an image from a process.

5. A user's text segment is reentrant and thus can be shared. Data and stack segments, on the other hand, are private. What does this mean? Why is it significant?

6. Why is the system data segment necessary? It is not part of the user's image. Why?

7. Explain how processes are created under UNIX.

8. The *fork* primitive creates two *identical* processes, yet those processes can yield very different results. Explain how.

9. Explain UNIX dispatching. Distinguish between an event and a process. How do time-slicing and interrupts affect the dispatching process?

10. Describe the UNIX swapping process.

11. Why does UNIX need a text table?

12. Explain how UNIX links a peripheral device and an application process.

13. Sketch the contents of a UNIX disk.

14. Explain how UNIX converts a file name to the file's location on disk. Why is the system file table necessary?

15. All block I/O takes place through a buffer pool. Explain.

16. Under UNIX, logical I/O and physical I/O are asynchronous. What does this mean? Why is it significant?

17. Explain how UNIX links the various segments that make up a process. Explain how that process is linked to its physical devices and files.

18. Sketch the Linux architecture.

19. Describe how the Linux task scheduler works.

20. Describe how Linux manages memory.

21. Discuss the Linux file system.

22. Briefly describe Linux multimedia support.

▪ Exercises

1. UNIX is highly portable. What is portability? What makes UNIX so portable? Why is portability important?

2. Under UNIX, a user can visualize his or her image running on a private pseudocomputer. Why is that visualization valuable?

3. Why do you suppose professional programmers find the consistency and elegance of UNIX so appealing?

4. How did the profit motive influence the design of Linux?

5. Figures 13.4, 13.13, and 13.14 are useful templates for organizing many of this chapter's key terms.

CHAPTER 14

Macintosh OS X Internals

When you finish reading this chapter you should be able to:

▶ Identify the four primary layers in the functional view of OS X.

▶ Distinguish between the functional and system software views of OS X.

▶ Identify Darwin's two basic layers.

▶ Define the terms task, thread, message, and message port from an OS X perspective.

▶ Explain the OS X thread scheduling process.

▶ Explain how OS/X manages memory.

▶ Explain how the virtual file system (VFS) allows OS X to support multiple file systems.

▶ Distinguish between HFS+ and UFS and describe the contents of an HFS+ volume.

▶ Distinguish between a user-space device driver and a kernel-space device driver.

▶ Explain how the services provided by I/O Kit support writing device drivers and populating the I/O registry.

◼ Introduction

When Apple introduced the Macintosh in 1984, it was the first system to feature an affordable graphical user interface (GUI). Today's Mac, powered by a 32-bit PowerPC chip manufactured by Motorola, represents the most successful non-Intel personal computer system in the marketplace and enjoys cultlike status within segments of the PC community. With its impressive graphic applications and its legendary ease of use, the Mac has long been a favorite of artistically oriented users, particularly for such applications as desktop publishing and multimedia, and many Mac devotees simply refuse to work with any other platform.

Over the years, Apple has steadily upgraded Mac OS, the Macintosh operating system, assigning each new release a different system number. An improved file system named HFS appeared with the release of OS System 3, cooperative multitasking was added to System 4, Internet and multimedia support were key features of System 7, and System 9 brought support for the PowerPC chip and some multiuser capability. Following the release of System 9, Apple decided to significantly change the Macintosh operating system's internals to keep up with developments in information technology, particularly enhanced hardware capabilities. In 1996, Apple rehired Steven Jobs, one of the company's founders, acquired his NeXT Corporation, and began to integrate features from OpenStep, the NeXT operating system, into the Mac. The end result, **Mac OS X,** combines the stability of UNIX with the Mac's legendary ease of use, incorporating such key features such as preemptive multitasking, memory protection, and symmetric multiprocessing while continuing to support classic Macintosh applications.

◼ OS X Architecture

OS X can be viewed from two different perspectives: a functional view that focuses on the functions the operating system provides to users and a system software view that focuses on the internal services the operating system provides.

The Functional View

From the functional or user-oriented point of view, OS X consists of four layers: Darwin, the graphics subsystem, the application environments, and the Aqua user interface (Figure 14.1).

Darwin, the lowest layer, is the open source UNIX base on which OS X is built; it represents the core of the operating system. Darwin is responsible for kernel and operating system services, memory protection, memory management, high performance file systems, networking, preemptive multitasking, symmetric multiprocessing, multi-threading, network kernel extensions, and device driver support.

The **graphics subsystem** is responsible for screen rendering; in other words, it controls what appears on the display and ensures that type fonts are smooth and not jagged. Within the graphics subsystem, Open GL is a widely adopted application programming interface (API) standard for developing interactive 2D and 3D applications, and Quartz is a 2D graphics environment that supports the portable document format (PDF). QuickTime, another graphics subsystem component, makes available such multimedia applications as creating, editing, and playing back video, audio, animation, graphics, and text and also supports a real-time streaming Web protocol that allows users to view both live and on-demand movies[1]. The graphics subsystem also provides the OS X window server, making windows and event routing services available to the application environments, assigning each application its own window, and routing input from the keyboard and the mouse to the appropriate application.

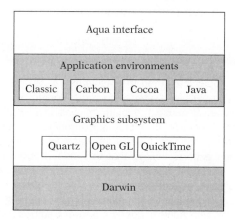

FIGURE 14.1

A functional view of OS X.

---

[1]QuickTime is available as a plug-in application for Windows and other operating environments.

Under OS X, an application program runs in one of four **application environments.** Existing System 9 applications run natively (rather than in emulation mode) within the Classic environment. Carbon makes it relatively easy to migrate System 9 applications to the OS X environment by providing nearly 70 percent of System 9's application programming interfaces, thus allowing older applications to take advantage of such OS X features as the Aqua interface, protected memory, and multiprocessing, often without modification. Cocoa supports native OS X applications and provides an object-oriented framework for rapidly developing those applications. The Java environment adds to Java programs a look and feel consistent with the Aqua user interface.

Aqua is the Mac OS X graphical user interface. It uses the windowing and 2D technology features provided by the graphical subsystem to create attractive controls and menus, photo-quality 128-pixel icons, windows, and drop shadows for menu bars, thus enhancing ease of use. Aqua manages the screen real estate and avoids modal windows to the extent possible. An example of a modal window is a warning message in a dialog box that requires the user to click on an option before the program continues. Aqua improves the user experience by providing nonmodal windows called sheets that attach themselves to the title bar of the document window like sticky notes. At first glance, a nonmodal window resembles a modal window, but a nonmodal window does not interfere with or interrupt the user work flow because the user can perform other tasks before responding.

Open and Closed Standards

Traditionally, Apple marketed the Macintosh as a closed platform, never publishing its flagship operating system's source code and never licensing its system software to anyone. Because the platform was closed, Apple was able to control virtually every aspect of its operating environment, a key factor in the company's ability to provide the user-friendly interface for which the Macintosh is famous. However, many experts believe that this closed environment explains at least in part why the Macintosh has such a limited market share while Microsoft's Windows (a comparable but, at least according to Mac devotees, technically inferior product) has become the dominant personal computer operating system.

In a break with Apple's closed platform tradition, OS X has multiple features that tap into the open source movement. For example, Darwin draws extensively from such open-source environments as Mach and FreeBSD, Apple has released Darwin under an open-source license, and there is a version of Darwin that runs on Intel platforms. OS X also supports other open source licensed software such as the Apache Web server, and Safari, the new OS X browser, is built on Konqueror's (KDE) code base (Chapter 9). The graphics subsystems, the application environments, and the Aqua interface are still proprietary, however, which protects the Macintosh look and feel.

The System Software View

OS X can also be viewed from a system perspective as a set of layers (Figure 14.2). At the top are the Classic, Carbon, Cocoa, and Java application environments you read about in the previous section. To the right of Figure 14.2 is the BSD (Berkeley Software Design) UNIX shell that supports a command line environment. (Because most users prefer a graphical user interface, BSD does not appear in the functional view.) Note that BSD interacts directly with the kernel and the Classic environment interacts directly with each of the other three layers. In contrast, Carbon, Cocoa, and Java interact exclusively with application services.

The **application services** layer provides graphical and windowing services to Classic, Carbon, Cocoa, and Java. Clearly distinguish between an application environment and an application service. Application programs run in an application environment. An application service is an operating system service that supports an application program. Note in Figure 14.2 that QuickTime bridges both layers. QuickTime is a hybrid—it requires a host environment (such as a browser) so it resembles an application service but it offers multimedia services that are found only in an application environment.

The **core services** layer provides all nonwindowing and nongraphical services that are common to all the application environments except BSD, giving OS X the ability to share code and data across environments. The core services layer also provides functions for managing lists, queues, and stacks, programming interfaces for managing processes and threads, and functions for creating and managing interprocess messages. Other core services enable a program to communicate with software running on remote machines using architecture-independent Internet and Web services (Chapter 17).

The bottom layer is the kernel environment provided by Darwin, the subject of the next section.

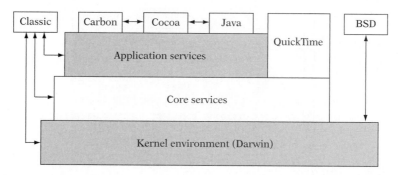

FIGURE 14.2

A system software view of OS X.

◾ Darwin

Darwin, the OS X kernel, is divided into two layers (Figure 14.3). **Mach 3.0,** the kernel's lowest layer, is a microkernel, a compact version of a kernel that implements a limited number of specific tasks and serves as a base for supporting any of several operating systems. The OS X process management services, memory management subsystem, device driver subsystem, and interprocess messaging services are implemented in Mach 3.0. **BSD (Berkeley Software Design) UNIX** is a popular open-source version of UNIX that represents Darwin's second layer. BSD incorporates the OS X networking services, file systems, and user management policies such as security.

Mach 3.0

Mach 3.0 assigns an address space (virtual memory) and the rights to access selected resources to a **task,** the basic OS X resource allocation unit. Each task has access to 4 GB of protected virtual address space. A task is a container for many **threads,** where a thread is the basic unit that Mach schedules for execution on the processor. For example, within a word processing task, spell checking, printing, and editing might be performed by different threads. The function of an OS X task is to manage memory, the virtual address space, and other resources and to provide a framework within which its threads run. The term process (from earlier chapters) typically implies a Mach task and one or more threads.

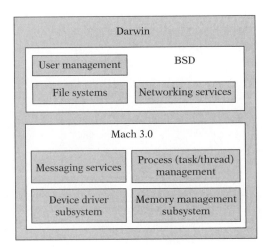

FIGURE 14.3
Darwin, the OS X kernel.

Client tasks access resources by sending **messages** to a **message port**, a secure channel for intertask or interprocess communication. Think of a message port as a protected mailbox or communication channel with its access rights managed by the kernel; in other words, a given task must have the kernel's permission to access a given port. In addition to interprocess communication, Mach's messaging feature also supports remote procedure calls to, as the term implies, procedures stored and executed on another machine. The threads within a task share resources, ports, and the address space. Mach also supports real-time services, provides a scheduler for symmetric multiprocessing (SMP), manages memory, and communicates with peripheral devices through the device driver subsystem. Mach and BSD services run in kernel mode. All other processes run in user mode.

BSD

One of Mach's design goals was portability. Systems designed with portability in mind often take a performance hit because of the need for constant communication and translation between the user mode and the kernel mode processes. To help improve performance, OS X adds a layer of BSD (Berkeley Software Design) UNIX services to the kernel and directly links Mach and BSD. The BSD layer is based primarily on FreeBSD, an open-source implementation of 4.4 BSD[2].

BSD views an active program as a process. Each process maps to a single Mach task and one or more Mach threads. Process management and file systems support are key BSD responsibilities, and because the Internet's underlying protocols (Chapter 17) were created on BSD UNIX systems, it makes sense to assign network services to the BSD layer. Additionally, OS X is a multiuser operating system and such security procedures as verifying user IDs and group IDs and controlling access to shared printers and other shared network resources are implemented in the BSD layer. BSD provides the OS X startup (boot), shutdown, and accounting procedures. Darwin also supports POSIX (the de facto standard portable operating system interface), adding much of the POSIX application programming interface (API) to the FreeBSD base.

---

[2]UC Berkeley's style places the release level first, as in 4.4 BSD, rather than last, as in OS X.

◼ Processor Scheduling

BSD implements processes on top of Mach's task management facility. A task provides a framework for running threads, so a thread represents the basic OS X computational unit.

Thread Scheduling

Mach provides thread support and schedules threads preemptively. A fixed priority thread runs for a fixed quantum of time and then moves to the end of the queue of threads with the same priority. To improve response time for interactive tasks, an alternative is to use a time-sharing policy to raise or lower a thread's priority based on its resource needs. For example, the priority of a thread waiting for input might be raised, while the priority of a compute-bound thread might be lowered.

A given thread is classified into one of four **priority bands** (Figure 14.4). Normal application threads are assigned normal priority. If a thread's priority has been raised by a time-sharing policy, it is assigned system high priority. Kernel mode priority is assigned to threads running in the kernel space. Real time threads are threads that consume a significant fraction of the available clock cycles; for example, an audio-playback program's thread might consume 2,500 of the next 10,000 clock cycles. If a real-time thread were allowed to run continuously it would prevent other threads from running, so real-time threads are typically limited to a percentage of the available clock cycles. Because of the time-sharing scheduling policy enforced by OS X, a given thread can move from one priority band to another, but most threads stay within a single band. For example, if a real-time thread

Priority bands	Characteristics
Normal	Normal application threads
System high priority	Threads whose priority has been raised above normal
Kernel mode threads	Threads created in the kernel that run at a higher priority than all user space threads.
Real-time threads	Threads that need a significant fraction of available clock cycles

FIGURE 14.4

Thread priority bands.

requests a reasonable number of clock cycles, it stays in the real-time band. However, if the real-time thread exhibits compute-bound behavior, its priority might be reduced to a normal thread level.

Multiprocessor Scheduling

Mach and OS X support multiple processors. Processors are grouped into processor sets, with a given processor assigned to only one processor set. A given task is allocated to a specific processor set, and all threads associated with that task execute within the assigned processor set. Each processor schedules its threads as described above.

■ Memory Management

OS X relies on Mach for memory management. A machine-dependent physical mapping module runs in the kernel and is responsible for managing the PowerPC's processor by coordinating the processor's memory cache and address translation operations. A machine independent virtual memory (VM) module also runs in the kernel and is responsible for processing page faults, managing address maps, and swapping pages.

A Mach task sees a large, sparsely populated, nonlinear, noncontiguous 4 GB virtual address space. The virtual address space is divided into text, data, stack, and mapped file regions that are separated by undefined, unallocated address spaces (Figure 14.5). The regions are themselves divided into pages, and it is the pages that are swapped between virtual memory and physical memory. If a thread accesses a region not currently in physical memory, Mach creates a page fault and swaps the appropriate address space into physical memory.

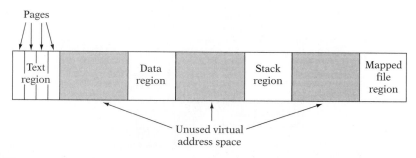

FIGURE 14.5

Virtual address space.

The kernel associates a **VM object** with each region in the virtual address space. The VM object is used to track and manage the resident (in physical memory) and nonresident portions of the memory region. Each VM object is managed by a **pager,** a task that is used to move data between the backing store (usually disk) and physical memory. Implicitly, each VM object is associated with a given pager through its memory object. A **memory object** is a specific source of data, such as a file. Logically, you can think of the memory object as a repository for data upon which various operations (read and write) can be performed.

The pager is the task that has the right to access the memory object's port. When a process needs data in its virtual address space, the VM object sends to the memory object a message requesting that the address be populated with data. The pager reads this request, and transfers the data to the address. When Mach needs to reclaim the page, it notifies the pager to transfer it back to disk.

OS X supports two pagers: a default pager and a vnode pager (Figure 14.6). The default pager is a system manager that maps nonresident virtual memory pages to the swap space and fetches them when requested. The default pager handles nonpersistent memory that exists only during the life of the task. The role of the default pager is swap space management. It stores dirty pages (pages with modified data) and finds the dirty pages when they are needed again.

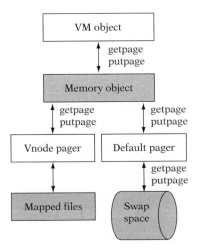

FIGURE 14.6

VM objects and pagers.

The vnode pager handles VM objects that map files accessed via a file system. When a page request is received, the pager loads the physical memory page with the file contents. When a vnode pager is asked to save a page, it simply writes the page back to the file. Thus, the vnode pager allows the task (or the process) to read and write the contents of the file as though it were reading and writing memory (Figure 14.6). You will read more about vnodes in the next section.

When a new task (or process) is created, it is cloned (or copied) from a parent. The underlying memory address space is cloned as well, so the new task inherits and either shares or copies the address space. Mach uses **copy-on-write,** a form of delayed copy, to speed up this process. Copy-on-write is done via protected sharing; in other words, both tasks are granted read-only access to the shared memory (Figure 14.7a). If either task modifies a portion of shared memory, Mach makes another copy of the modified range and gives the initiating task write access (Figure 14.7b).

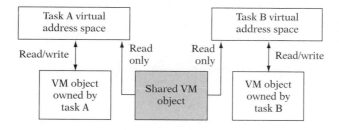

FIGURE 14.7

Copy on write.

a. When a new task is created, it is cloned (or copied) from a parent.

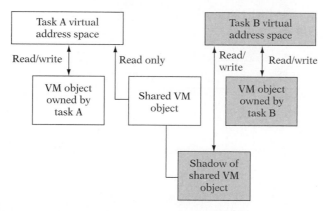

b. If a task modifies a portion of shared memory, Mach makes another copy and gives the task write access.

◼ File Systems

Before OS X was released, the standard Mac OS file system was called **hierarchical file system plus (HFS+),** also known as the extended file system (efs). OS X supports as its primary file systems both HFS+ and the BSD **UNIX file system (UFS).** Additionally, OS X supports several file systems that enable file sharing over a network, including network file system (NFS), a Microsoft Windows standard called server message block (SMB), and a proprietary Macintosh standard called AppleTalk filing protocol (AFP). Finally, two multimedia file systems are supported: ISO9660 for CD-ROM and universal disk format (UDF) for DVD.

OS X supports multiple file systems through a kernel layer **virtual file system** or **VFS** that separates file-system generic operations from specific implementations (Figure 14.8). VFS uses a file representation structure called a **vnode.** A vnode operation or VOP call is used to perform operations on a file within the file system (read, write, and so on); note that there is a unique vnode for each active file or folder. An operation or a request by a task to read from or write to a file is translated to a corresponding I/O request on the specific file system and the results are returned to the task. A VFS vnode resembles a UNIX i-node, but vnode ids are unique network wide while UNIX i-nodes are unique only within a specific file system.

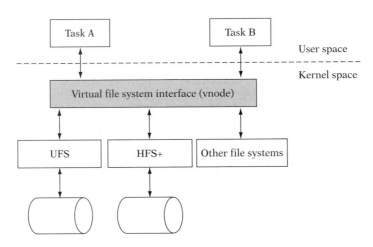

FIGURE 14.8

The virtual file system (VFS).

HFS+

An HFS file has two forks, a data fork and a resource fork, either or both of which can be empty (Figure 14.9). The data fork contains the same information as a regular file in UNIX or Windows. The resource fork contains Macintosh resources (data in a special format) that describe the menus, dialog boxes, icons, and so on associated with the file. The advantage of using a resource fork is that it enables such features as displaying menu items in the appropriate local language (English, French, Italian, Arabic...).

HFS+ specifies how a volume is stored on a disk by using a number of structures to manage the organization of data in the volume (Figure 14.10). Starting to the left of Figure 14.10, the first two sectors on every Macintosh volume are boot blocks. These blocks contain instructions and information essential to boot (start up) a system. The **volume header** is stored in sector 3 and contains information about the entire volume, including the number of files stored on the volume, the date and time the volume was created, and the location of other key structures. A copy of the volume header called the alternate volume header is stored in the next to last sector, 1024 bytes from the volume's end. The remaining structures can appear anywhere between the volume header and the alternate volume header.

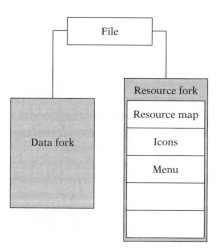

FIGURE 14.9

An OS X file has two forks.

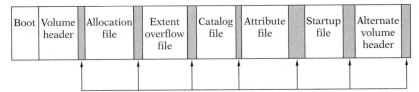

FIGURE 14.10

The contents of an HFS+ volume.

HFS+ allocates sectors in groups called allocation blocks. Typically, each allocation block holds 4 KB of storage space. The **allocation file** uses a bitmap (a bit for every block on disk) to indicate whether each block has or has not been used. An extent is a contiguous range of allocation blocks that is allocated to a fork. The first eight extents of a user file associated with a given fork are stored in the volume's catalog. The remaining extents are stored in an extent overflow file, another HFS+ volume structure. Defective portions of the medium (usually disk) are listed in a bad block file within the extent overflow file and not allocated.

The **catalog file** describes the volume's folder/file hierarchy, holds vital information about those files and folders in the files' data and resource forks, and enables quick searches for files in the hierarchy. Each file or folder name consists of up to 255 Unicode characters[3]. The attribute file contains additional data for a file or folder and is meant for future use for storing information about new forks. Finally, the startup file facilitates booting of non-Macintosh operating systems from an HFS+ plus volume.

UFS

HFS+ is the default file system on most Macintosh systems, but UFS (UNIX file system) is sometimes used instead, particularly in client/server environments. HFS+ stores data in multiple forks. In contrast, UFS stores only a single data fork. OS X provides commands to copy and move files between the two file systems and tries whenever possible to preserve the resource fork information within UFS. For example, when you move a file from an HFS+ to a UFS file system, OS X copies the data fork and resource fork separately and stores them as two separate files in the UFS system, using the same name for both but prefixing a dot underscore (._) to the resource fork name to distinguish them.

---

[3]Unicode is a 16-bit character set that can represent as many as 65,536 unique characters including the characters used in numerous foreign languages.

Other key differences involve file names and path names. UFS is case sensitive, so *Letters, LETTERS,* and *letters* are three different files. HFS+, in contrast, is case insensitive, so *Letters, LETTERS,* and *letters* are simply versions of the same file name. Within a path name, HFS+ uses a colon as a separator while UFS uses a slash (/). OS X can translate between the two as necessary.

Aliases and symbolic links are used to maintain references to files within a file system and allow you to refer to a file using a different name. In HFS+ an alias refers to both the path name and the unique file name, while UFS uses only the path name to store a symbolic link. If you move a UFS file from its original location you change the path name, so USF can no longer find the file. In contrast, HFS+ tries the path name first. If the file cannot be found, HFS+ uses the file's unique name and then updates the path name.

One advantage UFS enjoys is the ability to store sparse files efficiently. Space is allocated in 4 KB blocks, so a file that contains fewer than 4 KB will not fill the first allocation block. UFS can store the data without storing the unused space, but HFS+ fills the unused space and uses the entire 4 KB.

Device Drivers

A device driver provides an abstract view of a hardware device to the software layers above it. OS X supports two types of device drivers (Figure 14.11). As the names imply, a **user-space driver** runs in an application program's virtual address space and a **kernel-space driver** runs in the kernel's

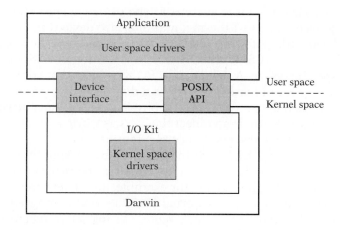

FIGURE 14.11

OS X supports user-space and kernel-space device drivers.

address space. User-space drivers are preferred because kernel-space drivers are difficult to write and if something goes wrong they can crash the system, but both types are used. For example, security considerations sometimes rule out direct user space access to a particular hardware device, and if multiple user programs frequently access the same device it makes more sense to use a shared kernel-space driver than it does to replicate a user-space driver in each application.

A user space driver communicates with the kernel either by calling a BSD POSIX procedure or by accessing a device interface that allows a program in user space to communicate with the kernel to control a specific device (Figure 14.11). For example, if an application wants to communicate with an SCSI (small computer system interface or "skuzzy") compatible scanner, the application calls the device interface which sends the request to the SCSI device driver via a communication channel called a nub (Figure 14.12). Nubs are more fully defined in the next section.

I/O Kit

The device files and device interfaces that support the OS X file systems are made available by **I/O Kit,** the OS X device driver subsystem. Device drivers are difficult to write. Not only do they require the programmer to know how to control a specific peripheral device, but other hardware components, such as buses, call for hardware-specific code, too. I/O Kit is an object-oriented framework (similar to an application programming interface) that simplifies the process of creating device drivers.

I/O Kit supports three major types of entities. **Family** is an object that provides a software abstraction common to all devices of a particular type. Think of a family as a library of methods and data associated with a particular class of device such as a type of bus, a class of disk devices, network services such as Ethernet, and interface devices such as the mouse and the keyboard. Note that the support provided by a family is generic; in other words, the SCSI family provides services for all SCSI devices but not for any specific device. A **driver** is an I/O Kit object that communicates with a specific piece of hardware such as a disk drive or a scanning device. Except for drivers that control a specific physical device, each driver is associated with a family. A **nub** is an object that acts as a bridge or communication channel between two drivers (hence two families).

Using I/O Kit's built-in software objects simplifies the task of writing a device driver. A good way to visualize the process is as a series of layers (Figure 14.13). Imagine, for example, an ink jet printer that is connected to the computer via an external USB bus that is plugged into an internal PCI bus. The top layer, which holds the ink jet printer driver and the ink jet printer family, is specific to the device—it drives the printer. The USB driver/USB family layer is more generic, holding methods and data that

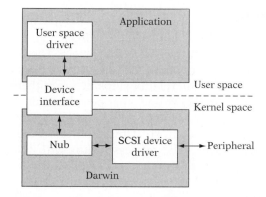

FIGURE 14.12

Accessing a device through the device interface.

apply to any USB connection, including the scanner, an ink jet printer, a mouse, and so on. At the bottom layer, the PCI bus driver and the PCI family are methods and data that apply to any PCI connection but not to the attached buses. Those three layers are connected by nubs. Rather than writing an ink jet printer driver that incorporates code to communicate with the printer, the USB bus controller, *and* the PCI bus driver, the programmer using I/O Kit writes only the printer-specific code and uses the USB and PCI code from the lower layers.

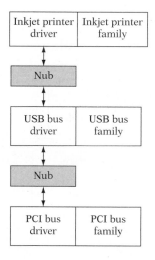

FIGURE 14.13

I/O Kit's objects as a series of layers.

I/O Registry

Inside OS X, the services provided by I/O Kit are used to provide an abstraction for each device attached to the system. These abstractions are stored in the **I/O registry,** a dynamic database that keeps track of active nubs and drivers and tracks the relationships between them. Active programs check the I/O registry to determine what peripheral devices are available.

The I/O registry is stored only in memory and is not archived when the computer is shut down, so it must be recreated each time the system is booted or restarted. The process begins with the I/O registry's root node, which starts the platform driver. The platform driver responds by creating a nub for each bus on the system (Figure 14.14). Each of those nubs then searches the **I/O catalog,** a library of the system's available device drivers, and loads the driver and associated family for each bus type. Each bus driver checks its bus and generates a nub for each peripheral or external bus card plugged into it; for example, the USB bus driver identifies each device attached to the USB bus and creates a nub for each one. Each of those nubs, in turn, loads the appropriate device driver and its associated family. The result resembles an inverted tree, with each lower level child driver/family linked to its parent driver/family by a nub.

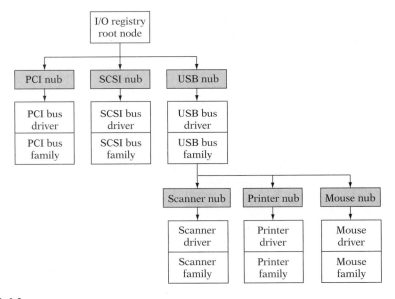

FIGURE 14.14

Building the I/O registry.

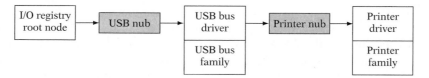

FIGURE 14.15

Adding a new device to the I/O registry.

After the system is running, if a peripheral is added to or removed from the system the registry is immediately updated with the new configuration. For example, imagine that the user plugs an ink jet printer into a USB port. Following a process that resembles the boot process, the printer's device driver is linked by nubs to the intermediate driver/family objects (Figure 14.15), and that path is stored in the I/O registry.

Windows Compatibility

In spite of its legendary ease of use and technically impressive architecture, sales of the Macintosh platform have consistently lagged behind Windows, accounting for less than five percent of personal computer sales. The reasons most often cited for the Mac's relatively poor market showing include Apple's closed platform strategy and the limited availability of Mac-compatible application software, but those issues are beginning to fade. Today, there are Mac-compatible versions of many popular applications including the Microsoft Office suite, Internet Explorer, and Quicken, and those programs use the same file formats on both the Windows and Macintosh platforms so file exchange is not a problem. More important, however, is the Mac's compatibility with such open source standards as the Internet (Chapter 17), the universal serial bus (USB), and Apple's own FireWire bus (a trademarked name for Apple's version of the IEEE 1394 standard). Such standards make it relatively easy for a Macintosh system and a Windows system to communicate and allow a Macintosh computer to operate transparently on a network designed with Windows platforms in mind. Networks are the subject of Part Five.

■ QuickTime

QuickTime is the OS X multimedia component that allows a user to play back audio, video, graphics, and animation. QuickTime supports most of the major file formats used for audio, video, and animation and it is portable across different environments, including Windows and Java.

QuickTime consists of a set of managers (Figure 14.16). Starting on the left, the Movie Toolbox provides functions that an application program can use to store, retrieve, edit, and play back movies. QuickTime provides a number of built-in components such as image processors, media handlers, and other utilities that enable multimedia to be played back and provide services to the managers and applications; for example, the sound manager can be used to play back audio tracks such as a movie's soundtrack. These components are registered with the component manager. Application programs access the various components through the component manager. Components are extensible; in other words, QuickTime makes it possible to develop new component processes and register them with the component manager. The image compression manager provides a set of device and driver independent functions to compress and decompress images. Most applications access and use QuickTime by calling functions in the Movie Toolbox.

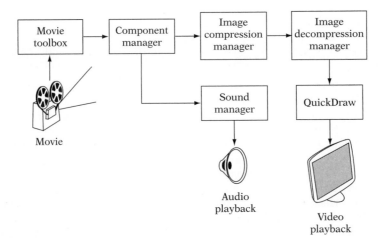

FIGURE 14.16

The QuickTime architecture.

◼ Summary

The four primary layers in the functional view of OS X are Darwin, the graphics subsystems, the application environments, and the Aqua interface. The application environments include Classic, Carbon, Cocoa, and Java. OS X can also be viewed from a system software perspective, with the application environments communicating with core services and Darwin via an application services layer.

Darwin is the OS X open source kernel. Within Darwin, Mach 3.0 is responsible for process, task, and thread management, memory management, intertask messaging services, and the device driver subsystem. BSD adds file systems, user management services, and networking services to Darwin, including the virtual file system (VFS), that allows OS X to support multiple file systems such as HFS+ and UFS. Device drivers can reside in user space or kernel space. The services provided by I/O Kit support writing device drivers and populating the I/O registry. QuickTime is the OS X multimedia component

◼ Key Words

allocation file	kernel-space driver
application environment	Mac OS X
application services	Mach 3.0
Aqua	memory object
BSD (Berkeley Software Design) UNIX	message
catalog file	message port
copy-on-write	nub
core services	pager
Darwin	priority bands
driver	QuickTime
family	task
graphics subsystem	thread
HFS+ (hierarchical file system plus)	UFS (UNIX file system)
I/O catalog	user-space driver
I/O Kit	virtual file system (VFS)
I/O registry	VM object
	vnode
	volume header

▉ Review Questions

1. Identify the four primary layers in the functional view of OS X.
2. What functions are performed by the OS X graphic subsystems?
3. Differentiate the Classic, Carbon, Cocoa, and Java application environments.
4. Distinguish between the functional and system software views of OS X.
5. What is Darwin? Identify Darwin's two basic layers.
6. Why is Darwin broken into two layers?
7. Define the terms task, thread, message, and message port from an OS X perspective.
8. Explain the OS X thread scheduling process.
9. Explain how OS/X manages memory.
10. How does the virtual file system (VFS) allow OS X to support multiple file systems?
11. Describe the contents of an HFS+ volume.
12. Distinguish between HFS+ and UFS.
13. Distinguish between a user-space device driver and a kernel-space device driver. User-space device drivers are preferred. Why? Under what conditions is a kernel-space driver considered a better choice?
14. Explain how the services provided by I/O Kit support writing device drivers.
15. Explain how the services provided by I/O Kit support populating the I/O registry.
16. What is QuickTime? What does QuickTime do?

▉ Exercises

1. How do you suppose a closed platform helped Apple maintain the Macintosh's user friendly interface?
2. Talk to a committed Macintosh user and ask why he or she prefers the Mac over such alternatives as a Windows platform. If you are not already aware, you might be surprised about how strongly Mac users feel about their platform of choice.
3. How does a closed platform help to explain the Macintosh's limited market success?
4. Relate I/O Kit families to the object-oriented inheritance principle.
5. What are the marketing implications of Apple's decision to adopt open source standards for OS X?
6. Looking beyond marketing, what factors do you suppose might have influenced Apple to adopt open standards for OS X? Note your initial thoughts now, and return to this question after you have completed Part Five.
7. Figures 14.2, 14.3, 14.10, and 14.14 are useful templates for organizing many of this chapter's key terms.

CHAPTER 15

MVS Internals

When you finish reading this chapter you should be able to:

▶ Identify the key fields in a traditional IBM mainframe's PSW.

▶ Describe how physical I/O is performed on a traditional IBM mainframe.

▶ Explain how the interrupt concept is implemented on a traditional IBM mainframe.

▶ Describe the relationship between software-generated interrupts and privileged instructions.

▶ Distinguish between a job and a task.

▶ Describe the functions performed by job management.

▶ Describe the functions performed by task management.

▶ Identify the key control blocks that support the dispatching process.

▶ Discuss the traditional IBM mainframe dispatching process.

◪ Traditional Mainframes

To this point, you have focused on personal computer operating systems[1]. Mainframes are different. This chapter is concerned with the internal workings of a traditional mainframe; more specifically on an early 1980s IBM mainframe running under an operating system called **MVS.** The intent is to give you a sense of how the dispatching process works on such a machine. In the days before PCs and the Internet, IBM's mainframes dominated the information technology marketplace. Initially, the mainframe operating systems were designed to concurrently process several batch applications. Over time, the number of concurrent applications increased and eventually such innovations as virtual memory, multiple virtual machines, time sharing, and interactivity enhanced the operating environment, but the underlying architecture of the operating system still reflected its batch processing roots.

In contrast, today's dominant distributed information technology environment (the subject of Part 5) is highly interactive, with a myriad of personal computers and workstations simultaneously communicating with a variety of remote service providers via the Internet and similar networks. Clearly, the operating systems that function in such a complex, distributed environment have outgrown their batch roots. Traditional batch-oriented operating systems still exist, however, running primarily as virtual machines under a higher-level operating system.

Although they represent old technology, traditional mainframe operating systems such as MVS do, however, offer one significant advantage—relative simplicity. A modern distributed system is incredibly complex and is best studied by focusing on the interrelated layers rather than on the contents of any given layer. It is, however, possible to understand the internal logic of an MVS operating system, and what happens within a stand-alone computer is a pretty good reflection of what happens inside one of those complex, distributed system's independent layers.

---

[1]Although UNIX can be scaled to run on virtually any platform, Chapters 9 and 13 were written from a microcomputer perspective.

IBM's Traditional Mainframes

To many experts, the modern computer era began in 1964 when IBM released the System/360 family of computers. For the first time, customers were presented with a set of architecturally compatible machines that allowed the organization to start small and upgrade to a more powerful mainframe without rewriting existing software or reformatting existing data. By the early 1970s, when the System/370 family replaced the System/360, IBM was clearly the dominant force in information technology, and its products defined a set of de facto standards that shaped the industry until the microcomputer revolution of the 1980s changed the landscape.

The first System/360 computers ran one of three batch-oriented, multiprogramming operating systems: DOS (*not* MS-DOS), OS/MFT, and OS/MVT. DOS was an entry level system that initially supported only two concurrent application programs and was not fully compatible with the other two operating systems. OS/MFT supported up to fifteen concurrent applications in fixed partitions, while OS/MVT supported up to fifteen applications in dynamically allocated regions. DOS evolved into DOS/VSE and, eventually, VSE. Over time, OS/MVT evolved into MVS, a sophisticated operating system that controlled multiple virtual systems. Although the batch processing era is clearly over, IBM's traditional mainframe operating systems helped to set the stage for today's interactive environments.

■ Traditional IBM Mainframe Operating Principles

Before you consider MVS internals, you must understand a few basic IBM mainframe operating principles. These principles reflect the mechanism by which the operating system layer communicates with the hardware layer.

The Program Status Word

A computer executes one instruction during each machine cycle. The instruction control unit looks to the instruction counter for the address of its next instruction. An IBM mainframe's instruction counter is called the **program status** word or **PSW** (Figure 15.1).

Three PSW fields are particularly relevant to this chapter. Bits 8-11 hold the **protection key.** Each partition is assigned its own unique protection key, and the operating system's memory management function uses the protection key to ensure that one task does not attempt to modify the space assigned to another task. Bits 14 and 15 indicate the task's state—more about that later. The last 31 bits hold the **instruction address,** the address of the next instruction to be executed. In generic terms, those 31 bits are the instruction counter.

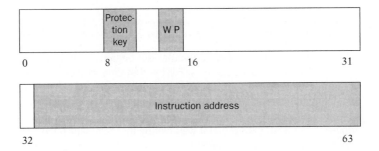

FIGURE 15.1

The program status word.

Physical I/O

External devices are attached to a traditional IBM mainframe through channels. A channel is a special-purpose computer. Because it has its own, independent processor, the channel can function in parallel with the main processor, thus freeing the mainframe to do other work.

Like any computer, a channel executes instructions. The channel's instructions are stored in a **channel program.** The channel's function is to transfer a certain number of bytes from a peripheral device into memory (or from memory to a peripheral device), so among the key parameters that must be included in the channel program are a byte count and a memory address. The channel program is stored in the main computer's memory and passed to the channel when the I/O operation begins.

A channel program consists of one or more **channel command words** (Figure 15.2). Each **CCW** contains a command code that specifies the operation to be performed (e.g., read, write, or seek), a data address, a byte count, and several flags. Programmers can write their own channel programs, but rarely do. Instead, the channel program is typically part of an access method.

Just before it starts a physical I/O operation, the mainframe operating system places the address of the channel program's first CCW in the **channel address word (CAW)** (Figure 15.3). Note that the CAW also holds the requesting partition's protection key. The protection key, remember, uniquely identifies the partition that originated the I/O request. Refer to Figure 15.4. When the channel's processor receives a start I/O (SIO) command from the main processor (1), it copies the channel address word into the channel's instruction counter (2). Then the channel fetches and executes the first channel command word (3).

The channel and the computer are asynchronous; in other words, they function independently. Consequently, the main processor has no way of knowing when the channel has completed its work unless the channel tells it. Thus, when the I/O operation is finished, the channel signals the main processor and reports its status to the operating system through the **channel status word** or **CSW** (Figure 15.5). Note again that the requesting partition's protection key occupies the first four bits in the channel status word.

FIGURE 15.2

The format of a channel command word (CCW).

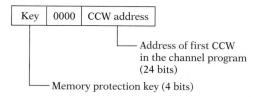

FIGURE 15.3

The channel address word (CAW).

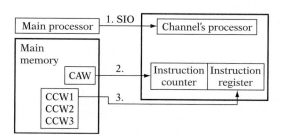

FIGURE 15.4

The channel's processor looks to the channel address word to find the first channel command word.

Key		Command address	Status	Byte count

FIGURE 15.5

The channel status word (CSW).

Interrupts

The signal that flashes from a channel to the processor is called an **interrupt.** A traditional IBM mainframe's hardware responds to an interrupt signal by switching PSWs. Three fields are involved: the **current PSW,** an **old PSW,** and a **new PSW.** The current PSW is the special register that holds the address of the next instruction to be executed. The old PSW is located in memory. The new PSW (also found in memory) holds the address of an interrupt handling routine in the operating system.

When an interrupt occurs, hardware stores the current program status word in the old PSW field and then loads the new PSW into the current PSW register (Figure 15.6). Note that following the interrupt, the current PSW points to the interrupt handling routine. Thus, as the processor begins its next machine cycle, it fetches the instruction whose address is in the program status word and starts the interrupt handling routine. Note also that the old PSW holds the address of the next instruction in the original application program, so after the interrupt is processed, the application program can be resumed.

Traditional IBM mainframes recognize six different interrupt types. Because the channels and the main processor work independently, the channel must signal the processor when an I/O operation is completed by sending it an **input/output (I/O) interrupt.** A **restart interrupt** allows an operator or another processor to intervene and start a program. An **external interrupt** comes from the operator's console, another processor, or the timer. A **machine check interrupt** occurs when the computer's self-checking circuitry detects a hardware failure.

Not all interrupts originate with hardware. A **supervisor call (SVC) interrupt** is issued when a program executes an SVC instruction, such as

```
SVC  17
```

The operand, in this case 17, requests a particular supervisor routine. An SVC interrupt is generated by a valid instruction. In contrast, a **program interrupt** is the result of an illegal or invalid instruction. Consequently, SVC and program interrupts are mutually exclusive because a given instruction cannot possibly be simultaneously valid and invalid.

Permanent Storage Assignments

The old and new PSWs, the channel status word, and the channel address word are stored in the same fixed memory locations on every traditional IBM mainframe (Figure 15.7). They, along with the computer's control registers, represent the primary interface between hardware and software.

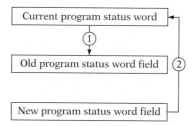

FIGURE 15.6
Switching PSWs.

Program States and Privileged Instructions

The computer, at any given time, is either executing an application program or a supervisor routine; in other words, it is either in the **problem state** or the **supervisory state.** PSW bit 15 indicates the computer's state—1 means problem and 0 means supervisory.

Address		Purpose
Decimal	Hexadecimal	
0	0	Restart new PSW
8	8	Restart old PSW
16	10	Unused
24	18	External old PSW
32	20	Supervisor call old PSW
40	28	Program old PSW
48	30	Machine check old PSW
56	38	Input/output old PSW
64	40	Channel status word
72	48	Channel address word
76	4C	Unused
80	50	Timer
84	54	Unused
88	58	External new PSW
96	60	Supervisor call new PSW
104	68	Program new PSW
112	70	Machine check new PSW
120	78	Input/output new PSW

FIGURE 15.7
Fixed memory locations.

Privileged instructions can be executed only in supervisory state. For example, because the instructions that directly control physical I/O are privileged, an application program must issue an SVC to request the operating system's support to perform an I/O operation. As you learned in Chapter 6, activating the operating system at the beginning and the end of each I/O operation is an important key to multiprogramming.

Additionally, a given program is either ready to resume processing or waiting for the completion of some event such as an I/O operation; in other words, it is either in a **ready state** or a **wait state.** A 0 in PSW bit 14 means ready; a 1 means wait.

Operating System Functions

In addition to key principles of operation, you must also understand the functions performed by several operating system routines.

Job and Task Management

To a programmer, a test run is a single job that generates a listing and a set of results. To the computer, this job involves three distinct steps or tasks: compile, link edit, and execute. A **task** is a single program or routine that has been loaded on the computer and is ready to run. A **job** consists of one or more related tasks. The programmer visualizes a job. The computer loads and executes tasks.

Within the operating system, the routines that dispatch, queue, schedule, load, initiate, and terminate jobs or tasks are part of **job management.** Note that job management is concerned with job-to-job and task-to-task *transitions*. Once a program or routine has been loaded into memory and started, **task management** supports it as it runs by handling interrupts.

The Master Scheduler

The **master scheduler** (Figure 15.8), a key job management routine, is the MVS dispatcher. With several application tasks sharing memory, it is inevitable that two or more will be ready to use the processor at the same time. The master scheduler resolves this conflict by following an algorithm to select the next task to run. The operator can issue an external interrupt to communicate with the master scheduler and thus override standard system action, perhaps improving the priority of a "hot" routine or canceling a task locked in an endless loop.

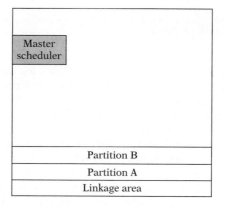

FIGURE 15.8

The master scheduler is the dispatcher.

The Initiator/Terminator

The **initiator/terminator** is a transient module that occupies memory only when needed (Figure 15.9). When a partition becomes available, the initiator/terminator reads the next job step from a queue and loads it into memory. Once the job step enters memory, it becomes a task. Later, the terminator cleans up the partition when the task ends. Because the initiator/terminator starts and ends tasks (two obvious transition points), it is part of job management.

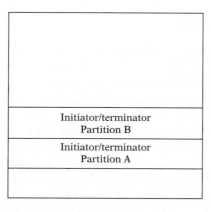

FIGURE 15.9

Each partition has its own initiator/terminator.

Job Control Language

IBM's traditional mainframe operating systems were designed to support a batch processing environment. In a batch environment, the complete job, including all the related programs or job steps and their peripheral device requirements, must be specified in advance and submitted to a computer operator or an operating system scheduler routine so it can be placed in a queue for eventual processing. The specifications are defined in a series of job control language (JCL) statements.

An OS/JCL job stream consists of three types of JCL statements. Every job begins with a JOB statement that defines such things as accounting parameters and the job's class or external priority. Each job step is defined by an EXEC (execute) statement that identifies the program to be loaded and executed. For example, a compile, link edit, and execute job would have three EXEC statements—one for the compiler, one for the linkage editor, and one for the load module. The peripheral devices needed to support a given job step are specified in a series of DD (data definition) statements that follow the step's EXEC statement. Think of each JCL statement as a single line command and a job's complete job stream as a batch file or a script.

Initially, the JCL statements were keypunched and a job was submitted to the computer center as a deck of punched cards. Over time, terminals replaced the keypunches, the JCL statements were typed with each card becoming one line, the complete job stream was stored as a file, and the file was submitted to the mainframe for processing. Although using a terminal was more convenient than punching cards, the JCL line command interface could hardly be called user friendly. In fact, the JCL statements were typically prepared and submitted by computer professionals and ordinary users rarely if ever worked with them. Today's graphical user interfaces can seem intimidating at times, but they are orders of magnitude more user friendly than batch JCL.

You will find a brief introduction to MVS JCL in Appendix D.

Task Management

Task management supports a program as it runs. A task management interrupt handling routine is activated following an interrupt. After the interrupt has been processed, task management calls job management's master scheduler, which selects the next task to be executed.

On a traditional IBM mainframe, interrupts are implemented by switching program status words, so the old PSW field provides a link back to the task that was executing at the time the interrupt occurred. Call the active task X. Following the interrupt, the master scheduler might start some other higher priority task before it restarts task X. Thus, the contents of the old PSW must be stored, because if another task is activated first, the link back to task X might be destroyed by a subsequent interrupt. Task management is responsible for saving the old PSW.

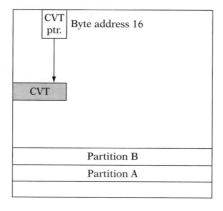

FIGURE 15.10

The communication vector table holds the addresses of key system control blocks.

Control Blocks

Job management, task management, and application program routines are linked through a series of **control blocks** that hold key control information in memory. The **communication vector table** or **CVT** (Figure 15.10) holds system constants and pointers. Each partition has its own **task control block** or **TCB** (Figure 15.11). The communication vector table points to the first partition's TCB, which points to the second partition's TCB, which points to the third, and so on, forming a linked list called a TCB queue.

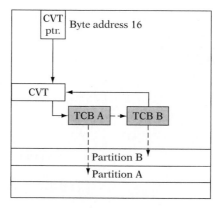

FIGURE 15.11

The TCBs are linked by pointers.

The contents of a given partition are described in a series of **request blocks** spun off the partition's task control block (Figure 15.12). The existence of a **program request block** or **PRB** indicates that the partition holds an active task. If a supervisor call interrupt is being processed in support of the partition, this fact is indicated by a **supervisor request block** or **SVRB,** so each TCB can have several request blocks attached to it. Note that each request block identifies one active task executing in or in support of the partition. Following any interrupt, task management stores the interrupted task's old PSW plus other key control fields in the appropriate request block. If the request block queue is empty, so is the partition. The terminator deletes no longer needed request blocks following task completion.

■ The Dispatching Process

At this point, you have enough information to following the MVS dispatching process through a few nanoseconds of system time. Quickly review the essential concepts before you begin.

The master scheduler is activated after any interrupt. It selects the next task by following the pointers through the task control block queue (or linked list). The communication vector table points to the high priority partition's task control block. If the task in the first partition is ready, the master scheduler starts it. If the task in the first partition is waiting, however, the master scheduler looks to the second partition's task control block. One by one, it follows the pointers from TCB to TCB, starting the first ready task it finds. Thus, on a system with fifteen active partitions, the task at the end of the TCB queue is allowed to execute only if the fourteen higher priority tasks are *all* in a wait state.

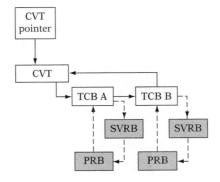

FIGURE 15.12

A request block queue is linked to each task control block.

Starting the First Task

As the example begins, the computer's two partitions, A and B, are both empty and the master scheduler is executing. The communication vector table points to the first (highest priority) task control block, which has no active request blocks (Figure 15.13). Because this first partition is empty, the master scheduler creates a program request block, loads the initiator/terminator into partition A, and starts it (Figure 15.14). The initiator/terminator, in turn, reads the first task from the job queue and loads it into the partition. For simplicity, ignore the time delay inherent in loading the task.

Soon, the application routine finds itself in need of input data, so it executes a supervisor call (SVC) instruction (Figure 15.15). The resulting SVC interrupt starts the SVC interrupt handling routine (Figure 15.16). The interrupt handler stores the old SVC PSW in the Class A partition's program request block and attaches a supervisor request block to the queue (Figure 15.17). After storing the channel program address in the channel address word, the interrupt handling routine executes a privileged start I/O instruction and then waits until the channel reports its status through the channel status word. Finally, the wait state bit in the original task's PSW (which is stored in the program request block) is set to 1 (wait state), and the master scheduler is called.

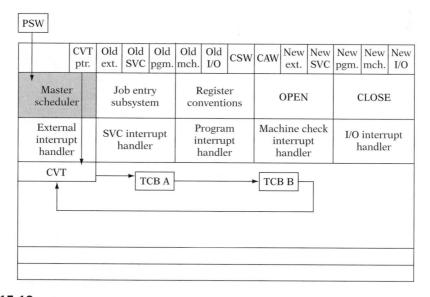

FIGURE 15.13

The master scheduler finds an open partition.

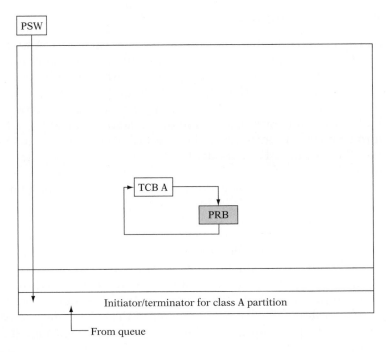

FIGURE 15.14

The initiator/terminator loads a task.

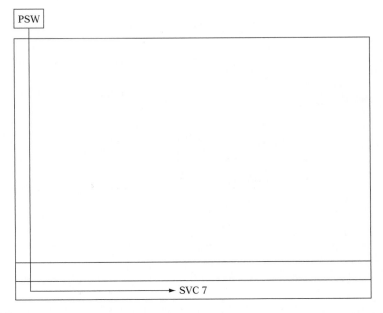

FIGURE 15.15

The application task executes an SVC instruction.

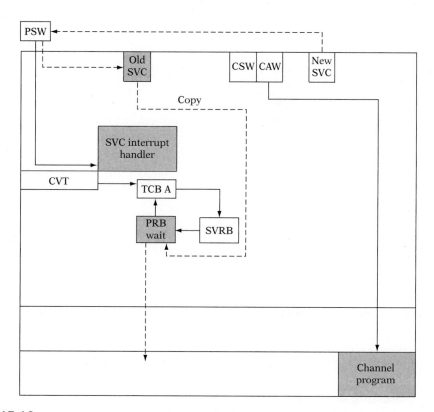

FIGURE 15.16

The interrupt handling routine starts the I/O operation.

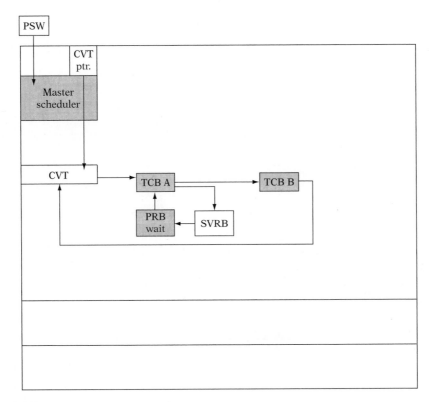

FIGURE 15.17

The task in the class A partition is in a wait state.

Starting a Second Task

Once again, the master scheduler searches the TCB queue. The communication vector table points to partition A's task control block. The partition is active (there are request blocks present), but the PSW field in the program request block indicates a wait state (Figure 15.17). Since the first partition's task is waiting, the master scheduler follows the pointer to the second task control block. Because no request blocks are chained off this second TCB, the master scheduler knows the partition is empty, so it loads the initiator/terminator into partition B (Figure 15.18) and the initiator/terminator subsequently loads a task (Figure 15.19).

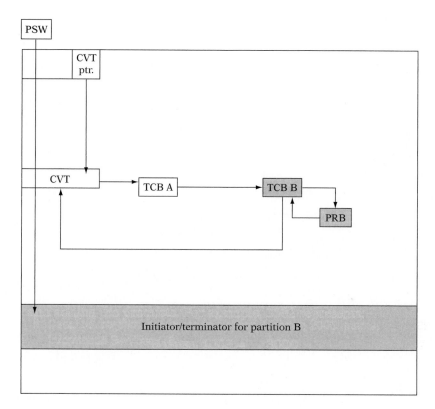

FIGURE 15.18

The master scheduler loads the initiator/terminator into partition B.

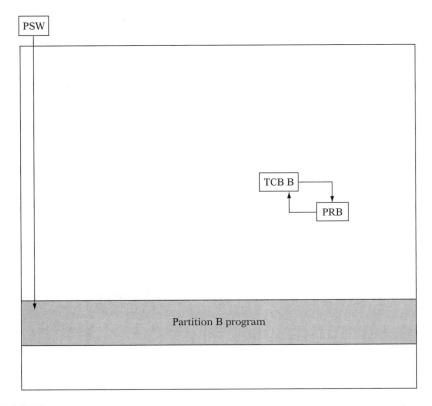

FIGURE 15.19

A second task begins executing.

Restarting a Task

Suddenly, the I/O operation that was started earlier is completed and an I/O interrupt occurs. After the PSWs are switched, the I/O interrupt handler, a task management routine, takes over (Figure 15.20). The old I/O PSW field, don't forget, still points to the program in partition B, and this program is in a ready state. Even so, the old PSW is copied to partition B's program request block.

The interrupt handling routine then checks the protection key in the channel status word, which uniquely identifies the partition that requested the I/O operation. By following the CVT/TCB/RB chain, the interrupt handling routine locates that partition's program request block, which holds the active task's most current program status word and resets its wait state bit to a ready state (Figure 15.21).

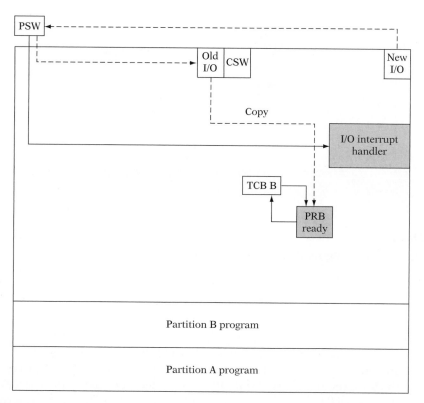

FIGURE 15.20

An I/O interrupt occurs.

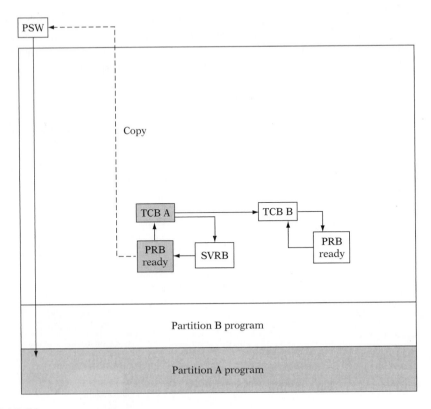

FIGURE 15.21

The I/O interrupt handling routine calls the master scheduler.

Once again, the master scheduler is called and begins searching the task control block queue. The first TCB is associated with the task in partition A. Because the task is ready, its PSW is loaded and task A resumes processing (Figure 15.21), even though the task in partition B, which was running at the time of the interrupt, is also ready.

Restarting a Second Task

Soon, the task in partition A is ready to output data to the printer, so it executes an SVC instruction. As a result, the SVC interrupt handling routine is activated (Figure 15.22). The SVC interrupt handler stores the old SVC PSW in the program request block, creates another SVRB, starts the output operation, sets the application task's PSW to a wait state, and calls the master scheduler (Figure 15.23).

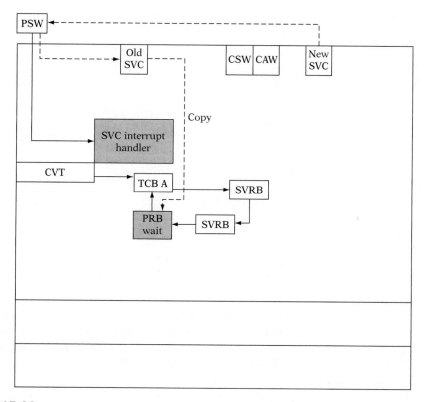

FIGURE 15.22

Another supervisor call interrupt occurs.

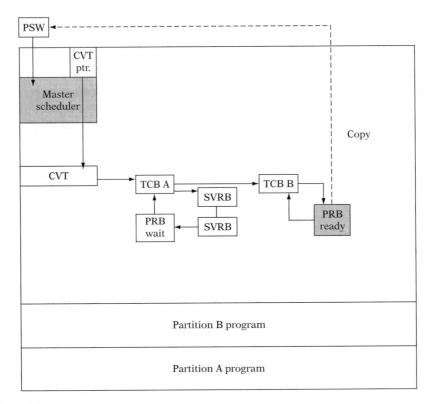

FIGURE 15.23

The master scheduler loads the PSW for the partition B task.

The master scheduler once again searches the TCB queue. The program in the first partition is in a wait state, so the master scheduler moves on to partition B's task control block. The partition B task is in a ready state, so task B's most current PSW is loaded from the PRB and task B resumes processing (Figure 15.24).

The Process

Note how predictable and repetitive the dispatching process is. Following any interrupt, the master scheduler is activated. It finds the address of the first task control block in the communication vector table. That first or high priority TCB marks the beginning of a linked list that ties together all the TCBs. The master scheduler follows the chain of TCB pointers and starts the first ready task it finds. That basic dispatching cycle is repeated over and over again from the instant the operating system is booted until it is shut down.

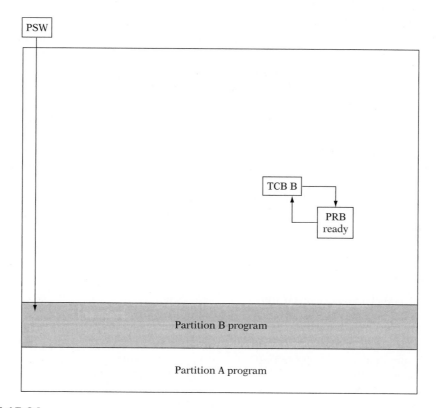

FIGURE 15.24

The partition B task begins executing.

▌ Summary

A traditional IBM mainframe's instruction counter is called the program status word. An application program starts an I/O operation by executing an SIO operation. The operating system responds by storing the address of the first channel command word in the channel address word and issuing a privileged start I/O instruction. When the I/O operation is completed, the channel notifies the processor by sending an interrupt and reporting its status through the channel status word. A traditional IBM mainframe responds to an interrupt by storing the current PSW in the old PSW field and loading the new PSW into the current PSW. Six types of interrupts are supported: external, I/O, machine check, restart, program, and SVC.

A task is a routine that is loaded into memory and ready to run. A job is a set of related tasks. Job management is concerned with job-to-job and task-to-task transitions. Task management supports the tasks as they run.

Job management includes the master scheduler and a transient routine called the initiator/ terminator. The master scheduler dispatches tasks, identifies empty or available partitions, loads the initiator/terminator in an empty partition, and communicates with the operator. The initiator/terminator loads tasks into memory. Task management is composed of interrupt handling routines.

The contents of each partition are defined in a task control block. The TCBs are linked in a fixed order, with the communication vector table pointing to the first TCB, the first TCB pointing to the second, and so on. The specific tasks active in a given partition are described by a chain of request blocks spun off the task control block. The master scheduler selects the next task to activate by following this chain. The MVS dispatching scheme was illustrated by an example showing a fraction of a second of computer time.

▌ Key Words

channel address word (CAW)
channel command word (CCW)
channel program
channel status word (CSW)
communication vector table (CVT)
control block
current PSW
external interrupt
initiator/terminator
input/output (I/O) interrupt
instruction address
interrupt
job
job management
machine check interrupt
master scheduler
MVS

new PSW
old PSW
privileged instruction
problem state
program interrupt
program request block (PRB)
program status word (PSW)
protection key
ready state
request block
restart interrupt
supervisor call (SVC) interrupt
supervisor request block (SVRB)
supervisory state
task
task control block (TCB)
task management
wait state

▌ Review Questions

1. Identify the key fields in a traditional IBM mainframe's PSW and explain the purpose of those key fields.

2. Explain how physical I/O is performed on a traditional IBM mainframe. Include in your response the access method, the channel program, the channel command word, the channel address word, the operating system, and the channel status word.

3. Explain how the interrupt concept is implemented on a traditional IBM mainframe.

4. List the types of interrupts recognized on a traditional IBM mainframe and identify the source of each type.

5. What are permanent storage assignments? Why are they necessary on a traditional IBM mainframe?

6. Describe the relationship between software-generated interrupts and privileged instructions.

7. Distinguish between a job and a task.

8. Distinguish between job management and task management.

9. What functions are performed by job management?

10. The initiator/terminator is a transient module. Why? What does transient mean?

11. What functions are performed by task management?

12. Identify the key control blocks that support the dispatching process.

13. How does the master scheduler discover if a partition is free or busy? Identify all the tables, control blocks, and pointers involved in this process.

14. How does the master scheduler determine which task to start next?

15. How does the master scheduler know when to start a new task?

■ Exercises

1. IBM's traditional mainframe operating systems were initially designed to support batch processing applications. Why?

2. IBM's mainframes dominated information technology until well into the 1980s. Why do you suppose IBM lost that dominant position? Or did they?

3. For those who might be interested in studying JCL in greater depth, appropriate material from earlier editions can be found on this textbook's companion Web site.

4. Describe the MVS dispatching process in terms of layering.

5. Figure 15.13 is a useful template for organizing many of this chapter's key terms.

6. An excellent way to gain a deeper understanding of this chapter's underlying concepts is to start with Figure 15.13, add a third partition to the example developed in the text, and explain how this third partition might change the flow of control through the system.

Distributed Systems

This section focuses on distributed operating systems and the software that controls inter-computer communication. Chapter 16 discusses basic communication and networking concepts. Chaper 17 focuses on the Internet, the evolving standard platform for intercomputer communications, and Chapter 18 presents client/server operating system concepts, principles, and security implications. Chapter 19, 20, and 21 introduce the user interface and key internal operating principles for three real-world network operating systems: Windows XP Server, Linux, and Novell NetWare.

CHAPTER 16

Data Communication and Networks

When you finish reading this chapter you should be able to:

▶ List and define the basic elements essential to data communication.

▶ Identify several common data communication media.

▶ Distinguish between a message and a signal and explain modulation and demodulation.

▶ Distinguish between analog and digital data communication.

▶ Explain packet switching.

▶ Distinguish between wired and wireless communication services and explain the last mile problem.

▶ Distinguish between a LAN and a WAN.

▶ Distinguish among polling, collision detection, token passing, and routing.

▶ Define internetworking and distinguish between a bridge and a gateway.

▶ Explain how a client/server network works.

◼ Layers

Many of today's information systems are spread over multiple computers that communicate with each other and share responsibility for information processing, storage, and retrieval. A good way to view such distributed systems is as a set of layers (Figure 16.1). The individual computers are linked by a communication infrastructure. The computers physically communicate via the underlying infrastructure following the rules imposed by a set of network protocols that reside in each computer's operating system. Each computer hosts a portion of the multiple-computer application, and those partial applications communicate with each other via their operating systems, their network protocols, and the data communication infrastructure. This chapter focuses on the communication infrastructure and key network principles.

◼ Data Communication

Data communication is the process of transferring data, information, or commands between two computers or between a computer and a terminal. Successful communication requires a message, a transmitter, a receiver, a medium, and a protocol (Figure 16.2). The **message** is the information being sent. The **transmitter** or sender is the source of the message and the **receiver** is the destination. The **medium,** sometimes called a line, a channel, or informally a pipe, is the path over which the message flows. A data

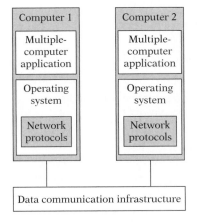

FIGURE 16.1

View multicomputer applications as a series of layers.

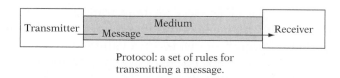

FIGURE 16.2
Communication requires a message, a transmitter, a receiver, a medium, and a protocol.

communication **protocol** is an agreed upon format or procedure (in effect, a set of rules) for transmitting a message over a communication medium. There are many different protocols, but the transmitter and the receiver must both use the same one. A protocol can be implemented in hardware, software, or both. Key issues include delivering messages efficiently and detecting and/or correcting errors.

Connectivity

Connectivity refers to the ability of a device or a program to communicate with other devices or software. *Physical* connectivity is achieved by establishing a connection between the transmitter and the receiver via some medium. *Logical* connectivity is achieved by using a common set of protocols to ensure that both the transmitter and the receiver follow the same rules and speak the same language. For example, when you answer the telephone, you say "hello." You and the caller then identify yourselves, and the conversation begins. Without really thinking about it, you both use the same language and you exchange information by taking turns. Finally, you say "goodbye" and hang up. Those informal telephone etiquette rules represent a primitive communication protocol. In this example, the telephone line is the medium. Combining a medium and a protocol enables connectivity.

Data Communication Media

There are two types of data communication media: cable and wireless. A **cable** medium physically links the transmitter and the receiver; examples include a twisted pair of wires, a coaxial cable, a fiber-optic cable, and so on. There is no physical connection when **wireless** media, such as radio, television, cellular telephone, Wi-Fi[1], microwave links, satellite links, and infrared beams, are used. A dedicated line is a permanent link between a sender and a receiver. A **switched line,** in contrast, links the sender and the receiver only while the message or a series of related messages are being exchanged.

---

[1]Intel's new Centrino mobile laptop technology comes with built-in Wi-Fi connectivity.

A given cable or wireless medium transmits messages in either baseband or broadband mode. A **baseband** line carries one message at a time. **Broadband,** in contrast, divides the medium into distinct channels that act much like independent wires and transmit simultaneous messages in parallel. For example, your cable television service allows you to select from many different stations all of which are transmitted over the same cable. Some sources use the term broadband as a synonym for high-speed communication, perhaps because most high-speed lines are broadband.

The speed of a communication line is a function of its **bandwidth,** the number of bits the line can transmit in a fixed amount of time. Bandwidth is usually expressed in bits per second (bps) or bytes per second (Bps). Each byte holds 8 bits, so 2,400 Bps is equivalent to 19,200 bps. Prefixes such as K (1000), M (1 million), or G (1 billion) are used to indicate order of magnitude; for example, 5 Mbps means 5 *million* bits per second. Figure 16.3 summarizes the communication speeds of several common media.

Compression

Line speed is a significant bottleneck in many applications. There are two ways to transmit a message more quickly. One is to increase the bandwidth of the connecting medium by switching to a faster line. The second, less obvious solution is to transmit fewer bits.

Connection type	Bandwidth
Local telephone line	56 Kbps
Wireless	
2G digital cellular	19.2 Kbps
2.5G digital cellular	144 Kbps
3G digital cellular	2 Mbps
Bluetooth	1 Mbps
Wi-Fi (802.11b)	Up to 11 Mbps
Home satellite service	400 Kbps
DSL	1.44 Mbps
Cable service	2 to 10 Mbps
Leased line (T-1, T-3)	1.5 to 43 Mbps
Fiber optic cable	Up to 10 Gbps

FIGURE 16.3

Bandwidth is a measure of the amount of data a line can transmit in a given period of time.

One way to reduce the size of a message is to use a **compression** algorithm. For example, Figure 16.4 shows a long form directory listing of two files. The first file is a 633 KB bitmap *(bmp)* of a digital photograph of a sunset. The second file is a compressed 70 KB *jpg* version of the same image. Compression typically reduces file size by 50 to 75 percent (or more), and smaller files mean fewer bits to transmit.

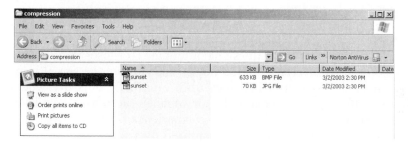

FIGURE 16.4

Compression.

Messages and Signals

A message consists of a header, a body, and a trailer (Figure 16.5). The header holds such system information as the source address and the receiving address. The body contains the message content; from the user's point of view the body is the message. The trailer, when present, holds additional system information such as an end-of-message marker. The precise format of the header and the trailer depends on the protocol.

A message moves over a communication line in the form of a **signal;** for example, the signal might consist of a fluctuating electric current or a flashing light. Variations in the signal represent coded information. The sending device creates the signal variations, and the receiving device interprets them.

FIGURE 16.5

A message consists of a header, a body, and a trailer.

Modulation and Demodulation

A direct link between two devices that are in close proximity to each other is called a local connection. For example, a sales associate might transfer the week's sales activity from his or her laptop to the office desktop by stringing a cable between the two machines and running a file transfer program. Communication over such local connections is similar to sending output data from a computer to a printer. Incidentally, most local connections are baseband.

Remote communication between two devices that are separated by more than a mile or two is much more complex, however. When data are transmitted over a distance, the signal attenuates (or loses intensity) and picks up electronic interference called noise. The further the signal moves from its source, the weaker it becomes until eventually it is overwhelmed by the noise. If you have ever tuned your vehicle's radio to a local FM station and driven away from town, you have experienced both attenuation and noise.

Messages are typically transmitted over a distance in the context of a carrier signal such as the sine wave pictured in Figure 16.6. One complete S-on-its-side pattern is called a cycle, the height of the wave is its amplitude, and the number of cycles per second (usually expressed in hertz) is its frequency. Because the carrier signal's frequency and amplitude are known, equipment can be designed to filter and boost it.

The task of transmitting a message in the context of a carrier signal is performed by a device called a **modem** (an acronym for modulator/demodulator) placed at both ends of the communication line (Figure 16.7). At the transmitter's end the modem adds the data (or the intelligence) to the carrier signal in a process called modulation. At the other end of the line, the receiver's modem demodulates the signal by subtracting out the carrier signal, leaving only the data.

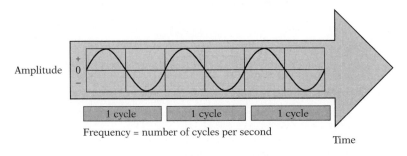

FIGURE 16.6

A carrier signal.

FIGURE 16.7

Modems are placed at both ends of the communication line.

Analog and Digital Data Transmission

A sine wave is a continuous analog signal, and analog signals are boosted by amplifying them. The problem is that when you amplify the signal, you also amplify the noise. As a result, an analog signal accumulates noise as it travels along a line, which makes it difficult to maintain signal quality. An option is to use digital technology.

Superficially, there is little difference between transmitting analog and digital data. In both cases, the transmitting modem adds the data to the carrier signal and the receiving modem subtracts the carrier signal to recover the data. What happens in between the modems, however, is what distinguishes analog from digital data transmission. An analog signal is boosted by amplifying it. A digital signal, in contrast, is electronically captured, reconstructed, and retransmitted, so most of the noise is automatically filtered from the signal. Just as a digital compact disk yields a clearer, sharper sound than an analog cassette or a vinyl LP, digital data transmission means better quality than analog data transmission.

Analog and Digital Sound

For many years, such analog media as vinyl LP and magnetic tape dominated the sound recording industry. Over the past decade, however, those analog media have been largely supplanted by digital media such as CD and DVD. Given that both the analog and digital recording processes start with the same analog sound patterns (a rhythm track, a lead guitar track, a lead vocalist track, and so on), why the change?

The analog process records a continuous signal. Play back the recording and you reproduce the original signal. The digital process, in contrast, samples the source signal, converts each sample to a pattern of digits, and records a series of discrete digital pulses. Imagine flipping a microphone on and off thousands of times a second and you have a pretty good mental image of the digital recording process. Note that in between samples, the digital process records absolutely

(continued)

Analog and Digital Sound *(continued)*

nothing, but if you sample frequently enough, when you play back the digital signal the listener hears what seems to be a continuous signal.

The problem with analog is that you record the *entire* signal, warts and all, and when you amplify the signal to play it back you also amplify any noise it might have picked up. That is why the background hiss gets louder when you crank up the volume on a cassette player, and that is why sound quality tends to deteriorate when you copy an analog recording.

Digital recording tends to produce a higher quality sound because any noise that occurs in between samples is ignored and the discrete digital pulses that are captured can be screened and filtered to remove unwanted sounds. Also, because the digital signal consists of a string of numbers, it can be stored and reproduced with no loss in quality (a fact that concerns the sound recording industry).

Are there any advantages associated with analog recording? Actually, there are. Many audiophiles prefer older analog recordings because they find digital sound a bit too cold and precise. Imagine a singer holding a note for several seconds. The sound waves produced by the singer are a continuous analog signal. The sampling process chops the signal into very brief digital pulses, but by its very nature the process misses any sounds that occur in between samples. Those inter-sample periods are not silent, of course. On most recordings, most listeners do not consciously notice the on/off nature of a digital signal, but a true audiophile might sense the enhanced warmth of the analog version.

Packet Switching

For any given sender, the typical data communication pattern consists of occasional bursts of activity separated by lengthy quiet times. The high bandwidth lines used for remote communication are quite expensive, so efficiency is a priority. Local lines are relatively inexpensive so low utilization is not a concern, but there is a risk that a single user might dominate a line. **Packet switching** achieves efficient message delivery by allowing numerous messages to share the line while preventing any single user from dominating it.

With packet switching, a message is divided into a set of small blocks called packets. Picture the communication line as a continuously moving escalator-like matrix of slots, each of which can hold one packet (Figure 16.8). Some of the slots hold packets from other messages. Some are empty. The first packet from the new message is dropped into the first available slot, the second packet goes into the next available slot, and so on; note how packets from numerous messages are intermixed. At the receiving end, the packets are reassembled to form the original message. Should transmission errors occur, only lost or erroneous packets must be retransmitted, which is much more efficient than resending the entire message.

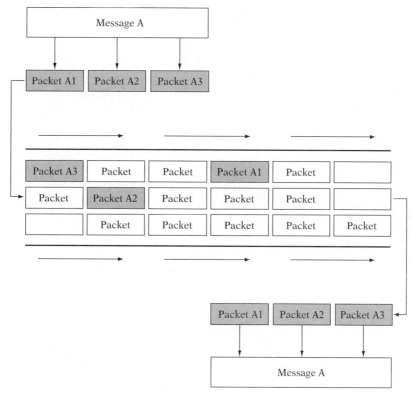

FIGURE 16.8
Packet switching.

■ The Public Communication Infrastructure

Think of a simple device-to-device link as the communication infrastructure's base layer. More complex communication systems are created by combining one or more of those basic links. A **common carrier** is an organization that provides the public communication services that define the higher levels of the communication infrastructure.

Plain Old Telephone Service

Today's best-known common carriers are the companies that provide **plain old telephone service (POTS).** The process of placing a call begins when the sender (a person or a computer) dials a number. The act of dialing generates a signal that travels from the originator's telephone over a wire (or cable) to the local telephone service provider's central office (Figure 16.9). Local calls are connected directly by the local provider. Long distance calls, however, are routed over a high-speed line to the destination telephone's central office, which completes the call. Think of the local and long distance segments as two independent layers. The local layer transmits the call between the sender and the sender's central office. The long distance layer transmits the message between the two central offices. The receiver's central office then passes the message to the receiver's local layer and on to the receiver.

Long distance carriers include such companies as AT&T, MCI, Sprint, Verizon, and many others. For a given call, the local service provider and the long distance service provider might or might not be the same company, and a long distance connection might use almost any combination of cable and wireless media. To the user, however, the specific path assigned to the connection is transparent and irrelevant. Incidentally, the long distance connection is an example of a switched line because the connection is established only for the length of the call.

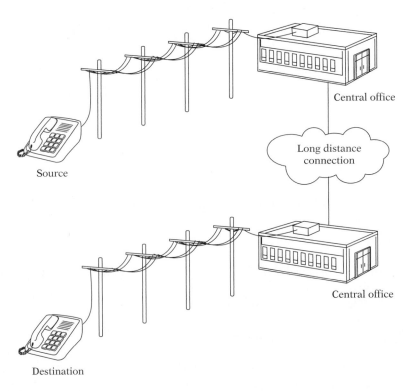

FIGURE 16.9

Plain old telephone service (POTS).

Perhaps you noticed that the long distance layer is visualized as a cloud in Figure 16.9. The cloud image suggests that the underlying infrastructure acts like a black box, an independent layer that can be used without fully understanding what happens inside the box. For example, when you call a friend, your voices flow between the two telephones and you could care less about what happens in between. As far as you are concerned, the call disappears into a cloud and emerges at the other end. Implementing the telephone system in layers allows you to ignore the underlying technology and makes mass telephone communication possible.

Communication Pricing

In the 1960s, the cost of a long distance telephone call was a function of time and distance. To help control costs, many homes (and even a few businesses) kept a three-minute egg timer next to the telephone, and cross-country calls were reserved for special occasions.

Today, the major telephone service providers offer rates as low as 7 cents per minute to anywhere in the United States, and in most parts of the country the local (free) calling area has expanded from a single community to a much larger region. Expect that trend to continue, with the "local" calling area expanding until, eventually, the pricing model resembles cable TV's, with unlimited calls anywhere within the country for a fixed monthly fee, plus additional charges for extra services such as call waiting, call forwarding, voice messaging, teleconferencing, and so on.

Why the trend toward fixed fee pricing? Monitoring the length of individual phone calls and printing multipage monthly bills is expensive. Shifting to fixed fee pricing significantly reduces administrative costs, leading to increased profits for the company and often lower bills for the customer—a classic win-win scenario.

Wireless Communication

In contrast to POTS, cellular telephones rely on wireless communication. When the originator dials a number on his or her mobile phone, an antenna picks up the signal and transmits it to a base station (Figure 16.10), which forwards the signal to a mobile switching center. If the receiving cell phone is in the same service area, the call is completed by the mobile switching center in much the same way a POTS central office completes a local call. If the call is to a wire-based telephone, it is transferred to the appropriate POTS central office, which makes the final connection. If the call is long distance, the mobile switching center routes it to a long distance carrier,

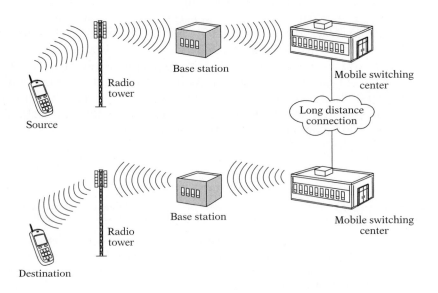

FIGURE 16.10

Wireless communication.

often one of the same companies that transmit traditional, wire-based telephone calls. Note that on a long distance call, both wire-based and wireless service providers access the same long distance infrastructure (Figure 16.11). Think of **POTS** and wireless services as independent layers that plug into the long distance layer.

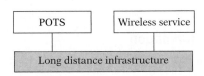

FIGURE 16.11

POTS and wireless are alternative access paths to the long distance communication infrastructure.

The Last Mile Problem

Using a modem, the current de facto standard for transmitting a message over a local telephone line is 56 Kbps. Wireless cell phones support comparable transmission rates, but quality is a problem and retransmitting errors cuts the effective speed. Once the message is transferred to a long distance service provider, however, it is sent on its way over high-speed (Mbps or Gbps) lines. The enormous speed disparity between a local line and a long distance line is called the **last mile problem,** where the "last mile" is the link between a home or office and the telephone service provider's local central office.

There are promising broadband alternatives for plugging into the long distance layer; several of them were summarized in Figure 16.3. First-generation cellular phones and second-generation digital cellular services are not quite fast enough or reliable enough for serious data communication, but third-generation wireless technology should be, and new wireless options such as Bluetooth and Wi-Fi are gaining users. Another wireless option, home satellite service, is widely available today.

A digital subscriber line (DSL) enables high-speed data communication on existing local telephone lines. Cable service bypasses the telephone company, offering connectivity from the subscriber's home or office via high bandwidth cable. Business, government, educational, and other large organizations sometimes bypass the last mile problem by leasing a high-speed (T-1 or T-3) line that links them directly to a central office or a long distance carrier, and fiber-optic cable looks very promising.

■ Networks

As individuals, we tend to see the act of communication (a phone call or an e-mail message) as a two-party process involving a sender and a receiver. On many modern information systems, however, a given computer or workstation often must communicate with many other computers or workstations. Imagine stringing separate lines linking every computer in the company to every other computer in the company. In addition to looking ugly and costing a fortune, the resulting spaghetti-like jumble of wires would be virtually impossible to manage and maintain.

The solution is to create a network. A **network** is composed of two or more (usually more) computers or other intelligent devices linked by communication lines in a way that allows them to communicate effectively.

Each device on the network is called a **node.** For a given message, one node is the transmitter or sender and another node (or set of nodes) is the receiver. The rules for sending the message from the transmitting node to the receiving node are defined in a communication protocol. In effect, networks are constructed on top of the communication infrastructure described earlier in this chapter.

LANs and WANs

A group of interconnected computers or workstations located in close proximity (for example within the same building or adjacent buildings) form a **local area network** or **LAN.** Each node has a unique address that distinguishes it from all the other nodes. The message header typically carries information for delivering the message, including the addresses of the source and the receiving nodes.

A **wide area network** or **WAN,** in contrast, links computers or LANs that are geographically disbursed. Most WANs utilize (at least in part) high-speed, broadband public communication services such as those provided by the telephone company and other common carriers.

Topologies

A LAN's topology describes its shape or form and defines its (typically baseband) connections or data paths (Figure 16.12). In a bus network, all the nodes share a common communication line called a bus. In a star network, all the nodes are linked to a central star node and all communications flow through the star node. For example, a local telephone service provider operates a star network with the central office computer as the star and your telephone as one of the other nodes. In a ring network, the nodes form a ring or loop and messages move around the ring from node to node.

Some local area networks transmit messages directly from the transmitting node to the receiving node. Others **broadcast** messages, sending every message to every node on the network. When a message reaches a given node on a broadcast network, the appropriate protocol checks the header, accepts (or receives) any messages addressed to it, and ignores messages addressed to some other node.

LAN Protocols

The nodes on a local area network are asynchronous; in other words, they operate independently. Consequently, it is possible for two (or more) nodes to transmit data simultaneously (or nearly simultaneously) over the same line. When that happens, the messages interfere with each other and both are rendered unreadable. Such interference is called a **collision.**

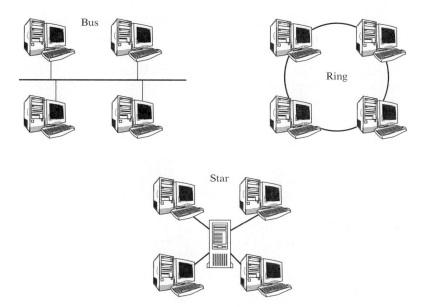

FIGURE 16.12

Some common LAN topologies.

One solution to the interference problem is to use a collision avoidance protocol that prohibits simultaneous message transmission. For example, on a **token passing** (or token ring) network, an electronic signal called the token moves continuously around the network and a node is allowed to transmit only when it holds the token. Since only one node can transmit at any given time, collisions cannot happen. Token passing is common on ring networks.

Polling is another collision avoidance protocol. On a star network, the primary or star node starts the polling process by sending a polling signal to node A. If node A is ready to transmit a message, it does so. If not, the star computer sends a polling signal to node B, then node C, and so on in round-robin fashion. Only one polling signal is active at any given time, and a node can transmit only when polled, so collisions are impossible.

On a **collision detection** network, in contrast, a given node can transmit whenever the line is clear. Because it takes time for a signal to traverse a line, however, two nodes might both sense a clear line and transmit simultaneously (or nearly simultaneously), so collisions *are* possible. When a collision occurs, it is detected electronically and the affected messages are retransmitted. Token passing and polling are most effective on a heavily loaded LAN. Collision detection is often a better option on a lightly loaded LAN, because fewer messages mean fewer collisions.

Ethernet is a popular, inexpensive, high-speed local area network collision detection protocol designed by Xerox Corporation for a bus or star topology. An Ethernet adapter card or network interface card is installed in each network node and assigned a unique (within the LAN) address. Each station is linked to a central wiring closet. For example, Miami University's School of Business Administration LAN has one wiring closet per floor (Figure 16.13). The wiring closets are connected to each other and (eventually) to the rest

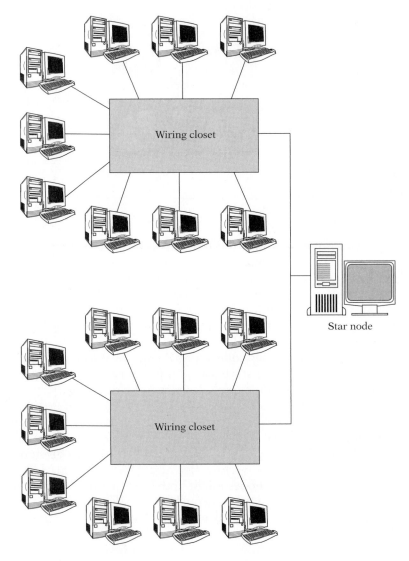

FIGURE 16.13

An Ethernet network.

of the network by coaxial or fiber optic cables that stretch from floor to floor and between buildings.

Routing

Most WANs lack an easily defined topology. For example, the Internet, a worldwide network of networks, is so vast that nobody knows exactly what it looks like. Lacking obvious connection paths, such networks (including some LANs) rely on point-to-point transmission, passing the message from node to node across the network in a series of hops (Figure 16.14). The intermediate nodes might be computers or routers, hardware devices that accept a message, examine the header, and forward the message to the next node without regard for the message's content.

The process of selecting the next node or set of nodes is called **routing.** For example, consider node 5 in the middle of Figure 16.14 and imagine that it just received a message from node 4. In addition to node 4 (which, we'll assume, cannot be the next target), node 5 has links to nodes 3, 6, and 7. How does it select the next node? The decision is often made by consulting a routing table; in effect, a list of routing rules. Static routing uses preset paths; for example, whenever node 5 receives a message from node 4 it might always forward the message to node 6. Sometimes the routing node is given a bit more flexibility. For example, node 5 might direct the message to node 7 if the path to node 6 is busy, or alternate between nodes 6 and 7 to achieve better load balancing. With dynamic or adaptive routing, the best path is computed based on real-time data such as the candidate destination nodes' utilization rates or failure rates.

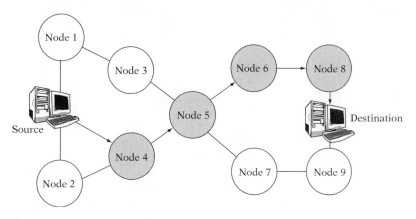

FIGURE 16.14

With point-to-point transmission, a signal is routed node-by-node across the network.

Internetworking

The process of linking two or more networks (LANs, WANs, or both) is called **internetworking.** A number of hardware devices are used to control and coordinate internetwork communication. A bridge is a node that links two or more similar networks (Figure 16.15). A gateway is a node that links dissimilar networks; for example, a local area network might be connected to a wide area network through a gateway. Note that the term Internet is an acronym for *internet*working.

Client/Server Networks

In addition to their physical configuration, most networks also have a logical configuration that defines the role played by each node. For example, on a **client/server network** (Figure 16.16), specialized computers called **servers** control access to all the network's shared resources, and the other nodes act as **clients.** When a client logs onto a network, the client node establishes a connection to a server and, subsequently, asks the server for help when it needs a shared resource. The server provides **services,** specific tasks (often system tasks) that support other programs.

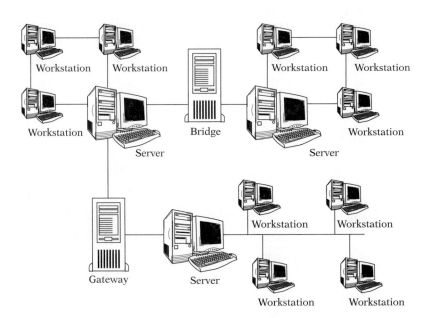

FIGURE 16.15

A bridge links two or more similar networks. A gateway links dissimilar networks.

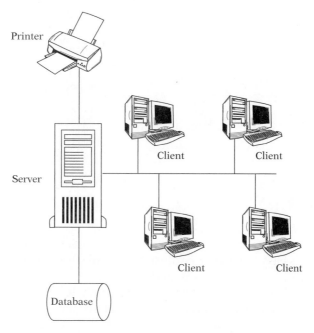

FIGURE 16.16

A client/server network.

A client/server network is an implementation of the more general client/server model. The basic idea of the client/server model is to assign a resource to the most appropriate computer or software routine (the server) and require other components (the clients) to access that resource through the server. For example, imagine that a mainframe controls access to a database and a microcomputer controls access to a high-speed laser printer (Figure 16.17). If the microcomputer needs information from the database, it is the client and the mainframe is the server. If, on the other hand, the mainframe generates a report that must be printed on the laser printer, the mainframe becomes the client and the microcomputer becomes the server. Note that the terms *client* and *server* relate to the function and not to the machine. A client requests support. A server fills the request.

Note also that the terms *client* and *server* do not necessarily refer to hardware. Consider, for example, the system pictured in Figure 16.18. There are two programs in memory. The user interface communicates with the user through the console and the database server manages access to the database. If a user requests information from the database, the user interface routine acts as the client and requests the data from the database server routine, which acts as the server.

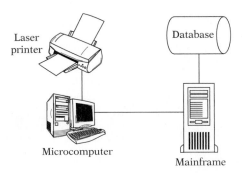

FIGURE 16.17

The client/server model.

Because the term server is commonly applied to both hardware and software, it is easy to become confused, particularly when you see advertisements for Dell's server hardware and Microsoft's server software. A computer designed to be a server (hardware) typically has a powerful processor, considerable memory, and vast amounts of secondary storage, but it is still a computer and, given the appropriate software, could be used as a client workstation. Server software, on the other hand, is an application program that allocates shared resources and provides services on request. Install a server software routine on any computer, and that computer becomes a server.

Peer-to-Peer Networks

In a peer-to-peer network (Figure 16.19) there is no dedicated server. Every computer on the network can be a server and a client, and each user can decide to share his or her files or printer resources with any other user. If

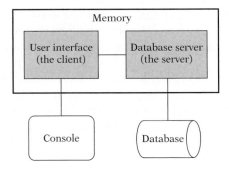

FIGURE 16.18

Software clients and servers.

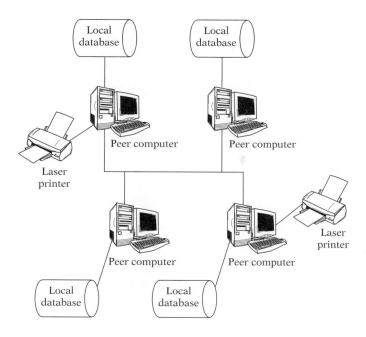

FIGURE 16.19
A peer-to-peer network.

you have ever accessed a Napster-like file sharing network, you have used a peer-to-peer network.

◼ Summary

Data communication requires a message, a transmitter, a receiver, a protocol, and a medium. Today's best-known connectivity options are plain old telephone service (POTS) and wireless. Broadband options such as DSL, cable service, home satellite services, and leased high-speed lines help to solve the last mile problem.

Each device on a network is called a node. A local area network's topology defines the communication links that connect its nodes. Token passing and collision detection are two options for ensuring successful message delivery on a LAN. Ethernet is a popular LAN protocol. Many wide area networks (WANs) rely on point-to-point transmission and routing. Internetworking uses bridges, gateways, and routers to link LANs and WANs. On a client/server network, the servers control access to various services and the clients request the services they need. On a peer-to-peer network, there is no central server.

◼ Key Words

bandwidth
baseband
broadband
broadcast
cable
client
client/server network
collision
collision detection
common carrier
compression
connectivity
data communication
internetworking
last mile problem
local area network (LAN)
medium
message

modem
network
node
packet switching
plain old telephone service (POTS)
polling
protocol
receiver
routing
server
service
signal
switched line
token passing
transmitter
wide area network (WAN)
wireless

◼ Review Questions

1. List and define the basic elements essential to data communication.
2. Identify several common data communication media. How is the speed of a data communication medium expressed?
3. What is compression? Why is compression valuable?
4. Distinguish between a message and a signal.
5. If you want to transmit data over a distance, you must boost and filter the signal. Why?
6. What are modulation and demodulation and why are they necessary?
7. Distinguish between analog and digital data.
8. Explain packet switching.
9. Distinguish between wired and wireless communication services and explain the last mile problem.
10. What is a network?
11. Distinguish between a local area network and a wide area network.
12. Briefly describe a bus network, a star network, and a ring network.
13. Distinguish among polling, collision detection, and token passing.
14. Define routing.
15. Define internetworking.

16. Distinguish between a bridge and a gateway.

17. Explain how a client/server network works.

18. Distinguish between server hardware and server software.

▌ Exercises

1. Take a digital picture or scan a photograph. Store the image on your hard disk as a bitmap file and again in the same folder as a *jpg* file. Then compare the sizes of the two files.

2. Listen to a recording on vinyl LP and then listen to the digital (CD or DVD) version of the same recording. Do you sense any differences? Note your impressions.

3. Why do you suppose the sound recording industry is so concerned about digital file sharing?

4. A chapter sidebar suggested that communication pricing may be moving toward the cable TV model, with a base price for standard service and additional fees for premium services. Do you agree or disagree? Why?

5. Do a little research and find out what broadband connectivity options are available in your town or on your campus.

6. Figure 16.1, perhaps supplemented by Figure 16.11, and Figure 16.15 are useful templates for organizing many of this chapter's key terms.

CHAPTER 17

The Internet and the World Wide Web

When you finish reading this chapter you should be able to:

▶ Describe the structure of the Internet's backbone and the services that link a user to the backbone.

▶ Read and understand a domain name and an IP address.

▶ Explain how the domain name system (DNS) maps a domain name to an IP address.

▶ Explain how the address resolution protocol (ARP) maps an IP address to a MAC (media access control) address.

▶ List the layers in the TCP/IP model and explain what happens at each layer.

▶ Explain the difference between an application program and an application layer protocol.

▶ Explain how a logical messaging port number establishes a link to a specific application protocol.

▶ Distinguish between a Web page, a home page, and a Web site.

▶ Explain how a browser and a Web server work together to transfer a Web page from a Web site to a client.

▶ Read and understand a Uniform Resource Locator (URL).

◼ The Internet's Infrastructure

The **Internet** is a vast network of networks layered on top of the global data communication network described in Chapter 16 (Figure 17.1). Accessible from virtually anywhere in the world, the Internet has effectively reshaped modern information technology. As a result, almost without exception modern operating systems are Internet enabled.

FIGURE 17.1

The Internet is layered on top of the global data communication network.

Internet Service Providers

Most users and many business concerns access the Internet through an **Internet service provider (ISP)** such as America Online, MSN, or one of thousands of others (Figure 17.2). The ISP, in turn, connects the user to the Internet much as a POTS central office or a mobile switching center links a caller to a long distance connection. Most ISPs offer additional services such as e-mail, data access, training, chat rooms, news, and so on. These services are implemented on host computers, where a **host** (or end system) is a computer attached to the Internet that runs (or hosts) application programs such as server software.

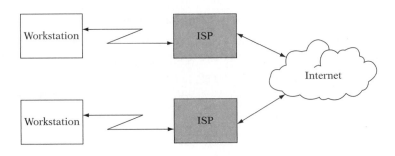

FIGURE 17.2

Most users access the Internet through an Internet service provider (ISP).

The Backbone

The **backbone** is a network of high-speed communication lines that carries the bulk of the traffic between major segments of the Internet (Figure 17.3). In the United States, backbone service is provided by a number of commercial **network service providers (NSPs),** and the major ISPs lease service from and access the Internet though one of the NSPs. Among the primary NSPs are many long distance telephone service providers.

Each NSP operates its own (national) wide area network of high-speed communication lines. Because those WANs are independently owned and operated, it is often necessary to transfer a message from one NSP to another. The network service providers are interconnected and exchange data through **network access points (NAPs).** Some major Internet service

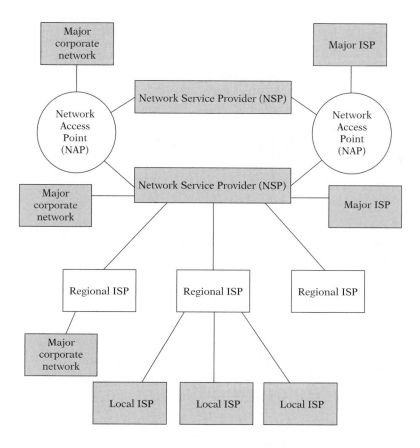

FIGURE 17.3

The backbone.

providers and a few large organizations such as universities, research centers, and corporations connect directly to a network access point, but most access the Internet through an ISP or a regional ISP.

A **regional ISP** operates a statewide or regional backbone and (typically) connects to the Internet by leasing bandwidth from a network service provider. Many local ISPs access the Internet through a regional ISP, and large organizations sometimes lease a direct broadband connection to a regional ISP or even an NSP.

Local Networks

At Miami University, each division (Arts & Science, Business, Education, Engineering…) has its own local area network (Figure 17.4). The divisional LANs are all linked to a university host named *muohio* that serves as a

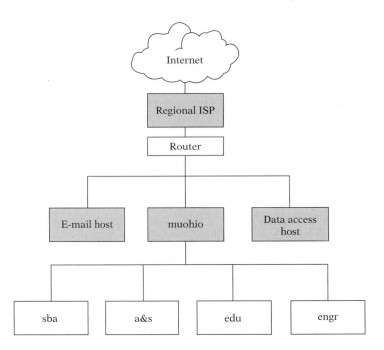

FIGURE 17.4

Miami University's network structure.

LAN-to-LAN bridge or gateway. Other university hosts support e-mail and data access. Access to the Internet (pictured as a cloud) is through a router connected to a high-speed leased line that links Miami to a regional ISP.

Note that the divisional LANs and their workstations are not directly connected to the Internet. Instead, much as a home user accesses the Internet through an ISP, they access the Internet through a host *(muohio)* that serves as a gateway to the Internet. Because the host is the only node known to the Internet, anything that happens behind the host is the responsibility of the local network and not the Internet. In other words, the Internet delivers the message to the host, and the local network forwards the message to the receiving node.

Internet Addressing

Your school's network might link hundreds, perhaps even thousands of computers, and a large company's network links even more. Even the biggest corporate network appears insignificant when compared to the Internet, however. In order to route a message across the Internet (or any network for that matter), each connected device must have a unique address that distinguishes it from all the other nodes. The Internet could not function without an effective system for assigning, maintaining, and retrieving those addresses.

Domain Names

A **domain** is a set of nodes that are administered as a unit; for example, all the networked computers belonging to Miami University form one domain and all the networked computers belonging to Microsoft Corporation form another. A **domain name** consists of two to four words separated by dots (Figure 17.5). Starting at the right is a top-level domain name such as *edu* for an educational institution, *com* for a commercial entity, *org* for a non-profit group, *gov* for a government service, and so on. Moving to the left are the entities within the domain. For example, in the domain name *sbaserver1.sba.muohio.edu*, *edu* is the top-level domain, *muohio* is Miami University's domain (part of the edu domain), *sba* is the School of Business Administration subnet (a network that forms a part of a larger network) within the *muohio* domain, and *sbaserver1* is a server within the *sba* subnet. Note how the various elements of the domain name correspond to the network structure pictured in Figure 17.4.

The top-level domain names are assigned by the Internet Corporation for Assigned Names and Numbers (ICANN); Figure 17.6 lists several. An organization's domain name (for example, *muohio* or *aol*) is assigned to a

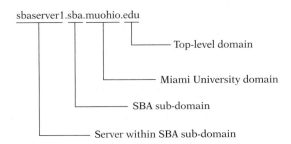

FIGURE 17.5

A domain name.

host computer that is linked to the Internet 24 hours a day. To the left of the domain name, the subnet and server names are assigned by the domain and consequently have meaning only within the domain. For example, the Internet can deliver a message to *muohio*, but it is *muohio's* responsibility to pass the message to *sba*, and *sba's* responsibility to pass the message to *sbaserver1*.

Domain	Signifies	Domain	Signifies
aero	Air-transport industry	au	Australia
biz	Business organization	br	Brazil
com	US commercial	ca	Canada
coop	Cooperatives	cn	China
edu	US educational	de	Germany
info	Unrestricted	fi	Finland
gov	US government	fr	France
mil	US military	gb	Great Britain
museum	Museums	in	India
name	Individuals	it	Italy
net	US network	jp	Japan
org	US non-profit	ru	Russia
pro	Professionals	za	South Africa

FIGURE 17.6

Some top-level domain names.

Domain Name Registration

To avoid duplication, domain names are registered with a central authority and kept in a central registry. In the United States, responsibility for top-level *com, net,* and *org* domain name registration rests with the Internet Corporation for Assigned Names and Numbers (ICANN). Together with Network Solutions, Inc. (NSI), ICANN accredits the organizations that perform the actual registration process, usually for a fee. Other governments are responsible for allocating domain names in their own domains; for example, Japan controls the top-level domain *jp,* Germany controls *de,* and Italy controls *it.* Because the supply of unique names is limited, an organization's domain name is a valuable piece of intellectual property that can be bought and sold, often through a domain name brokerage. For example, a few years ago Delta Airlines purchased the rights to *delta.com* from the insurance company that previously (and legitimately) owned it, and if your local television station has a domain name ending in *tv,* the station (directly or indirectly) purchased the name from the tiny South Pacific country of Tuvalu. Such new top-level domains as *biz, coop,* and *pro* should help increase the supply of appropriate domain names.

The IP Address

An **IP address** is a number that uniquely identifies a specific node. The Internet uses this number to route packets to the node. An IP address consists of four numbers separated by dots (Figure 17.7). For example, in the address 134.53.40.2, the first number, 134, is the top-level domain *(edu);* 53 designates Miami University's domain; 40 is the School of Business Administration subnet; and 2 is a server within this subnet.

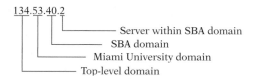

FIGURE 17.7

An IP address.

The Domain Name System

The actual physical transmission of a message across the Internet requires an IP address, not a domain name. Fortunately, a given node's domain name and IP address convey exactly the same information (Figure 17.8), and the **domain name system (DNS)** takes advantage of that relationship to convert domain names to IP addresses. The domain name system is implemented by a DNS protocol and by a hierarchy of DNS servers that store tables of domain-name-to-IP-address mappings that allow each layer to find the IP addresses for the next higher and next lower layers.

Imagine, for example, sending a message to *service.microsoft.com* from within the Miami University School of Business network *(sbaserver1.sba.muohio.edu)*. The search begins with the *sba* DNS server (Figure 17.9, step 1). The *sba* DNS server knows the next higher layer's IP address so the request is sent to *muohio* (2). The *muohio* DNS server knows the IP addresses of its next higher layer (the top level domains) so it sends the request to *com* at IP address 207 (3). The top level DNS server knows *microsoft's* IP address (207.46) because *microsoft* is at the next lower level, but it does not know *service* because *service* is two levels down. Thus, *com* sends Microsoft's numeric IP address (207.46) back to *muohio* (4). Miami's DNS server then sends a request to Microsoft (5). *Microsoft.com* knows the IP address for *service* (one level down) and completes the address translation (6). The IP address (207.46.140.71) is then returned to the originating server *(sba)* (7), which (finally) sends the message.

Following the initial address translation, the participating domain name systems cache or save the domain name and its matching IP address. Consequently, the next time a user in the SBA lab types the domain name *service.microsoft.com*, a cached copy is in *sba* and the address translation is done immediately rather than being forwarded up the ladder. Similarly, if another Miami user not on the SBA subdomain requests *service.microsoft.com*, another cached copy is available on *muohio*, so the university computer's DNS does the address translation.

sbaserver1.sba.muohio.edu ⟶ 134.53.40.2

FIGURE 17.8

A domain name and an IP address convey the same information.

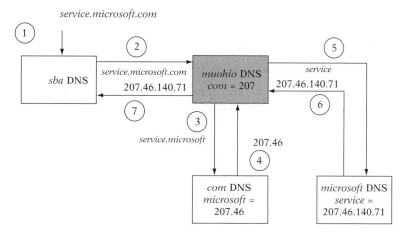

FIGURE 17.9

The domain name system.

The Media Access Control Address

An IP address points to a specific computer, router, or (more generally) node on the Internet. However, the ultimate destination of most messages lies *off* the Internet within a local domain. The IP address of any node not directly connected to the Internet (for example, a user workstation on a subnet) is assigned by and has meaning only within the local domain. As a result, physically transmitting a message to its final destination node (the last hop) requires the physical **media access control (MAC)** address of that node. For example, in an Ethernet LAN an Ethernet card is installed in each workstation and each card has a unique MAC address that is hard-coded by the card's manufacturer. To cite another example, if the last hop from an ISP to a client workstation is via a dial-up telephone line, the physical address of the modem is the MAC address. On the final hop from the destination server to the destination computer, the **address resolution protocol (ARP)** translates the workstation's IP address to a MAC address. The message is then routed to the destination computer.

Address Translation

Quickly review the relationship between the three types of Internet addresses (Figure 17.10). The task of transmitting a message begins when a user identifies the destination node's domain name by typing it, selecting it

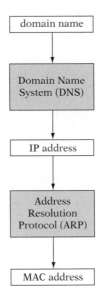

FIGURE 17.10

Internet address translation.

from a list, or clicking on a hyperlink. The Internet uses numeric IP addresses to route packets from node to node, so the domain name system (DNS) converts the domain name to an IP address.

At the other end of the connection, the final hop takes the packet from a server to the destination node. Because the destination node is inside the local domain, its IP address is assigned by and has meaning only within the domain. Thus the server's address resolution protocol (ARP) maps the final node's IP address (which means nothing to the Internet) to a physical media access control (MAC) address. Note that the address translation process starts with a relatively easy to remember logical name and ends with the numeric physical address of a specific device.

▪ TCP/IP, the Internet's Protocols

As you learned in Chapter 16, if two devices are to communicate, both the transmitter and the receiver must use the same protocols. Although it links *millions* of computers worldwide, messages still move over the Internet in a series of node-to-node hops, and the common protocol rule applies to each of those hops. The Internet simply could not exist without a set of widely accepted standard protocols.

The TCP/IP (Internet) Model

The **TCP/IP** or **Internet model** (Figure 17.11) specifies a set of layered packet switching protocols that define the rules for communicating over the Internet. (In fact, the Internet is sometimes defined as the set of interconnected computers that use TCP/IP.) The top two layers deal with the complete message and the bottom two layers work with individual packets. As you are about to learn, Internet access only *seems* easy; an incredible number of tasks are hidden beneath the surface. Because of TCP/IP's layered architecture, however, the underlying complexity is largely transparent, making Internet access available even to nontechnical users. As you read about the TCP/IP protocols, note how each protocol layer builds on the standards implemented in the layer below it. That is the essence of layering.

The TCP/IP model resembles the International Organization for Standardization's seven-layer Open Systems Interconnect (OSI) reference model for packet switching, computer-to-computer communication (Figure 17.12). Although rarely implemented precisely as specified, the OSI model is a useful blueprint for designing and creating networking hardware and software. In the OSI reference model, the top three layers deal with the complete message. The fourth layer, transport, breaks the message into packets on the sending computer and reassembles the packets to reform the complete message on the receiving computer. The bottom three layers route, format, deliver, and receive the packets.

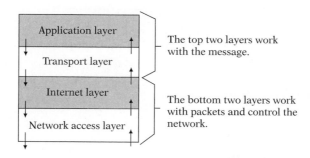

FIGURE 17.11

The TCP/IP model.

OSI layer	Responsibilities
The top three layers work with the message.	
Application	Provides a logical link between an application program and the lower-level protocols.
Presentation	Performs necessary data representation and/or syntax conversions; e.g., encryption/decryption.
Session	Establishes, maintains, and terminates a connection.
The transport layer breaks the message into packets and reassembles the packets at the receiving end.	
Transport	Breaks the message into packets. Ensures error free, end-to-end delivery of the complete message.
The bottom three layers work with packets.	
Network	Determines the best route for sending a packet from the source node to the destination node.
Data-link	Formats a packet for transmission to the next node.
Physical	Interfaces with the physical communication medium.

FIGURE 17.12

The Open Systems Interconnect (OSI) model.

The Application Program

A typical Internet transaction begins and ends with an application program. For example, if you use an e-mail program to send a message to a friend, your friend on the other end of the line must use a compatible e-mail program to read that message. Similarly, if you use an FTP program to transfer a file from a file server, you can safely assume that you are communicating with a compatible FTP program because if you aren't, the file transfer will not work. Basically, the user initiates a transaction through the application program's user interface, and the application program calls and passes parameters down to the appropriate application layer protocol.

For example, imagine using the FTP protocol to download a file from a file server to your computer. After launching the FTP application program, you indicate the file server's domain name address, identify the file to be transferred, and start the file transfer process. The FTP program responds by calling the application layer's FTP protocol and passing it the target domain name and file path name.

The Application Layer

The TCP/IP **application layer** holds protocols that directly support application programs (Figure 17.13). Several well-known application layer protocols, including the FTP protocol, are summarized in Figure 17.14. On the sending computer, an application layer protocol accepts the parameters passed down from an application program and creates the parameters needed by the next layer down. At the other end of the line, the application layer protocol accepts information from the next layer down and passes it up to an equivalent application program on the receiving machine.

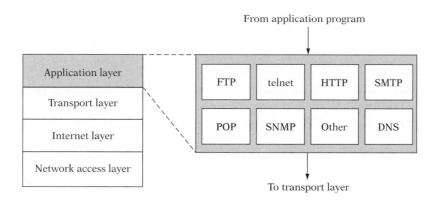

FIGURE 17.13

The application layer protocols directly support application programs.

Acronym	Name	Function
DNS	Domain name system	Translate a domain name to an IP address.
FTP	File transfer protocol	Download a file from or upload a file to another computer.
HTTP	Hypertext transfer protocol	Request and download a web page. HTTP is the standard Web surfing protocol.
POP	Post office protocol	Deliver accumulated mail from a mail server to the recipient's computer.
SMTP	Simple mail transfer protocol	Send an e-mail message from the originator's computer to the recipient's mail server.
SNMP	Simple network managment protocol	Monitor the activity of a network's hardware and software components.
Telnet	Terminal emulation protocol	Log into a remote computer. System operators use telnet to remotely control a server.

FIGURE 17.14

Some common application layer protocols.

The lower TCP/IP layers require IP addresses, not domain names. The responsibility for translating the domain name passed down from the application program into an equivalent IP address is assigned to the application layer's DNS protocol. The DNS protocol relies on the domain name system pictured in Figure 17.9 to accomplish its task.

The IP address allows the FTP message to be transmitted to the correct node, in this example to the file server host. At the receiving end, the message is passed to the correct application program by referencing a port number. As you know from Chapter 4, a device port is a physical interface or plug; for example, you plug your printer into a printer port. In the TCP/IP model, a **port** is also the endpoint of a *logical* connection (a program-to-program link), and every application layer protocol is associated with a logical **messaging port** number. Often, the word port is used without qualification and the type of port referenced is implied by context. A device port links physical hardware components such as a network access line and an Ethernet card. A messaging port links logical software routines such as the transport layer's TCP protocol and the application layer's FTP protocol.

TCP/IP supports up to 64K unique messaging ports, but port numbers below 1024 are assigned by the Internet Assigned Numbers Authority (IANA) and are considered well-known ports. Figure 17.15 lists several well-known port assignments.

Port	Used for:	
5	RJE	Remote job entry
20	FTP	File transfer protocol data
21	FTP	File transfer protocol control
23	Telnet	Terminal emulator
25	SMTP	Simple mail transfer protocol
79	Finger	Given e-mail address, identify user
80	HTTP	Hypertext transfer protocol
110	POP3	Post office protocol, version 3
119	NNTP	Network news transfer protocol

FIGURE 17.15

Some well-known port assignments.

For example, the telnet protocol connects port 23 on the sending computer to port 23 on the receiving computer (Figure 17.16). A file transfer protocol (FTP) exchange uses two ports: 20 for the data and 21 for control signals (Figure 17.17). Using FTP is more efficient than attaching a file to an e-mail message because the FTP data and control signals simultaneously travel over separate connections in parallel. Superficially, e-mail seems like a simple application, perhaps because mail programs like *Outlook* and *Eudora* are so familiar, but transferring an e-mail message is actually a relatively complex two-step operation (Figure 17.18). First, the simple mail transfer protocol (SMTP) transfers a single message from port 25 on the sending computer to port 25 on the recipient's e-mail server. Subsequently, the recipient uses a post office protocol such as POP3 to transfer accumulated e-mail from port 110 on the e-mail server to port 110 on his or her own workstation.

Getting back to the FTP application, the application layer's FTP protocol adds to the message passed down from the application program a header that contains information needed by the receiving node's FTP protocol (Figure 17.19) and passes the header, the FTP request, the IP address, and the port number (20 or 21) down to the transport layer. At the other end of the line, when the message reaches the receiving node (the file server), the receiving application layer's FTP protocol strips off the header, uses the header contents, and passes the request up to the FTP application program.

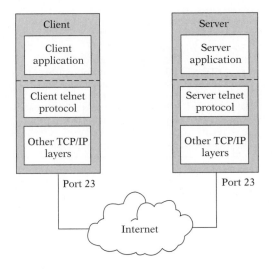

FIGURE 17.16

The *telnet* protocol uses port 23.

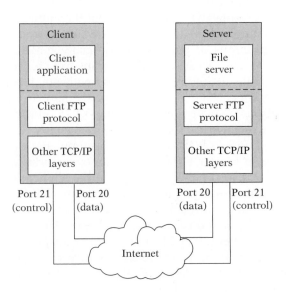

FIGURE 17.17

The *FTP* protocol uses ports 20 and 21.

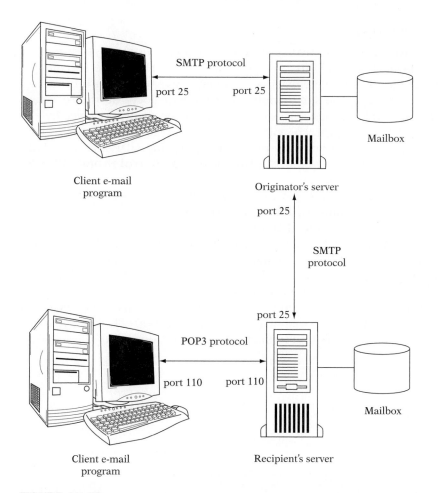

FIGURE 17.18

Sending an e-mail message is a two-step process.

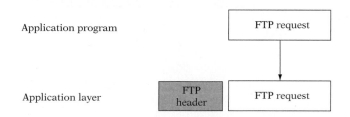

FIGURE 17.19

The application layer *FTP* protocol adds a header to the FTP request.

The Transport Layer

The next layer down, the **transport layer**, also known as the host-to-host transport layer (Figure 17.20), is responsible for ensuring successful end-to-end delivery of the complete message from an application layer protocol on the sending node to the same application layer protocol on the receiving node. For example, a message passed down to the transport layer by the application layer FTP protocol will be passed up to the receiving node's FTP protocol. Several transport layer protocols (including UDP, the user datagram protocol) can be used, but the **transmission control protocol (TCP)** is by far the most common.

The "message" passed down to the transport layer consists of the application layer's header plus the message created by the user. TCP breaks the message into packets (note that only the first packet contains the FTP header) and adds a TCP header to each packet (Figure 17.21). The TCP header (Figure 17.22) holds the source port number, the destination port number, and a sequence number. The port number, remember, is linked to a specific application layer protocol—in this example, the header to a packet carrying FTP data would reference port 20 and a packet carrying all or part of an FTP control signal would reference port 21. The sequence number is assigned by TCP to indicate the proper sequence of the packets.

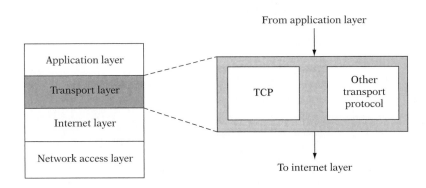

FIGURE 17.20

The next layer down is the transport layer.

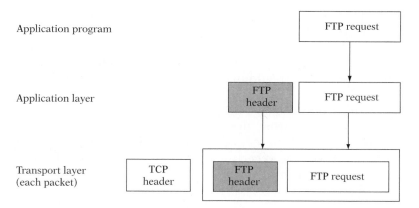

FIGURE 17.21

TCP adds its own header.

Byte	Contents
00 01	Source port number
02 03	Destination port number
04 05 06 07	Sequence number
08 09 10 11	Acknowledgement number
12	Header length
13	Control bits
14 15	Window size
16 17	TCP checksum
18 19	Pointer

FIGURE 17.22

The format of a TCP header.

At the receiving end, the destination computer's transmission control protocol (TCP) checks each packet for errors and uses the sequence numbers to reassemble the packets in the proper order. When the message is fully assembled, TCP passes it up to the application layer protocol associated with the port number in the TCP header, in this example, the FTP protocol.

On the sending side, TCP guarantees error free message delivery by waiting to receive from the destination computer's transport layer an acknowledgement for every packet sent and resending individual packets as necessary. On the receiving side, the sequence numbers in the TCP header help to ensure delivery of the *complete* message by highlighting lost packets.

Note that the application and transport layers deal with the entire message. Below the transport layer, the Internet and network access layers work with the packets created in the transport layer.

The Internet Layer

The **Internet** or **network layer,** the second layer from the bottom (Figure 17.23), uses the **Internet protocol (IP)** to route packets by selecting the next node on the path that leads (eventually) to the receiving node. The Internet layer accepts a packet from the transport layer (the next higher layer) and adds its own IP header (Figure 17.24) which holds the IP addresses of the source and destination nodes (Figure 17.25). Note that each packet contains an IP header that identifies the sending and receiving IP addresses and a TCP header that identifies the sending and receiving ports, so the path from an application protocol on the sending node to an application protocol on the receiving node is fully defined.

Once the Internet layer has added its header to the packet, it passes the packet down to the network access layer. At each of the intermediate nodes (and there may be many), the IP protocol selects the next node, replaces the old IP header with a new one, and passes the packet down to the network access layer. Once the packet reaches the destination node, it is passed up to the transport layer, where TCP reassembles the packets.

Note that the address resolution protocol (ARP) is an Internet layer protocol, because each packet must be routed to its final destination before the packets are reassembled at the transport layer. Note also that IP routes packets; it does not deliver them. Packet delivery is the responsibility of the next layer down, the network access layer. Finally, note that the source computer's IP protocol does not receive an acknowledgement from the receiving node. Guaranteeing delivery is TCP's job.

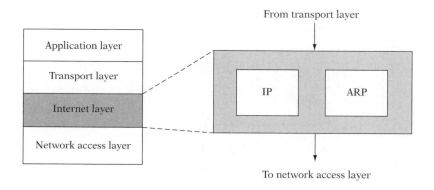

FIGURE 17.23

The Internet layer uses the Internet protocol (IP).

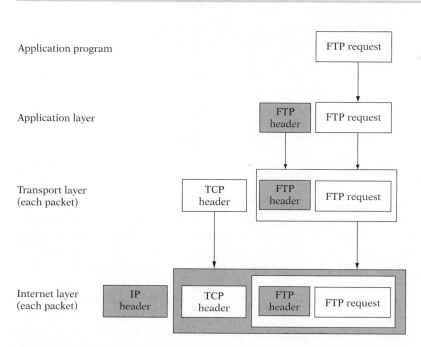

FIGURE 17.24

IP adds its own header.

Byte	Contents
00	Version/Header leader
01	Type of service
02 03	Length (bytes)
04 05	Identification
06	Flags/Offset address
07	Offset address
08	Time to live
09	Protocol
10 11	Header checksum
12 13 14 15	Source IP address
16 17 18 19	Destination IP address

FIGURE 17.25

The format of an IP header.

The Network Access Layer

The **network access** or **physical layer** is where packets are transferred from a node to the physical communication line and sent on to the next node. Like the other layers, the network access layer accepts a message from its immediate upper layer (Internet) and adds its own header containing the address of the current node and the next node (Figure 17.26). The TCP/IP model recognizes several data communication protocols that support numerous technologies (including Ethernet, collision detection, and token ring) for routing messages within a subnetwork (or subnet), and the precise content of a network access layer header varies with the physical network structure. Because the interface with the physical network is fully contained within the network access layer, however, the upper layers are independent of the physical network structure.

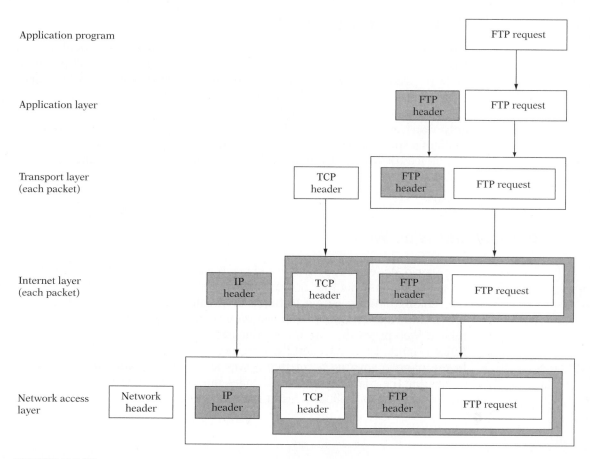

FIGURE 17.26

The network access layer adds another header.

Note in Figure 17.26 that each packet moving from one node to the next node over a communication line carries three headers, one each for the transport, Internet, and network access layers. (Generally, only a message's first packet carries an application layer header.) Each header holds control information appropriate to its layer. When the message reaches the destination node, the network access layer uses the information from the network header; the Internet layer uses the information from the IP header, and so on. Once the message is reassembled at the transport layer and passed up to the application layer, the application protocol (in this case, FTP) uses the application header embedded in the message. That is how each layer communicates with its peer layer on the other node.

The User Datagram Protocol

UDP (user datagram protocol) is an alternative transport protocol to TCP. UDP is not so accurate or reliable as TCP, primarily because it skips much of TCP's error checking, but it is significantly faster. The extra speed makes UDP particularly attractive for multimedia applications. For example, if one video frame out of every 30 fails to arrive or arrives out of order, you probably won't even notice the missing frame. In contrast, one missing piece renders a spreadsheet unusable, so the more reliable TCP protocol is a better choice for transmitting spreadsheets and similar nonmultimedia, non-streaming files.

◼ The World Wide Web

The **World Wide Web,** or **Web** for short, is a client/server application layered on top of the Internet that provides simple, standardized protocols for naming, linking, and accessing virtually everything on the Internet. The basic unit of information on the Web is a **Web page.** A **Web site** is a set of closely related Web pages that are interconnected by logical pointers called **hyperlinks** (Figure 17.27). Generally, one page is designated as the Web site's **home page,** a starting point that serves as a table of contents or index for navigating the site, and most Web pages incorporate hyperlinks to pages on other Web sites as well. The result is a vast, global "Web" of *billions* of pages.

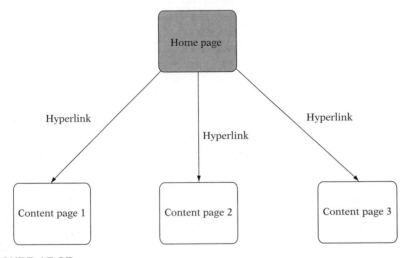

FIGURE 17.27
A Web site consists of a set of related Web pages.

Browsers and Web Servers

The World Wide Web supports communication between a browser and a Web server (Figure 17.28). A **browser** is an application program such as Internet Explorer or Netscape that runs on the client computer and requests and displays Web pages. A **Web server** is a server-side application program that runs on a host computer and manages the Web pages stored on the Web site's database.

Typically, the browser requests an initial home page from the Web server and displays the page. Once the initial home page is displayed, the user can begin surfing the Web. Hidden behind each hyperlink is the address of another Web page. Clicking on a hyperlink sends a page request from the browser (the client) to the desired page's Web server. The Web server responds by returning a copy of the requested page to the client's browser. The browser then displays the page.

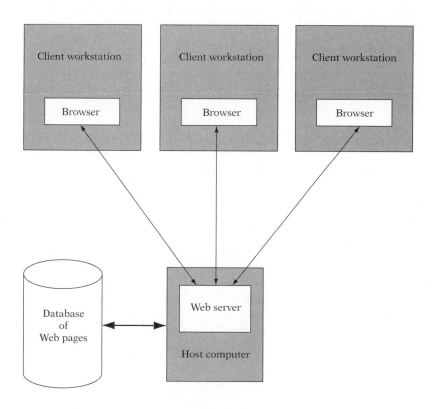

FIGURE 17.28

The World Wide Web links a browser and a Web server.

For example, imagine requesting a Web page from a major corporation like Microsoft (Figure 17.29). The client workstation resides on a LAN and is running a browser program (1). The user clicks on a hyperlink to Microsoft and the browser responds by generating a page request. The page request then flows from the workstation to the LAN server[1] (2), crosses the Internet, and makes its way to Microsoft's host computer (3). On Microsoft's host (hardware), a Web server (software) retrieves the requested page from a database of Web pages (4) and returns it via the Internet (5) to the LAN server (6) and on to the client workstation (7), where the browser displays the page.

The term "Web server" is sometimes used to refer collectively to an organization's Internet host and its hardware, software, and data components, but you will find the Web much easier to understand if you clearly distinguish between server hardware and server software. When you think of server hardware, picture a computer system designed and marketed to perform the server role in a client/server network. When you think of server software, picture an application program that runs on a server or a host computer and provides the requested service. The name of a server software application usually reflects its function; for example, a Web server returns Web pages, a file server retrieves files, an e-mail server manages e-mail, a database server controls access to a database, and so on. Unless the authors specify otherwise, the word server implies server software throughout the balance of this book.

The Uniform Resource Locator (URL)

Every page on the World Wide Web is assigned a unique address called a **uniform resource locator (URL)** (Figure 17.30); this is the Web page address that hides behind a hyperlink. Starting at the left, the first parameter names the access method or protocol to be used. **Hypertext transfer protocol (HTTP)** is the standard TCP/IP application layer protocol for requesting and transmitting Web pages between a client browser and a Web server via port 80. The colon is a separator, and the double slash indicates that a system address (rather than a file address) follows. The host computer's domain name comes next. To the right of the domain name is the path name of the host file that holds the requested Web page. The path name is a list of subdirectories that lead to the file. Note that a URL follows the UNIX standard, using regular slashes (rather than backslashes) to separate fields.

---

[1]Technically, there should be a gateway host or a router (or both) between the LAN server and the Internet in Figure 17.29, but for simplicity we'll ignore them.

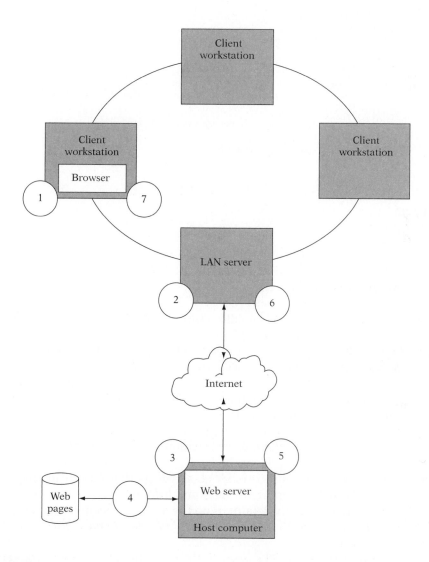

FIGURE 17.29

Downloading a Web page.

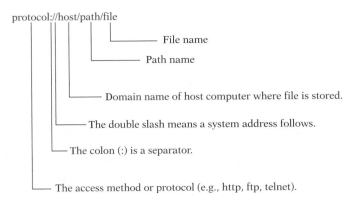

FIGURE 17.30

A URL.

For example, in the URL

http://www.anyco.com

http is the protocol, *www* (a conventional name for a publicly accessible Web server) is the name of Web server application program that runs on the host computer that holds the desired Web page, *anyco* is the local domain, *com* is the top-level domain, and dots or periods are used to separate the parts of the domain name. In the URL

http://employees.anyco.com/help.html

employees is a different *anyco* Web server (perhaps a private, password protected server for employees only) and *help.html* is the name of a Web page stored on the host. By default, if no file name is specified the server assumes an initial page (or home page) named *index.html, index.htm, default.html,* or *default.htm.*

Although most URLs begin with *http,* other protocols can be referenced. For example, the URL

ftp://archives.anyco.com/myfile

uses FTP, the file transfer protocol, to initiate a request for a file named *myfile* from *archives,* an *anyco* file server. Once again, the leftmost parameter in a URL defines the access method or protocol that supports the transaction.

Downloading a Web Page

The task of downloading a Web page from a server to a client is accomplished by the standard TCP/IP protocols. The process starts with the client's browser (Figure 17.31). The user identifies the desired page by clicking on a hyperlink, selecting a link from a bookmark or a *Favorites* file, a list of recently accessed URLs, or a history file, or by typing a URL on the address line. The request is passed to the TCP/IP application layer via port 80, where the HTTP protocol prepares a request for the selected page, calls on the application layer's domain name system (DNS) to convert the domain name specified in the URL to an equivalent IP address, adds a header, and passes the request down to the transport layer. The transport layer establishes a connection with the destination host, breaks the request into packets, and passes the first packet to the Internet layer. The Internet layer then adds its header, routes the packet to the next node, and passes the packet down to the network access layer, which adds a final header and drops the packet on the communication line.

The packet is routed through numerous intermediate nodes as it moves across the Internet. Once it reaches the target host, the network access layer removes it from the communication line and passes it up to the Internet layer, which checks the packet and passes it up to the transport layer. At the transport layer, the packets are collected and the message (a page request) is reassembled and passed, via port 80, through the application layer to the Web server, an application program. The Web server then retrieves the requested page and passes it down through the application, transport, Internet, and network access layers for transmission back to the client. When the packets that make up the requested Web page reach the client node, the client's network access layer takes each packet off the line and passes it up to the Internet layer. Subsequently, the transport layer assembles the packets and passes the message to the application layer via port 80, where HTTP passes it to the browser. Finally, the browser displays the page.

Note that the link between the client and the server is temporary. It is established when the client sends a page request to the host server and is terminated when the requested page is returned to the client. To the user there appears to be no difference (ignoring time delays) between loading a page from a local hard disk, another computer on the same local area network, or a remote host located halfway around the world because the various lower-level protocols operate transparently (and very quickly).

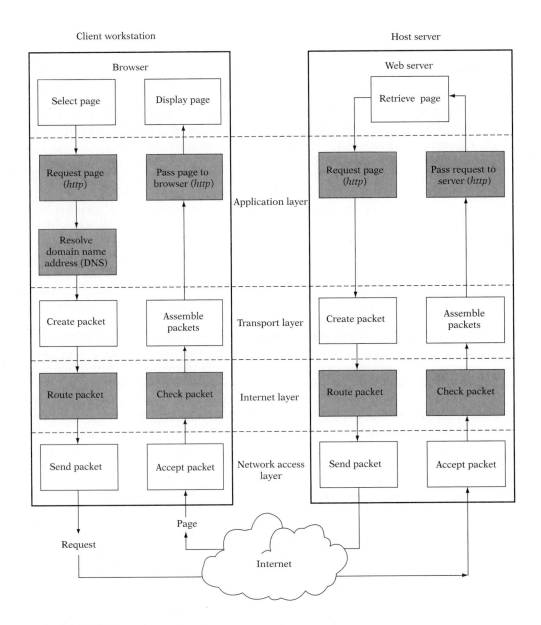

FIGURE 17.31
Using TCP/IP protocols to download a page.

Bottlenecks

Although it is convenient to think of each Internet and Web layer as an independent black box that performs its assigned task instantly, the reality is quite different. In Chapter 16 and this chapter you learned about the numerous intermediate computers and routers that participate in transmitting packets across the Internet and the TCP/IP protocols that run on each of those machines. Note that delays are possible within any layer on any device. An unacceptably long response time might be traced to the client's browser, one or more of the client's TCP/IP layers, the client's hardware, the client's local Internet service provider, backbone congestion, an intermediate router, the server's local Internet access provider, the server's hardware, the server's TCP/IP layers, the server software, and so on.

It is important to remember that the infrastructure is a complex, integrated system of many parts. What good is a super-fast computer if excessive traffic clogs the backbone? What good is a beautifully designed, highly interactive Web page if the user's underpowered computer (or modem, or local service provider) slows the page display process to such an extent that the user abandons the download? Layering makes it possible to deal with a complex system by allowing people to focus on one layer at a time, but those layers are still interconnected, and at some point they must function together or the system will not work well.

Web Page Contents

A basic Web page is a text file of **hypertext markup language (HTML)** tags (Figure 17.32) and embedded text that tells the client's browser how to display the page elements. HTML is a standard formatting language that all browsers understand. Consequently, any browser can display any Web page written in standard HTML.

HTML was originally designed to support text, but plain text can be boring. To make a page more interesting, hyperlinks to image, animation, sound, and multimedia files can be inserted into the HTML. For example, imagine a real estate agency's Web site that features photographs of available properties, one per page. The HTML for each page consists of several lines of text that describe the property and a hyperlink to an image file. When a customer selects the property by clicking on a hyperlink, the browser responds by requesting the appropriate page and the Web server returns an HTML file. The browser then maps the file's contents to the screen (Figure 17.33), scans the HTML for any embedded files, extracts the hyperlink, and sends another request to the Web server. The Web server responds by returning the image file, and the browser displays it (Figure 17.34).

Tag	Description	Tag	Description
<APPLET>	Java applet	<HEAD>	Document header
<B>	Bold	<HTML>	HTML document
<BIG>	Big text	<I>	Italics
<BODY>	Body of document	<IMG>	Image file
 	Line break	<LINK>	Hyperlink
<CENTER>	Center element	<MENU>	Menu list
<EMBED>	Embed a plug-in	<META>	Metatag
<FIG>	Figure (gif or jpeg)	<P>	Paragraph break
<FONT>	Define type font	<SCRIPT>	Insert script
<FRAME>	Define a frame	<SMALL>	Small text
<FRAMESET>	Define a frameset	<Tab>	Insert tab
<H1>	Level 1 heading	<TABLE>	Table of data
<H2>	Level 2 heading	<TITLE>	Page title
<H3>	Level 3 heading	<U>	Underline

FIGURE 17.32

HTML tags.

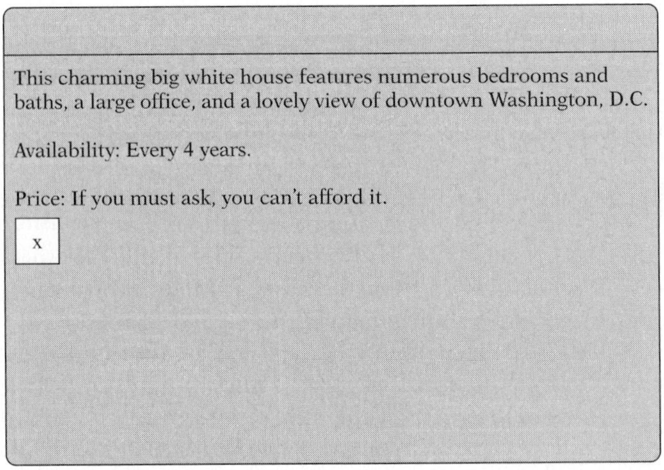

This charming big white house features numerous bedrooms and baths, a large office, and a lovely view of downtown Washington, D.C.

Availability: Every 4 years.

Price: If you must ask, you can't afford it.

x

FIGURE 17.33

The text is displayed first.

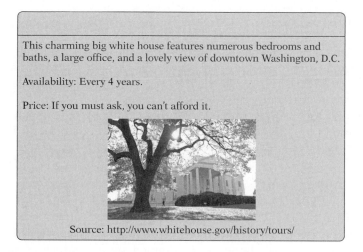

This charming big white house features numerous bedrooms and baths, a large office, and a lovely view of downtown Washington, D.C.

Availability: Every 4 years.

Price: If you must ask, you can't afford it.

Source: http://www.whitehouse.gov/history/tours/

FIGURE 17.34

The browser requests the embedded file and displays its contents.

Page Load Time

Page load time is the elapsed time between the act of clicking on the first hyperlink and the appearance of the finished page on the client's screen. Because downloading each embedded file takes time, page load time increases as the number and size of the embedded files increases. One consequence is that the Internet's default is to transfer only compressed files using such formats as *jpg* and *gif*.

Another way to speed up the page loading process is to use a **proxy server,** an intermediate server located on the client side of the connection that accepts a transaction from a user, forwards it to the appropriate server, and returns the response to the originator. To the real client, the proxy server appears to be the server. To the real server, the proxy server appears to be the client. Thus, the proxy server performs an intermediate role.

A proxy server can be used to perform such functions as screening transactions, maintaining a log, and performing virus and security checks, but in the context of the current topic, its most valuable function is caching pages to reduce page load time. The first time a given page is requested by a client, the proxy server forwards the request to the Web server and then caches (or saves) the returned page. Subsequently, should any client on the local network request the same page, the proxy server responds by returning the cached copy, thus bypassing the time delays inherent in transmitting the page across the Web.

▤ An Expanded Layered View

As you learned in the first part of this chapter, the Internet is a worldwide network of networks layered on top of the global communication network (Figure 17.35). The World Wide Web is a client/server application layered on top of the Internet, and Web-based systems, the subject of Chapter 18, are built on top of that base. Each of those layers can be expanded to multiple sublayers, of course, but such high-level views help to clarify the relationships between the layers.

▤ Summary

Internet connectivity is achieved through an Internet service provider (ISP). The Internet's backbone is maintained by a number of network service providers (NSPs) who lease bandwidth to regional ISPs. NSPs exchange messages at network access points (NAPs).

A domain is a set of nodes that are administered as a unit. Each domain is assigned a domain name. The domain name system (DNS) converts domain names to the numeric IP addresses used by the Internet. The address resolution protocol matches the IP address to a physical MAC (media access control) address.

The TCP/IP or Internet model defines a set of standard packet switching protocols. The application layer protocols directly support application programs. The transport layer uses TCP and ensures successful end-to-end delivery of the complete message. The Internet or network layer uses IP to route packets. The network access or physical layer transfers packets to and from the physical network.

The basic unit of information on the World Wide Web is a Web page. A Web site consists of a set of related Web pages. Web pages and page requests are transferred between a client-side browser and a server-side Web server by following the standard TCP/IP protocols. Every page on the World Wide Web is assigned a unique address called a Uniform Resource Locator

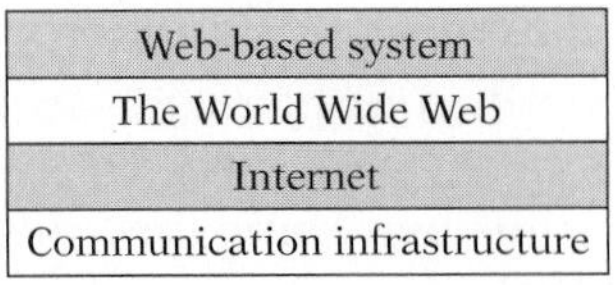

Web-based system
The World Wide Web
Internet
Communication infrastructure

FIGURE 17.35

An expanded layered view.

(URL). The hypertext transfer protocol (HTTP) is the standard protocol for requesting a Web page from a server. Web pages are created using HTML. Hyperlinks to image, animation, sound, and multimedia files can be inserted into the HTML. Page load time increases with the number and size of embedded files.

◼ Key Words

address resolution protocol (ARP)	media access control (MAC) address
application layer	messaging port
backbone	network access layer
browser	network access point (NAP)
domain	network layer
domain name	network service provider (NSP)
domain name system (DNS)	physical layer
home page	port (logical)
host	proxy server
HTML (hypertext markup language)	regional ISP
	TCP/IP model
HTTP (hypertext transfer protocol)	transmission control protocol (TCP)
	transport layer
hyperlink	UDP (user datagram protocol)
Internet	uniform resource locator (URL)
Internet layer	Web page
Internet model	Web server
Internet protocol (IP)	Web site
Internet service provider (ISP)	World Wide Web, or Web
IP address	

◼ Review Questions

1. What is the Internet?

2. What functions does an Internet service provider (ISP) perform?

3. What is the Internet's backbone? Who maintains the backbone? How does a user gain access to the backbone?

4. How is a workstation on a local network linked to the Internet?

5. What is a domain? Explain what each part of your school or organization's domain name means.

6. What is an IP address? Explain what each of the numbers in an IP address means.

7. Explain how the domain name system (DNS) maps a domain name to an IP address.

8. Explain how the address resolution protocol (ARP) maps an IP address to a MAC (media access control) address.

9. List the layers in the TCP/IP model and explain what happens at each layer.

10. What is a protocol? What functions are performed by TCP (transmission control protocol)? What functions are performed by IP (Internet protocol)?

11. What is UDP? Why is UDP used?

12. Explain the difference between an application program and an application layer protocol.

13. Explain how a logical messaging port number establishes a link to a specific application layer protocol.

14. Identify at least five application layer protocols and their port assignments.

15. Distinguish between a Web page, a home page, and a Web site.

16. What is a browser? How does a browser work?

17. What is a Web server? Explain how a Web server and a browser work together to download a page from a Web site.

18. Explain each element in the URL *http://www.muohio.edu/admissions.html*.

19. Describe the process of downloading a Web page in terms of the TCP/IP layers.

20. Explain how page load time is affected by the number and size of the files referenced on a page.

▌ Exercises

1. Access the Web site *www.thelist.com* and identify several nearby Internet service providers and the types of services they offer.

2. Cybersquatting is the act of registering a domain name someone else might want with the intent of selling it rather than using it. Why would anyone want to do that?

3. Use a dial-up line to access a Web site that features numerous graphical images. Watch as the images appear one by one, and explain what is happening.

4. If you are using Windows, investigate the Internet by issuing the following commands at the MS-DOS prompt. Look for *Command Prompt* on the *Accessories* menu if you are using Windows 2000 or Windows XP or MS-DOS *Prompt* on the *Programs* menu if you are using Windows 98.

    a. Find your computer's IP address by issuing the command *ipconfig/all*. Explain what the various parts of the IP address mean.

    b. If you are using Windows XP, issue the command *nslookup domain.top* (for example, *nslookup muohio.edu*) to find the equivalent IP address. Substitute your school or employer's domain name.

  c. To determine if a remote host is active, issue the command *ping domain.top* (for example, *ping muohio.edu*).

  d. Trace the path of a packet as it travels over the Internet by issuing the command *tracert www.muohio.edu*. Feel free to substitute another domain name of interest to you.

5. To view source information for an e-mail message, launch your mail program and select the message you want to read. Then pull down the *File* menu and click on *Properties*. The *General* tab summarizes key information about the message's source. Click on the *Details* tab to view source information in greater detail, and click on the *Message Source* button at the bottom of the *Details* window to see an enlarged view of the information. You might not understand everything listed, but much of it will make sense.

6. To view source information on a Web page, first launch your browser. When your initial home page appears, pull down the *File* menu and click on *Properties*. The contents of the *Properties* window should make sense. To see the source HTML, pull down the *View* window and click on *Source*. Even if your experience with HTML is limited, you should be able to connect at least portions of the HTML stream with the content displayed on the Web page.

7. Figures 17.3, 17.9, 17.26, and 17.31 are useful templates for organizing many of this chapter's key terms.

CHAPTER 18

Client/Server Information Systems

When you finish reading this chapter you should be able to:

▶ Define the term Web information system.

▶ Explain the concept of partitioning a Web information system's logic.

▶ Identify several different types of services.

▶ Explain how middleware enables complex Web applications.

▶ Define security. List and define seven key security criteria.

▶ Identify several common network vulnerabilities.

▶ Explain how antivirus software works.

▶ Describe the functions performed by a firewall.

▶ Distinguish between symmetric and asymmetric cryptography. Distinguish a public key, a private key, and a secret key.

▶ Discuss the need for security services.

◪ Web Information Systems

Today's state of the art in information technology features sophisticated interactive **Web information systems,** also known as **client/server information systems,** that rely on communication between asynchronous client-side and server-side application routines. A **Web-based** application is designed and built specifically to take advantage of the Internet and the World Wide Web. A **Web-enabled** application is a non-Web application, often a legacy application, to which a Web interface has been added, thus enabling a level of Web interactivity.

Web information systems follow the client/server model. Visualize a set of interconnected layers (Figure 18.1). The client platform and the server platform are linked by the underlying data communication infrastructure, the Internet, and the World Wide Web. An operating system and a Web application program run on both the client platform and the server platform. Those two Web applications, linked by the underlying infrastructure, form the Web information system.

Most operating systems (including Windows, UNIX, and Linux) can be used to support a client/server network, and the client and the server do not necessarily have to run the same operating system. However, if they are to communicate, both the client operating system and the server operating system must use the same set of communication protocols, and for Web applications the TCP/IP protocol suite is by far the most common choice (Figure 18.2). Most server operating systems come with the TCP/IP protocols preinstalled, and for a home computer user (the client), the installation program on an Internet service provider's activation CD typically installs and/or activates the TCP/IP protocols. The odds are very good that you have seen one of those ubiquitous AOL CDs, and most ISPs provide a comparable self-installation option.

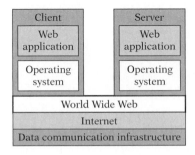

FIGURE 18.1

Web information systems are built on the infrastructure defined by the Internet and the World Wide Web.

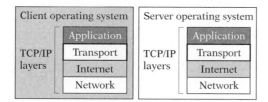

FIGURE 18.2

The client and the server both use the TCP/IP protocols.

Services

By definition, a Web information system incorporates at least two computers—a client and a server. Consequently, applications can be **partitioned** so that some of the logic is executed on the client and some on the server. On the client side, the logic is typically performed by an application program such as a browser. On the server side, the logic is typically implemented as one or more services, where a **service** is a routine that performs a single task, such as returning a Web page or downloading a file, in support of another program. Several common services are described below.

Web Services

A Web server is a server-side application program that provides **Web services,** such as retrieving Web pages in response to a request from a client (Figure 18.3) or supporting the ability to run scripts[1] on both the client side and the server side. When you browse the Web, you use a client-side browser program to communicate with a server-side Web server.

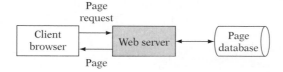

FIGURE 18.3

A Web server.

---

[1]A script is a programlike set of precoded commands.

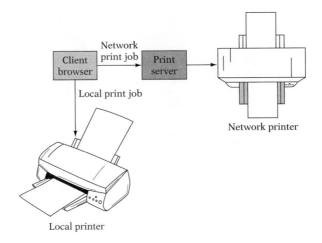

FIGURE 18.4

Print services.

Print Services

On many local area networks, client workstations have the option of sending a print job to a local printer or to a networked printer (Figure 18.4). Often the local printer is an inexpensive printer that is adequate for short, draft-quality print jobs, while the networked printer (or printers) is both faster and more effective for large print jobs and finished-quality documents. The networked printer is typically controlled by a print server that performs **print services.**

Sending a print job to a networked computer is similar to printing to a local client-side printer. When the user issues a print command, the client-side operating system routes the job to the local printer or to the print server. Jobs that are routed to the print server are stored temporarily on a print queue (Figure 18.5). Some time later when the printer is free and can service the job, the print server sends the print job to the networked printer. The print queue acts as a buffer and allows multiple clients to share the same networked printer.

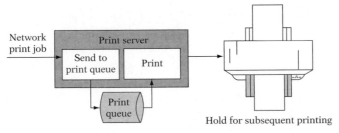

FIGURE 18.5

The print queue.

Many print servers also support bi-directional communication with the networked printers, allowing users to access the print queue to find the status of their jobs. Once printing is complete, the print server might send a confirmation message to the client machine. On some systems, users can request notification when certain events (such as low toner) occur.

E-Mail Services

E-mail services predate Web services. Think of an e-mail server as an electronic post office that accepts and stores messages, notifies clients when their mailboxes contain mail, and distributes the mail on request. Additional e-mail services might allow a user to look up the addresses of other users, broadcast messages, and so on. The user reads, writes, and replies to the messages through a client-side mail program.

File Services

File services enable a user to create, retrieve, and update data on the network file server, often by accessing a virtual disk. For example, in addition to the usual A (diskette), C (local hard disk), and D (CD-ROM) drives, a student or faculty member accessing a workstation connected to the Miami University's School of Business Administration's local area network can access a virtual G drive. Faculty members post course materials to the G drive, and students (who have read-only access) can retrieve those materials twenty-four hours a day, seven days a week. To a user, there is no apparent difference between accessing the G drive and accessing the C drive, even though the G drive is physically stored on a central host and accessed via a file server. In addition to supporting centralized sharable files, a file server can be used to provide backup for both private and shared files, specify access and control information, and provide file compression and data migration utilities.

Like print services, modern file services are designed to make the physical location of a file largely irrelevant, ignoring transmission time of course. On the client side, the user requests access to a file as though the file was stored on a local, client-side hard disk (Figure 18.6). If the file is available on the client-side (for example, on drive C), the client's operating system simply calls the local file system, which returns the file. If, however, the file is located on a remote computer, (virtual drive G, for example) the request is directed to the client's network interface (TCP/IP), which sends the request to the file server. The file server then retrieves the file and returns it to the client.

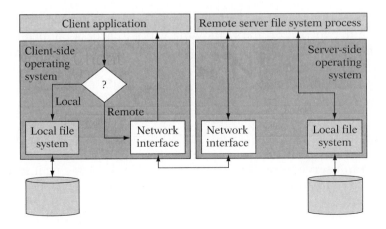

FIGURE 18.6
File services.

Directory Services

Modern business organizations and other large organizations have offices and users all over the world. Ideally, all these users should be able to access such network resources as files, databases, applications, and information without worrying about where a given service is physically located or through which server it is accessed. In other words, the users expect the network's resources to be location independent.

A **directory service** is a database of objects and users that organizes the network resources and makes them available to all the users. In effect, directory services help to manage interpersonal and internetwork relationships, network devices, network applications, and other network-based information by providing a single logical view of the network's resources and services. The directory database might be distributed over several nodes, with different portions stored on different servers. An alternative is to replicate the directory database, storing identical copies on multiple servers for faster access.

For example, imagine that a user working at a client workstation in Cincinnati wants to route a document to a laser printer located in a Los Angeles branch office. By working through directory services, the user can select the proper printer and send a print job to that printer as though the printer was directly connected to his or her computer. Directory services make the details associated with transporting the document across the network transparent to the user.

Management Services

For many modern organizations, the network has become a mission-critical resource. For example, a large business concern simply cannot tolerate network downtime because downtime means that employees lose access to applications, the central database, print services, e-mail, and other services essential to performing their jobs. Even worse, network downtime means that customers cannot access the system, and that can mean lost business. **Management services,** a collection of modules that support system management, play a crucial role in reducing network downtime by helping the system manager maintain the network and recover from service interruptions quickly and with minimal disruption.

Typically, management services allow the responsible administrator to access and manage all the desktop (client) services without leaving his or her office. For example, a system administrator might use management services to electronically distribute a software upgrade from a central source, which is significantly more efficient than individually installing the upgrade on each client machine. Other management services allow the system administrator to manage and monitor the use of licensed software to ensure that no violations of licenses take place, track software usage, and shut down and start services remotely. Additionally, management services sometimes support load balancing algorithms designed to spread the workload over multiple servers. For example, if a given server's processor is fully utilized, management services can shift work to another server.

Updating Application Software

One of the first reasons why many organizations (including many schools) installed a client/server LAN was to simplify the task of maintaining application software. Imagine, for example, that your academic division's computer lab has 100 workstations. In the pre-LAN days, application programs such as Word or Excel were independently installed on each of those 100 workstations, so when a bug was discovered, it had to be patched 100 times. When the supplier released an updated version of the software, the technical support group faced a difficult decision: install the new software 100 times or stay with the old version. As you can imagine, the decision was often to stay with the old version, so the students who used the lab were stuck with outdated software.

Contrast the old system with a LAN-based system. Key applications are still installed on each of the 100 workstations. However, when an update or a patch is received, the system administrator updates the server copy and then sets up a program that copies the update from the server to the user's machine the next time the user logs onto the network. Using a LAN significantly reduces software maintenance costs.

Content Management Services

Content management services allow the responsible individuals to add, delete, modify, and generally maintain the content of a Website. Often, three (or more) versions of the Website are maintained—the public or active version, a backup version that can be activated if the public version is corrupted, and a test or development version.

There are two common approaches to Website content management: centralized and decentralized. In the centralized approach, content experts submit updates to a technical expert who converts the information to HTML form and updates the site. As the amount of content grows, however, the technical expert can become a bottleneck. The decentralized approach shifts the responsibility for generating the HTML to the content experts. Distributing responsibility to multiple sources can introduce inconsistencies in the look and feel of a Website's pages, however, which can create navigational problems for users. In an attempt to overcome the disadvantages of both approaches, some organizations use a hybrid approach, allowing the content experts to generate the content in HTML form and assigning a centralized group the responsibility and authority to enforce consistency across the Website.

Database Services

In a distributed client/server environment, the results of a database query might be displayed in a spreadsheet, incorporated in a Web page, merged into a word processing document, and so on. **Database services** are an important key to enabling such applications. The aim of database services is to allow users to easily access, integrate, and use a system's data resources. For example, if client's query is passed to a database server, the database server responds by retrieving the requested information and passing the results back to the client (Figure 18.7). In addition to queries, a database server might allow a user to manage the contents of the database by issuing transactions to add, delete, and modify information. Report generation is another common feature.

Application Services

An application server (or application platform suite) performs a variety of **application services** that integrate many of an organization's day-to-day tasks. Additionally, most application service providers support a system development environment for client/server applications. The application services concept is still evolving so the definition remains a bit imprecise, but the intense competition among such major players as BEA (WebLogic),

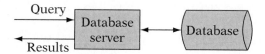

FIGURE 18.7

Database services.

Hewlett-Packard (OpenView), IBM (WebSphere), Microsoft (.Net), Oracle, Rational, Sun Microsystems, and others suggests that the potential for such software is enormous.

■ Middleware

In a basic Web information system, surfing the Web for example, a client-side application program (a browser) communicates with a single service (a Web server) on the server side. In contrast, more sophisticated Web information systems often rely on **middleware** to link multiple servers and/or custom application routines, where middleware is software that connects two dissimilar applications and allows them to exchange data or intercommunicate.

For example, consider a Web information system that involves accessing a database (Figure 18.8). The client's browser initiates the database query. A browser communicates with a Web server using HTML, so the query flows across the Internet to the Web server in HTML form. In addition to the Web server, the host computer also runs a database server that requires a database language such as SQL (structured query language), so the HTML query is converted to a form acceptable to the database server by a middleware routine. Subsequently, the database server's results are converted back to HTML form by the middleware routine before the Web server returns them to the client browser for display.

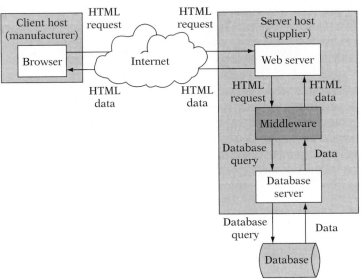

FIGURE 18.8

Middleware connects two otherwise separate applications.

Note that multiple servers can run on a single host computer (Figure 18.9). For example, one Web server might manage access to the organization's public Website, a second Web server might be available only to authorized customers and business partners who know the proper password, and access to a third Web server might be restricted to the organization's own employees. Add a file server and an e-mail server, and you have five server applications running on the same host. It is also possible to run each server on a separate host (Figure 18.10) or spread the five servers over two, three, or four hosts. Using middleware, those servers can be linked to form complex Web information systems.

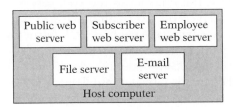

FIGURE 18.9

Multiple servers can run on the same host.

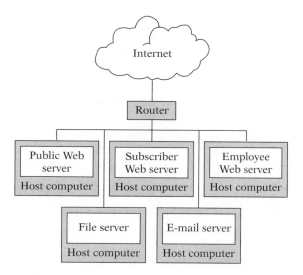

FIGURE 18.10
Multiple servers can run on multiple hosts.

Security

The ability to partition a Web-based application over multiple, interconnected computers is the key to creating sophisticated Web information systems, but there are significant security implications associated with such systems. It might be possible to prevent unauthorized users from gaining physical access to a system's clients, server hosts, and other nodes by using doors, locks, guards, and other access control tools. However, once those nodes are connected to a network and begin communicating over the public Internet, logical access control is lost because both legitimate users and cybercriminals can access the Internet from virtually any computer located anywhere in the world. Usually, the advantages of using the Internet outweigh the risk, but it is dangerous to ignore the risk.

What Is Security?

According to Merriam-Webster's *Collegiate Dictionary* (the online version), **security** is "the quality or state of being secure," which includes "freedom from danger" and "freedom from fear or anxiety." Security also means "something that secures," including "measures taken to guard against espionage or sabotage, crime, attack, or escape." In an information technology context, security is a set of procedures, techniques, and safeguards designed to protect the hardware, software, data, and other system resources from unauthorized access, use, modification, or theft.

Somewhat hidden by the apparently straightforward definitions is a clear sense of security as a series of trade-offs between conflicting objectives. Users want convenience, ease of use and no downtime. Consequently, system administrators are under constant pressure from management and users to keep the system up and running, and security is essential to achieving that objective. But security adds an extra layer of overhead that makes system access more difficult and less convenient. The key to effective security is balancing those conflicting objectives.

Figure 18.11 summarizes several key security criteria. The first criterion, **access,** focuses on the user. The principle is simple: security must not interfere with the user's primary activities. The purpose of **authentication,** the act of verifying a user's credentials and confirming that the user is who he or she claims to be, is to ensure that only authorized people are allowed access to a network, a service, a system, or a facility. The purpose of the **integrity** criterion is to ensure that the message was not modified during transmission, while the purpose of the **privacy** criterion is to ensure that only the sender and the receiver know the contents of a transaction. **Nonrepudiation** prevents the sender from denying that he or she sent the message. If the message can be repudiated, it is possible for the sender or someone posing as the sender to commit fraud. The **recovery** criterion calls

FIGURE 18.11

The objectives of security.

Criterion	To ensure that:
Access	Each user has reasonable access to all the system resources he or she needs to perform a task.
Authentication	Only authorized users are allowed access to a network, a service, a system, or a facility.
Integrity	The message was not modified during transmission.
Privacy	The contents of the message are known only to the sender and the recipient.
Nonrepudiation	The sender cannot deny that he or she sent the message.
Recovery	Procedures are in place to quickly get the system back on line after a security breach has occurred.
Auditability	The security procedures can be audited.

for effective backup and recovery procedures to quickly get the system back on line after a security breech has occurred. Finally, the key to **auditability,** a measure of the extent to which a set of procedures can be audited, is consistent, accurate data collection.

Hackers and Malware

Back in the 1970s, to be called a **hacker** was a compliment. In those days, a hacker was an expert programmer with a knack for quickly creating elegant solutions to difficult problems. Today, however, the term is more commonly applied to someone who illegally breaks into computer systems.

True hackers (in the expert programmer sense) resent that characterization. They divide themselves into white-hat and black-hat categories. The white-hat hackers follow an unwritten code of ethics. They believe that a hacker should cause no harm and should not profit financially from his or her hacking activities. Black-hat or dark-side hackers, on the other hand, break into computers with malicious intent; they are the Internet's cyberterrorists, industrial espionage agents, free-lance spies, and troublemakers.

Once they gain access, hackers sometimes introduce destructive software called **malware** into a computer system. A logic bomb is a program that (symbolically) blows up in memory, often taking the contents of a hard disk, selected data, or selected software with it. A variation called a time bomb executes on a particular date or when a particular condition is met. A rabbit is a program that replicates itself until no memory is left and no other programs can run. For example, one well-known rabbit copies itself twice and then launches the copies. A few nanoseconds later there are four rabbits running. Then eight, then sixteen, then.... By the time the operator realizes what is happening, the rabbit is out of control.

A backdoor is an undocumented software routine (less frequently, a hardware trap) deliberately inserted by a system's designer or a hacker that allows undetected access to a system. Sometimes called a trap door or a wormhole, a backdoor is a legitimate programming, testing, and debugging tool, but sometimes, programmers and system administrators forget to properly close a backdoor after they finish using it. Hackers use such backdoors to gain access to a system, and they sometimes leave behind a backdoor for future use following an initial intrusion by some other means.

A Trojan horse is a seemingly harmless program that invites an unsuspecting user to try it. Trojans typically enter a system in the guise of a computer game or a cool graphic attached to an e-mail message or available for free download from a mysterious Web site. A Trojan horse is often used as a delivery vehicle for a payload that might hold a logic bomb, a time bomb, a rabbit, a backdoor, or a similar piece of destructive software.

Perhaps the biggest fear among Internet users and corporate network managers alike is the uncontrolled spread of a virus or a worm. A **virus** is a program that is capable of replicating and spreading between computers by attaching itself to another program. Viruses typically spread through infected diskettes, downloaded copies of infected programs, or e-mail attachments. They are parasites that require a host program to reproduce and survive. A **worm,** in contrast, is a viruslike program that is capable of spreading under its own power.

Network Vulnerabilities

Before a hacker can launch a piece of malware, he or she must first gain access to the target computer. Physically secure information systems, networks, and access points are an essential starting point for system security, but even the most physically secure system can be successfully attacked. Often, the easiest way to gain access to an unauthorized computer is to log in using the ID and password of someone who has the appropriate rights.

The hacker's most common source of passwords is carelessness. Obvious passwords are easy to remember, but they are also easy to guess. In the lab, a hacker might watch a student and steal a password by reading the keyboard, a technique called shoulder surfing. Often, a user writes down and then throws away a password. Unfortunately, hackers do not hesitate to hunt through the paper trash, an activity they call dumpster diving. Some users write their password on a sticky-back note and paste it to their display screen, visible to anyone who might walk by including a visitor or an insider hacker. It is surprising how many people simply tell others their password. The act of convincing someone to divulge his or her password by taking advantage of the target's apathy, courtesy, curiosity, good nature, greed, gullibility, or ignorance is a form of what hackers call social engineering. Standard patterns give the hacker another potential source of passwords and software designed to crack passwords, can be downloaded from the Internet.

Not all illegal access is the fault of a careless user, however. Many network operating systems contain well-known **vulnerabilities** that allow a hacker to gain access. For example, computers are typically shipped with default passwords (such as *system, setup, startup, sysop,* and so on) that are used by the system operator to initialize the operating system. Once the system is properly initialized and ready to use, the system operator is expected to assign new passwords and disable the defaults, but sometimes the operator forgets. Once a hacker discovers a vulnerable system, he or she can simply log on using the default password and gain system operator (sysop) or root status (a common hacker objective), giving the hacker the ability to access and change virtually anything on the system.

Other possible access points must remain open to support common applications. For example, e-mail has become an accepted way of communicating and conducting business, so the e-mail messaging port must be active. That is why hackers rely on e-mail attachments to insert Trojan horses, viruses, and worms into a system.

Instant messaging is a growing problem. The technology relies on presence detection and buddy lists to identify currently online friends, colleagues, and contacts and allows a user to send instant messages to them, thus eliminating phone tag and crossing e-mail messages and making possible an effective, ad hoc form of data conferencing. Users like instant messaging because it improves efficiency and makes their lives easier. However, the popular instant messaging services are maintained by such public domain service providers as AOL, Microsoft Network, and Yahoo, so the supporting software is outside the organization's or the user's control.

Good Passwords

Your password is your first line of defense against hackers, so pick a good one. A good password is easy to remember and difficult to guess. Longer is better—6 to 9 characters is a good target. Mix different types of characters (letters, digits, special characters) to increase the number of possibilities a cracking program must test. Give your password a challenging meaning by using an acronym formed from a phrase; for example, "my first dog's name was Spot" becomes *m1dnws,* where the second character is the digit 1. To thwart password-cracking programs, avoid dictionary words, proper nouns, and foreign words; if you can find it in a dictionary, don't use it. Incidentally, sticking a digit or two at the beginning or the end of a dictionary word or substituting ph for f will not confuse a good password cracker. Stay away from personal information, too; a determined hacker can easily locate your telephone number, your mother's maiden name, your significant other's name, your pet's name, the last four digits of your social security number, and similar information. To limit the damage caused by a cracked password, avoid using the same password on multiple accounts. Finally, it only takes a few minutes to change your password, so change it regularly. Quarterly is reasonable for most users, but people with access to sensitive information should change their passwords more frequently.

Antivirus Software

These days, it is folly to access the Internet without up-to-date **antivirus software** installed on your system. A good antivirus program protects a system in three ways. First, it scans incoming and outgoing messages and files (and files stored on disk) for code patterns called **virus signatures** that uniquely identify a given virus. When a virus is detected, the software sounds an alarm, and many antivirus programs can isolate and destroy the virus before it even enters the system. The software also incorporates heuristic logic that continuously monitors the system for abnormal activity such as an attempt to modify the Windows registry. Finally, most antivirus programs include facilities that help a system manager to recover from a virus attack. New viruses are created almost daily, so it is important to keep your antivirus software up to date by regularly downloading new virus signatures and heuristics.

Perhaps the most effective approach is to implement virus protection in layers. Placing a router between the host server and the Internet and screening incoming and outgoing messages on that router provides a measure of networkwide protection. Antivirus software running on the host server represents a second layer of protection. Personal antivirus software running on each workstation forms a third line of defense. On such defend-in-depth systems, the lower-level filters are likely to stop any virus that manages to slip by the higher layers.

Firewalls

A **firewall** isolates a private network from a public network by controlling how clients from outside can access the internal servers. Often, the firewall software runs on a router or a bastion host (a host computer that is directly linked to the Internet and thus fully exposed to attack) that sits between the host server and the Internet and blocks potentially dangerous or questionable transactions from getting in or out (Figure 18.12). Another common configuration allows unrestricted access to Web servers, FTP servers, and similar public services but restricts access to the corporate network or a local area network (Figure 18.13), and proxy servers are often firewall-protected, too. Additionally, users often install personal firewall software on their workstations.

A packet filtering firewall works by screening incoming and outgoing packets at the TCP/IP Internet level. It accepts or rejects packets based on

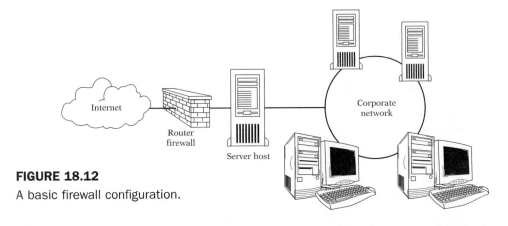

FIGURE 18.12

A basic firewall configuration.

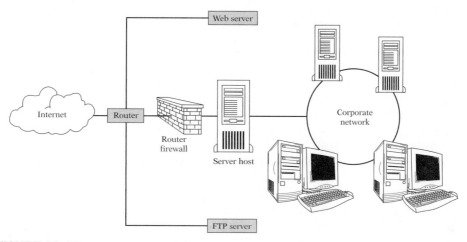

FIGURE 18.13

An alternative firewall configuration.

criteria stored in the message headers such as protocol (reject all *telnet* transactions), sending IP address, outgoing IP address, incoming port (reject all packets that do not come through port 80, the HTTP port), and so on. Most packet filtering firewalls are stateless; in other words they treat each packet as an independent entity and accept or reject it without considering related packets.

Other firewalls run at the application level and function as content filters, perhaps enforcing the organization's acceptable use policies. Sometimes called stateful firewalls, they rely on a proxy server to cache related packets, reconstruct the original message, and inspect the message content. Stateful firewalls tend to make better, more intelligent accept/reject decisions. For example, by screening content a stateful firewall can reject messages or pages with a possible sexual content by looking for such key words as breast and sex. One problem with such screens, however, is that they can reject legitimate information such as articles about breast cancer or biographical information about John Sexton, and they do cause some performance degradation. Once again, security is a series of tradeoffs.

A good firewall significantly improves security, but even a good firewall has weaknesses. They are particularly vulnerable to inside attack. Carelessness is perhaps the most serious risk, however, with system operators failing to remove default passwords, users choosing easy-to-guess passwords or writing their passwords on paper, users failing to disable Windows printer and file sharing, and users failing to update their antivirus software. One possible solution is to take responsibility away from the user and automate such tasks as software updates and regular password changes, but some tasks require human intervention.

Encryption

No matter how well a network is protected, some intrusion attempts will succeed—the question is not if but when. Consequently, it is wise to add another layer of protection to sensitive information stored on disk or while in transit. Cryptography is a potential solution.

Cryptography is the science of encrypting or otherwise concealing the meaning of a message to ensure the privacy and integrity of the information transfer. An unencrypted message is called **plain text.** The originator uses a secret code or cipher to **encrypt** the message into encoded or ciphered form. A code replaces one word or phrase with another; for example, the Secret Service assigns a code name to the President. A cipher replaces each letter or digit with another, for example substituting Q for A. On the other end of the line, the recipient reverses the process, **decrypting** the message by converting it back into plain text. Cryptographic techniques can also be used to protect the contents of a database from an intruder.

Symmetric encryption techniques such as **secret-key cryptography** use the same key to both encrypt and decrypt a message (Figure 18.14). Secret-key algorithms can be almost unbreakable, and both the encryption and decryption processes are relatively fast. However, both the sender and the receiver (at least two people) must know the key and getting the right key to both parties (the key exchange process) represents a significant security risk.

In contrast to symmetric single-key encryption, asymmetric encryption uses different keys to encrypt and decrypt a message. **Public-key cryptography** (Figure 18.15) is a good example. The encryption and decryption keys are distributed in related pairs. The receiver keeps one, the **private key,** and publishes the other, the **public key.** A message is encrypted using the *receiver's public* key (which is known to everyone) and decrypted using the *receiver's private* key (which is known only to the recipient).

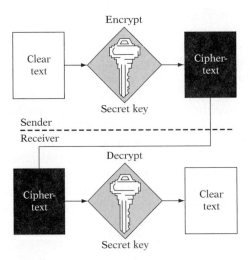

FIGURE 18.14

Secret-key cryptography.

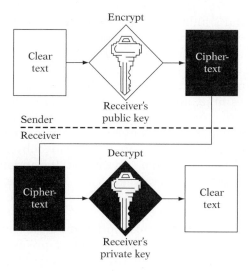

FIGURE 18.15

Asymmetric public-key cryptography.

Public-key algorithms are more complex and use longer keys than secret-key algorithms. Consequently, they are much slower (perhaps thousands of times slower) than secret key algorithms, making them unsuitable for encrypting real-time or lengthy messages. They are more secure than secret key algorithms, however, primarily because there is no need to exchange keys. Often, the solution is a hybrid approach that uses secret-key encryption to encode the message and public-key encryption to exchange the key.

The Secure Sockets Layer

The **secure sockets layer (SSL)** is a protocol that runs in the context of the standard TCP/IP protocols. It uses public-key encryption techniques to send a secret key to the recipient and then establishes a secure symmetric secret key connection between a client and a server for the duration of a session. The next time you pay for an e-commerce purchase by submitting your credit card number over the Internet, look for a closed lock icon near the bottom of your screen. It indicates that SSL is active. Check the protocol field in the URL, too; it should read *https*.

Security Services

The nature of security attacks is incredibly dynamic, with new system vulnerabilities, viruses, worms, and other malware appearing daily. Application, operating system, and security software suppliers respond to these threats by releasing a steady stream of patches, updates, new virus signatures, and similar fixes. Generally, it is the responsibility of the network administrator or system operator to ensure that these fixes are installed in a timely manner, because the failure to do so leaves the system vulnerable to attack. The problem is the sheer volume of patches, updates, virus signatures, and similar fixes that must be identified and installed. Each fix takes time, and system operators are often so overwhelmed with just keeping the system up and running that they don't have time for proper maintenance. The result can be disastrous.

A subscription model is often used to deliver patches and updates. Perhaps you have access to a service that, for an annual fee, automatically downloads at regular intervals new virus signatures and/or firewall patches to your personal computer, and similar subscription services are available at the server level.

The problem with the subscription model is that each service typically provides patches and updates for a single supplier. A user might find it relatively easy to deal with two or three subscription services to obtain patches and updates for an operating system, an application suite, and a security suite, but a system operator responsible for a large network might have dozens, even hundreds of software suppliers.

An important trend on modern network operating systems is to install a set of **security services** that help to automate all or part of the security maintenance task. For example, Opsware, a product of Loudcloud Corporation and the latest brainchild of Marc Andreessen, the creator of Netscape, is designed to monitor and track changes to numerous servers, in effect automating server operation and maintenance. Other security services monitor key Web sites and file servers for new patches and automatically download and install them.

◼ Summary

Today's state of the art in information technology features sophisticated interactive Web information systems that rely on communication between asynchronous client-side and server-side application routines. A Web information system can be partitioned so that some of the logic is implemented on the client and some on the server. A server is an application program that runs on the server side and performs services, such as Web services, print services, e-mail services, file services, directory services, management services, content management services, and database services. A Web information system's application programs are linked by middleware.

Security involves balancing conflicting objectives. Hackers use a variety of malware tools to attack computer systems and networks. E-mail, instant messaging, and Web surfing are considered potential sources of network vulnerability because access to those tools cannot be fully controlled. Antivirus software works by scanning for virus signatures, monitoring for viruslike patterns of activity, and supporting recovery. Firewalls are commonly used to help minimize the risk of intrusion. Symmetric, secret-key cryptography requires that both the sender and the receiver share the same secret key, but it is relatively fast and the algorithms are difficult to break. With asymmetric public-key encryption, two different keys are used for encryption and decryption—the public key (known to everyone) and a companion private key (known only to the key holder). Public-key encryption is relatively slow, but it solves the key exchange problem.

Key Words

access	partition
antivirus software	plain text
application services	print services
auditability	privacy
authentication	private key
client/server information system	public key
content management services	public-key cryptography
cryptography	recovery
database services	secret-key cryptography
decrypt	Secure Sockets Layer (SSL)
directory services	security
e-mail services	security services
encrypt	service
file services	virus
firewall	virus signature
hacker	vulnerability
integrity	Web-based
malware	Web-enabled
management services	Web information system
middleware	Web services
nonrepudiation	worm

Review Questions

1. What is a Web information system?

2. Distinguish between Web-based and Web-enhanced applications.

3. Explain the concept of partitioning a Web information system's logic between the client and the server.

4. What is a service? What is a server?

5. What functions are performed by a Web server?

6. What are print services?

7. What functions are performed by a file server? How does a file server make the physical location of a file transparent to the user?

8. What are directory services?

9. What are management services? Why are management services necessary?

10. What are database services?

11. What is middleware? Explain how middleware enables complex Web applications.

12. What is a hacker? Describe several common hacker tools.

13. What is a vulnerability? How do hackers find vulnerabilities?

14. What is security? List and define seven key security criteria.

15. Why are e-mail, instant messaging, and Web surfing considered potential sources of network vulnerability?

16. How does antivirus software work?

17. What is a firewall? What is a stateful firewall?

18. What is cryptography? Distinguish between symmetric and asymmetric cryptography.

19. What are the primary advantages of symmetric, secret-key cryptography? What is the biggest weakness of this technique?

20. What is the primary advantage of asymmetric public-key encryption? Distinguish a public key, a private key, and a secret key.

▌ Exercises

1. Investigate your school's network and determine how the technical support people update software.

2. Determine what services are available on your school's (or your company's) network.

3. Why do you suppose that an active Web site's content must be carefully managed?

4. Discuss the relative advantages and disadvantages of centralized and decentralized Web site content management.

5. What are the characteristics of a good password?

6. A good password is easy to remember and difficult to guess, but those two criteria conflict. How do you balance those criteria when you define your own passwords? In your experience, how do other people balance those criteria?

7. Security is a series of tradeoffs between conflicting objectives. What does that statement mean? Why is it important?

8. Do you have antivirus software installed on your personal computer? If not, install some; free versions are available for download via the Internet. If you do, how often do you update your virus signatures?

9. The intelligence community tried to keep public-key encryption secret. Why? Do you agree with the intelligence agencies or with the people who decided to take public-key encryption public? Why?

10. Figure 18.8 is a useful template for organizing many of this chapter's nonsecurity key terms. Study Figures 18.11, 18.13, 18.14, and 18.15 to review the security concepts.

CHAPTER 19

Windows 2003 Server

When you finish reading this chapter you should be able to:

▶ Briefly explain the functions performed by the protocols that operate at each level of the Windows 2003 network model.

▶ Define domain, domain tree, and forest.

▶ Describe the purpose of the Windows 2003 Active Directory.

▶ Describe the functions performed by the Windows 2003 Common Internet File System (CIFS).

▶ Explain the purpose of a shared folder.

▶ Identify the purpose of the Distributed file system (Dfs).

▶ Describe the primary components of the Windows 2003 Internet Information Services (IIS).

▶ Identify the tasks performed by clustering services.

▶ Identify several common features for managing Windows 2003 Server.

▶ Describe several Windows 2003 features and services you can access from a client computer.

Introduction

In Chapters 8 and 12 you studied Windows XP Professional running on a workstation in a client environment. This chapter focuses on the server features incorporated in Windows 2003, an enhanced, highly robust version of Windows XP. There are several different Windows 2003 Server editions, including: (1) the small business Standard Edition, (2) the Enterprise Edition, which is generally used as a departmental or enterprise server in a client/server network, (3) the Data Center Edition, which is designed to support mission critical applications that require a high degree of availability and scalability, and (4) the Web Edition, which is designed to host Web application services. The examples in this chapter feature the Enterprise edition.

Unless stated otherwise, the term server will be used to refer to software. Clearly, there is a hardware component called a server in a client/server network, but what makes a server host computer (hardware) a server is the software that runs on it, and given other software that computer could just as easily be used as a client.

The Windows 2003 Network Architecture

The network architecture supported by Windows 2003 (Figure 19.1) is based on the seven layer OSI model you encountered in Chapter 17 (Figure 17.12). Rather than having each of the seven layers implemented as distinct modules, Windows 2003 is divided into broad interfaces, with each interface straddling multiple layers of the OSI model.

The topmost layer, the application interface layer, runs in user mode. Some of the standard application programming interfaces (APIs) are implemented through user mode dynamic link libraries and others utilize both user mode libraries and kernel mode drivers.

Network APIs must use transport protocols such as TCP/IP to communicate information across the network. Other transport protocols such as Novell's IPX/SPX and Apple's AppleTalk are also widely used, so Windows 2003 must support multiple protocols. The network APIs use the **transport driver interface (TDI)** to provide a protocol-independent way for applications to communicate over the network. A transport driver implements a specific protocol such as TCP/IP and exposes the TDI interface to the network API clients.

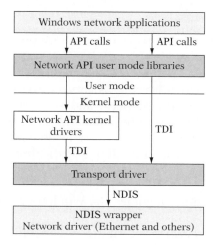

FIGURE 19.1

Windows 2003 network architecture.

The transport driver is independent of the underlying network hardware and communicates with the network card using the **network driver interface specification (NDIS).** NDIS describes the interface used to communicate with underlying hardware or network interface card. NDIS drivers are responsible for interfacing TDI transports to a particular network adapter and allow network card vendors to ensure that their drivers are compatible with Windows.

Domains

In most organizations, groups of users require access to shared resources. For example, students at a university might want access to a faculty member's PowerPoint presentations, and they might need to share printers and disk space to perform group work. In this example, different groups require different access rights. The faculty member must have read/write access to the PowerPoint files, but students must be restricted to read-only access. In contrast, all the students in a given workgroup require read/write access to their shared disk space, but they must not be able to access other workgroups' shared workspaces.

Windows uses the notion of a **domain** to manage the user workgroups, where a domain is a group of computers that share an **Active Directory** database and have a common security policy (Figure 19.2). The Active Directory is a hierarchical database that holds information about all the objects on the network, such as servers, users, shared volumes, printers, domains, applications, services, and security policies. The domain controller is a computer running Windows 2003 Server that hosts the Active Directory. The Active Directory is replicated across all domain controllers, so if the main **domain controller** fails the directory is not lost. Servers that are in the same domain but do not host an Active Directory are called member servers.

Each domain has a name. The Windows naming scheme resembles the Internet domain name system, so a university might have a domain name such as *university.edu*. The **namespace** is the set of all names that are unique within a network. In a contiguous namespace, each child object contains the name of its parent object; for example, the business school domain within the university might be named *business.university.edu*.

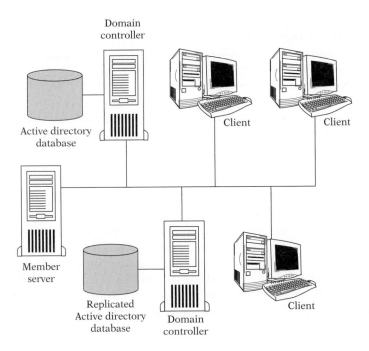

FIGURE 19.2

The basic unit of a Windows 2003 client/server network is a domain.

A **domain tree** is a hierarchical organization of different domains. For example, the business school and the engineering school might each have a domain and those two domains might be integrated to form a domain tree. A domain tree is characterized by a shared Active Directory database and a shared contiguous namespace. For example, the university might use *university.edu* as its Internet name, the business school might use *business.university.edu*, and the engineering school might use *eng.university.edu*. Additionally, each domain within the tree has a trust relationship with other domains; in other words each trusts the other to authenticate users within their domains, allowing users to access any network resource within the tree for which they have rights.

A domain tree is associated with a contiguous namespace, while a **forest** (a group of one or more domain trees) is associated with a noncontiguous (disjointed) namespace. Imagine, for example, that company X purchases or merges with company Y. Prior to the merger, both companies have their own, independent domain trees, *X.com* and *Y.com*. After the merger, employees at Y must be able to access and use resources on X's domain tree, and vice versa. A forest is used to bring together and link the independent domain trees of such disjointed namespaces and enable communication across the entire organization. All domains in a forest share a common global catalog. Each domain tree within the forest has a trust relationship with the other domain trees that allows authentication in one tree to carry over to the other trees.

Active Directory Service

A service is a specific task, often a system task that supports another program. A **network service** is a service that supports a system task over a network. A **directory service** is a network service that makes a directory available to users, system administrators, and applications.

Under Windows 2003 Server, all objects exist within a domain and Active Directory is a directory service installed on a Windows 2003 domain controller. The main Active Directory object is the **domain component (DC).** Network resources (such as users, printers, files, and applications) are found at the end of the hierarchical tree structure and are called **leaf objects.** Organizational units, such as companies, divisions, and departments are **container objects;** they contain other containers and leaf objects and are used to divide and organize the tree structure into branches. **Access control lists** are permissions assigned to the resource that identify which users have access to the object and the specific actions each user can perform on the object. Active Directory associates an access control list with each container, object, and object attribute within the directory.

Every object has a **distinguished name (DN)** that uniquely identifies the object. The DN includes the common name associated with the object and its ancestors in the tree. For example, in Figure 19.3, user *DavisW* is in the container *Users,* which is in the container *Business School,* which is in the *University* domain. Hence, its DN might be

/DC=University/OU=Business School/OU=Users/CN=DavisW

where *DC* means domain component, *OU* means organization unit, and *CN* means common name.

Since users are objects, logon authentication is provided by Windows using the information in the Active Directory. Each user has a single logon name within the domain and has access to all the network resources to which he or she has rights. Active Directory user objects can also be mapped to their corresponding Passport identification, if it exists. Passport is a Microsoft service that allows users to log on once on the Web and use that logon and profile information at multiple participating Web sites. All user account and security information is stored centrally in the Active Directory.

Active Directory provides a **global catalog** that allows users to find any object for which they have access rights. A user can use the global catalog to search for objects within the Active Directory; for example, a user can find the e-mail address of another user using the global catalog. The catalog is also the primary mechanism by which a user logs onto the network.

▪ File Services

File services allow users to share files stored on the server and access a single point of backup. Windows 2003 uses the **Common Internet File System (CIFS)** to share files. CIFS defines a standard remote file system access protocol for use over the Internet, enabling groups of users to share documents (files). Standard network functions, such as read, write protection, and so on, are implemented within CIFS. Generally, servers that provide file services are installed as member servers rather than domain controllers (in other words, they do not store a copy of the Active Directory).

Shared Folders

To share files on the server, you create **shared folders.** When a folder is shared, users (with the appropriate permissions) can read, create, and modify the files in the shared folder. Shared application folders hold applications installed on the server. The client computers download and use these applications, so they need not be installed on every client computer. Client computers store configuration information for the shared applications on their own machines. Shared data folders are created when users wish to

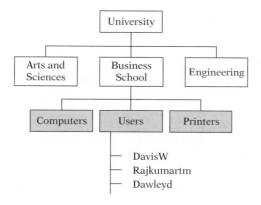

FIGURE 19.3

Active Directory is a directory service installed on a Windows 2003 domain controller.

Net and Passport

Windows 2003 is the first Windows operating system to integrate Microsoft's .Net framework. In fact, for a few months before it was released, .NET was called *.net-server.*

A major benefit of .Net is that it facilitates the development of Web services, applications that can be used over the Web. Businesses use these Web services as building blocks to help develop applications. At the heart of .Net is the Common Language Runtime (CLR). Programs written in languages such as Visual Basic, C, and C# are first compiled into the Microsoft Intermediate Language (MSIL), which defines instructions for the CLR. The CLR then translates the MSIL code into machine language before it is executed. The advantage of this approach is that objects from different languages can be mixed and combined to create a single application. For example, a program can have a Windows form written in Visual Basic call a service from a C# object. The CLR also provides memory management and security features. In addition to the CLR, .Net contains a library of classes that provide a variety of reusable components such as buttons, list boxes used by Windows forms, database connections, tools to help build applications that can talk to databases and html-form elements, image objects, and other Web application tools.

Many Web sites require users to register and log in with a user ID and a password to access services, and remembering multiple user IDs and passwords is difficult. Incorporated within .NET is a Web service called Passport that provides a single login service that makes signing in to Web sites fast and easy. Passport uses encrypted cookies on the client machine to allow authentication credentials to travel with the user to other Web sites that participate in Microsoft's passport system.

exchange data. Working data folders are created for small work teams. Public data folders are created for large groups within the organization.

The system administrator has special rights and privileges on a shared folder. The users who are connected to a computer can be monitored and disconnected if necessary, and the administrator can close files.

Distributed File System

Distributed file system (Dfs) allows a network administrator to link together files that exist on physically different servers to form a single namespace (Figure 19.4). Defining a single namespace simplifies user access because all the files appear to be on a single server and the user need not know where the file is located or how to specify access.

Using Dfs, Windows 2003 can link files managed by servers that are not necessarily Windows-based. The Dfs client and server both use the Common

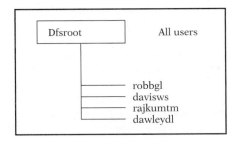

FIGURE 19.4

Distributed file system (Dfs) allows a network administrator to link together files that exist on physically different servers to form a single namespace.

Internet File System (CIFS) to decide which file server the client is accessing. Once the non-Windows server has been identified, that server's protocol (for example, UNIX file system) is used to access the file.

Shadow Copy

Windows 2003 uses **shadow copies** to maintain previous versions of files. With the appropriate client, users can see all previous versions of their files and restore a previous version if necessary. Windows 2003 provides a volume shadow copy service for backup applications. Once the service receives a backup request, it temporarily freezes the programs/applications that are writing to the file, performs the backup, and restarts the programs/applications. Thus Windows 2003 ensures consistent data on backups.

▪ Print Services

As the name implies, a **print server** is server program running under Windows 2003 Server that manages printers. A printer can be connected to a server computer, a client computer, or directly to the network. The print server software makes the printer visible on the network and accepts and schedules print jobs from client computers. Windows 2003 Server supports plug and play, which simplifies printer installation. Active printers are defined as objects in Active Directory.

Windows 2003 supports print pools, allowing a print job to be submitted to a logical printer that connects to a set of physical printers. The job is then printed on the first available printer. Additionally, print priorities can be enabled and administrators can specify user permissions and priorities.

▪ Web Services

An **application service** is a network service that provides a computing platform on which day-to-day applications can run smoothly. As the term implies, a **Web service** is an application service that utilizes the World Wide Web.

Under Windows 2003, the key Web services component is a Web server named **Internet Information Services (IIS)** (Figure 19.5). One key kernel-mode IIS component, **http.sys**, responds to http connection requests that arrive via port 80 and places each request on a queue for subsequent processing. In a simple two-tier Web surfing application, IIS returns to the queue a static (predefined) Web page. In an n-tier application, IIS might activate a middleware routine responsible for consolidating information from a file server or database server into a template page, creating a dynamic (constructed in real time) page, and placing the dynamic page on the queue. Http.sys subsequently returns the dynamic page to the client.

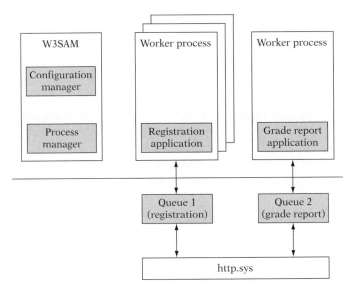

FIGURE 19.5

IIS architecture.

When http.sys receives a request that requires a middleware routine to be run, a second IIS component, World Wide Web Service Administration and Monitoring (W3SAM) starts a **worker process** that hosts and executes the middleware routines. Since different middleware routines can be assigned to run within a worker process, IIS allows the administrator to name the worker process and associate it with a specific middleware routine or application. A named worker process is called an application pool. Note that each application pool services a single queue (a single application).

Http.sys places different application requests in different queues. For example, a student registering for a course at a university might be serviced by a process associated with queue 1, while a student checking his or her grades might be serviced by a process associated with queue 2. It is also possible for a given queue to be serviced by more than one worker process. For example, at registration time multiple students are likely to be registering simultaneously and multiple processes might serve the single registration queue to improve response time and share the workload.

Application pools work in isolation and are separated from other application pools by process boundaries. Thus, if a faulty Web application runs in the application pool, it crashes only that application pool and not the entire Web server. Each worker process also runs in a default account with very few privileges and has no access to command line tools, thus reducing the potential for security violations or break-ins. These features improve the stability, security, and reliability of Web services in Windows 2003.

W3SAM allows the Web administrator to determine which applications will run and helps configure those applications. For example, by default an application pool has only one process, but the administrator can configure the number of processes within an application pool. Additional parameters such as memory usage, scheduled process run times, caching, and so on can be configured using W3SAM.

◗ Media Services

An optional module called **media services** can be used to configure Windows 2003 Server as a streaming server. In contrast to a Web server, which delivers the contents of a file, a **streaming server** is designed to broadcast live information (music, sound, video) in real time, encoding, compressing, and transmitting the information at a constant, predictable rate so that playback glitches (like dropped phrases and broken or frozen images) can be minimized. Streaming servers often use UDP (User Datagram Protocol) rather than TCP at the transport layer. Because the UDP protocol skips some of the TCP protocol's error checks, a streaming server effectively sacrifices quality for speed. On the client side of the connection, the user's media player application offers such controls as pause and rewind, and the streaming server must have the ability to respond to such commands. Also, a streaming server must be able to transmit information at different bit rates to accommodate both broadband and dial-up clients.

A Windows server using Media Services establishes publishing points to link clients to the server. A broadcast publishing point is used to stream live content to the client, and an on-demand publishing point is used respond to such client commands as rewind and pause. Server side play lists containing a list of contents and advertisements are specified for each publishing point using a variation of XML. Such information as content security and the maximum number of clients that can connect to a given publishing point are configured and set by the system operator, and additional plug-ins can be used to provide such services as authentication and logging.

■ Clustering Services

A **cluster** is a group of computers (hardware) that act like a single system to provide services to clients (Figure 19.6). The computers in the cluster are connected using high-speed network links and run server software such as the Windows 2003 operating system. To the clients or users who log on to the cluster, the computers that form the cluster appear as though they are a single unified resource. Each computer in the cluster is referred to as a node or host.

Note that a cluster links several computers—hardware. The word "server" generally implies software, but it is sometimes applied to the host computer that runs a server program, and you'll encounter that second meaning in the next paragraph. To help avoid confusion, we'll selectively use the term "server host" or "host" to make clear that we are talking about hardware. Note, however, that if you read Microsoft's source documentation, the term "server" is used without qualification.

When one of the hosts in the cluster goes down, a client request is routed automatically to another host without the client being aware of the switch, thus increasing reliability and availability. Under Windows, each server host in the cluster operates independently on its copy of the data and shares nothing with the other hosts. Devices that can be shared, such as a disk, are selectively owned and managed by a single server host. Windows provides load balancing so that each server host performs similar amounts of work. For example, the first request for a Web page might go to server host 1, the second to server host 2, and so on. However, once an application is assigned to a given host, further service requests from the client go to the same host. Windows 2003 can handle up to eight server hosts in a cluster.

One benefit of the World Wide Web is that customers can use self-service twenty-four hours per day, seven days per week rather than relying on the Web site's employees to complete work for them. Applications calling for such high availability are well suited to clustered services. In fact, many popular Web sites such as *cnn.com, ibm.com,* and *microsoft.com* use clustered Web servers called Web farms to share the load among computers and keep the system available. For example, if you issue the command

nslookup cnn.com

from the command line, multiple **IP** addresses will be returned reflecting different computers working together to provide a single Web service.

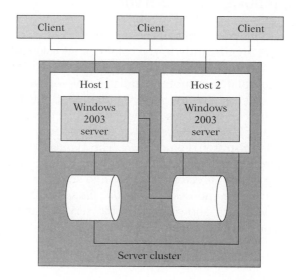

FIGURE 19.6

A cluster consists of two or more host computers running Windows 2003 Server.

◼ Peer-to-Peer Networks

Although client/server networks are much more common, both Windows 2003 Server and Windows XP Professional can be used to support a peer-to-peer network. A peer-to-peer network is called a **workgroup** in Windows terminology. Each computer maintains its own **security database** that contains information on users and resource security. All network administration is decentralized, and a user who wants access to multiple machines must have accounts and permissions on each machine. The advantages of running a peer-to-peer network include ease of setup and the ability to share such resources as files and printers. Such networks are effectively limited to connecting perhaps twenty-five computers, however.

Managing Windows 2003 Server

Organizations must control the total cost of ownership, and administration contributes significantly to the total cost of ownership as a network grows in size. Windows 2003 provides numerous administrative aids such as security templates, remote installation of software on the client's desktop machine, software update services, command line controls, and elimination of duplicate copies of files to reduce storage costs.

Windows 2003 provides a *Start* menu option, *Manage Your Server,* for the system administrator (Figure 19.7). The *Manage Your Server* option is a single location from which the administrator can manage a file server, an application server, the Active Directory, security, and so on (Figure 19.8). For example, if the administrator chooses *Manage this file server* (from the right panel), a new window will open showing other file server management options such as *Backup File Server, Configure Shadow Copies,* and so on (Figure 19.9).

FIGURE 19.7

Select *Manage Your Server.*

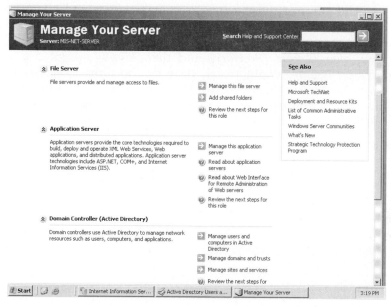

FIGURE 19.8

The *Manage Your Server* option.

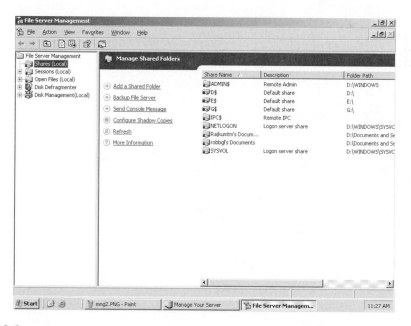

FIGURE 19.9

The *File Server* window.

The administrator can also manage users and client computers by accessing the information in the Active Directory. Click the left-pointing arrow to return to Figure 19.8. If the administrator chooses *Domain Controller (Active Directory)* and then *Manage users and computers in Active Directory* (right panel, near the bottom), a screen displaying all users is shown (Figure 19.10). By selecting a user and that user's properties, the administrator can change the information for any given user (Figure 19.11).

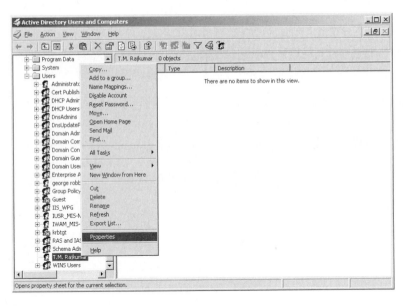

FIGURE 19.10

The *Active Directory Users and Computers* screen.

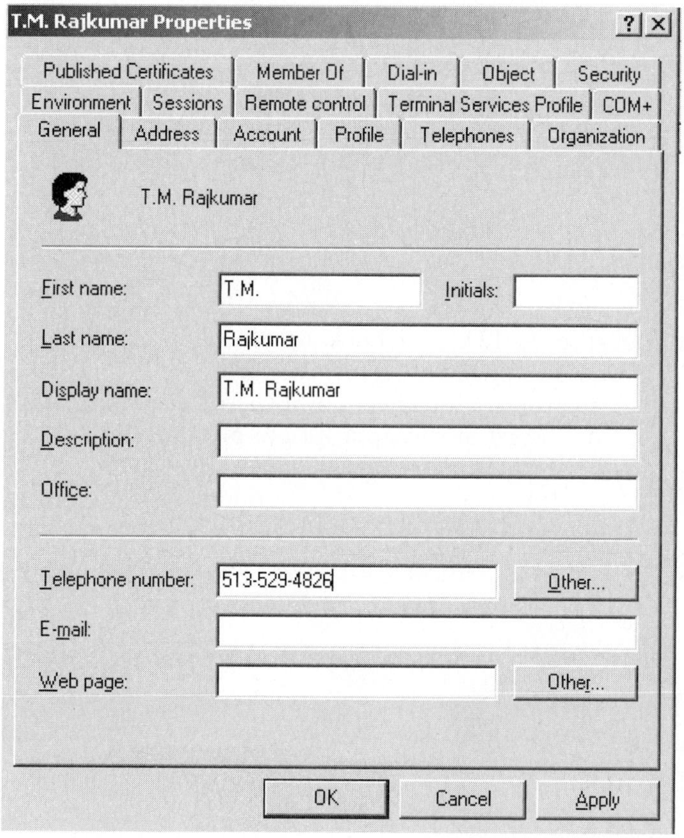

FIGURE 19.11

The administrator can change the information for any given user.

Using Windows 2003 Server from a Client Computer

The preferred client for Windows 2003 Server is the Windows XP Professional product. In this section, you will use the Windows XP client to perform some simple and standard operations with the Windows 2003 Server. Most users log in to the network, retrieve and manipulate network files, and use network printers. The network is transparent to the user and regular Windows tools such as *Explorer* are used when accessing network resources such as files or printers. As you read the material, try (with your instructor's permission) to work through the examples given here. Since every network is unique, you might have to adapt the material to the specific situation in your lab.

Logging onto the Network

Simultaneously press the *Ctrl+Alt+Delete* keys to display the login screen (Figure 19.12), and click on the Options button to reveal your choices. Choose *Logon to Servername* from the drop down menu; check with your instructor for the appropriate server name. Enter your user name and password at the appropriate prompts. Click on *OK* to log onto the network.

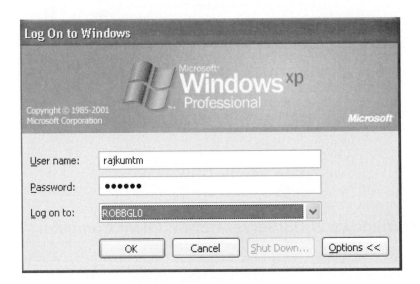

• Some commands available on Windows XP

• Access logon window by pressing *ctrl-alt-del*

FIGURE 19.12

The logon window.

Browsing Network Resources

Since the Windows XP client is integrated within the Windows interface, you can use Windows features such as *My Network Places* and *Explorer* to browse the resources on the network. *My Network Places* allows you to browse the resources of all networks to which your computer is connected. *Explorer* allows you browse through folders in a hierarchical fashion.

Accessing Network Resources Using My Network Places

Click on Start and select *My Network Places* (Figure 19.13). Choose *Entire Network* from the next screen (Figure 19.14) and double click *Microsoft Windows Network* (Figure 19.15) to reveal the domains available on your network (Figure 19.16). Depending on your environment, your domains and choices will almost certainly be different. Check with your instructor for the correct domain name and double click on the domain where your server is located (it's *robbgl0* in Figure 19.16) to open it. You will see a list of computers within the selected domain (Figure 19.17).

FIGURE 19.13

Select *My Network Places.*

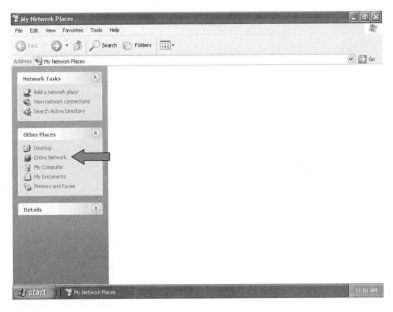

FIGURE 19.14

Choose *Entire Network.*

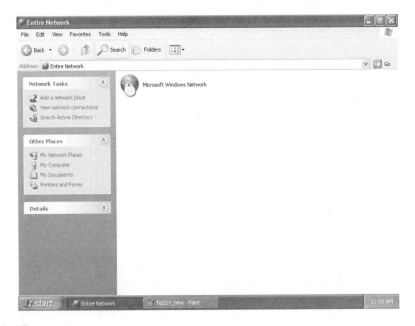

FIGURE 19.15

Double click *Microsoft Windows Network.*

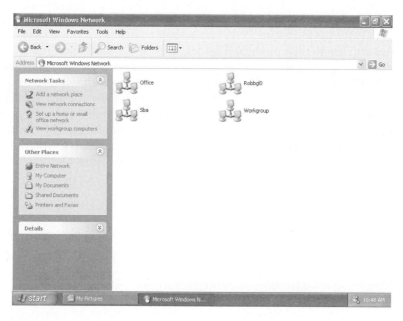

FIGURE 19.16

The domains available on the author's network.

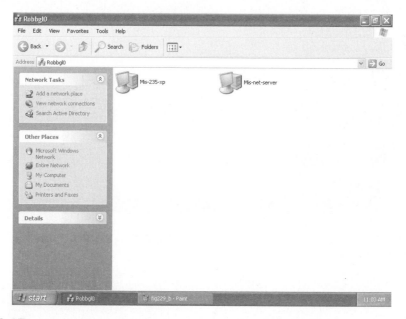

FIGURE 19.17

A list of computers within the selected domain.

Check with your instructor for the correct choice on your system (it's *Mis-net-server* in Figure 19.17) and double click the icon to open your server. You will see the list of shared folders that are available on the server (Figure 19.18). By default, certain shared folders (such as *NETLOGON* and *SYSVOL)* are always available, and other shared application and data folders might be listed. Check with your instructor for the name of the shared data folder you are to use and double click the folder name (the example in the book uses *rajkumtm's documents)*. You should see the contents of the shared folder (Figure 19.19); note that the author's shared folder is currently empty. You can now access or add to the contents of this folder as you would any other folder.

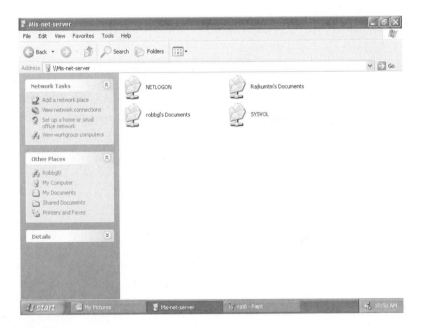

FIGURE 19.18

A list of shared folders.

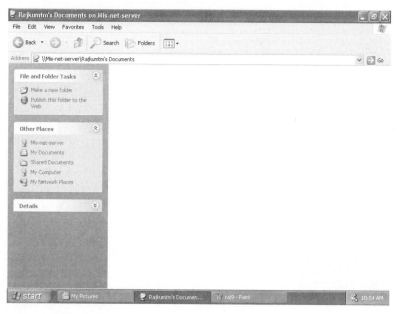

FIGURE 19.19

The contents of the author's (currently empty) shared folder.

Mapping a Folder

If you want repeated access to a shared folder, you can map the folder to a drive on your system. Mapping makes the shared folder on the server appear to your system as though it were a local drive. Once you map it to a drive (for example the G drive), the shared folder can be accessed from within *Explorer* by referencing the drive letter.

To map a shared folder, click on *Tools/Map Network Drive* (Figure 19.20) to start a wizard (Figure 19.21). Choose G on the first pull down list box *(Drive)* and enter the server address or browse to the shared folder (Figure 19.22) in the second pull down list box *(Folder)*. Check the *Reconnect at logon* box to ensure that every time you log onto the system the shared folder will be available as the G drive. Click on *Finish* to map the drive. Once the mapping takes place you can reference the G drive much as you reference your C drive.

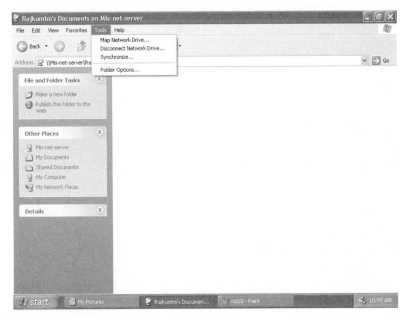

FIGURE 19.20

Mapping a network drive.

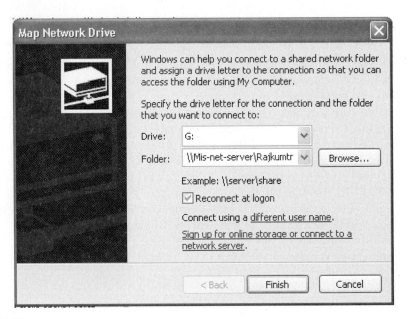

FIGURE 19.21

The mapping wizard.

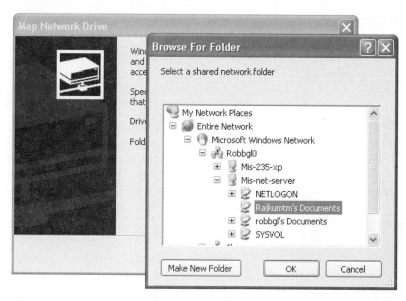

FIGURE 19.22
Browsing for the folder.

Windows *Explorer* and Mapped Shared Folders

Open Windows *Explorer* and select the drive G to make the files within the shared folder visible (Figure 19.23). Provided you have the appropriate rights, you can create files, rename files, delete files, or execute files from the shared folder. In other words, all normal file operations can be performed.

Using the Mapped Drive

A mapped drive can be opened and used to read and write files. To test this facility, create a file with Notepad and store it on the network drive. Click on *Start/Programs/Accessories/Notepad* to open *Notepad* and enter the text shown in Figure 19.24. Click on *File/Save* as and save the file on the G drive (your mapped drive) as *test.txt*. You can copy, rename, and perform other normal operations on the file using the techniques you learned in Chapter 8.

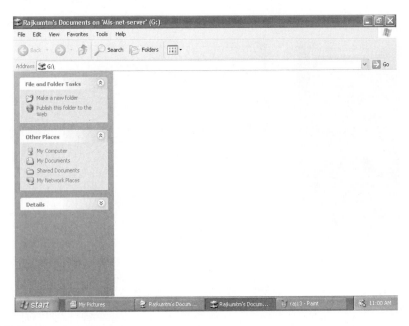

FIGURE 19.23

The files within the shared folder accessed via drive G.

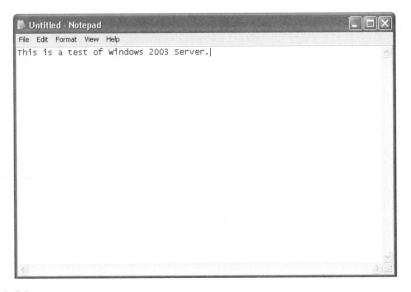

FIGURE 19.24

A test file.

Printing with a Network Printer

Printing within the network is seamless as long as the printer driver is installed on your machine. To print a file, simply return to *Explorer,* choose the *test.txt* file on the *G* drive, right click on the file name, and choose *Print* (Figure 19.25).

Disconnecting a Mapped Drive

To disconnect from a mapped drive, open Windows *Explorer* and choose *Tools/Disconnect Networked drive* (Figure 19.26) to access a screen that lists all networked drives (Figure 19.27). Select drive G, and click on *OK*. The mapping will be removed.

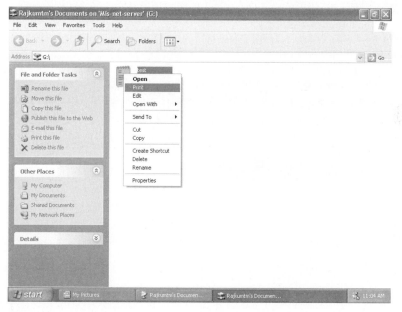

FIGURE 19.25
Printing the test file.

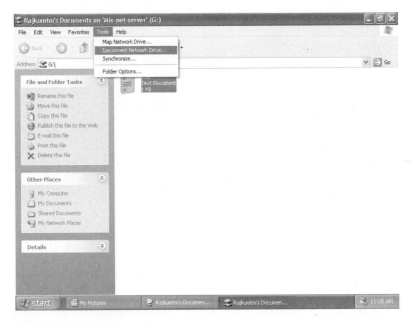

FIGURE 19.26

Disconnecting from a mapped drive.

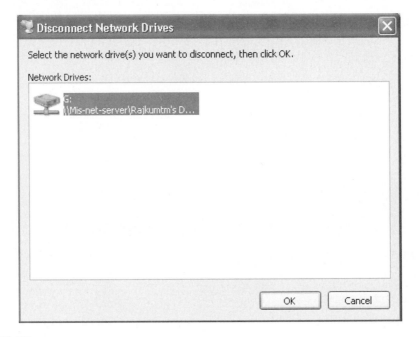

FIGURE 19.27

A list of all networked drives.

Creating a Shared Folder

You may or may not have the appropriate rights to create a shared folder. Unless your instructor tells you to perform the following tasks, please read this subsection and do not follow the step-by-step instruction.

Open *My Computer (Start/ My Computer)* and click on *Shared Documents* to select the default shared documents folder. Select *File/New Folder* from the menu and create a new folder. Name the folder *testsharing*. Your screen will resemble Figure 19.28.

Highlight testsharing, right click the mouse, and select *Sharing and Security* to access the *Sharing* window (Figure 19.29). Click on *If you understand the security risks* option under *Network sharing and security* to display the screen shown in Figure 19.30. Choose *Just enable file sharing,* click on OK, and the screen shown in Figure 19.31 appears. Check the *Share this folder on the network* option, leave the *Allow network users to change my files* box unchecked, and click on OK. You have now created a shared folder that other users on the network can see and use. However, they cannot modify the files on the folder. Accessing this shared folder is similar to accessing a shared folder on the server.

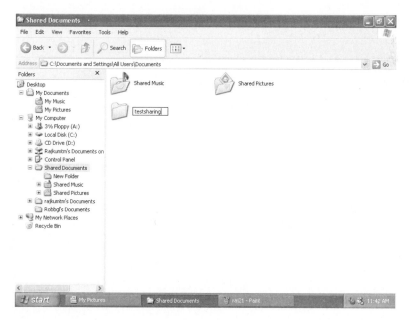

FIGURE 19.28

Name the new folder *testsharing*.

- Highlight *testsharing*

- Right click icon

- Select *Sharing and Security*

- Click *If you understand ...*

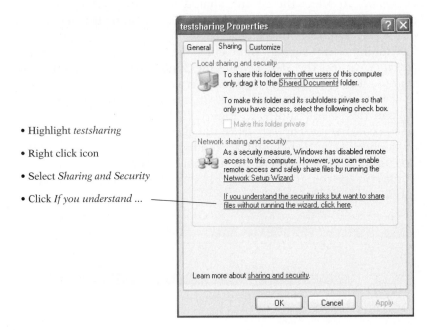

FIGURE 19.29

The *Sharing* window.

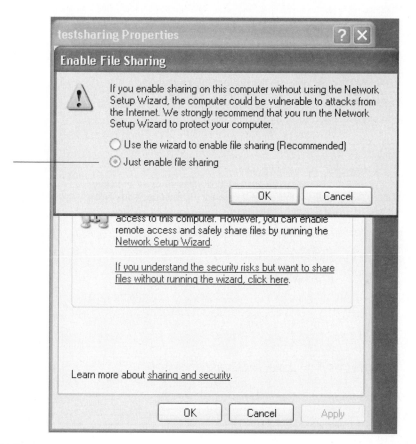

FIGURE 19.30

Enabling file sharing.

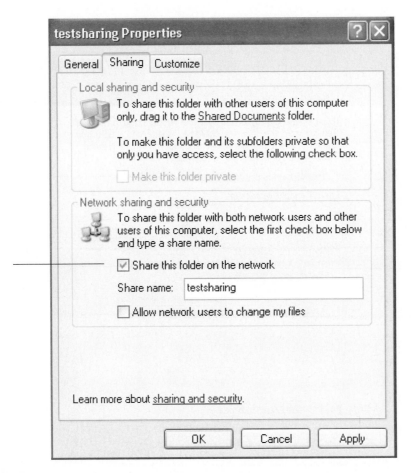

FIGURE 19.31

Check *Share this folder on the network.*

> ### Shared Files
>
> You can use Windows XP to share files with other users on your computer (such as your family members) by storing the files within shared folders. By default, there are two standard shared folders, *Shared Music* and *Shared Pictures,* under *Shared Documents* and, as you discovered in Figures 19.29 through 19.31, you can make any folder a shared folder. To share a file, simply drag it to the appropriate folder.
>
> In contrast to sharing files on a single computer with people you know, the files under the shared folder option in this section enable you to share files with other users on your entire network, whether or not they hold an account on your Windows XP machine. Unless you trust everyone who has access to your network, be careful about providing network access to your files.
>
> File sharing provides numerous benefits including the ability to read and modify one another's work and perform other group tasks. There are risks, however. You must ensure that only authorized users have access to your files. Most networks are connected to the Internet and it is possible for some unknown person to stumble onto your files and change them without your knowledge. It is also important to realize that when you access a file from someone else's computer, you run the risk of acquiring a virus. Thus, it is essential that you protect the shared folders with strong passwords, share those passwords only with those you trust and who need access to the files, and always use virus scanning software on all files downloaded from other computers.

Logging Off a Client

When you are finished with this brief tutorial, log off by choosing *Start/Log off*. Click *Log off* to complete the process (Figure 19.32).

FIGURE 19.32

Logging off.

▣ Summary

Windows 2003 supports a number of network transport protocols, including TCP/IP. The Network Device Interface Specification (NDIS) communicates with network card drivers. All transport protocols use the transport driver interface (TDI) to expose their services to the upper layer. Application programs use application interfaces to access services.

The basic unit of a Windows 2003 client/server network is a domain. A domain controller is a computer running Windows 2003 Server that contains the Active Directory database. Servers that are in the same domain but do not have an Active Directory are called member servers. A domain tree is a hierarchical organization of different domains. A forest consists of one or more domain trees.

Active Directory is a directory service installed on a Windows 2003 domain controller. A directory service is a network service that makes the directory available to users, administrators, and applications. Every object has a distinguished name (DN) that uniquely identifies it. Active Directory provides a global catalog that allows users to find any object for which they have access rights.

Windows 2003 uses the Common Internet File System (CIFS) to share files by creating shared folders. Shared application folders hold applications. Shared data folders are created when users wish to exchange public and working data. Windows 2003 provides Distributed file system (Dfs) to let the network administrator link files that exist on physically different servers to form a single namespace. A print server is a computer running Windows 2003 Server that manages printers. Windows 2003 supports print pools.

A Web service is an application service that utilizes the World Wide Web. Under Windows 2003, the key Web services component is a Web server named Internet Information Services (IIS). One key kernel-mode IIS component, http.sys, responds to http connection requests and places each request on a queue for subsequent processing. When http.sys receives a request that requires a middleware routine to be run, a second IIS component, World Wide Web Service Administration and Monitoring (W3SAM) starts a worker process that hosts and executes the middleware routines. A named worker process is called an application pool.

An optional module called media services can be used to configure Windows 2003 Server as a streaming server. A cluster is a group of computers (hardware) that act like a single system to provide services to clients.

A peer-to-peer network is called a workgroup in Windows terminology and can share resources such as files or printers. Each computer maintains its own security database that contains information on users and resource security.

The rest of the chapter consisted of examples illustrating the management and client-level use of Windows 2003 Server.

◼ Key Words

access control list	Internet Information Services (IIS)
Active Directory	leaf object
application service	media services
cluster	namespace
Common Internet File System (CIFS)	network device interface specification (NDIS)
container object	network service
directory service	print server
distinguished name (DN)	security database
Distributed file system (Dfs)	shadow copy
domain	shared folder
domain component (DC)	streaming server
domain controller	transport driver interface (TDI)
domain tree	Web service
forest	worker process
global catalog	workgroup
http.sys	

◼ Review Questions

1. Briefly explain the functions performed by the protocols that operate at each level of the Windows 2003 network model.
2. What is a domain? What is a domain tree? What is a forest?
3. What is the Active Directory? What is its purpose?
4. What is a distinguished name? Distinguish between leaf objects and container objects.
5. What functions are performed by the Windows 2003 Common Internet File System (CIFS)?
6. What is a shared folder? What is its purpose? Distinguish between a shared data folder and a shared application folder.
7. What is the purpose of the Distributed file system (Dfs)?
8. Why are shadow copies useful?
9. What functions are performed by a print server? What is a print pool?
10. What are Web services?
11. Describe the primary components of the Windows 2003 Internet Information Server (IIS).
12. What functions are performed by media services?
13. What is a cluster? What tasks are performed by clustering services? What is a Web farm?

14. Distinguish between a client/server network and a peer-to-peer network. Briefly describe a peer-to-peer network under Windows 2003.

15. Identify several common features for managing Windows 2003 Server.

16. Describe several Windows 2003 features and services you can access from a client computer.

▊ Exercises

1. With your instructor's permission, complete the brief tutorial starting with the header "Using Windows 2003 Server: A Client's Perspective."

2. Turn back to Figure 17.12 and review the seven-layer OSI model. Then relate the OSI model to the Windows 2003 network architecture.

3. Cite at least two benefits associated with Microsoft's .NET and Passport services.

4. Would you be willing to sign up for Microsoft's Passport service? Why or why not?

5. What are some of the risks associated with sharing files? What can you do to minimize those risks?

6. Figures 19.1, 19.5, and 19.6 are useful templates for organizing many of this chapter's key terms.

CHAPTER 20

Linux Networking

When you finish reading this chapter you should be able to:

▶ Identify the services performed by *inetd*.

▶ Explain how file sharing is achieved by Linux/UNIX.

▶ Discuss the Linux/UNIX Network File System (NFS).

▶ Identify the purpose of Server Message Block (SMB).

▶ Identify the functions performed by *smbd* and *nmbd,* the two primary Samba daemons.

▶ Distinguish between Postscript and Ghostscript.

▶ Distinguish between *lpd,* the line printer daemon, and the Common UNIX Printing System (CUPS).

▶ Explain how a kernel-based Web server such as *khttpd* and a user-mode Web server such as Apache work together to fill page requests.

▶ Explain the Apache pre-forking model.

▶ Distinguish between a single system image and a Beowulf cluster.

▆ Introduction

Traditionally, UNIX and Linux systems have dominated enterprise networking, providing file services, remote printing, mail services, Web services, and a wide variety of other services. For example, Apache, a popular Web server that runs under Linux/UNIX, powers more than half the Web sites in the world[1], and popular mail services such as Hotmail and Yahoo mail started on UNIX systems. Key reasons for this dominance include the configurability (the ability to customize a system to fit a unique set of needs), scalability (the ability to serve an increasing number of users without increasing response times), and stability (the ability to avoid system crashes) of UNIX applications and systems. This chapter will consider some common network services that are available under Linux.

Although Linux/UNIX enjoys a significant server-side presence, most client computers run Windows. Consequently, because few students have access to a server-side host, this chapter will not feature a tutorial.

▆ Network Services

Services are programs that run on Linux/UNIX machines and wait for clients to connect using specific network ports. For example, most Web servers use the *http* protocol that generally connects at port 80. These services run with little or no human intervention.

Daemons

Within the UNIX world, services that run in the background are known as **daemons,** and the names of these programs traditionally end with *d* (for daemon). For example, the *http* service is enabled by a daemon program named ***httpd.*** Generally, daemons are started when the system starts, stop when the system is shut down, find the information they need in configuration files, and record error information in an error log file. Daemons usually sit idly until a client connects, consuming computing resources only when they are active.

---

[1]Netcraft.com, *http://news.netcraft.com/archives/2003/05/05/may_2003_web_server_survey.html.*

In a typical Linux system there may be many such daemons waiting and listening for client connections. Rather than have each of these daemons wait for connections, Linux provides a superserver daemon named ***inetd*** (Internet services daemon) that functions as an intermediary, listens for connection requests for certain ports, and starts the appropriate service program when a request reaches a port (Figure 20.1). The *inetd* daemon maintains a configuration file that links port numbers to the associated server daemon. For example, if a Web page is requested by a client via port 80, *inetd* checks the configuration table to find the daemon associated with port 80 and starts *httpd*, which handles the Web page transfer and stops on completion of the transfer of the Web page data. If, in contrast, a file transfer is requested via port 21, *inetd* starts *ftpd*, the file transfer daemon, to handle the file transfer request. Using a superserver such as *inetd* insures that less memory is consumed because there is only one listener running. Also, *inetd* helps improve system security by supporting filters for incoming requests.

Since, *inetd* must start and stop the other server daemons there is a slight delay inherent in the Linux/UNIX approach. Thus, *inetd* is often not used for high demand daemons. For example, a university Web site that gets numerous page hits might not run the *http* service daemon under *inetd*. However, an individual faculty member's Web server is likely to get relatively few hits per day, making the *inetd* option more efficient.

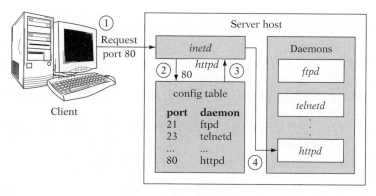

FIGURE 20.1

Linux provides a super-server daemon named *inetd*.

UNIX Naming Conventions

UNIX line commands tend to be quite cryptic, which can be intimidating to a beginner. Remember, however, that UNIX was not designed with beginners in mind. It was designed to simplify the work of professionals, such as system administrators, system operators, and system programmers. For example, UNIX line commands are typed all lowercase because typing all lowercase simplifies typing.

If you look carefully at a UNIX line command, its meaning is actually quite clear. Generally, the commands are acronyms composed of a few key letters or the first letter of each word in the command. Thus, *cd* means change directory, cp means copy, *http* is the hypertext transfer protocol, *httpd* is the hypertext transfer protocol daemon, *ftp* is the file transfer protocol, and *ftpd* is the file transfer protocol daemon. If you use such cryptic commands on an everyday basis (as system professionals do), they soon become second nature.

Even words like daemon begin to make sense when you think about them. "Daemon" is an archaic spelling of the word "demon" that often appears in swords and sorcery games. In mythology, a demon is a dark-side being that does negative things. Primitive, text-based computerized swords and sorcery games were very popular among the computing pioneers and hackers who helped UNIX evolve back in the late 1960s and 1970s, so they were familiar with daemons. Service programs (usually) perform useful functions, but sometimes they misbehave. A misbehaving service program can literally crash a system, so it makes perfect sense to call it a daemon.

Improving Security

Many Linux distributions install numerous server daemon programs by default. To reduce security exposure, before they complete the system initialization process, system administrators are urged to review the *inetd* configuration file (typically stored in */etc/inetd.conf*) and remove any unnecessary daemons.

Linux systems also place a program named TCP Wrappers between the *inetd* server and the other server daemons (Figure 20.2) by modifying the *inetd* configuration file to refer to the TCP Wrappers application instead of the server daemons. The TCP Wrappers application daemon *(tcpd)* examines each request and either grants or denies access to the server daemon based on a set of criteria that the system administrator specifies. The criteria for each network service typically include a set of allowable clients *(/etc/hosts.allow)* and a set of clients to which the service is denied *(/etc/hosts.deny)* and can be defined separately for each network service. TCP *Wrappers* can also log (in a system log file) every network request, recording the date/time stamp, the service that was requested, the client address and name, and the decision (grant or deny service).

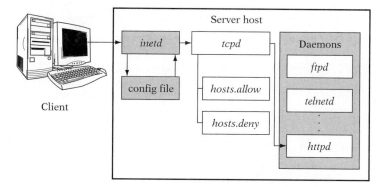

FIGURE 20.2

TCP Wrappers sits between *inetd* and the other server daemons.

▪ Linux File Services

File sharing is the process of making available one or more of the directories (or folders) on a local computer to a user on a remote computer. The directories that a client might want to share, such as the */home/sharedfolder* directory, are **exported** by creating an entry in the */etc/exports file*. When a directory is exported, all the files and any folders inside it are also exported. Exported folders are made available to other clients over the network, appearing as though they were available locally to each participating client subject to the limitations imposed by UNIX file system permissions and ownerships.

Linux/UNIX file sharing is achieved either by using an FTP program (Chapter 17) or by using the **Network File System (NFS).** You can use NFS when you want to share files with other Linux/UNIX systems. For example, in an enterprise that supports only Linux/UNIX servers, a user might be able to use NFS to access all his or her files from virtually any computer in the organization.

Under Linux, the NFS server daemon *knfsd* and NFS client tools can run in kernel mode (the leading k on the daemon name), improving response time to clients. As you discovered in Chapter 13 (Figure 13.17), Linux uses the virtual file system to direct read or write requests from applications to the appropriate file system. The NFS client is a virtual file system (Figure 20.3). When a client application requests a read (or write) operation for an NFS file, the NFS client uses the network to contact the NFS server daemon *(knsfd)*. The NFS server then sends the request to the virtual file system on the server, which uses the server's file system to retrieve the file from the disk. The NFS server then returns the file to the client.

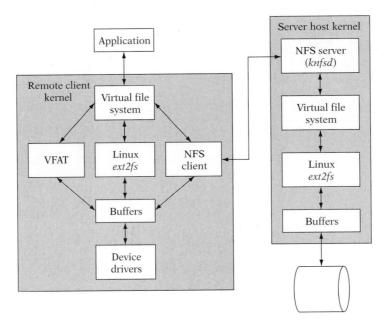

FIGURE 20.3

NFS client server is a virtual file system.

The system administrator specifies the folders to be exported in the */etc/exports* file by recording for each file such information as the folder name, its read and/or write permissions, and an optional list of hosts that are allowed to access the specified folders. NFS restricts the hosts from which connections can be made but relies on the client operating system to authenticate the user.

A Linux/UNIX file is owned by the file's creator. Each Linux user account has a numeric user ID (UID) in addition to a user name, and file ownership is defined by the UID. File ownership in NFS follows standard UNIX techniques and is based on the UIDs of each file and directory in the path name. Thus it is important that the user IDs associated with the user names on the client and server be coordinated so that a file that belongs to one user is not erroneously associated with a different user.

For example, Figure 20.4 lists a set of users and their user IDs on two Linux hosts named *os6e* and *mis*. On *os6e,* user *bill's* files are associated with the UID 1002, but on the *mis* host *bill's* files are associated with UID 1003. Assume *bill* is working on the *os6e* host. If he tries to access a file stored on host *mis,* he will erroneously access user *don's* files because the UID 1002 is associated with user *don*. The system administrator can correct this problem by issuing the appropriate *usermod* (user modify) commands on the *mis* host or by setting up a map file that associates each remote user with his or her correct UID.

User	User ID *os6e*	User ID *mis*
george	1001	1001
bill	1002	1003
don	1003	1002

FIGURE 20.4

Three users' IDs on two Linux hosts.

A client computer that wants to access a file via NFS must run the NFS client and be listed in the NFS server host's */etc/exports* file. A user must know where the shared folder is located in order to be able to mount it by issuing a *mount* command at the line prompt. (In other words, the user cannot browse or search for the shared folder on the network.) Once the shared folder is mounted, the files in the server's exported folder can be accessed by the client from the mount point like any other local directory.

NFS differs from many other types of file sharing in that, like the *http* protocol, it is stateless. Each NFS request is completely self-contained and need not refer to prior connections or requests. The stateless nature of NFS allows it to survive server crashes. For example, assume a client had previously sent a request to read file X on the server, but the server crashed. Because the server is down, the client does not receive a response. Rather than crashing, the client responds by intermittently repeating the request to the server. Once the server comes back up, it can handle the request as though all those independent, unanswered requests never happened. Thus, while the client might experience a delay, the data will eventually be delivered.

▣ Windows Interconnectivity

NFS is useful for sharing files with other UNIX or Linux systems. However, in most enterprises most of the client workstations run Windows.

Server Message Block (SMB) is a client/server protocol for file sharing, printing, and login services that is commonly found in Windows. SMB corresponds to the application and presentation level protocol within the OSI model and runs on most transport and network protocols such as TCP/IP. A number of commands within the SMB protocol support file sharing, printer sharing, authentication, and authorization services. In the mid-1990s, Microsoft updated their SMB protocol and called it Common Internet File System (CIFS) (Chapter 19). However, in the Linux world what Microsoft calls CIFS is still widely known as SMB.

Windows XP (Chapter 19) includes CIFS clients and servers that enable a user to create shared folders. The SMB server for the UNIX and Linux world is called **Samba,** and the client is known as *smbclient*. Samba and *smbclient* allow Windows and UNIX clients to access shared files as though they were stored locally. In other words, Samba allows Windows clients to access UNIX files.

A **share** is a server resource such as a file or printer that is made available to SMB clients for network sharing. The system administrator can place security restrictions on access to shares, and users might be asked to enter a user name and password before they can access the share. (This is also the level of security prevalent in Windows XP.) File services are created by setting up file or folder shares. You can access files and folders from a server over a share as though the files were stored locally.

Figure 20.5 shows an example of a server host running Linux server software. Stored on the server is a shared directory resource named \\server\group. The client machines can use SMB to map this resource to their file directories as a virtual drive (for example, the G drive). To the applications that run on the clients, the files on the G drive are accessed just like a file stored on the local hard drive (C). When the client needs a file on the server, the client sends an SMB request and receives an SMB response containing the file.

Samba Components

Under Samba, the *smbd* daemon is responsible for file and print services (Figure 20.6). In addition, *smbd* implements user authentication and access to the shares; note that Windows domains might provide additional authentication. Samba and *smbd* can work with the Windows domain controller (Chapter 19) so that once a user logs into the Windows domain, he or she can also access Samba shares. Samba can also perform the functions of a Windows domain controller.

The second primary Samba daemon, *nmbd*, implements name resolution and browsing. The *nmbd* daemon resolves names such as \\server to their corresponding IP (Internet protocol) address and keeps track of which names correspond to which IP address. Clients can then use the *nmbd*

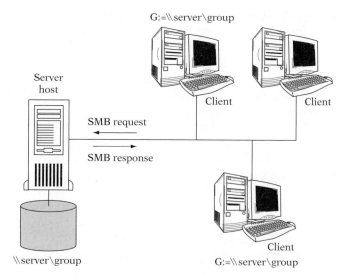

FIGURE 20.5
Samba share mapping.

mappings to open an SMB request directly with the server. Note that *smbd* and *nmbd* are linked by a shared routine named *libsmb* that implements the *smb* protocol routines.

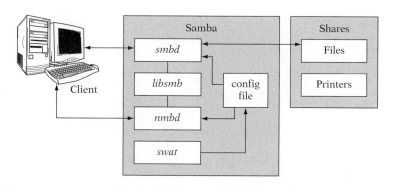

FIGURE 20.6
Samba's architecture.

Under Windows, users can use the *My Network Places* application to browse a domain list (note, not the Internet) for shared resources. When a Linux host runs a Samba server, the Linux machine appears to a Windows client as a resource within the *My Network Places* application (Figure 20.7), and clicking on an option can take you to the exact resource you need (Figures 20.8). Depending on how the Samba share is set up, a username and password may or may not be required to reach Figure 20.8. Otherwise, the Windows user sees little or no difference between the Linux machine and the Windows system. For example, the only hint that *os6e* in Figures 20.7 and 20.8 is a Linux machine can be gleaned from the title bar near the top of Figure 20.8. The *nmbd* daemon implements the service announcements that make the Linux machine available for browsing with the SMB protocol.

Samba Web Administration Tool (SWAT) can be used to administer and manage Samba using a Web browser. SWAT allows the system administrator to easily change the Samba configurations, designate shares, set authentication requirements (user name and password) for the shares and so on. Configuration information is stored on a *config* (configuration) file that is accessed by *smbd* and *nmbd*.

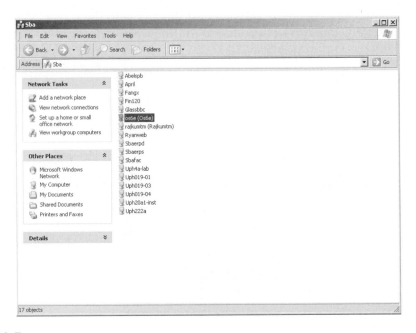

FIGURE 20.7

A Windows client can browse the Linux system like a network resource.

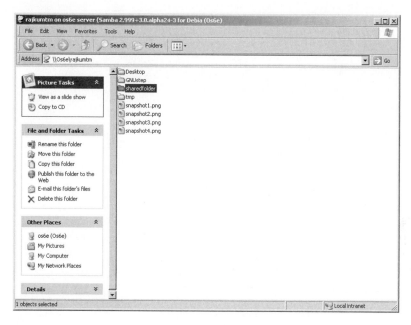

FIGURE 20.8

The Linux system's shared folder.

Samba Clients

SMB file sharing works both ways. If you are using a Windows client, you can mount on a file share that is stored on a Linux/UNIX server. Similarly, you can make a shared folder that is stored on a Windows system available to a Linux client. *Smbclient* works like an *ftp* client and allows you to transfer files to and from a Windows server. *Smbfs* is a Linux/Unix driver that allows you to mount the remote file share as a local mount point in Linux. Once the file share is mounted, files can be read and written as though the file share were local. Two command line utility programs, *smbmount* and *smbumount*, make it simple to mount and dismount (the *umount* command means unmount in UNIX) the file share.

Konqueror, the KDE file manager (Chapter 9), allows you to view the file share graphically using the SMB protocol (Figure 20.9). In order to use Konqueror, you must know the location of the file share. In contrast, *LinNeighborhood* is a graphical utility similar to *My Network Places* in Windows that allows users to browse for SMB resources (Figure 20.10). *LinNeighborhood* uses the *smbfs* and *smbmount* programs.

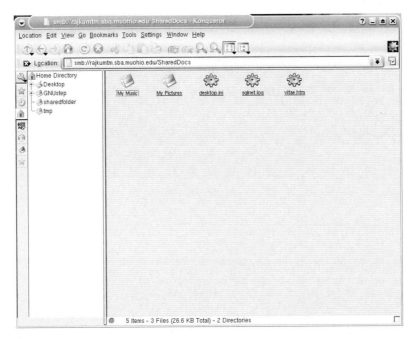

FIGURE 20.9

Viewing a Windows shared folder with Konqueror.

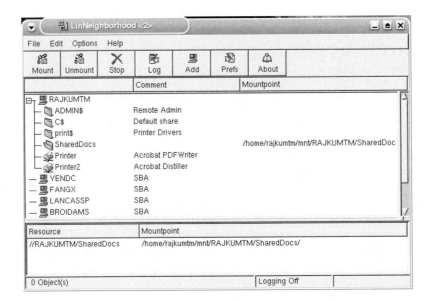

FIGURE 20.10

Browsing with LinNeighborhood.

■ Print Services

Under Linux/UNIX, when you choose the print option from an application program the program generates a Postscript file. **Postscript** is a device independent page description language that specifies the layout of the text and graphics on the page. Most modern printers print a raster image composed of pixels or dots. Page description languages are abstract and must be converted to a raster image before they can be printed. A Postscript printer's raster image processor (RIP) is a Postscript interpreter that converts the Postscript language to a raster image.

Not all printers are Postscript compatible; for example, most common inkjet printers do not understand Postscript. In such cases, Linux uses a software filter that converts one print format to another. Typically, a filter called **Ghostscript** is used to convert the Postscript document to a raster image for use by a specific, non-Postscript printer. Figure 20.11 outlines the flow of a typical printing operation in Linux.

Postscript is *not* a Windows standard, so a Windows client that sends output to a printer server on a Linux system must ensure that a Postscript printer driver is installed on the Windows client. On demand, Samba 3 (the latest version of Samba) allows the necessary printer driver to be downloaded from the server to a Windows client and installed before the output is sent to the SMB print share.

The Line Printer Daemon

Typically, when an application program issues a print command, a client-side operating system routine named lpr (line printer) transfers the file to a

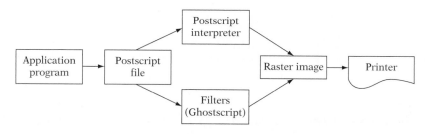

FIGURE 20.11
Postscript is the Linux/UNIX page description language.

local (client-side) print server (Figure 20.12). (Yes, it is possible to have a print server residing on the client. Remember the client/server concept.) Each active printer is identified by a queue name and has an associated spool subdirectory that specifies whether the printer associated with the print queue is local or networked. The line printer daemon (lpd) watches this directory and listens on port 515 for requests from lpr clients. Every time lpd receives a request, it finds the file on the spool subdirectory and either passes the print job to a local Postscript printer, through a filter such as Ghostscript to a local non-Postscript printer, or, if the request is for a remote printer, to the lpd server running on the remote (networked) computer to which the printer is attached.

CUPS

Linux's default printing system is *lpd*, but it has drawbacks. For example, *lpd* does not use printer drivers, which means the user cannot take advantage of such printer-specific features as printing on both sides of the paper. Consequently, **Common UNIX Printing System (CUPS)** (Figure 20.13) is a recommended replacement for traditional lpd-based print servers.

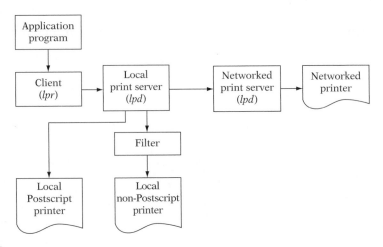

FIGURE 20.12

The line printer daemon is *lpd*.

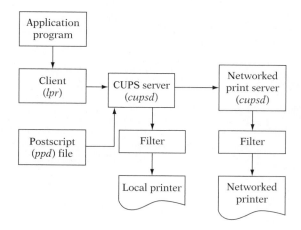

FIGURE 20.13

CUPS is a replacement for *lpd* print services.

CUPS can work with **Postscript printer description (PPD)** files, which are simple text files that describe the device-dependent features and contain commands that a Postscript printer understands. The CUPS server, *cupsd,* incorporates a raster image processor based on Ghostscript filters that allows non-Postscript printers to print documents initially formatted in Postscript using PPD.

CUPS also supports the **Internet printing protocol (IPP),** a protocol that runs on top of *http* and allows for bi-directional communication between client and server. Using IPP allows clients to browse for available printers on the network (Figure 20.14) and to get status and other detailed information about a printer. A Web-based interface available at port 631 (Figure 20.15) allows the system administrator to configure every aspect of CUPS. IPP supports access control and authentication using the CUPS configuration file *(/etc/cups/cupsd.conf)* that specifies which clients are allowed to access a given server host. CUPS can also be configured to store usage logs for specific printers and provides accounting capabilities. Finally, CUPS offers a compatibility layer called *cups-lpd* to support work with older *lpd*-style clients and provides the *cupsadsmb* utility to share CUPS printers using Samba. Because CUPS can work with most UNIX facilities, it is the recommended Linux/UNIX printing system.

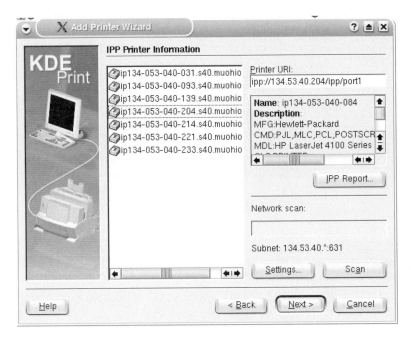

FIGURE 20.14

IPP allows a client to browse the network for available printers.

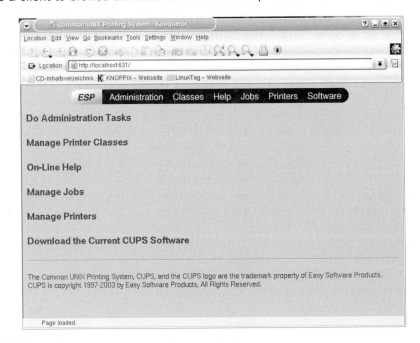

FIGURE 20.15

The CUPS Web interface for system administration.

Samba Print Shares

In Samba, print shares behave very much like file shares. In order to print to a network printer, the client sends the file to the print share. The server then treats the file as though it originated locally and passes it through its (the server's) print system. Many features, such as access control, work equally on both file and print shares.

◼ Apache Web Server

Linux/UNIX systems are frequently used as Web server platforms. **Apache,** a freely available, open source Web server, is a popular software choice.

A Web server is an application-layer program that runs on the host server computer in a client/server network. As you read earlier in this chapter, under Linux/UNIX a Web server daemon called *httpd* listens for connections at port 80 (Figure 20.16). Apache is a Web server daemon, a specific version of *httpd*. When a client makes a connection, httpd responds by serving a static or dynamic (created on demand by middleware) HTML file back to the client. The client's browser then receives and displays the page.

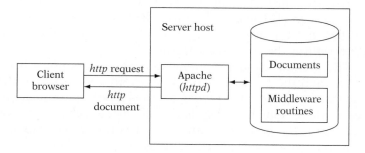

FIGURE 20.16
Apache is a Web server daemon *(httpd)*.

So You Want to Host a Web Site?

DSL and cable modems provide different speeds for transferring data upstream (from your computer) and downstream (to your computer). In general, downstream speeds are faster, which is fine for browsing the Internet. If you want to host a Web site on your computer, however, you must run a Web server, and Web servers spend most of their time uploading files to clients. In other words, if you want to host a Web site, you'll need fast upstream speeds. You'll also need a domain name such as *yourcompany.com* mapped to your Web site and to a static IP address.

Security is another consideration. Opening any port for service can create system vulnerabilities. Security holes are occasionally found in Web server software and, in addition to maintaining the system and the Web site, you'll find it necessary to spend time installing patches and fixes. (Security issues were discussed in Chapter 18.) If you are serving only a few pages, you might consider renting space and service from an Internet service provider rather than running your own Web server.

Kernel-Based Web Servers

Most *httpd* daemons such as Apache run in user mode. However, user mode processes carry considerably more overhead than processes that run inside the kernel. For example, kernel mode processes can be started and stopped much more quickly.

Many user mode Web servers actually perform a significant part of their work in kernel mode. For example, an *http* request on port 80 is initially sensed by the kernel and not by the user mode *httpd* process (Figure 20.17). The kernel then forwards the request to the user mode process. Assuming the requested page is static, the *httpd* daemon sends a request for the *html* file to the kernel. The kernel returns the *html* file to the daemon, which creates the *http* response (the page), and forwards it to the kernel. Finally, the kernel returns the page to the client.

The overhead and communication that takes place between the user process and the kernel can be significantly reduced by running a kernel-based Web server such as *khttpd*, a kernel mode Linux daemon that provides Web services. Note, however, that kernel-mode Web servers can only provide static pages. Dynamic pages are created by user mode middleware routines.

Kernel-based Web servers such as *khttpd* (for kernel *http* daemon) can run in conjunction with other Web servers such as Apache. In such systems, khttpd is configured to monitor port 80 for *http* requests and the Apache

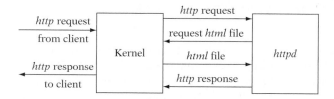

FIGURE 20.17

The Web server *(httpd)* must communicate with the kernel to fill a request for a static Web page.

httpd listens on a different port such as 8080. If the request is for a static page, then *khttpd* serves the page back to the client (Figure 20.18) without involving the user mode Web server. If, however, the request is for a dynamic page, then *khttpd* forwards the request to the user mode daemon (Apache), which responds.

While kernel mode Web servers can speed up the serving of static pages, they have drawbacks. If there is a bug in the kernel mode server, it can bring the entire system down. In contrast, user based processes are inherently more stable because an error will bring down only a single user process (the Web server) and not the entire system.

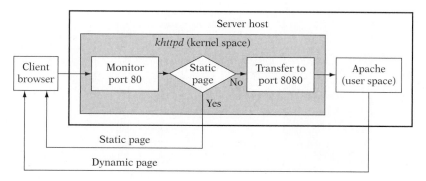

FIGURE 20.18

A kernel mode Web server *(khttpd)* passes dynamic page requests to a user mode Web server (Apache).

The Apache Pre-Forking Server Model

Apache supports a particularly robust server model called the **pre-forking model** (Figure 20.19). New UNIX processes are created via calls to *forks* (Chapter 13), but it takes time for a child process to be created. To speed the process, Apache creates in advance a main parent process and several child processes to handle client requests. Note that all the processes share a common pool of memory.

A child process can serve either a static page or a dynamic page, but serving a dynamic page calls for a middleware routine that runs within the child process. If the middleware routine fails, then only that child process fails, and the Web server and the other child processes remain unaffected and stable. Isolating errors in this way is what makes the pre-forking model robust.

Figure 20.20 is a screen capture that shows the Apache processes in use on the authors' system. The main Apache process has a process id *(pid)* of 13603, and the eight child processes have *pids* ranging from 13604 to 13612. Each of the child processes also references (in the column labeled PPID) the parent process, 13603. Note also (in the STIME column) that all the child processes were started immediately after the main process was started.

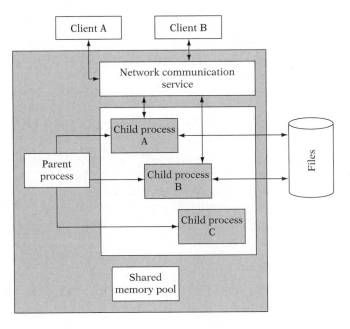

FIGURE 20.19

The Apache pre-forking model.

```
UID          PID  PPID   C  STIME  TTY             TIME  CMD
root        13603     1   0  08:36  ?           00:00:00  /usr/sbin/apache
www-data    13604 13603   0  08:36  ?           00:00:00  [apache]
www-data    13605 13603   0  08:36  ?           00:00:00  [apache]
www-data    13606 13603   0  08:36  ?           00:00:00  [apache]
www-data    13607 13603   0  08:36  ?           00:00:00  [apache]
www-data    13608 13603   0  08:36  ?           00:00:00  [apache]
www-data    13610 13603   0  08:37  ?           00:00:00  [apache]
www-data    13611 13603   0  08:37  ?           00:00:00  [apache]
www-data    13612 13603   0  08:37  ?           00:00:00  [apache]
```

FIGURE 20.20

A screen capture showing Apache pre-forking in use.

Each child process has one thread and can service only one request at a time. When all the child processes are busy, the main parent process creates an additional child process to handle a new request. When a system administrator shuts down the service, the parent process uses signals to shut down the child processes.

Apache Multiprocessing Model

Apache is a cross-platform Web server that runs on UNIX/Linux, Windows, and numerous other platforms. A number of different processing models can be substituted for the pre-forking model on non-Linux/UNIX systems, and the system administrator can choose and configure the model that works best on his or her system.

Apache provides the *winnt* model for Windows platforms. The *winnt* model is multithreaded and runs as a single task or process that creates child threads (rather than child processes) to handle client requests. Threads are faster and less demanding, and consume fewer resources than processes, so *winnt* is the default processing model for Windows.

Apache Modules

The Apache daemon uses a modular architecture (Figure 20.21). A core module provides basic *http* functionality and other modules are incorporated to provide additional functionality. For example, the code that performs process/thread management is provided as a platform-specific multiprocessing module. If the platform is Linux, the pre-fork model is present. If, on the other hand, the platform is Windows, then the *winnt* model is present.

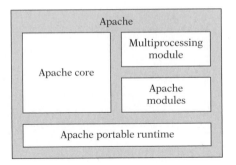

FIGURE 20.21

Apache's architecture.

Other modules can be incorporated statically (compiled along with the server) or dynamically, on demand. Apache supports dynamic shared objects that permit the loading of external modules at run time, and modules can be specified for inclusion at startup or re-start or added or removed without recompiling the server. Many different dynamic modules are available. For example, if you need encryption, the secure sockets layer (Chapter 18) is available as a module. Middleware routines that run applications might be written in such languages as perl, php, and so on, and each of these languages is available as a module that links the language's run-time libraries to Apache.

Like an operating system, Apache provides an application programming interface implemented in the Apache portable run-time layer. For example, Windows and Linux/UNIX handle files, locking, processes, and threads differently. The Apache portable run-time layer provides file input/output, network input/output, its own memory management routines, and so on. Using the Apache API allows a system administrator or a programmer to fully customize the version of Apache that runs on a given platform, and if programs are written to be consistent with the Apache API, the modules can be easily ported from one platform to another.

Apache Filters

When an Apache thread or process receives a request, it delegates the request to a single content handler module that sends the data back to the client. Based on the type of request, different content handlers are invoked. For example, if the request is for an image, an image-handler module transmits the image to the client. If, on the other hand, the request is for a middleware routine, a corresponding middleware module transmits the output to the client.

Generally, the modules work independently of each other, but it is sometimes necessary for one module's output to be modified by another module. For example, it is common for a middleware routine to generate a dynamic page that incorporates server-side *include* tags, template directives included within the html such as the date and time that are processed and filled by a server-side *include* module. Apache takes advantage of the UNIX filters concept (Chapter 9) to support such applications. The output of the first middleware module (the dynamic page generator) is sent to the second module (the server-side *include* module) using the same mechanism UNIX uses to send the output of a line command to the *sort* filter. The server-side *include* module then sends the finished dynamic page to the client. Apache can be configured to specify the sequence of modules that support different types of requests.

Clustering

A **cluster** consists of multiple computers, each with its own operating system, working together over a high speed network. The network interconnections are typically gigabit Ethernet connections that are specifically configured for the cluster. The goals of clustering are high performance, high availability, load balancing, scalability, and manageability. For example, Google, the Internet search engine, uses a cluster of 4000 Linux systems to support its Web services. Linux/UNIX clustering is similar to Windows clustering (Chapter 19).

Beowulf Clusters

High performance clustering refers to a tightly connected network of computers all dedicated to the solution of a single problem. A **Beowulf cluster** links multiple inexpensive computers in an effort to achieve the performance of a conventional supercomputer at a much lower price.

For example, to find all the prime numbers between 1 and 1,000,000, you might divide the problem into ten groups (1 through 100,000, 100,001 through 200,000, and so on), give a portion of the task to each of ten different computers, and assign one computer responsibility for coordinating and merging the results. In such a Beowulf cluster, ten systems (nodes) might be connected via Ethernet, with each running a copy of Linux. The nodes in the cluster are usually connected to the outside world through the single master node (Figure 20.22).

On such a system, the individual nodes lose their individuality and the operating system is tuned to make a single parallel program run efficiently across the entire cluster. Multiple messages are passed between the nodes,

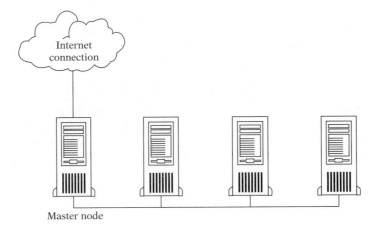

FIGURE 20.22
A four-node Beowulf cluster.

so high speed proprietary networks are typically used to link the nodes. All the programs that run inside this high performance computing environment must be modified to use message passing interface (MPI) commands.

Single System Image

A **single system image (SSI)** is a form of distributed computing in which multiple heterogeneous resources such as networks, distributed databases, or servers appear to the user as one, more-powerful, unified resource[2]. The nodes in an SSI cluster are linked to form a peer-to-peer network and do not share a client-server relationship. In an SSI cluster, it does not matter with which node a given resource is physically associated, because to the user the entire cluster appears as one global resource managed by the operating system's kernel.

The goal of an SSI cluster is to provide better performance for both sequential and parallel applications. The operating system is modified to support group scheduling of parallel programs by identifying global unused resources such as processors and memory and by managing access to those resources. Processes are automatically moved from one node to another, so the load is balanced across multiple machines. Unlike the Beowulf clusters,

---

[2]Based on *http://www.webopedia.com/TERM/S/single_system_image.html*.

it is not essential for the programs to be modified to use MPI. Regular programs can be run without any modification, and they need not be cluster-aware to take advantage of the cluster's benefits.

▐ Summary

The *http* service is run by a daemon named *httpd*. Linux provides a super-server daemon named *inetd* (Internet services daemon) that functions as an intermediary between client requests and the daemons. Linux systems also place a program named TCP Wrappers *(tcpd)* between the *inetd* server and the other server daemons.

Linux/UNIX file sharing is achieved either by using an FTP program or by using the Network File System (NFS). Server Message Block (SMB) is a client/server protocol for file sharing, printing, and login services that is commonly found in Windows. A share is a server resource such as a file or printer that is made available to SMB clients for network sharing. Windows XP includes SMB clients and servers that enable a user to create shared folders. The SMB server for the UNIX and Linux world is called Samba. Two daemons named *smbd* and *nmbd* implement most of Samba's key features.

Under Linux/UNIX, the default page description language is Postscript. A filter called Ghostscript is used to convert the Postscript document to a raster image for use by a specific, non-Postscript printer. When an application program issues a print command, a client-side operating system routine named *lpr* (line printer) transfers the file to a local (client-side) print server. The line printer daemon *(lpd)* either passes the print job to the appropriate local printer or to the remote (networked) computer to which the appropriate printer is attached. Common UNIX Printing System (CUPS) is a recommended replacement for traditional *lpd*-based print servers. In SMB, print shares behave very much like file shares.

Apache is a user-mode Web server daemon, a specific version of *httpd*. The overhead and communication that takes place between the user process and the kernel can be significantly reduced by running a kernel-based Web server such as *khttpd*. Apache supports a particularly robust server model called the pre-forking model. The Apache daemon uses a modular architecture. It is sometimes necessary for one module's output to be modified by another module using the UNIX filters concept.

A Beowulf cluster links multiple inexpensive computers in an effort to achieve the performance of a conventional supercomputer at a much lower price. A single system image (SSI) is a form of distributed computing in which multiple heterogeneous resources such as networks, distributed databases, or servers appear to the user as one, more-powerful, unified resource.

▌ Key Words

Apache	Internet printing protocol (IPP)
Beowulf cluster	line printer daemon (lpd)
cluster	Network File System (NFS)
Common UNIX Printing System (CUPS)	Postscript
	Postscript Printer Description (PPD)
daemon	pre-forking model
export	Samba
Ghostscript	Server Message Block (SMB)
httpd	share
inetd	single system image (SSI)

▌ Review Questions

1. What is a daemon? What is *httpd?*

2. What is *inetd?* What services are performed by *inetd?*

3. What functions are performed by TCP Wrappers?

4. How is file sharing achieved by Linux/UNIX?

5. What is the Network File System (NFS)? What is *knfsd?* What does the *k* imply?

6. NFS requests are stateless. What does that mean? Why is it significant?

7. What is the purpose of Server Message Block (SMB)? What is Samba? What is a share?

8. What functions are performed by *smbd* and *nmbd,* the two primary Samba daemons? What functions are performed by SWAT?

9. What is Postscript? What is Ghostscript? Why is something like Ghostscript necessary?

10. What does *lpd,* the line printer daemon, do?

11. What is the Common UNIX Printing System (CUPS)? What advantages are gained by replacing *lpd* with CUPS?

12. What is the Internet Printing Protocol (IPP)?

13. What is Apache? How is Apache related to *httpd?*

14. Why are kernel-based Web servers such as *khttpd* used? How do *khttpd* and a user-mode Web server such as Apache work together to fill page requests?

15. How does the Apache pre-forking model save time?

16. Why does a modular architecture make sense for a Web server like Apache?

17. What is the purpose of an Apache filter ?

18. What is a cluster?

19. What is a Beowulf cluster? Why are Beowulf clusters used?

20. What is a single system image? Distinguish between a single system image and a Beowulf cluster.

▌Exercises

1. Apache, a popular Web server that runs under Linux/UNIX powers more than half the Web sites in the world. However, most client computers run under Windows. Why do you suppose that is true?

2. Why do you suppose so many computing professionals prefer cryptic line commands to the more user-friendly interface provided by a GUI?

3. How is it possible to have a print server running on a client computer?

4. Distinguish between downstream and upstream. Why does a Web server host require faster upstream speed than a client?

5. Why would anyone want to create a Beowulf cluster?

6. Compare file sharing under the Common Internet File System (CIFS) described in Chapter 19 and Linux/UNIX Samba file sharing.

7. Compare Windows clustering from Chapter 19 to Linux/UNIX clustering.

8. Figures 20.2, 20.6, 20.12, and 20.18 are useful templates for organizing many of this chapter's key terms.

CHAPTER 21

Novell NetWare

When you finish reading this chapter you should be able to:

▶ Identify NetWare as the operating system on a Novell network server.

▶ Identify TCP/IP as NetWare's native protocols and briefly explain SPX/IPX.

▶ List the functions performed by the NetWare control protocol (NCP).

▶ Explain how the traditional Novell file system works.

▶ List several advantages of using Novell distributed print services (NDPS).

▶ Explain the purpose of Novell's directory services (NDS).

▶ Distinguish between a leaf object and a container object.

▶ Define a distinguished name.

▶ Distinguish between object rights and property rights.

▶ Describe the purpose of a network provider or network client.

◧ NetWare

Novell's **NetWare** is a commonly used networking operating system on local area networks. It provides robust services for the general business, including file services, print services, and application services. This chapter describes NetWare Version 5 and includes a section on NetWare 6.5.

NetWare is the server's operating system (Figure 21.1). Each client computer runs its own primary operating system (Windows XP, for example). A NetWare module runs under the client's operating system and communicates with NetWare on the server.

NetWare Kernel

NetWare's kernel (filename *server.exe*) runs on the server and provides such basic operating system functions as input/output management, interrupt processing, memory management, and thread and process management. The kernel (currently) can support up to 32 processors and can run on both multiprocessor and single-processor machines. It runs in protected mode at privilege level 0 on an Intel Pentium processor. Its scheduler provides for preemptive multitasking.

Networking Protocols

NetWare is based on the TCP/IP model (Chapter 17), and uses TCP and IP as its native protocols. Previous versions of NetWare used SPX/IPX, and NetWare continues to support these two protocols.

The **IPX** protocol occupies the Internet layer of the TCP/IP model and the network layer of the OSI model (Figure 21.2). Like IP (and similar protocols at this level), IPX addresses and routes packets from one location to another. IPX uses the address information in its header to forward the packet to its destination node or to the next router that provides a path to its destination.

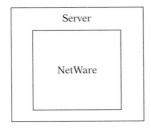

FIGURE 21.1

NetWare is the server's operating system. A NetWare module also runs on the client computer.

IPX provides a **connectionless datagram** service (as does IP). Datagram means each packet is independent of other packets and has no logical or sequential relationship with other packets. Connectionless means that when a process running on a particular node communicates with a process on another node, no connection is established between the two nodes. Consequently, when IPX packets are sent to their destination, successful delivery is not guaranteed.

Like TCP, **SPX** occupies the transport layer of both the TCP/IP model and the OSI model (Figure 21.2) and provides a virtual circuit or connection oriented service. **Connection oriented** implies that when SPX is used by a process on one node to communicate with a process on another node, a dedicated connection is established between the two nodes. Consequently, SPX guarantees delivery of packets to their destination and delivers them in their proper sequence. Since SPX carries a high overhead, NetWare avoids using it whenever possible.

Consistent with the TCP/IP model, the presentation and session layers are not present in NetWare. The data link and physical layers of the OSI model correspond to the physical layer in the TCP/IP model and are provided in the network interface cards.

The application layer is provided through the **NetWare control protocol (NCP)** (Figure 21.2), which enables NetWare clients and servers to communicate. NCP provides its own session control and sequence control, avoiding the overhead of SPX. The client issues NCP requests for file access and transfers, virtual drive mappings, directory searches, and so on. The server responds to these requests and replies to NCP. When the server finishes processing the request, the client terminates the connection. Under NetWare 5, NCP can run with either IPX or IP. If an IP connection is made, NCP uses TCP (transmission control protocol) for communication.

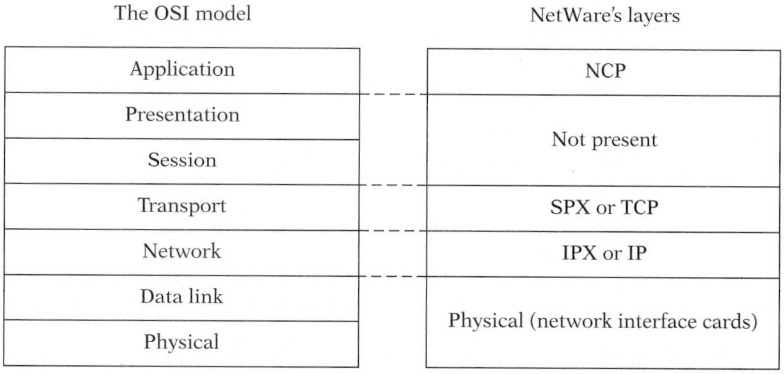

The OSI model	NetWare's layers
Application	NCP
Presentation	Not present
Session	Not present
Transport	SPX or TCP
Network	IPX or IP
Data link	Physical (network interface cards)
Physical	Physical (network interface cards)

FIGURE 21.2

NetWare and the OSI model.

NetWare Loadable Modules

NetWare loadable modules (NLM) are object modules linkable at run time. They can be loaded and unloaded at will, and once loaded they become part of the network operating system. Many pieces of NetWare run as NetWare loadable modules, including software to support TCP/IP and printing services. In NetWare 5, NetWare loadable modules run in the protected address space at Pentium privilege level 3. Optionally, they can run at privilege level 0, along with the kernel.

Memory Architecture

NetWare is a 32-bit operating system and can access 4GB of address space. NetWare provides protected memory and uses Intel's logical memory addressing (Chapter 10). Page translation tables are used to translate logical addresses to physical addresses. NetWare also supports virtual memory and swaps least recently accessed pages to disk as needed.

NetWare keeps its kernel *(server.exe)* in memory and allocates the rest of the memory for cache (Figure 21.3). The cache is used for all the server's processing needs, such as creating protected address spaces, storing programs (including NetWare loadable modules), storing file and directory entries, and storing user data files. Memory is allocated from the cache when a program requires memory and is returned to the cache pool when the program releases the memory. Cache is always allocated as fixed 4KB pages called cache buffers.

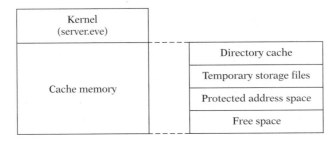

FIGURE 21.3

NetWare keeps its kernel in memory and allocates the rest of the memory for cache.

When the server receives a request for data on disk, it retrieves the data and stores it in a file cache buffer. The file cache buffers are organized to form a linked list. The most recently used buffer is placed at the head of the linked list and is stamped with the current time. As new buffers are added to the head of the list, the older buffers move down the list. Whenever the server requires a buffer, it retrieves the oldest buffer from the tail of the list, stores the new data in the buffer, and moves the buffer to the top of the list. When the server receives a request for data already in a cache buffer, it retrieves the data from the buffer, stamps the buffer with the new time, and moves the buffer to the head of the list. Consequently, the most recently used buffers are found at or near the top of the list and the least recently used buffers gather at the bottom.

A portion of the cache memory is used as the protected address space. The kernel's memory protection subsystem prevents a module in a protected address space from having direct access to anything outside its address space. All protected address spaces use virtual memory, and each one has its own page translation table to provide logical addressing. When data are moved from memory to disk they are stored in a swap file. The kernel is never swapped out of memory.

File Systems

NetWare provides two compatible file systems that allow a user to store, access, retrieve, and manage data on the network using files: the traditional **NetWare file system** and **Novell Storage Services (NSS).** The basic object in either file system is a **volume,** a fixed amount of space on one or more disks. Physically, a volume is divided into segments, where a segment is an area of physical storage. The segments that make up a volume can reside on different physical devices. For example, a 32-segment volume can be physically stored on 32 different devices.

NetWare reads and writes data in blocks, where a block is the smallest number of bytes that is read from or written to the disk. The block size is determined at installation time, generally based on the size of the volume. The larger the volume size, the larger the block size.

Logically, a volume is divided (by network supervisors and users who have the appropriate rights) into directories that contain files and subdirectories (Figure 21.4). When the server is booted, the volume is mounted and becomes visible to users who log into the system.

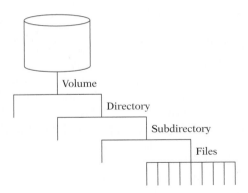

FIGURE 21.4
A volume is divided into directories that contain files and subdirectories.

The Traditional NetWare File System

Like MS-DOS (Chapter 11), NetWare maintains a file allocation table (FAT) to support allocating files on disk. The FAT is cached in RAM as long as the volume is mounted. Since the number of files on a volume can be large, NetWare caches the directory table on an as-needed basis, and caches the file entry whenever a file is opened. NetWare uses a least recently used algorithm to erase old entries from the caches. It relies on a hashing algorithm to improve initial search time through the directory table by constructing a numeric key for each file name and using the numeric key to locate the file.

A directory or a file is located by following its **path** (Figure 21.5). A fully defined path consists of the server name, the volume, the directory, any subdirectories, and the file name. Parameters are separated by backslashes, except for the volume and the directory, which are separated by a colon.

Since specifying such long names can become tedious, drive pointers or mappings are used to simplify file access. A **mapped drive** is a convenient way to reference a particular subdirectory on the network with a single letter. For example, if you map the letter Z to the MS-DOS subdirectory, instead of typing *Server\sys:Public\DOS* to fully specify the subdirectory, you can just type the letter Z followed by a colon (Z:). In effect, when you access the Z drive, you are really accessing the MS-DOS network subdirectory. Later in the chapter you will learn how to map drives.

servername\volume:directory\subdirectory\filename

FIGURE 21.5
A directory or a file is located by following its path.

Novell Storage Services

In addition to the traditional file system, NetWare supports Novell storage services (NSS), which enables the management of large files, volumes, name spaces, and storage devices. NSS uses a 64-bit file system and can support larger capacity disk drives than are prevalent today, with file sizes up to 8 terabytes, volumes that hold up to 8 trillion files, and up to 1 million open files per server. Free space on multiple disk drives can be combined to create a storage pool, and NSS volumes can be created within this storage pool. An additional advantage is that NSS volumes mount faster than traditional file systems while consuming less memory. For example, CD-ROMs can be mounted as NSS volumes, allowing faster access to multiple CDs in CD towers.

Disk Management

All disks on the server are managed by the NetWare operating system. Each server must contain at least one **NetWare partition** (Figure 21.6) that stores the system files using the traditional file system. Any unused space can be allocated to a **Novell storage services partition.** Additionally, at least one disk on the server must contain a **boot DOS partition.** The kernel file, *server.exe,* is stored in the boot partition. Each server must contain at least one NetWare partition that stores the system files using the traditional file system.

Fault Tolerant Features

NetWare has some built-in support for fault tolerance, the ability to recover from errors. **Disk duplexing** is the use of a redundant disk as a mirror. Everything written to the primary disk is also written to the redundant disk. If the primary disk fails, the system switches to the redundant disk. **Read after write** keeps data in the buffer after the write operation has completed. It then reads the data again and compares them against the buffer. If an error occurs, it rewrites the data. **Hot fix** detects the presence of bad sectors on the disk and moves the data from the defective area to an error-free location. These fault tolerant features must be turned on explicitly and work only in the traditional file system.

NSS partition
NetWare partition
Boot DOS partition

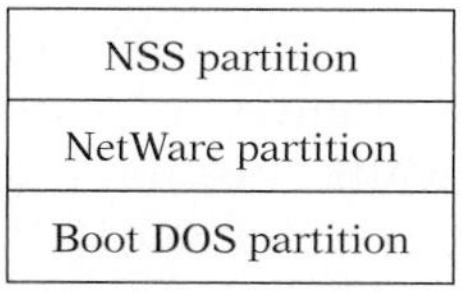

FIGURE 21.6

Hard disk partitions.

Storage Management Services

NetWare provides enhanced backup services, too. It can back up and restore files stored on the server or a client workstation to (or from) a target storage device. The files can be on a traditional NetWare file system, NSS, or client file systems. As a user, you must follow good backup practices, performing regular backups to ensure that critical data are never lost. Full backup ensures all the data are backed up. Differential (also known as incremental) backup backs up all data since the last full backup.

■ Printing Services

NetWare supports the traditional print queue-based printing and a new service called Novell distributed print services (NDPS).

Queue-Based Services

NetWare's queue-based print services use printers, print queues, and a print server. A print queue is essentially a subdirectory on a print server where the data are stored while waiting to be sent to a printer. The network administrator creates the queues and manages each individual printer separately. The user downloads and installs the driver needed for the central printer on his or her client machine. When a user prints from an application to a print queue, the data are sent directly to the queue or redirected from a local print port to a queue.

The redirection of printed data to a queue has several advantages. The user can resume working with the application without waiting for the print job to complete, print jobs can be sequenced so that higher priority jobs get routed to the printer first, and large print jobs can be stored and printed later.

Novell Distributed Print Services (NDPS)

Novell distributed print services (NDPS) allow the network administrator to manage network printing more efficiently than queue-based services. A system administrator creates a printer object as a resource on the network. Printers can be configured and designated for certain users, and drivers can be automatically installed and set up for the users. The administrator sets up a printer agent that allows a user to submit a job directly to the printer and enables bi-directional feedback between the client and the printer. Consequently, the client can check on the status of a print job, but the printer can also inform the client that toner is low, the paper tray is empty, and so on, and status messages can be routed to a third party or a printer administrator. NDPS also allows the client to schedule jobs on the printer based on time of day, job size, availability, and so on.

■ Novell Directory Services

Novell directory services (NDS) is a method of storing and retrieving service and other information in a distributed database. Instead of keeping all the service information in the same location, each directory server contains a portion of the database. Each directory server, however, has access to all the service information in the entire directory database.

NDS is organized logically as a hierarchical database (a tree structure) and stored on the server (Figure 21.7). Network resources, such as disk volumes, printer agents, servers, users, and workstations, are represented as objects. Each of these objects has properties that define its characteristics, such as identification, login restriction, mailbox, rights to files and directories, and so on. Entries for these properties are known as values.

Network resources (such as those just identified) fall under the category of **leaf objects.** They are found at the end of the hierarchical tree structure. Organizational units, such as companies, divisions, and departments, are **container objects,** which contain other containers and leaf objects. They are used to divide and organize the tree structure into branches. Generally, the container objects mirror the business unit's organizational structure, although an exact match is not necessary.

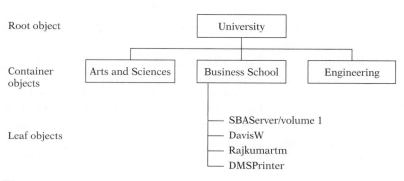

FIGURE 21.7

NDS is organized logically as a hierarchical database.

Novell directory services (NDS) objects are referenced by using their position in the tree. For example in Figure 21.7, user *DavisW* is in the container *Business School,* which is in the container *University*. Thus, users can be referenced by their **distinguished name,** such as *DavisW.Business School.University.*

Rights are associated with NDS objects. Whenever a user requests an NDS object, the system checks the user's rights before granting access. **Object rights** control what the user can do with an object, such as browse, create, rename, supervise, and so on. **Property rights** control access to information fields that define an object, such as supervise, read, write, and so on. Rights can be assigned to or denied to users, groups, or containers, and can be inherited. For example, if you specify rights at the container level, those rights flow to all the leaf objects in that container.

A **partition** is a logical division of the NDS tree that contains one or more complete branches. These partitions can be pruned and stored on different servers. The NDS tree might be partitioned on the basis of geographical location; for example, resources at the Los Angeles branch of a company might be in the Los Angeles tree and those at the Cincinnati branch might be in the Cincinnati tree. This arrangement provides better performance because Cincinnati users are most likely to use Cincinnati resources. However, because NDS is global, Cincinnati users can see and use the Los Angeles resources if needed.

Replication is the act of storing of a copy of an NDS partition on a different server. Replication provides for fault tolerance because the replicated copy can be used in case the primary server fails. Replication does not replicate the file system resources; only information about NDS is replicated.

Before a new user can access a Novell network, the network administrator must create an account for the user through Novell Directory Services. The first step is to identify the user's container and unique id (or login name) within the container. Then the login name, home directory, and additional parameters and properties are defined. The new user can also be assigned to one or more groups, and the user inherits all properties that are set for the group. For example, if the group has read access to certain folders, the new user automatically gets access to those folders.

NDS allows Internet addresses and resources on the Internet to be managed as NDS objects. It also allows each user to have a single login to the network. Once you log in at one location, you have access to all the servers and other resources to which you have rights. This global login feature saves the user from having to create multiple accounts on multiple servers. Additionally, if your network and desktop settings are stored in NDS, then your working environment can be recreated wherever you log into the network.

◼ Network Management

Zero Effort Networks (ZENworks) is the part of NetWare that supports desktop management. With ZENworks, the network administrator can use the Novell directory services to automate application management, remote management, and workstation management. These features reduce the time and effort a network administrator spends managing the network because they can solve many user problems without physically visiting the user's workstation.

Application management allows the administrator to distribute software and customize the software for each group or individual user. Applications can also be launched automatically by creating scheduled actions for users. **Workstation management** is the ability of the user's desktop to follow the user. This facility allows a user to log on at multiple clients; for example, a faculty member might log on through his or her office computer and also from a computer laboratory and see the same services at all locations. **Remote management** allows the network administrator to control the user's workstation remotely from his or her desktop to troubleshoot a problem.

◼ Novell Netware 6.5

NetWare 6.5 is the latest version of Novell NetWare. With this release, Novell addresses enterprise concerns such as strong support for Web application services, business continuity, and reliability with clusters and virtual office support.

Virtual office support provides a **portal** for end users. Using the portal, users access files and applications, print documents, and communicate with other team members via the Internet. Printing and sharing files are greatly simplified in NetWare 6.5; for example, with iPrint, users can print to any printer on the Internet. Users find their closest printer using Web pages set up by administrators, automatically download drivers and configure the printer, and print to the printer as if it were local. With iFolder, users can synchronize their files on any client device by accessing the NetWare server over the Internet. NetWare's iFolder provides a virtual centralized file repository. Every time the user logs in with the iFolder client, both client and server are checked for updates, and the data on the client device are synchronized with the server.

Novell directory services (NDS) has evolved to Novell eDirectory. NDS was originally restricted to managing users, servers, printers, print queues, and applications within NetWare. eDirectory can manage users, servers, printers, print queues, and applications not only within NetWare, but also within UNIX and Windows. It provides a single view for all the resources within an organization and provides a secure identity management that runs across multiple platforms. eDirectory provides both Web-based and wireless management capabilities, allowing all resources to be managed with a Web browser or a handheld device. The directory is physically stored as a set of database files on a server. Similar to NDS, the directory is organized in a tree structure.

In NetWare 6.5, Netware Storage Services (NSS) is robust and can recover fully after a system crash. NSS also allows storage devices to be added dynamically. NSS supports both directly attached storage (a hard disk connected to the server), and network attached storage (a dedicated data server that provides centralized storage access for users and application servers). NetWare provides preconfigured solutions for network attached storage that allow for Web-based sharing of and access to files using a variety of protocols, and browsers.

NetWare 6.5 provides Novell **cluster** services to manage clusters that combine two or more servers into a single group. If one server in the cluster should fail, another server automatically takes over for the downed server and runs in its place. The second server recovers the downed server's applications, services, IP addresses, and volumes, so users are not aware of the failure of the first server. NetWare 6.5 has the capability to cluster up to 32 Netware servers into a single high availability group. The workload can be balanced among the NetWare servers in the cluster, and resources can be dynamically allocated to any server in the cluster. Figure 21.8 shows an example of a cluster using a shared disk system.

NetWare 6.5 includes Novell Web and Application services (NWAS), a mix of open source and Novell products integrated within NetWare that uses Apache 2.0 (Chapter 20) as its basic Web server. Apache is available as a custom NetWare loadable module and is tightly integrated with eDirectory. In addition, NWAS also supports Secure Sockets Layer encryption. The integration of Apache with eDirectory and SSL provides a secure means of sharing company information over the Internet. Other supported open source products include the MySql database management system, the PHP scripting language, and the Tomcat server, which can host Java server pages. These open source products are enhanced with Novell's NetWare Web Search Server (NWSS), which lets you add search and print functionality to any Web site in your organization. Additionally, for high end application server needs (for example, complex Java API support), NetWare includes the ExteNd Application server. The Apache Web server is also used internally within NetWare to provide Web-based administration to eDirectory, Novell Storage solution, and other services.

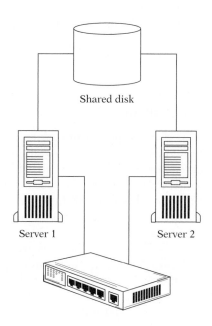

FIGURE 21.8

A shared volume cluster.

Novell and Linux

In November 2003, Novell announced plans to acquire Suse, a major Linux vendor, and to support Novell services on Linux. Earlier in the year (August 2003), Novell acquired another Linux vendor, Ximian, and ported Novell's e-mail system, Groupwise, to run on the Linux platform. The latest acquisition will allow eDirectory, Novell storage, and print solutions all to be available on the Linux platform. These acquisitions appear to be consistent with Novell's usage of high quality open source products, enhanced by the company's own products.

◼ Using NetWare

An excellent way to grasp how NetWare works is to use it to perform a few simple operations. With your instructor's permission, much of the balance of this chapter can be run as a tutorial similar to the chapters in Part 3. Note, however, that (for security reasons) many network administrators prefer that students not work directly with network commands.

The Client/Server Structure

The structure of the client/server connection that will be used to illustrate this example is shown as Figure 21.9. Novell's NetWare (as outlined in this chapter) is the server's operating system, providing print services, management services, and file and storage services, all coordinated by NetWare directory services. Your (client) workstation can run under any of several different primary operating systems, such as Windows or UNIX/Linux. Windows XP will be assumed in this example.

A subset of Novell's NetWare called the **network provider** or the **network client** runs under the client computer's primary operating system. The network provider is integrated within the desktop environment of Windows. When a user accesses a Novell NetWare network through *Explorer* or *My Computer* or *My Network Places,* the information is routed to the Novell network provider.

The network provider is a dynamic link library that uses the network redirector (Figure 21.9, client operating system) to access services from the network. The redirector is a file system driver under the I/O manager services of Windows XP. The redirector sends information to and returns information from the NetWare network to the provider. The provider and redirector together form the Novell client and provide access to the NetWare network, making it possible to perform network functions via the familiar Windows interfaces.

This section illustrates the use of the Novell client running under Windows XP to perform some simple and standard operations with the NetWare operating system. Since every network is unique, you might have to adapt the material to the specific situation in your lab. Finally, please do not perform these functions without the explicit permission of your instructor or system administrator.

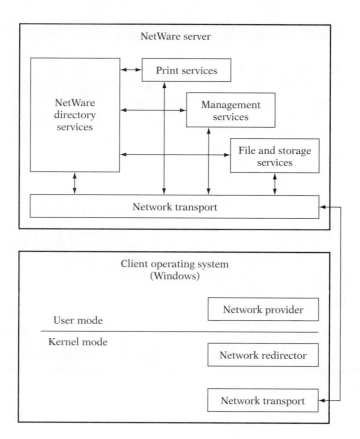

FIGURE 21.9

The client/server connection.

Logging In

In order to access the network, you must first login (Figure 21.10), generally to a Novell directory services tree rather than a specific server. The login step enables NDS to authenticate you once and use that authentication to provide access to any and all resources on the network for which you have rights. If the machine is already on, you can get to the login prompt by clicking on

Start/All Programs/Novell (Common)/Novell Login

(Figure 21.11). Enter your *userid* and *password,* and click *OK* to login to the network.

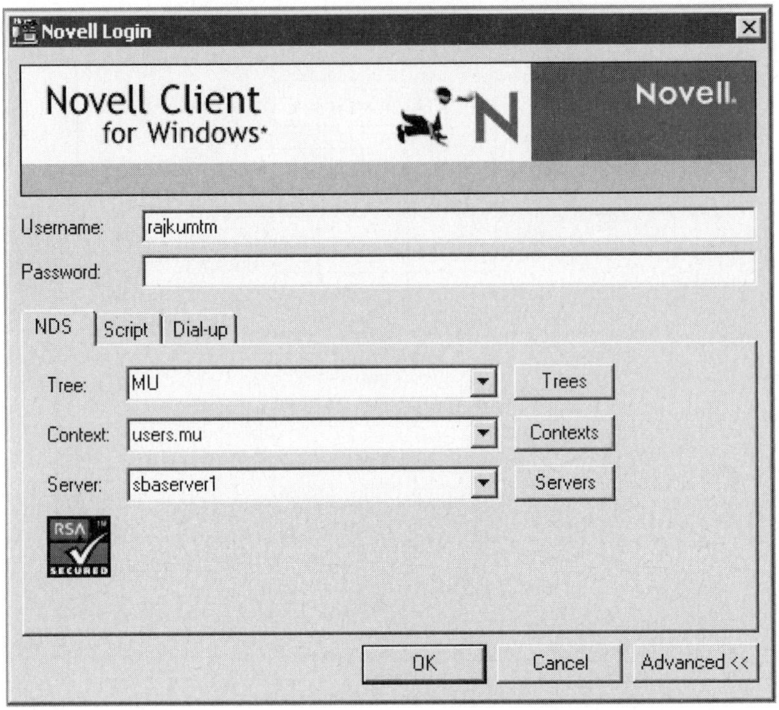

FIGURE 21.10
The login screen.

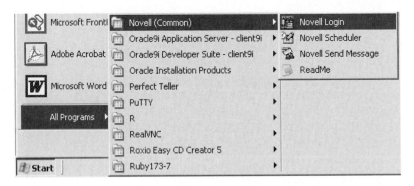

FIGURE 21.11
The path to the login screen.

Accessing Network Resources Using My Network Places

My Network Places allows you to browse resources on the entire network, be they Windows 2003 servers, Novell servers, or the Internet. Click the *Start/My Network Places* icon on the desktop (Figure 21.12) to open *My Network Places* (Figure 21.13). Open the *Tools* menu and click on the *Folder* options to bring up the *Options* window (Figure 21.14) and ensure that *Open each folder in same Window* is selected under the *Browse Folder* options. Then click *OK*.

FIGURE 21.12

My Network Places.

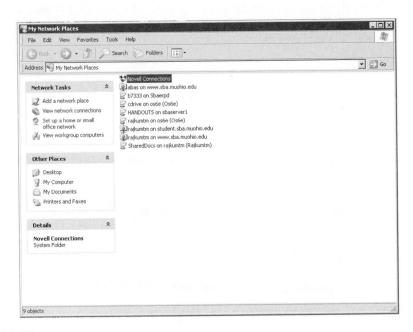

FIGURE 21.13

The *My Network Places* screen.

FIGURE 21.14

The *Options* window.

Double click on *Novell Connections* (Figure 21.13) to display the available trees. Select a tree that you know you have access to (Figure 21.15) and open it. (For example, the authors selected *MU* for Miami University; ask your instructor for help if necessary.) *Double click* on the organizational unit container (screen not shown) that holds your server. The authors selected SBA (for School of Business Administration). Then select your server (Figure 21.16). For example, the folder for the primary student server at Miami University is found in the SBA container and is called SBASERVER1_SYS. Your system is likely to be different, so please check with your instructor for information on what container, server, and folder to use. Generally, you can choose any sys folder for a server, because all servers have a sys folder that contains NetWare system files.

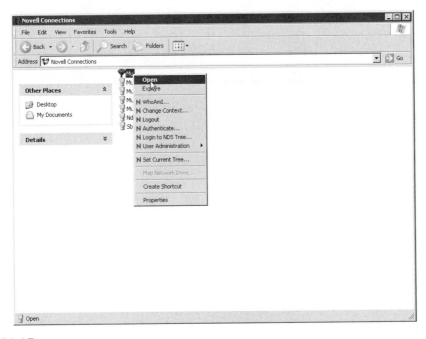

FIGURE 21.15

Novell Connections.

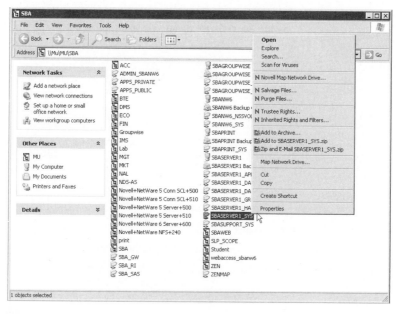

FIGURE 21.16
The authors' server.

Mapping a Network Drive

Once you have identified the server and system folder, *right click* on the folder (Figure 21.16) and you will see a variety of Novell client options. Choose *Novell Map Network Drive* and the system will allow you to map the drive (Figure 21.17). The system (by default) picks the first available letter. To be consistent, please use the pull down menu for drives and choose *O* as the drive letter to map. To add drive *O* to the search path, click on the check box *Map Search Drive*. Then click on Map, to map the drive, and the network drive *sbaserver1_sys* is available to you as your *O:* drive (Figure 21.18). You can then open folders and work with the *O* drive using *My Computer* or *Explorer*.

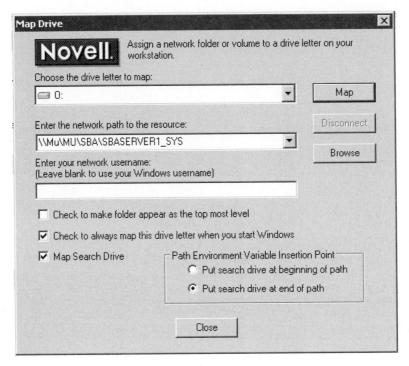

FIGURE 21.17

Mapping a drive.

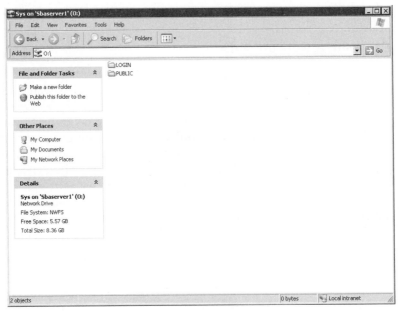

FIGURE 21.18

It is now the *O* drive.

Volume Information

Click on *Start/All Programs/Accessories/Windows Explorer* to open *Explorer*. Note that the mapped drive *O* created earlier is now visible on the left panel (Figure 21.19). *Right click* on the *O* drive to bring up the menu (Figure 21.20) and choose *Properties* to see the general volume information for this folder (Figure 21.21). The *General tab* shows the file system in use (NWFS) and the amount of used and available disk space. Click on some of the other tabs and browse through the information provided. Click on *Cancel* to close the properties window.

Mapping with *Explorer*

You can also map drives with Windows *Explorer*. Choose *Tools/Map Drive* from the *Explorer* menu to bring up the map screen (Figure 21.22). Note that the next drive, *P,* is selected by default. Click on *Browse* and then click on *Novell Connections* (Figure 21.23) to browse for your data folder. (If necessary, check with your instructor to identify your data folder.) In contrast, to the sys folder, you can read, write, and share files on your data folder. Click *OK* to select your data folder. Then click *Finish* to map it.

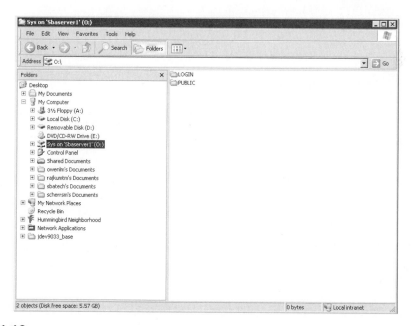

FIGURE 21.19

The mapped drive on *Explorer*.

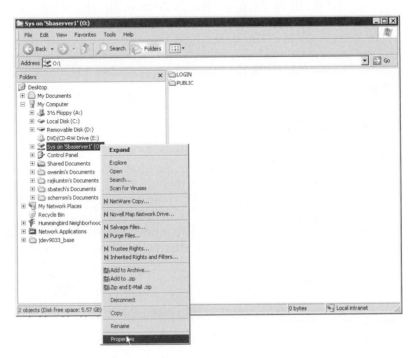

FIGURE 21.20

Select *Properties.*

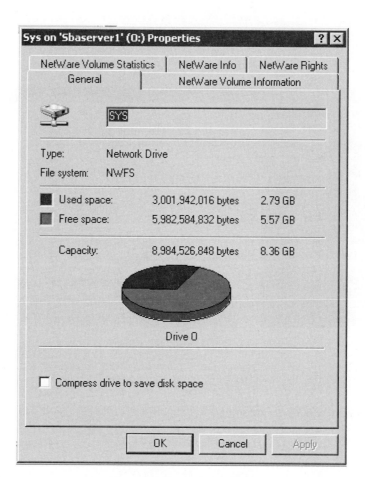

FIGURE 21.21

General information about the O drive.

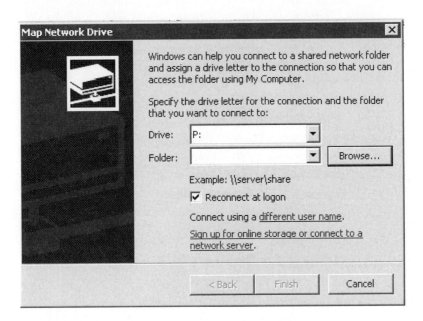

FIGURE 21.22

Mapping drives with Windows *Explorer*.

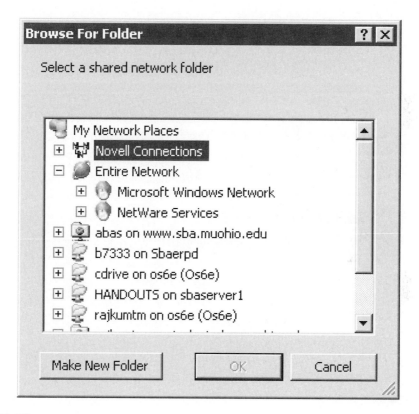

FIGURE 21.23

Browsing for your data folder.

Disconnecting a Mapped Drive

To disconnect from a mapped drive, choose *Tools/Disconnect Networked Drive* (Figure 21.24). The resulting screen lists all networked drives (Figure 21.25). Select drive *P*, and click on *OK* to remove the mapping. Choose *View/Refresh* from the *Explorer* menu to repaint the screen and show that the mapping has been removed. Repeat these steps for drive *O*.

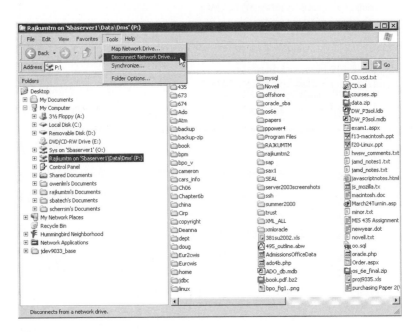

FIGURE 21.24

Disconnecting from a mapped drive.

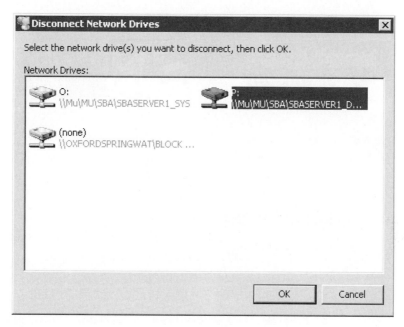

FIGURE 21.25
All networked drives.

Logging Out

To log out from the network, click on *Start/Windows Security* to bring up the Netware security window (Figure 21.26). Click on *logout* to log out of Novell and Windows. The system will ask for confirmation. Choose *OK* to close all active applications, log you out, and return you to the *Novell Login* Window.

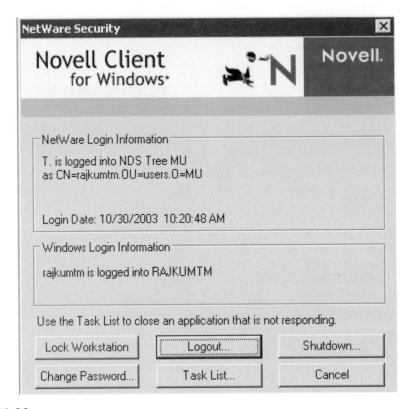

FIGURE 21.26

Logging out.

Summary

Novell's NetWare is a common local area network operating system. NetWare's kernel runs on the server and provides basic operating system functions. The Internet protocols (TCP and IP) are NetWare's native protocols, but previous versions used SPX/IPX. The application layer is provided through the NetWare control protocol (NCP). NetWare loadable modules (NLM) are object modules linkable at run time. NetWare is a 32-bit operating system and can access 4GB of address space. NetWare keeps its kernel in memory and allocates the rest of the memory for cache. A portion of the cache memory is used as the protected address space.

The basic object in a Novell file system is a volume. In the traditional NetWare file system, NetWare maintains a file allocation table (FAT) to support allocating files on a disk volume and caches the directory table on an as-needed basis. A directory or a file is located by following its path. A mapped drive is a convenient way to reference a particular subdirectory on the network with a single letter. A search path is a path to a directory on another computer. Novell Storage Services (NSS) enables the management of large files, volumes, name spaces, and storage devices.

All disks on the server are managed by NetWare. NetWare's queue-based print services use printers, print queues, and a print server. Novell distributed print services (NDPS) allows the network administrator to manage network printing more efficiently than queue-based services.

Novell directory services (NDS) is a method of storing and retrieving service and other information in a distributed database. Network resources, found at the end of a hierarchical tree structure, are called leaf objects. Organizational units, such as companies, divisions, and departments, are container objects used to divide and organize the tree structure into branches. Users can be referenced by their distinguished name.

Object rights control what the user can do with an object, such as browse, create, rename, supervise, and so on. Property rights control access to information fields that define an object, such as supervise, read, write, and so on. A partition is a logical division of the NDS tree containing one or more complete branches. Replication is the act of storing a copy of an NDS partition on a different server. Before a new user can access a Novell network, the network administrator must create an account for the user through Novell Directory Services. Zero Effort Networks (ZENworks) is the part of NetWare that supports desktop management. NetWare 6.5 is Novell's latest version.

A subset of Novell's NetWare called the network provider or the network client runs under the client computer's primary operating system. The chapter ended with a brief example using NetWare.

▋ Key Words

application management
boot DOS partition
cluster
connectionless datagram
connection oriented
container object
disk duplexing
distinguished name
hot fix
IPX
leaf object
mapped drive
NetWare
NetWare control protocol (NCP)
NetWare file system
NetWare loadable module (NLM)
NetWare partition

network client, or network provider
Novell directory services (NDS)
Novell distributed print services (NDPS)
Novell storage services (NSS)
Novell storage services partition
object rights
partition
path
portal
property rights
read after write
remote management
replication
SPX
volume
workstation management
Zero Effort Networks (ZENworks)

▮ Review Questions

1. What is the operating system on a Novell network server? What operating system(s) can be used on the client computers?

2. What are NetWare's native protocols? What is SPX/IPX?

3. What functions are performed by the NetWare control protocol (NCP)?

4. Explain the purpose of cache buffers. Explain how file cache buffers work.

5. Briefly explain how the traditional Novell file system works. What is a mapped drive?

6. What is fault tolerance? Briefly explain several fault tolerance techniques.

7. Explain how queue-based print services work.

8. What advantages (over traditional queue-based print services) are gained by using Novell distributed print services (NDPS)?

9. Briefly explain the purpose of Novell directory services (NDS).

10. Distinguish between a leaf object and a container object.

11. What is a distinguished name?

12. Distinguish between object rights and property rights.

13. What is a network provider or network client?

14. What is the purpose of ZENworks?

15. Briefly outline the key differences between NetWare Version 5 and NetWare 6.5

▮ Exercises

1. Turn back to Figure 17.12 and review the seven-layer OSI model. Then relate the OSI model to the NetWare architecture.

2. Apache, a popular Web server that runs under Linux/UNIX and is available under NetWare, powers more than half the Web sites in the world. However, most client computers run Windows. Why do you suppose that is true?

3. With your instructor's permission, complete the brief tutorial at the end of the chapter. What container, server, and folder did you use? Note any interesting properties associated with the drive you mapped. What data folder did you map with *Explorer*?

4. Figure 21.9 is a useful template for organizing at least some of this chapter's key terms.

Number Systems, Data Types, and Codes

■ Number Systems

A decimal number consists of a series of digits (0, 1, 2, 3, 4, 5, 6, 7, 8, 9) written in precise relative positions. The positions are important; for example, although they contain the same two digits, 23 and 32 are clearly different numbers because the digits are in different relative positions. The value of a given number is found by multiplying each digit by its place or positional value and adding the products. For example, 3582 represents:

$$
\begin{array}{rrr}
3 \text{ times} & 1000 = & 3000 \\
+5 \text{ times} & 100 = & 500 \\
+8 \text{ times} & 10 = & 80 \\
+2 \text{ times} & 1 = & \underline{2} \\
& & 3582
\end{array}
$$

Generally, any number's value is the sum of the products of its digit and place values.

Take a close look at the decimal place values 1, 10, 100, 1000, 10000, and so on. The pattern is obvious. Rather than writing all those zeros, you can use scientific notation, for example, writing 10000 as 10^4. Because any number raised to the zero power is (by definition) 1, you can write the decimal place values as the base (10) raised to a series of integer powers:

$$
\ldots\ 10^8\ \ 10^7\ \ 10^6\ \ 10^5\ \ 10^4\ \ 10^3\ \ 10^2\ \ 10^1\ \ 10^0
$$

A few general rules can be derived from this discussion of decimal numbers. First is the idea of place or positional value represented by the base (10) raised to a series of integer powers. The second is the use of the digit zero (0) to represent "nothing" in a given position. (How else could you distinguish 3 from 30?) Third, a total of ten digits (0 through 9) are needed to write decimal values. Finally, only values less than the base (in this case, 10) can be written with a single digit.

Binary Numbers

There is nothing to restrict the application of these rules to a base-10 number system. If the positional values are powers of 2, you have the framework of a binary or base-2 number system:

$$\ldots \quad 2^8 \quad 2^7 \quad 2^6 \quad 2^5 \quad 2^4 \quad 2^3 \quad 2^2 \quad 2^1 \quad 2^0$$

As in any number system, the digit zero (0) is needed to represent nothing in a given position. Additionally, the binary number system needs only one other digit, 1. Given these digit and place values, you can find the value of any number by multiplying each digit by its place value and adding these products. For example, the binary number 1100011 is:

$$
\begin{array}{rl}
1 \text{ times } 2^6 = 1 \text{ times } 64 = & 64 \\
+1 \text{ times } 2^5 = 1 \text{ times } 32 = & 32 \\
+0 \text{ times } 2^4 = 0 \text{ times } 16 = & 0 \\
+0 \text{ times } 2^3 = 0 \text{ times } 8 = & 0 \\
+0 \text{ times } 2^2 = 0 \text{ times } 4 = & 0 \\
+1 \text{ times } 2^1 = 1 \text{ times } 2 = & 2 \\
+1 \text{ times } 2^0 = 1 \text{ times } 1 = & \underline{1} \\
& 99
\end{array}
$$

The decimal number 2 is 10 in binary; the decimal number 4 is 100. Decimal 5 is 101 (1 four, 0 twos, and 1 one).

Octal and Hexadecimal

Other number systems, notably octal (base 8) and hexadecimal (base 16) are commonly used with computers. The octal number system uses powers of 8 to represent positional values and the digit values 0, 1, 2, 3, 4, 5, 6, and

7. The hexadecimal number system uses powers of 16 and the digits 0, 1, 2, 3, 4, 5, 6, 7, 8, 9, A, B, C, D, E, and F. The hexadecimal number FF is:

$$
\begin{array}{rr}
15 \text{ times } 16^1 = & 240 \\
+15 \text{ times } 16^0 = & \underline{15} \\
& 255
\end{array}
$$

There are no computers that work directly with octal or hex; a computer is a binary machine. These two number systems are used simply because it is easy to convert between them and binary. Each octal digit is exactly equivalent to three binary digits (Figure A.1); each hexadecimal digit is exactly equivalent to four binary digits (Figure A.2). Thus, octal and hex can be used as shorthand for displaying binary values.

Octal	Binary	Octal	Binary
0	000	4	100
1	001	5	101
2	010	6	110
3	011	7	111

FIGURE A.1

Each octal digit is exactly equivalent to three binary digits.

Hex	Binary	Hex	Binary
0	0000	8	1000
1	0001	9	1001
2	0010	A	1010
3	0011	B	1011
4	0100	C	1100
5	0101	D	1101
6	0110	E	1110
7	0111	F	1111

FIGURE A.2

Each hexadecimal is exactly equivalent to four binary digits.

◾ Data Types

The binary patterns stored inside a computer can be interpreted as several different data types.

Numeric Data

Because binary numbers are so well suited to electronic devices, computers are at their most efficient when working with pure binary values. A typical computer is designed around a basic unit of binary data called a word (usually 16, 32, or 64 bits). Normally, the high-order bit is set aside to hold a sign (0 for +, 1 for -), and the remaining bits are data bits. For example, the biggest binary value that can be stored on a 32-bit word computer is

> 0111 1111 1111 1111 1111 1111 1111 1111

which is 2,147,483,647 in decimal. The limit on a 16-bit machine is

> 0111 1111 1111 1111

or 32,767 in decimal. There is no provision for a decimal point. Decimal point alignment is the programmer's responsibility.

Binary integers are fine for many applications, but at times very large, very small, and fractional numbers are needed. With scientific notation, numbers are written as a decimal fraction followed by a power of 10; for example, the speed of light, 186,000 miles per second, is written as 0.186×10^6. Many computers can store and manipulate binary approximations of scientific numbers called real or floating-point numbers.

Certain applications, particularly business applications, demand precisely rounded decimal numbers. While any data type will do for whole numbers or integers, floating-point and binary numbers provide at best a close approximation to decimal fractions. Thus, many computers support a form of decimal data. Generally, computers are at their least efficient when processing decimal data.

String Data

Computers are not limited to storing and manipulating numbers. For example, many applications call for such data as names, addresses, and product descriptions. These string values (sometimes called character values) are typically stored as sets of individual characters, with each character represented by a code. Most modern computers use the ASCII code (Figure A.3). On many computers, a single coded character occupies one byte, so the name *Lopez* would be stored in five consecutive bytes.

It is important to note that strings and numbers are different. For example, if you type the digit 1 followed by the digit 2, each character will be stored as a 1-byte string in memory. On a computer that uses the ASCII code, these two characters would appear as:

00110001 00110010

That is *not* the number 12. On a 16-bit computer, a pure binary 12 is stored as

0000000000001100

(Try using the "digit-times-place-value" rule.)

Character	ASCII	Character	ASCII
0	0011 0000	I	0100 1001
1	0011 0001	J	0100 1010
2	0011 0010	K	0100 1011
3	0011 0011	L	0100 1100
4	0011 0100	M	0100 1101
5	0011 0101	N	0100 1110
6	0011 0110	O	0100 1111
7	0011 0111	P	0101 0000
8	0011 1000	Q	0101 0001
9	0011 1001	R	0101 0010
A	0100 0001	S	0101 0011
B	0100 0010	T	0101 0100
C	0100 0011	U	0101 0101
D	0100 0100	V	0101 0110
E	0100 0101	W	0101 0111
F	0100 0110	X	0101 1000
G	0100 0111	Y	0101 1001
H	0100 1000	Z	0101 1010

FIGURE A.3

The ASCII code for digits and uppercase letters.

Numbers and strings are different. That is why programmers and even spreadsheet users must distinguish strings from numbers. The positional value of each digit in a number is significant. In contrast, as you move from byte to byte, the positional values of the individual bits have no meaning in a string. (The order of the bits is significant, but defined by the code.)

Data normally enter a computer through an input device in string form. Most computers have special instructions to convert strings to numbers. Arithmetic operations are performed on the numbers, and the results are converted back to string form before they are sent to an output device. Most programming languages automatically perform these data type conversions for you. Assembler languages are an exception.

Images

Imagine laying a fine screen over a line drawing, chart, graph, photograph, or similar image. Each hole in the screen is one dot, or pixel, and numbers can be used to record each pixel's brightness, color, and other appearance parameters. For example, visualize an electronic scoreboard that displays the score by turning on and off selected light bulbs to form a pattern. Represent each unlit bulb as a 0 and each lit bulb as a 1, string those bits together, and you have a good mental model of a digital image.

A bitmap or raster image is a digital version of that dot pattern stored in memory. Bitmaps can be very large. For example, at one byte per pixel, a high-resolution, 1024 by 768 pixel bitmap occupies 786,432 bytes of memory. Such large files can quickly fill a hard drive and slow the download process.

To save space, bitmaps are usually compressed. Some compression algorithms, such as GIF (graphics interchange format) are lossless; in other words, following compression they retain every bit in the original bitmap. Others, such as JPEG (Joint Photographic Experts Group) are lossy—they lose some content during the compression process. Generally, lossy algorithms yield smaller files.

Rather than storing bitmaps, vector graphics relies on geometric formulas to represent images; Macromedia's Flash (SFW) format is an example. Prior to displaying or printing an image, the necessary pixel or dot values are computed from the formulas. Because the formulas require less space than an equivalent bitmap, a vector graphics file requires less memory and downloads faster than an equivalent raster graphics image. It is difficult to define a set of formulas for a complex image such as a photograph, however, so vector graphics is used primarily for lines and geometric shapes.

Figure A.4 lists several common graphics formats.

Extension	Description
AVI	Microsoft's audio video interleaved format. Used for movies and videos, with soundtrack. Access through Windows Media Player.
BMP	Microsoft Windows bitmap. No compression.
GIF	Graphics interchange format. A de facto Web standard developed by CompuServe for compressing bitmapped graphics and pictures. Lossless. Limited to 256 colors.
JPG or JPEG	Joint Photographic Experts Group. A de facto Web standard for compressing bitmapped still images and photographs. Lossy.
MOV	QuickTime movie file. The Apple Macintosh video format, now supported by Windows.
MPG or MPEG	Motion Picture Experts Group. A highly compressed format for storing movies.
PDF	Portable Document Format. Adobe Acrobat's page definition format. Download Acrobat Reader to view a PDF file.
PNG	Portable network graphics. A proposed replacement for GIF. Lossless, with better compression than GIF.
QTW	QuickTime for Windows. Movie files.
SVC	Scalable vector graphics. An open, XML-based vector graphics standard.
SWF	Macromedia Shockwave Flash file. Flash is a proprietary, scalable, vector graphics file format. Requires a downloadable plug-in.
TIF or TIFF	Tagged image (or information) file format. A bitmap format popular in desktop publishing applications. No compression.

FIGURE A.4

Some common graphics formats.

Note that AVI, MPEG, and QTM (Figure A.4) incorporate a sound track.

◼ Sounds

The idea of representing a visual image as a pattern of dots makes sense to most people, but sounds are different. By their very nature, sound waves are continuous (analog), not discrete (digital). How can sound be digitized? Sound is digitized through a sampling process. Imagine turning a microphone on and off thousands of times per second. During the time the microphone is on, it captures a brief pulse of sound, and for each sound pulse such parameters as tone, pitch, frequency, and so on are represented as numbers. Later, playing back the sound pulses in the proper order reproduces the original samples, and as long as the time between samples is sufficiently short, a human listener hears continuous sound.

Audio files can be huge. For example, to create an audio CD, the sound is sampled 44,100 times per second. Two bytes are used to store the information generated by each sample, so one second of sound consumes 88.2 KB and each minute fills 5.292 MB (that's megabytes) of storage. Consequently, audio files are almost always compressed. Figure A.5 lists several common audio formats.

Extension	Description
AIF	Audio interchange format. An Apple Macintosh format.
AU	Audio file. An early Internet sound format.
MID or MIDI	Musical instrument digital interface. Access through Windows Media Player.
MP3	MPEG, audio layer 3. MP3 uses a compression algorithm that shrinks CD-level sound files by a factor of 12 with no loss in sound quality. A popular format for swapping audio files.
RA or RAM	RealAudio file. Used for Internet streamed audio and video.
WAV	Waveform. Sound file for Windows. Access through Windows Media Player and Sound Recorder.

FIGURE A.5

Some common audio formats.

Summary of MS-DOS Commands

◼ General

▶ Command format

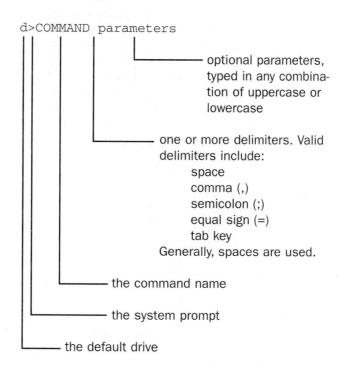

`d>COMMAND parameters`

optional parameters, typed in any combination of uppercase or lowercase

one or more delimiters. Valid delimiters include:
space
comma (,)
semicolon (;)
equal sign (=)
tab key
Generally, spaces are used.

the command name

the system prompt

the default drive

▶ Rules for defining a file name

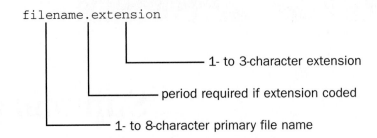

`filename.extension`

— 1- to 3-character extension

— period required if extension coded

— 1- to 8-character primary file name

▶ legal characters

A-Z a-z 0-9 $ & # % ' ( ) @ ^ { } ~ ` ! _

▶ illegal characters

? . , ; : = * / \ + " < >

▶ lowercase letters converted to uppercase

▶ primary file name padded with spaces to 8 characters

▶ extension padded with spaces to 3 characters

▶ wild-card characters

? any single character

* any group of 1 to 8 characters

▶ Rules for defining path names

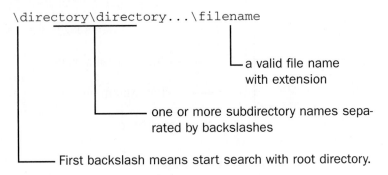

`\directory\directory...\filename`

— a valid file name
with extension

— one or more subdirectory names separated by backslashes

— First backslash means start search with root directory.

▶ To define a subdirectory name, use the rules for defining a file name without an extension.

▶ Maximum path name length is 64 characters.

▶ If path name does not start with a backslash, search begins with current working directory.

▶ Reserved device names

CON   PRN   LPT1   AUX   COM1

LPT2   LPT3   COM2   NUL   CLOCK$

▶ Conventional file name extensions

ASM	assembler source	EXE	executable file
BAK	backup file	FOR	FORTRAN source
BAS	BASIC source	LIB	library source
BAT	batch file	LST	ASCII list file
BIN	binary file	MAP	ASCII load module
COB	COBOL source	OBJ	object module
COM	command file	OVR	overlay file
DAT	ASCII data file	REF	cross reference
DIF	difference file	TMP	temporary link
DOC	ASCII document	$$$	temporary work
DVD	device driver		

▶ Redirection parameters

Parameter	*Meaning*	*Example*
<	Change source to a specified file or device.	<MYFILE.DAT
>	Change destination to a specified file or device.	>PRN
>>	Change destination, usually to an existing file, and append new output to it.	>>HOLD.DAT
|	Pipe standard output to another command or to a filter.	DIR | MORE

■ Selected Commands

▶ CHDIR changes the current working directory.

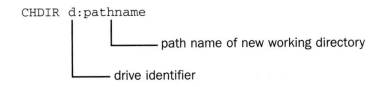

```
CHDIR  d:pathname
```
path name of new working directory

drive identifier

▶ . designates the current working directory.

▶ .. is the parent of the current working directory.

▶ CHDIR with no parameters displays name of current working directory.

▶ CHKDSK checks a disk's directory and reports on its contents.

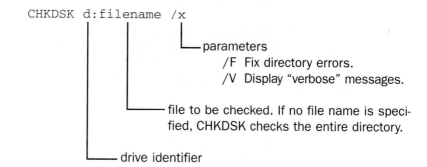

```
CHKDSK  d:filename  /x
```
parameters
/F Fix directory errors.
/V Display "verbose" messages.

file to be checked. If no file name is specified, CHKDSK checks the entire directory.

drive identifier

▶ CLS clears the screen.

```
CLS  (no parameters)
```

▶ COMP compares two files.

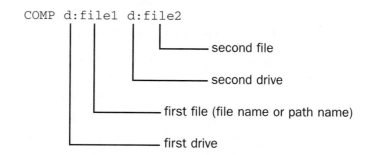

```
COMP  d:file1  d:file2
```
second file

second drive

first file (file name or path name)

first drive

COMP is often used after COPY to verify results.

▶ COPY copies one or more files from a source to a destination.

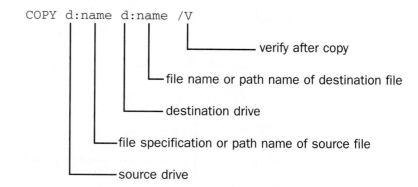

```
COPY  d:name  d:name  /V
```
verify after copy

file name or path name of destination file

destination drive

file specification or path name of source file

source drive

▶ If the destination file name is blank, the source file name is used and the drives must be different.

▶ The source and destination must differ in some way (file name, drive, and/or directory).

▶ **DATE** checks and/or sets the system date.

```
DATE
```

```
DATE mm-dd-yy
```

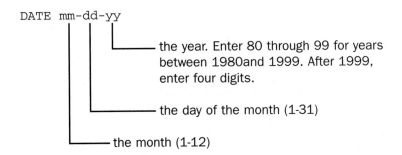

the year. Enter 80 through 99 for years between 1980and 1999. After 1999, enter four digits.

the day of the month (1-31)

the month (1-12)

▶ **DIR** displays a directory's contents.

```
DIR d:name /x
```

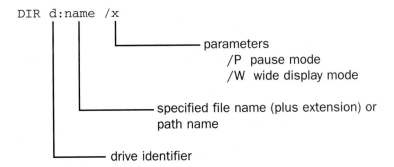

parameters
/P pause mode
/W wide display mode

specified file name (plus extension) or path name

drive identifier

▶ Default drive selection

`A:` selects drive A.
`B:` selects drive B, and so on.

▶ **DISKCOMP** compares the contents of two complete diskettes.

```
DISKCOMP d: d:
```

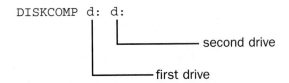

second drive

first drive

▶ Note: a /V option on a DISKCOPY command implies DISKCOMP.

▶ DISKCOPY copies the contents of one disk to another.

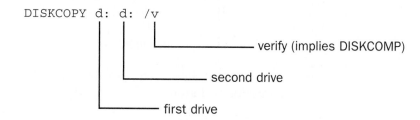

```
DISKCOPY d: d: /v
```
— verify (implies DISKCOMP)
— second drive
— first drive

▶ ECHO controls the display of batch file commands and displays comments on the screen.

ECHO ON	commands displayed
ECHO OFF	commands not displayed
ECHO message	message displayed

▶ ERASE (or DEL) erases a file or files.

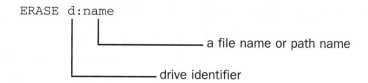

```
ERASE d:name
```
— a file name or path name
— drive identifier

▶ FORMAT formats a disk.

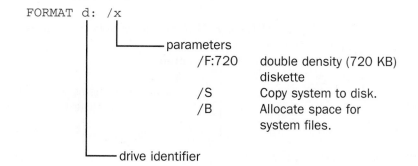

```
FORMAT d: /x
```
— parameters
/F:720 — double density (720 KB) diskette
/S — Copy system to disk.
/B — Allocate space for system files.
— drive identifier

▶ **MKDIR** creates a new directory.

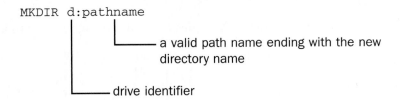

```
MKDIR d:pathname
```
— a valid path name ending with the new directory name

— drive identifier

▶ **RECOVER** salvages useful portions of a file or files on a disk containing bad sectors.

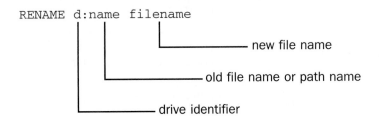

```
RECOVER d:file
```
— file name or path name

— drive identifier

▶ Note: if no file is specified, all files stored on the specified or default disk are recovered.

▶ **RENAME** (or **REN**) renames an existing file.

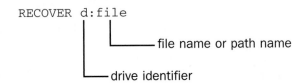

```
RENAME d:name filename
```
— new file name

— old file name or path name

— drive identifier

▶ **RMDIR** (or **RD**) removes the specified directory.

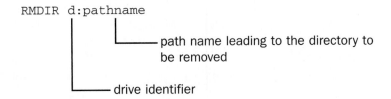

```
RMDIR d:pathname
```
— path name leading to the directory to be removed

— drive identifier

▶ Note: the directory to be removed must be empty.

▶ **SCANDISK** checks a disks surface, files, and directories for errors and corrects some errors.

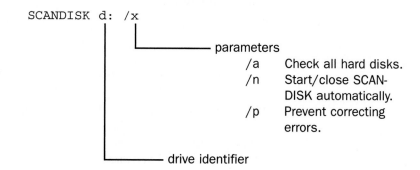

```
SCANDISK d: /x
```

— parameters

/a   Check all hard disks.
/n   Start/close SCAN-
     DISK automatically.
/p   Prevent correcting
     errors.

— drive identifier

▶ **TIME** checks and/or sets the system time.

```
TIME
```

```
TIME   hh:mm:ss.cc
```

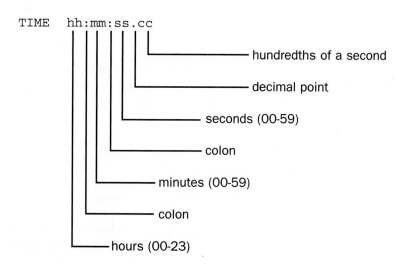

— hundredths of a second

— decimal point

— seconds (00-59)

— colon

— minutes (00-59)

— colon

— hours (00-23)

▶ **TYPE** displays the selected file's contents on the screen.

```
TYPE d:name
```

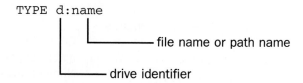

— file name or path name

— drive identifier

▶ VER displays the MS-DOS version number.

```
VER  (no parameters)
```

■ Selected Filters

▶ CIPHER encrypts and decrypts files for security.

```
CIPHER  keyword>d:name
CIPHER  keyword<d:name
CIPHER  keyword<d:name1>d:name2
```

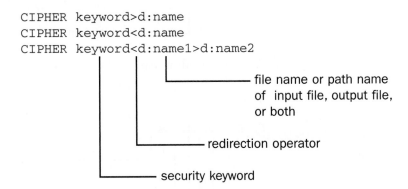

file name or path name
of input file, output file,
or both

redirection operator

security keyword

▶ Note: read the detailed documentation carefully before using
   CIPHER.

▶ FIND searches the specified file or files for a string, and displays
   all lines containing that string.

```
FIND /x "string" name1 name2 ...
```

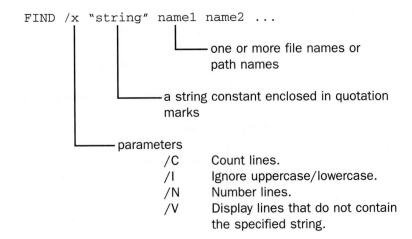

one or more file names or
path names

a string constant enclosed in quotation
marks

parameters
/C	Count lines.
/I	Ignore uppercase/lowercase.
/N	Number lines.
/V	Display lines that do not contain the specified string.

▶ MORE reads text from the standard input device and displays it one screen at a time.

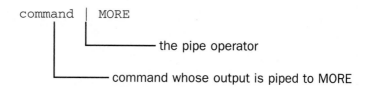

the pipe operator

command whose output is piped to MORE

▶ SORT sorts data into ascending order.

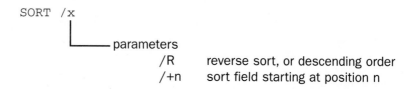

parameters

/R   reverse sort, or descending order

/+n   sort field starting at position n

Summary of UNIX Commands

◾ General

▶ Format of a command

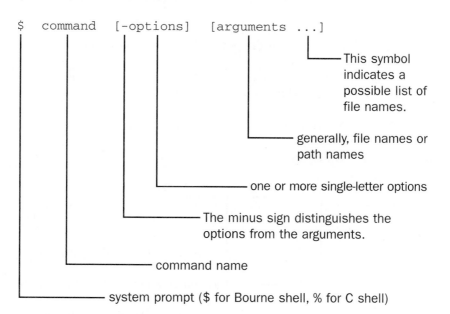

▶ Fields are separated by one or more spaces.

▶ Fields enclosed in brackets [..] are optional.

▶ Rules for defining a file name

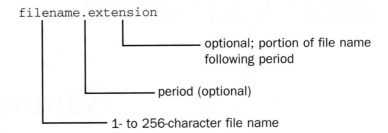

▶ Suggested characters include A-Z, a-z, 0-9, comma (,), and underscore (_).

▶ Avoid using slash (/) characters in a file name.

▶ Don't start a file name with a minus sign (-).

▶ UNIX distinguishes between uppercase and lowercase.

▶ If you include a period in the file name, the characters following the period form the extension.

▶ The period and the extension count against the 256-character limit.

▶ You can code more than one period.

▶ Rules for defining path names

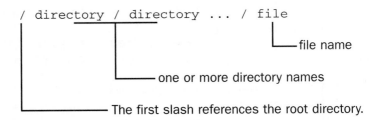

▶ A directory is a special type of file; thus the rules for defining a directory name are the same as the rules for defining a file name.

▶ If the path name starts with a directory name instead of a slash, UNIX starts searching with the working directory.

▶ Redirection parameters

Parameter	Meaning	Example
<	Change source to a specified file or device.	<myfile
>	Change destination to a specified file or device.	>tempfile
>>	Change destination, usually to an existing file, and append new output to it.	>>master.pay
|	Pipe standard output to another command or to a filter.	cat file1|sort

▶ Access Permissions

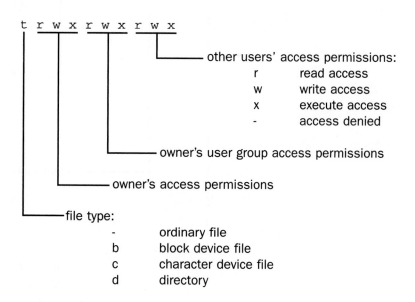

■ Commands and Utilities

▶ cat displays the contents of a file or files.

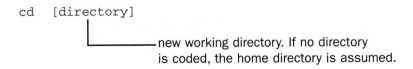

▶ cd changes the working directory.

▶ chmod changes a file's access permissions.

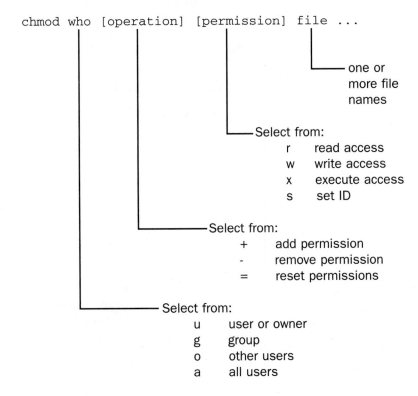

▶   cp copies a file or files.

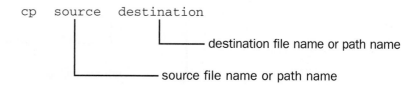

```
cp   source   destination
```
— destination file name or path name
— source file name or path name

▶   csh activates the C shell.

```
csh
```

—no options or parameters

▶   date displays the system date and time.

```
$ date
```
—no options

▶   ln creates a link.

```
ln file1 [file2]
```
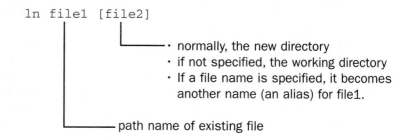
· normally, the new directory
· if not specified, the working directory
· If a file name is specified, it becomes
  another name (an alias) for file1.

—path name of existing file

▶   logout logs a user off the system.

```
logout
```
—no options or parameters

Note: on most systems, press control-D to log off.

▶ `lpr` sends the contents of a file to the printer.

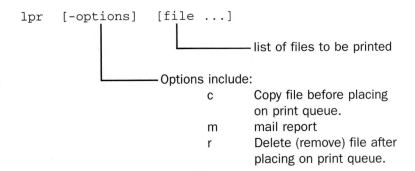

```
lpr  [-options]  [file ...]
```

list of files to be printed

Options include:

c	Copy file before placing on print queue.
m	mail report
r	Delete (remove) file after placing on print queue.

▶ `ls` lists the contents of a directory or directories.

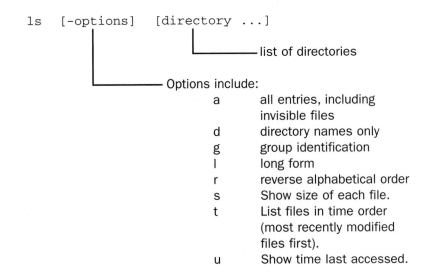

```
ls  [-options]  [directory ...]
```

list of directories

Options include:

a	all entries, including invisible files
d	directory names only
g	group identification
l	long form
r	reverse alphabetical order
s	Show size of each file.
t	List files in time order (most recently modified files first).
u	Show time last accessed.

▶ `mail` allows a user to send or receive electronic mail.

  ▶ To send mail, use:

```
mail  user-list
```

login IDs of users to receive mail

▶ To receive mail, use:

```
mail   [-options]
            └────────── Options include:
                            p       Display mail without
                                    prompts.
                            q       Quit.
                            r       View mail in reverse
                                    (chronological) order.
```

▶ man displays the UNIX manual page for the indicated command.

```
man   name
          └────── command or utility name
```

▶ mkdir creates one or more directories.

```
mkdir   directory ...
                └────────── one or more directory names
```

▶ more displays a file one screen at a time.

```
more   file ...
            └────── list of files to be displayed
```

▶ mv moves or renames a file.

```
mv   file   file
          │       └────── new file name or path name
          └────────────── old file name or path name
```

▶ passwd changes a user's password.

```
passwd
      └────── no options
```

▶ `pr` prepares standard input or a file for printing.

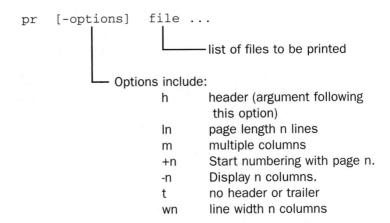

```
pr  [-options]  file ...
```

list of files to be printed

Options include:

h	header (argument following this option)
ln	page length n lines
m	multiple columns
+n	Start numbering with page n.
-n	Display n columns.
t	no header or trailer
wn	line width n columns

▶ `ps` displays the status of a process.

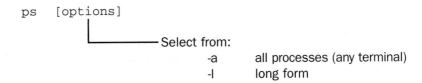

```
ps  [options]
```

Select from:

-a	all processes (any terminal)
-l	long form

If no options are coded, displays status of all processes controlled by user's terminal.

▶ `pwd` displays the user's current working directory.

```
pwd
```

no options

▶ `rm` deletes a file by removing a link.

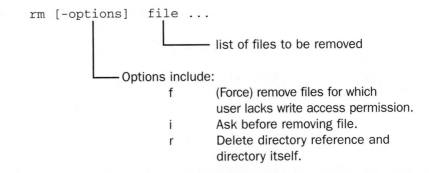

```
rm [-options]  file ...
```

list of files to be removed

Options include:

f	(Force) remove files for which user lacks write access permission.
i	Ask before removing file.
r	Delete directory reference and directory itself.

▶ `rmdir` deletes one or more directories.

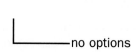

```
rmdir   directory ...
```
└─── path names of one or more
empty directories

▶ `sh` activates the Bourne shell.

```
sh
```
└─── no options

▶ `sort` sorts the contents of a file.

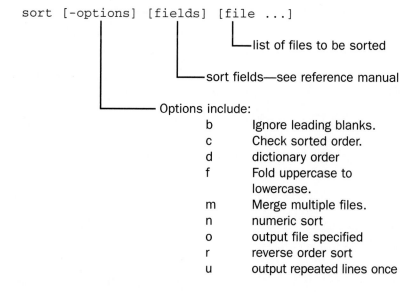

```
sort [-options] [fields] [file ...]
```
└─ list of files to be sorted

└─ sort fields—see reference manual

└─ Options include:

b	Ignore leading blanks.
c	Check sorted order.
d	dictionary order
f	Fold uppercase to lowercase.
m	Merge multiple files.
n	numeric sort
o	output file specified
r	reverse order sort
u	output repeated lines once

▶ `spell` checks a file for spelling errors.

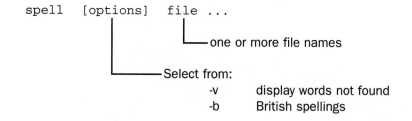

```
spell  [options]   file ...
```
└─ one or more file names

└─ Select from:

-v	display words not found
-b	British spellings

▶ `vi` activates the visual editor.

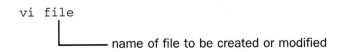

▶ `who` displays the names of users currently logged on the system.

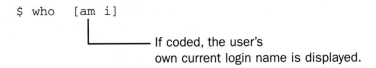

▶ `write` sends a message to another user in real time.

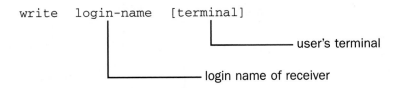

IBM OS/JCL

◾ Job Control Language

During the 1960s and much of the 1970s, the dominant computer applications included such accounting tasks as payroll, accounts receivable, accounts payable, and general ledger. These applications were (and still are) run on a scheduled basis, so most computer systems of that era were batch oriented. Punched cards were the standard input medium. A programmer prepared a deck of cards containing program source statements and data for a group of related application programs, arranged them to form a unit of work called a job, and submitted the job to the computer center. Instructions to the operating system for running the job were coded in a set of job control language (JCL) statements that were integrated into the job stream.

There are three basic types of IBM/OS JCL statements:

1. JOB statements separate and identify jobs. Secondary functions include passing accounting and priority information to the operating system.
2. EXEC (or execute) statements identify the programs (or job steps) to be executed.
3. DD (or data definition) statements define, in detail, the characteristics of each and every peripheral device used by each job step.

A job must begin with a JOB statement, and can contain almost any number of job steps. Each job step calls for one EXEC statement. Within a job step, one DD statement must be coded for each peripheral device accessed by the program.

JCL Statement Format

The basic format of a JCL statement is shown in Figure D.1. The first two columns must contain slash characters, and the name field must begin in position 3. The job name (the name associated with a JOB statement), step name (the name associated with an EXEC statement), or DD name (the name associated with a DD statement) is chosen by the programmer using a combination of from 1 to 8 letters, digits, or national characters (@, $, #). The first character may *not* be a digit.

Continuing to the right in Figure D.1, one or more blanks (or spaces) separate the name field from the operation field, which must be JOB, EXEC, or DD. One or more blanks separate the operation field from the operands, which consist of a series of parameters separated by commas. One or more blanks separate the operands from the optional comments. The JCL statement ends with column 71. Historically, columns 72 through 80 were reserved for sequence numbers, just in case a large deck of cards was dropped.

Note carefully that blanks are used to separate fields. Stray blanks are the beginner's most common JCL error. They *will be* interpreted as field separators. For example, coding

```
//  STEP2 EXEC COBOL
```

results in a strange error message—there is no such operation as STEP2 (only JOB, EXEC, and DD are valid). Try

```
//STEP2 EXEC COBOL
```

with no blanks between the // and the name field.

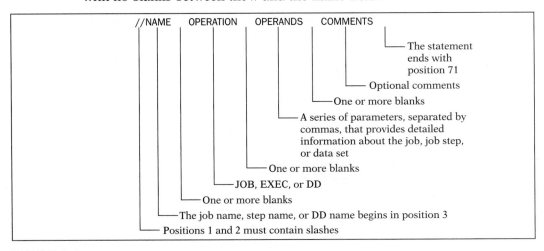

FIGURE D.1

An OS/JCL statement.

JOB Statements

The function of a JOB statement (Figure D.2) is to identify and mark the beginning of a given job, thus separating it from all other jobs. The job name is required, and must be unique. It must start with a letter or a national character; otherwise, any combination of from 1 to 8 letters, digits, and national characters is legal. In many computer centers, job names are assigned by the operating system to eliminate the risk that two or more jobs might have the same name. The job name and the operation (JOB) are the only required fields.

Positional Parameters

One important secondary function of the JOB statement is passing information to an accounting routine. Accounting information is a positional parameter that (if present) is always the first parameter. The meaning of a positional parameter is determined by its relative position in the operands field. For example, the statement

```
//JOB396 JOB 1234
```

indicates that the cost of running job JOB396 is to be charged against account 1234. Often, multiple accounting subparameters are coded. For example,

```
//MU435 JOB (1234,875)
```

might mean that job MU435 is to be charged against account number 1234, user number 875. When more than one subparameter is coded, commas are used to separate them. Note also the use of parentheses. When more than one subparameter is coded, parentheses are *required*.

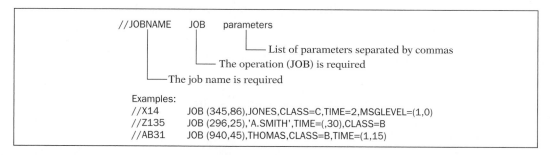

FIGURE D.2

A JOB statement.

The exact content of the accounting information parameter is up to the installation, and each computer center can define its own accounting subparameters. Note that the subparameters are also positional—in other words, they must be coded in a prescribed order.

On a batch processing system, programmers (and users) submit complete jobs and come back for the results some time later. To simplify programmer identification, the programmer's name is coded as a second positional parameter, for example,

```
//MU098 JOB (2987,235),DAVIS
```

or

```
//MU1735 JOB (2195,235),'W.S. DAVIS'
```

The programmer name parameter can contain up to 20 letters or digits, including a single period. The apostrophes (or single quotation marks) are needed when special characters, such as commas, blanks, or additional periods, are part of the programmer's name. Your computer center may have a preferred format.

Keyword Parameters

A job's class indicates the partition or region in which it runs. Another way to think of a job class is as a set of default limits on such parameters as execution time, memory space, types of peripherals accessed, and so on. For example, a simple, I/O-bound compilation job that reads source statements, compiles the code, prepares a compiler listing, and writes the object code to a library might run in a class A partition, while a complex application that requires mounting multiple disks and/or tapes might run in a less restrictive but lower priority class D partition. The various job classes supported by a given computer system are defined by the system operator at startup time.

A programmer indicates a job's class by coding a CLASS parameter, for example,

```
//MU741 JOB (3984,444),SMITH,CLASS=A
```

CLASS is a keyword parameter. It derives its meaning not from its position, but from the key word CLASS. Unlike positional parameters, which must be coded in a prescribed order, keyword parameters can be coded in any order.

Most batch systems automatically cancel a program caught in an endless loop after a reasonable time has passed. Often, an estimate of the job's likely run time is reported to the operating system in a TIME parameter. For example,

```
TIME=(5,30)
```

asks for 5 minutes and 30 seconds of processor time, while

```
TIME=5
TIME=(5)
TIME=(5,0)
```

are *all* requests for exactly five minutes. Note the use of parentheses. When the first subparameter alone is coded (minutes), they can be skipped. However, when more than one subparameter is coded, parentheses must be used.

Minutes and seconds are positional subparameters; in other words, they are defined by their relative positions. Minutes come first; seconds come second. For example, to request exactly 30 seconds, code

```
TIME=(,30)
```

The comma indicates the absence of the "minutes" positional subparameter. Because both the comma (indicating the absence of the first positional subparameter) and the second positional subparameter (seconds) are coded, parentheses are required.

CLASS and TIME are themselves keyword parameters. The key words CLASS and TIME give them meaning independent of their position. For example, the following JOB statements are all legal:

```
//X14   JOB  (345,86),JONES,CLASS=C,TIME=2

//Z135 JOB  (296,25),'A. SMITH',TIME=(,30),CLASS=B

//AB31 JOB  (940,45),THOMAS,CLASS=B,TIME=(1,15)
```

The accounting information must come first, followed by the programmer name. They are positional parameters, and derive their meaning from their relative positions. CLASS and TIME are keyword parameters that can be coded in any order.

On some systems, a job's priority is determined, in part, by the amount of space it requires. The programmer can request space by coding a REGION parameter. For example,

```
REGION=128K
```

represents a request for a 128K region. Modern memory management systems have largely eliminated the need to prespecify a region size.

The MSGLEVEL Parameter

Programmer-coded JCL statements, the JCL statements included in a cataloged procedure, and messages indicating the operating system's actions are valuable to the programmer, but once the program is released they are meaningless to the user. The MSGLEVEL (message level) parameter (Figure D.3) allows the programmer to select which JCL and device allocation messages are to be printed. For example,

```
MSGLEVEL=(1,1)
```

means to print everything, while

```
MSGLEVEL=(0,0)
```

means print only the JOB statement unless the job fails, and

```
MSGLEVEL=(1,0)
```

tells the system to print all JCL statements but to skip allocation messages.

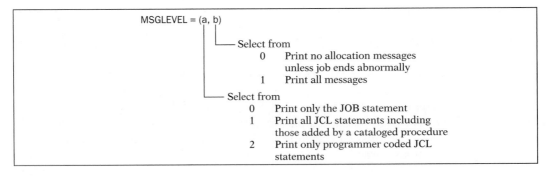

FIGURE D.3
MSGLEVEL specifies which JCL statements and messages are to be printed.

Instead of requiring the programmer to code numerous parameters each time a job is submitted, most computer centers rely on defaults. If the programmer fails, for any reason, to code a particular parameter, the system assumes a value. Often, only accounting information, the programmer's name, and the job class are required. Defaults are typically based on the job class with, for example, all CLASS=A jobs assigned a 640K region and a 30 second time limit, while CLASS=B jobs get 512K and a 2 minute time limit. To override a default, simply code the appropriate parameter.

Continuing a JCL Statement

Consider the following JOB statement:

```
//C1234567 JOB (3998,659),'A.B. JONES',CLASS=A,
//         TIME=(5,30),REGION=128K
```

It's too long to fit on a single line, and thus must be continued. The rules for continuing a JCL statement are:

1. Interrupt the field after a complete parameter or subparameter, including the trailing comma, has been coded. (In other words, stop after *any* comma in the operands field.)
2. *Optionally* code any nonblank character in position 72. Position 72 can be left blank; the continuation character is optional.
3. Code slashes (//) in positions 1 and 2 of the continuation line.
4. Continue coding in any position from 4 through 16. Position 3 must be blank and coding must be resumed no later than position 16.

In other words, just break after a comma and resume coding on the next line. The same rules hold for any type of JCL statement.

■ EXEC Statements

An EXEC statement (Figure D.4) marks the beginning of a job step. Its purpose is to identify the program or cataloged procedure (a set of precoded JCL statements stored on a library) to be executed. The step name is optional; if coded, the rules for a step name are the same as the rules for a job name. The first parameter must be a program or procedure name, for example,

```
// EXEC  PGM=SORT6
```

or

```
//    EXEC    PROC=COBOL
```

The keyword **PROC** can be skipped, for example,

```
//    EXEC    COBOL
```

If a program is referenced, the keyword **PGM** must be coded. Often, the program or cataloged procedure name is the only parameter coded on an EXEC statement.

When a cataloged procedure is referenced, the operating system searches the procedure library and replaces the programmer's EXEC statement with a set of precoded JCL. For example, the cataloged procedure FORTRAN is replaced by all the EXEC and DD statements needed to support three job steps—compile, link edit, and go (execute the resulting load module).

If you have ever programmed in a traditional compiler language, you may have noticed something called a severity code on your compiler listing. A program containing severe errors will almost certainly not run. The compiler passes the highest severity code to the system by placing a condition code in a register. The operating system can check this condition code prior to loading and executing a job step, skipping the step if the condition code is not acceptable. The programmer sets the limits for this comparison through a **COND** (condition) parameter.

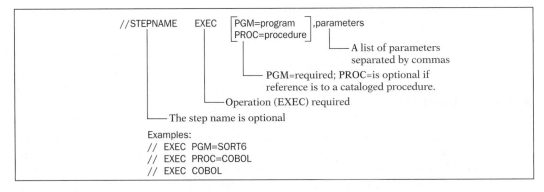

FIGURE D.4

An EXEC statement.

Other EXEC parameters allow the programmer to pass accounting information to a job step or set a dispatching priority for the step. Some parameters can be coded on the JOB statement or on an EXEC statement. For example, the programmer has the option of specifying a time limit, a region size, restart options, and other conditions for the complete job or for each job step independently.

Programmers often encounter a PARM parameter in a cataloged procedure. For example, in the FORTRAN procedure,

```
//   EXEC   FORTRAN,PARM.FORT='NODECK,LIST'
```

the PARM parameter informs the FORT job step (the compiler) that no object deck (at one time, a real deck of cards) is to be output and that a listing is to be printed. Information on the meaning of parameters for any compiler language can be found in the programmer's guide to that language.

◼ DD Statements

On a traditional IBM mainframe, one data control block is coded inside the program for each external device accessed by the program. The DCB contains only those parameters that must be known before the program is loaded. The actual physical devices are defined outside the program in DD statements. A program and its peripherals are not physically linked until run (open) time.

The UNIT Parameter

The general format of a DD statement is shown in Figure D.5. The UNIT parameter specifies the physical input or output device. One option is coding an actual unit address. Every peripheral attached to a traditional IBM system is identified by a three-digit hexadecimal number. For example, if a printer is device 8 on channel 0, its unit address is 008, and the DD statement

```
//PRINTER   DD   UNIT=008
```

references it. The unit address form implies that no other device will do; given the DD statement illustrated above, if device 008 is busy, or for some other reason not available, the program must wait to be loaded. This form of the UNIT parameter is rarely used.

```
//DDNAME   DD   UNIT=device,
                DCB=(parameters),
                DSNAME=name,
                VOLUME=SER=number,
                DISP=(a,b,c),
                SPACE=(parameters)
```

FIGURE D.5

A DD statement.

If a programmer wants a 3330 disk, and any 3330 disk will do, a device type can be specified; for example,

```
//OUTS   DD   UNIT=3330
```

The program can be loaded and run as soon as any 3330 is free. If a system has more than one of a particular device, specifying a device type is less restrictive than specifying a unit address.

A third choice is referencing a group name. For example, the DD statement

```
//XYZ   DD   UNIT=SYSDA
```

might represent a request for any available disk. It is the most general form of the UNIT parameter, and thus the most frequently used.

The DCB, DSN, and VOL Parameters

DCB parameters can be coded on the DD statement or in the program DCB. Both UNIT and DCB are keyword parameters. They can be coded in any order.

In the 1960s, IBM coined the term dataset to encompass both traditional files and libraries. To simplify retrieving cataloged or passed datasets, the programmer can give a file a unique name by coding a DSNAME (or DSN) parameter. A valid dataset name consists of from one to eight letters, numbers, or national symbols and must begin with a letter or a national symbol. Temporary, life-of-job files are assigned dataset names beginning with an ampersand (&); for example,

```
DSNAME=&&TEMP
```

To avoid confusing them with assembly language macro parameters, temporary dataset names normally begin with a double ampersand.

The VOLUME (or VOL) parameter specifies a particular disk volume (or pack). Each volume has a unique serial number. To request pack number MU1234, a programmer would code

```
VOL=SER=MU1234
```

The VOLUME parameter is coded only if the application demands a specific disk or magnetic tape volume.

The DISP Parameter

The DISP (disposition) parameter (Figure D.6) tells the system what to do with a disk file after the job step is completed. The first positional subparameter describes the file's status before the job step is executed. If a file is to be created, it's NEW. An existing file is OLD. Some files (a library for example) might be concurrently accessed (but not modified) by more than one program. Such files are shared (SHR). Disposition MOD allows a program to add more data to an existing file.

The second subparameter specifies system action following *normal* job step completion. If there is no further need for the data, the programmer can DELETE the file. KEEP means that the file will be retained. If the data are needed by a subsequent step within the same job, the programmer can PASS the dataset. The file can be entered on a catalog (CATLG) and retained, or removed from a catalog (UNCATLG) and deleted.

The third DISP subparameter defines the file's disposition following *abnormal* job termination. Options include DELETE, KEEP, CATLG, or UNCATLG. If the third subparameter is not coded, the normal termination disposition is assumed.

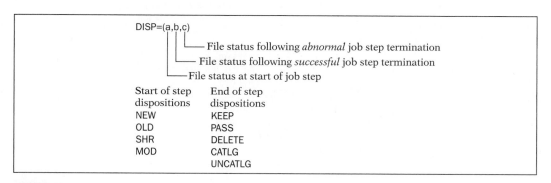

FIGURE D.6

The disposition (DISP) parameter specifies the file's status.

The SPACE Parameter

It makes little sense to load and execute a program unless adequate direct access space is available. Thus programmers are required to estimate their space requirements by coding a SPACE parameter (Figure D.7). Space can be requested in tracks, cylinders, or blocks. The first positional subparameter identifies the unit and the second positional subparameter indicates the number of units. For example,

```
SPACE=(TRK,20)
```

is a request for 20 tracks, while

```
SPACE=(CYL,14)
```

asks for 14 cylinders, and

```
SPACE=(200,10)
```

asks for ten 200-byte blocks (for a total of 2000 bytes).

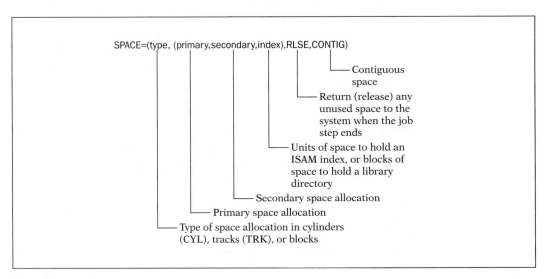

FIGURE D.7

The SPACE parameter.

Estimating space requirements can be difficult. To ensure sufficient space, a programmer might be tempted to request a bit more than the program needs, thus tying up a limited resource. Fortunately, there is another option. The parameter

```
SPACE=(TRK,(10,2))
```

requests a *primary* allocation of 10 tracks, and a *secondary* allocation of 2 tracks. Should the initial 10 tracks be filled, an additional 2 will be allocated, if available. If those 2 are filled, 2 more are allocated. The system will make a maximum of 15 secondary allocations, so the parameter coded above could represent as many as 40 tracks (10, plus 2 times 15).

The primary space allocation is made before the program is loaded. The secondary allocation is filled on an as-needed, if-available basis *after* the job step begins executing. A job step may be canceled for insufficient direct access space even though its primary and secondary requests are more than adequate if space is not available at the time of the secondary request.

Note that the primary and secondary subparameters are enclosed in parentheses. Both deal with the number of units of direct access space and thus should be treated as a single entity. (In effect, the primary and secondary allocations are *sub*parameters. When two or more subparameters are coded, a set of inner parentheses is needed.)

Requesting too much space can tie up a limited resource. The programmer can return unused space to the system at the end of a job step by coding a RLSE (release) subparameter, for example,

```
SPACE=(CYL,(5,1),RLSE)
```

RLSE is a positional subparameter that must follow the primary and secondary allocations.

To optimize disk input and output, space is sometimes requested in contiguous units. The parameter

```
SPACE=(TRK,(5,2),RLSE,CONTIG)
```

asks for 5 contiguous tracks, with a secondary request for 2 more, and returns unused space to the system at the conclusion of the job step. Without RLSE, this parameter would be coded

```
SPACE=(TRK,(5,2),,CONTIG)
```

Note the extra comma indicating the absence of a positional subparameter.

System Input and Output

A great deal of input and output takes place through relatively few devices. On some systems, a terminal keyboard and screen are the standards. On others, spooling routines create temporary disk files to insulate application programs from such slow devices as keyboards and printers. Default parameters are often used to access the standard system input and output devices.

For example, the system input device is normally defined by a statement such as

```
//SYSIN   DD   *
```

The asterisk indicates that the data follow this DD statement in the job stream. There is nothing sacred about SYSIN; it's just a DDNAME. The programmer can use any DDNAME for the system input device, as long as it matches the name coded in the program's internal data control block. Many compilers and utilities use SYSIN to reference the system input device, however, so it has become a de facto standard.

To spool data to the system output device, code

```
//SYSOUT   DD   SYSOUT=A
```

or

```
//SYSPRINT DD SYSOUT=A
```

Device A generally implies eventual printer output, but an installation can choose its own symbols to indicate the various system devices.

Job Step Qualification

Sometimes two or more DD statements, each in a different job step but still within the same job, are assigned the same DDNAME. For example, on a compile, link edit, and go job, both the compiler and the go step might get input from the system input device. Thus, both can contain a

```
//SYSIN DD *
```

statement. To distinguish these two statements, the DDNAMEs are qualified. The FORTRAN procedure contains three job steps: FORT (the compiler), LKED (the linkage editor), and GO (the program load module). FORT.SYSIN is the name of a DD statement attached to the first job step. GO.SYSIN is attached to the GO step. Qualified DDNAMES can be used only within a cataloged procedure.

A Complete Job

Figure D.8 lists the job control language statements needed to support a three-step assemble, link edit, and go job. The statements have been numbered to simplify reference. Statements submitted by the programmer begin with //. Statements added by the cataloged procedure begin with XX. Read through the statements one at a time and make sure you understand the purpose of each parameter.

1. The programmer's JOB statement.
2. The programmer's EXEC statement. ASMFCLG is a three-step catalogued procedure (assemble, link edit, and go).
3. This execute statement is added by the catalogued procedure. It references the assembler program, IEUASM.
4. The SYSLIB DD statement is added by the catalogued procedure. It allows the assembler program to access the system's macro library.
5. A work file added by the catalogued procedure. The assembler program uses this file to hold intermediate results as it assembles the program.
6. Another work file.
7. Another work file.
8. The SYSPRINT DD statement allows the assembler program to print a source statement listing.
9. The SYSPUNCH DD statement allows the assembler program to output the object module as a deck of punched cards. At one time this was a common option.
10. The SYSGO DD statement defines the disk file where the object module will be stored. The temporary dataset name &&LOADSET allows the linkage editor to find the object module in the next job step (see statement 15).
11. The ASM.SYSIN DD statement is coded by the programmer. It precedes the source code and is inserted into the ASM job step because the DDNAME SYSIN is qualified by ASM.
12. The programmer's source code.
13. The /* statement is an end-of-data marker coded by the programmer. It marks the end of the source code.
14. The second EXEC statement added by the catalogued procedure. This one references the linkage editor program, IEWL.
15. The SYSLIN DD statement tells the linkage editor where to find the just-created object module (see statement 10). Note the reference to dataset name &&LOADSET.
16. Note that this DD statement has no DDNAME. Consequently, it is treated as a continuation of the previous DD statement, SYSLIN. It tells the linkage editor that in addition to the object module file

1	//MU132	JOB	
2	//	EXEC	ASMGCLG
3	XXASM	EXEC	PGM=IEUASM
4	XXSYSLIB	DD	DSNAME=SYS1.MACLIB,DISP=SHR
5	XXSYSUT1	DD	...
6	XXSYSUT2	DD	...
7	XXSYSUT3	DD	...
8	XXSYSPRINT	DD	SYSOUT=A
9	XXSYSPUNCH	DD	SYSOUT=B
10	XXSYSGO XX XX	DD	DSNAME=&&LOADSET,DISP=(NEW,PASS), SPACE=(400,(100,20)),UNIT=SYSDA, DCB=(LRECL=80,BLKSIZE=400,RECFM=FB)
11	//ASM.SYSIN	DD	*
12	Source code		
13	/*		
14	XXLKED	EXEC	PGM=IEWL
15	XXSYSLIN XX	DD	DSNAME=&&LOADSET,DISP=(OLD,DELETE), DCB=(LRECL=80,BLKSIZE=400,RECFM=FB)
16	XX	DD	DDNAME=SYSIN
17	XXSYSLMOD	DD	DSNAME=&&GOSET(GO),DISP=(NEW,PASS), SPACE=(1024,(50,20,1)), UNIT=SYSDA
18	XXSYSUT1	DD	...
19	XXSYSPRINT	DD	SYSOUT=A
20	/*		
21	XXGO	EXEC	PGM=*.LKED.SYSLMOD
22	//GO.OUTPUT	DD	SYSOUT=A
23	//GO.DISK	DD	Parameters for program disk file
24	//GO.SYSIN	DD	*
25	Data		
26	/*		
27	//		

FIGURE D.8

A complete set of JCL for an assemble, link edit, and go job.

(&&LOADSET), additional input (other object modules, linkage editor commands) might be found following the DDNAME SYSIN later in the job stream. Had the programmer chosen to code an LKED.SYSIN DD * statement, he or she could have included additional linkage editor input. In this case, the SYSIN statement was not coded so there is no additional input. See the linkage editor reference manual for more information on linkage editor commands and object modules.

17. The SYSLMOD DD statement defines a temporary library named &&GOSET and adds one member named GO to that library. This is the load module. It will be referenced in the final EXEC statement (statement 21).

18. SYSUT1 is a work file used by the linkage editor to hold intermediate results.

19. The SYSPRINT DD statement allows the linkage editor to print messages.

20. The /* statement is an end-of-data marker. Technically it isn't needed because no SYSIN DD * statement was coded within the LKED step. It acts as a job step separator.

21. The final EXEC statement. The * following the key word PGM is a backward reference. Reading from left to right, the reference says to look back to the LKED step, find a DD statement named SYSLMOD (statement 17), and execute the load module stored on that dataset. The load module in question is member name GO on the temporary library &&GOSET.

22. The programmer coded this DD statement to allow the program to generate printed output.

23. The programmer coded this DD statement to define a disk file.

24. The programmer coded this DD statement to allow the program to get input data from the system input device.

25. The programmer's input data go here.

26. The /* statement is an end-of-data marker.

27. The // statement marks the end of the job.

If you can understand the purpose of each of these JCL statements, you have a pretty good grasp of job control language.

Glossary

. Under MS-DOS, a reference to the active directory.

.. Under MS-DOS, a reference to the active directory's parent directory.

Absolute address A physical address defined relative to the first byte in memory.

Abstraction A simplified view of an object that ignores the internal details.

Access The security criterion that each user has reasonable access to all the system resources required to do his or her task.

Access control list A list of permissions assigned to a resource that identifies which users have access to the object and the specific actions they can perform on the object.

Access method A subroutine that performs application-dependent portions of the logical to physical I/O translation process.

Active Directory A directory service installed on a Windows 2003 domain controller.

Address A number that represents the physical location of a unit of memory.

Address resolution protocol (ARP) An Internet protocol that operates at the network layer and is used to find the data link layer's hardware address; also known as the media access control (MAC) address, for a known IP address.

Allocation file A file on an HFS+ volume that uses a bitmap (a bit for every block on disk) to indicate whether each block has or has not been used.

Antivirus software Software that can recognize certain code patterns (called virus signatures) or heuristically recognize viruslike activity and sound an alarm when a virus is detected.

Apache A freely available, open source Web server popular on Linux/UNIX platforms.

Application environment Under Mac OS X, one of four environments (Classic, Carbon, Cocoa, or Java) for running application programs.

Application layer (1) The highest OSI layer. Users interact with the application layer by executing application programs to fetch and transmit data. (2) In the TCP/IP model, the layer that supports application programs.

Application management A Novell network management tool that allows the administrator to distribute software and customize the software for each group or individual user.

Application programming interface (API) A set of routines, protocols, and other tools that programmers, writing in a variety of languages, can use to build applications consistent with the underlying operating environment.

Application service(s) (1) A network service that provides a computing platform on which day-to-day applications can run smoothly. (2) A set of Web-based services that integrates many of an organization's day-to-day tasks. (3) In the system software view of Mac OS X, the layer that supports the Carbon, Cocoa, and Java application environments.

Application starter In the Linux K-Desktop Environment, an icon that opens a menu that lists all available programs.

Aqua The Mac OS X graphical user interface.

Architecture The interconnections and relationships between a computer's components.

Arithmetic and logic unit (ALU) The processor component that executes instructions.

Assembler language A programming language in which the programmer codes one source statement for each machine-level statement.

Asynchronous mode An operating mode in which an I/O request is handed off to an operating system routine and the process or thread that made the request continues to execute while the request is being processed.

Auditability The security criterion that requires that security procedures can be audited.

Authentication The process of identifying users or network components to each other and ensuring that they are who they say they are.

Backbone A network of high-speed communication lines that carries the bulk of the traffic between major segments of the Internet.

Background A region of memory that holds a low priority program.

Backup A copy used to recover data or software in case the original is lost. The act of producing such a copy.

Bandwidth A measure of the speed of a communication line, usually the number of bits the line can transmit in a fixed amount of time.

Base address The absolute address of a routine's,or set of data's entry point. Typically, the base address is stored in a register.

Baseband A communication mode in which the line carries one message at a time.

Batch file A set of commands saved in a file that can subsequently be executed by typing the file name.

Beowulf cluster A type of cluster that links multiple inexpensive computers in an effort to achieve the performance of a conventional supercomputer at a much lower price.

Bit A binary digit (0 or 1).

Black box A component whose contents are unknown.

Block Two or more logical records stored as a single physical record.

Boot The program that loads the operating system into memory.

Boot DOS partition A Novell NetWare disk management partition.

Bridge A computer that links two or more similar networks.

Broadband A communication mode in which the medium is divided into distinct channels that act much like independent wires and transmit simultaneous messages in parallel.

Broadcast A communication technique in which a message is sent to every node on the network.

Browser An application program such as Internet Explorer or Netscape that runs on the client computer and requests and displays Web pages.

BSD (Berkeley Software Design) UNIX A popular open-source version of UNIX. Under Mac OS X, Darwin's second layer.

Buffer Temporary memory or storage used to adjust for the speed differential between adjacent devices.

Bus A ribbonlike set of parallel electrical lines or wires that can carry several bits at a time. Used to physically link a computer's internal components.

Bus network A network in which the server, the workstations, and various peripheral devices all share a common bus.

Byte A unit of memory that contains enough bits (usually eight) to represent a single character. On many computers, the basic addressable unit of memory.

Cable A physical connectivity medium such as a wire, a coaxial cable, or a fiber-optic cable.

Cable modem A modem that links a computer to a high-speed, broadband communication line such as cable.

Cache, or cache memory High-speed memory that acts as a staging area for the processor.

Caching A technique for increasing performance by holding information in memory (rather than on disk) in case the information is needed a second time.

Catalog file A file on an HFS+ volume that describes the volume's folder/file hierarchy, holds vital information about those files and folders in the files' data and resource forks, and enables quick searches for the files in the hierarchy.

cd A UNIX command that changes the current working directory.

Change directory (CHDIR or CD) command An MS-DOS command that changes the current working directory.

Channel A device that handles device-independent I/O functions, usually on a mainframe computer.

Channel address word (CAW) On an IBM mainframe, a fixed memory location that holds the address of the channel program.

Channel command word (CCW) On an IBM mainframe, one instruction (or command) in a channel program.

Channel program A series of channel commands executed by a channel's processor.

Channel status word (CSW) On an IBM mainframe, a fixed memory location through which the channel passes status information to the computer.

Child A UNIX process that is created by another process (the parent).

Client In client/server mode, the module or node that requests a service.

Client/server information system Another name for a Web information system, an application system that relies on communication between asynchronous client-side and server-side application routines.

Client/server mode An operating mode in which each server module performs a single service such as file service, memory service, and so on. A client module requests a service by sending a message to the server module. The server module executes the request and sends the reply to the client module.

Client/server network A network in which a dedicated machine acts as the network server and all the other computers (the clients) request services from the server.

Clock A processor component (or an independent chip linked to the processor) that generates precisely timed electronic pulses that synchronize the other components.

clone A Linux utility similar to *fork* that gives a process a new identity but does not call *exec*.

Close The act of terminating a link to a file. In response to a close command, the file system updates the directory to indicate such information as the file's length and ending address.

Cluster (1) On an MS-DOS system, the basic unit of disk space allocation. (2) One or more (generally, a power of 2) contiguous sectors. (3) Under Windows 2003 Server, a group of computers (hardware) that act like a single system to provide services to clients. (4) Multiple computers, each with its own operating system, working together over a high speed network.

Collision The condition that occurs when simultaneous (or nearly simultaneous) messages interfere with each other and are rendered unreadable.

Collision detection A network management technique that allows the workstations to send messages whenever they want. Collisions are detected electronically and the affected messages are retransmitted.

Command A request to the operating system for a service.

COMMAND.COM The MS-DOS command processor or shell, consisting of a command interpreter and a number of resident operating system routines.

Command interface, or command line interface A user interface that requires the user to type brief, cryptic commands or acronyms.

Command language A set of available commands and their syntax rules.

Command line A Windows interface that provides access to all the features of MS-DOS.

Command processor Another name for the user interface or shell.

Commit The time when a process first uses a unit of memory it was allocated.

Common carrier An organization that provides the public communication services that define the higher levels of the communication infrastructure.

Common Internet File System (CIFS)
A standard remote file system access protocol that enables groups of users to share documents (files) over the Internet.

Common UNIX Printing System (CUPS) A recommended replacement for traditional *lpd*-based print servers on Linux/UNIX systems.

Communication services A set of operating system routines that support intercomputer communication.

Communication vector table, (CVT)
An IBM MVS table that holds system constants and pointers to most of the key control blocks.

Compiler A program that converts each source instruction into one or more machine-level instructions.

Compression To use an algorithm to reduce the size of a file.

Configuration table A UNIX table that lists all the devices attached to the system, including their major device number and minor device number.

Connectionless datagram A communication protocol in which each packet is independent of other packets and has no logical or sequential relationship with other packets. Consequently, when a process running on a particular node communicates with a process on another node, no connection is established between the two nodes.

Connection oriented A communication protocol in which, when a process on one node communicates with a process on another node, a dedicated connection is established between the two nodes, thus guaranteeing delivery of packets to their destination in their proper sequence.

Connectivity The ability of a device or a program to communicate with other devices or software.

Container object In a horizontal directory structure, an organizational unit, such as a company, a division, or a department, that contains other containers and leaf objects.

Content management services A set of service routines that allow the responsible individuals to add, delete, modify, and generally maintain the content of a Web site.

Context switching A multitasking technique in which a thread executes until it is interrupted by the operating system or must wait for resources. When a thread is interrupted, the system saves the context of the thread, loads the context of another thread, and executes the new thread.

Control block A set of data that holds a partition's key control flags, constants, variables, and other information required to resume executing the program following an interrupt.

Control unit (I/O) A device that handles device-dependent I/O functions, usually on a mainframe computer.

Controller A chip that controls the information transfer process between a bus and memory, a bus and a peripheral, and so on.

Coprocessor A special-purpose processor that assists the main processor on certain operations. For example, a math coprocessor performs mathematical computations, and a graphics coprocessor manipulates graphic images.

COPY command An MS-DOS command that copies a file or files.

Copy-on-write A form of delayed copy used by Mach 3.0 (Mac OS X) when a task modifies a portion of shared memory.

Core services A layer that provides nonwindowing and nongraphical services that are common to all the application environments except BSD, giving Mac OS X the ability to share code and data across environments.

cp The UNIX copy utility.

Cryptography The science of encrypting or otherwise concealing the meaning of a message to ensure the privacy and integrity of the information transfer.

Current directory The directory on the default drive in which the user is currently working.

Current PSW On an IBM mainframe, the register that holds the address of the next instruction.

Daemon A UNIX service routine that runs in the background.

Darwin The OS X kernel.

Data communication The process of transferring data, information, or commands between two computers or between a computer and a terminal.

Data element A single, meaningful unit of data, such as a name, a social security number, or a temperature reading.

Data segment A segment of a UNIX image that holds data.

Data structure A rule (or set of rules) for organizing data. A set of data elements that are stored, manipulated, or moved together.

Database A set of integrated, related files.

Database services A set of Web-based services that allows users to easily access, integrate, and use a system's data resources.

date A UNIX utility that displays the system date and time.

Deadlock A problem that occurs when two (or more) programs each control a resource needed by the other. Neither program can continue until the other gives in, and if neither is willing to give in, the system, almost literally, spins its wheels.

Decrypt To convert a message from encoded or ciphered form back into plain text.

Default drive The working or current drive.

Delimiter A character (often a space) that separates a command from its parameters and (if there are several) the parameters from each other.

Demand paging Bringing pages into memory only when they are referenced.

Descriptor table In the Intel architecture, a table that holds the segment descriptors for all the segments.

Desktop The Windows and KDE metaphor.

Device driver, or driver A special file that defines the linkage to a physical device.

Device port An access point for attaching a peripheral device (hardware) to an interface card or board.

Device management A set of operating system services responsible for communicating with the system's peripheral devices, such as the keyboard, the display screen, the printer, and secondary storage.

Device number On a UNIX system, a number that uniquely identifies a device.

Direct access Processing data without regard for their physical order. Also known as random access.

Directory A list of the files stored on a disk or other device. Often used to convert a file name to a physical address.

Directory (DIR) command An MS-DOS command that lists the contents of a directory.

Directory management A set of functions and routines for managing directories.

Directory service(s) (1) A database of objects (network resources) and users that organizes the network resources and makes them available to the users. (2) A network service that makes a directory available to users, system administrators, and applications.

Dirty The state of a buffer to which data has been written.

Disk A thin circular plate coated with a magnetic material and used to store and retrieve data. See also diskette and hard disk.

Disk duplexing The use of a redundant disk as a mirror.

Diskette A thin circular piece of flexible polyester coated with a magnetic material and used to store and retrieve data.

Dispatcher The operating system routine that determines which application routine or task the processor will execute next.

Displacement A location relative to a base address.

Distinguished name A complete name for a file or other object, similar to a path name or a URL.

Distributed file system (Dfs) A Windows 2003 Server facility that lets network administrators link together files that exist on physically different servers to form a single namespace.

Domain (1) A set of nodes administered as a unit; for example, all the networked computers belonging to Miami University form one domain and all the networked computers belonging to Microsoft Corporation form another. (2) Under Windows 2003 Server, a group of computers that share an Active Directory database and have a common security policy.

Domain component (DC) The main object in Windows 2003 Active Directory.

Domain controller A computer running Windows 2003 Server that contains the directory database.

Domain name A logical name consisting of two or more (generally up to four) words separated by dots that equates to an IP address.

Domain name system (DNS) (1) An Internet protocol that runs at the application layer and converts domain names to IP addresses. (2) The Internet's facility for converting domain names to IP addresses.

Domain tree A hierarchical organization of different domains.

Driver *See* device driver.

Dynamic address translation The process of converting a relative address (e.g., a segment/displacement address) to an absolute address as a program is executed.

Dynamic link library A library that contains frequently used executable routines and data. From the programmer's perspective, the application program interface defines the rules for calling the dynamic link library's functions.

Dynamic memory management A memory management technique in which the transient area is treated as a pool of unstructured free space and a region of memory just sufficient to hold a program is allocated from the pool when the program is loaded.

Dynamic storage A feature that allows a user to resize a disk without restarting Windows XP.

E-mail services An electronic post office that accepts and stores messages, notifies clients when their mailboxes contain mail, and distributes the mail on request.

Encapsulation Hiding implementation details by requiring other objects to obtain an object's data through one of that object's methods.

Encrypt, or encryption A process that ensures the privacy of an information transfer by converting the original, plain text message into encrypted text by using a key.

Environment subsystem A Windows XP subsystem that emulates different operating systems.

E-time, or execution time The time during which the current instruction is executed by the arithmetic and logic unit.

Event In UNIX, an occurrence (such as the death of a process) that produces a signal.

event-wait A UNIX routine that responds to an event by searching the process table and waking (setting to a ready state) every process waiting for that event.

Exception A synchronous event that is generated when the processor detects a predefined condition, such as division by 0.

exec A UNIX routine, called by fork, that overlays the child's text and data segments with the contents of a new file.

Executive, or executive services Windows XP's top kernel mode layer.

exit A UNIX routine that marks the death of a process.

Explorer A Windows tool that provides a hierarchical view of the directories on a system.

Export Under Linux/UNIX, the act of making a file or folder available for sharing.

ext2fs The native Linux file system,

Extension An optional addition to a file name. The extension usually follows a period and often identifies the type of file.

External bus A bus that links several external peripheral devices to a system through a single port.

External interrupt On an IBM mainframe, an interrupt that comes from the operator's console, another processor, or the timer.

External paging device On a virtual memory system, the disk space that holds application programs and transient operating system pages that will not fit or are not currently needed in real memory.

Family Under the Mac OS X I/O Kit, an object that provides a software abstraction common to all devices of a particular type.

FAT The original MS-DOS file system. See file allocation table.

FAT32 An enhancement of FAT that allocates the disk space in smaller units, creating a more efficient file system.

Fault tolerance The ability of a computer system to recover following errors.

File A set of related records.

File allocation table (FAT) On an MS-DOS system, a linked list that links the clusters that make up a file. The FAT contains one node for each cluster on the disk.

File descriptor On a UNIX system, a small, nonnegative integer number that identifies an open file to the user's process.

File management *See* file system.

File name A logical name assigned to a file.

File services Network services that enable a user to create, retrieve, and update data on the network file server, often by accessing a virtual disk.

File system A set of operating system services that allows the user or programmer to create, delete, modify, and manipulate files and programs by name.

File transfer protocol (ftp) A protocol that enables the transfer of files between two computers.

Filter A command that accepts input from the standard input device, modifies (or filters) the data in some way, and sends the results to the standard output device.

Firewall A set of hardware and software that controls how clients from outside can access an organization's internal servers.

Fixed-partition memory management A memory management technique that divides the available space into fixed-length partitions, each of which holds one program.

Flat memory model A single continuous address space called the linear address space. Generally used to model real memory. The base address is always 0. Hence, the offset is the actual physical address and is called a linear address.

Folder A subdirectory.

Forest A group of one or more domain trees.

fork The UNIX system primitive that creates a process.

Format To prepare a disk for use.

FORMAT command An MS-DOS command used to format a disk.

Fragmentation A problem that occurs over time when little chunks of unused space are spread throughout memory.

Gateway A computer that links dissimilar networks

Ghostscript Under Linux/UNIX, a filter used to convert a Postscript document to a raster image for use by a specific, non-Postscript printer.

Global catalog A catalogue that allows users to find any object located anywhere on the network for which they have access rights.

Graphical user interface (GUI) A user interface that presents the user with a selection of windows, icons, menus, and pointers.

Graphics subsystem The Mac OS X subsystem responsible for screen rendering, controlling what appears on the display and ensuring that type fonts are smooth and not jagged.

Hacker A person who illegally breaks into computer systems.

Hard disk One or more thin circular plates coated with a magnetic material and used to store and retrieve data. A hard disk is faster and has a higher storage capacity than a diskette.

Hardware abstraction layer (HAL) A Windows XP layer that hides the underlying hardware and provides a virtual machine interface to the other processes, thus supporting portability to different hardware environments by implementing functions such as interrupt controllers and I/O interfaces that are processor specific.

Hardware/software interface The point where hardware and software communicate. A function often performed by the operating system.

HFS+ (hierarchical file system plus) The standard Mac OS file system before OS X was released.

Home directory A user's initial working directory.

Home page A starting page that serves as a table of contents or index for navigating a Web site.

Host (1) In a wide area network (such as the Internet), a computer that performs end-user tasks. (2) A node on a wide area network.

Hot fix A fault tolerant feature that detects the presence of bad sectors on a disk and moves the data defect to an error-free location.

HTML (hypertext markup language) The standard markup language used to define Web pages.

HTTP (hypertext transfer protocol) A TCP/IP application layer protocol that defines the format of World Wide Web requests from a browser and replies by the server.

httpd The Linux/UNIX http daemon.

http.sys Under Windows 2003 Server, a key kernel-mode Internet Information Services (IIS) component that responds to http connection requests that arrive via port 80 and places each request on a queue for subsequent processing.

Hyperlink A logical pointer that links to a Web page. Typically, a URL lies behind the hyperlink.

Hyperthreading Executing tasks in parallel.

Icon A graphical symbol that represents either a program or a file.

IIS. *See* Internet Information Services.

i-list A UNIX table of i-nodes.

Image On a UNIX system, an execution environment that consists of program and data storage, the contents of general-purpose registers, the status of open files, the current directory, and other key elements.

Independent Self-governing.

inetd The Internet services daemon. Under Linux/UNIX, a superserver daemon that functions as an intermediary, listens for connection requests for certain ports, and starts the appropriate service program when a request reaches a port.

init A UNIX utility that creates one system process for each terminal channel. For example, if the system supports twenty concurrent terminals, twenty processes are created.

Initiator/terminator An IBM job management routine that starts and ends tasks.

i-node On a UNIX system, a 64-byte file definition that lists the disk addresses of blocks associated with a single ordinary file and the major and minor device numbers of a special file.

i-node table A UNIX table that holds the i-nodes of all open files. Also known as the system file table.

Input The act of sending data into a computer. Data ready to be entered to a computer.

Input/output control system (IOCS) The operating system module that communicates directly with the computer's peripherals.

Input/output (I/O) interrupt On an IBM mainframe, an interrupt sent by a channel to the main processor to signal the completion of an I/O operation.

Input output manager (I/O manager) A Windows XP module that manages the file systems, the cache, hardware drivers, and network drivers, works with the virtual memory manager (VMM) to provide memory-mapped file I/O, and manages the buffers for requests to the installed file system.

Instruction One step in a program that tells the computer to perform one of its basic functions.

Instruction address A field in an IBM mainframe PSW that holds the address of the next instruction to be executed.

Instruction control unit (ICU) The processor component that fetches and decodes instructions from memory.

i-number On a UNIX system, an i-node's offset from the beginning of the i-list.

Integral subsystem A Windows XP subsystem that provides protection and system services.

Integrity The security criterion that requires that the message not be modified during transmission.

Interface (1) A component that translates the signals moving from one device to another. (2) The point of linkage between two electronic devices and/or software routines.

Internet A vast network of networks layered on top of the global data communication network.

Internet Information Services (IIS) The Web server under Windows 2003.

Internet layer In the TCP/IP model, the layer responsible for routing and delivering packets to their destinations. The Internet layer roughly corresponds to the OSI model network layer and is typically implemented using the Internet protocol (IP). Sometimes called the network layer.

Internet model *See* TCP/IP model.

Internet printing protocol (IPP) A protocol that runs on top of http and supports bi-directional communication between client and server. Using IPP allows a client to browse for available network printers and to get status and other detailed information about a printer.

Internet protocol (IP) The protocol responsible for routing packets of data over the Internet.

Internet service provider (ISP) A service that provides Internet connectivity.

Internetworking The process of linking two or more networks.

Interpreter A program that works with one source statement at a time, reading it, translating it to machine level, executing the resulting binary instructions, and then moving on to the next source statement.

Interrupt An electronic signal that is sensed by hardware. The hardware responds by saving the control information needed to resume processing the current program and starting an operating system routine that responds to (or handles) the interrupt.

Interrupt descriptor table (IDT) An Intel Pentium table that associates each interrupt vector with an interrupt descriptor.

Interrupt handler An operating system routine that processes interrupts.

Interrupt vector table An MS-DOS table that occupies the first 1K bytes of memory and holds the addresses (interrupt vectors) of up to 256 different interrupt processing modules, most of which are found in MSDOS.SYS or IO.SYS. See also interrupt descriptor table.

I-time, or instruction time The time during which an instruction is fetched by the instruction control unit.

Invalid page A page that does not reside in physical memory because it has been swapped out to disk or has not yet been swapped into memory.

I/O catalog Under Mac OS X, a library of the system's available device drivers.

I/O Kit The Mac OS X device driver subsystem.

I/O registry Under Mac OS X, a dynamic database that keeps track of active nubs and drivers and tracks the relationships between them.

I/O request packet (IRP) A request for service from the Windows XP I/O manager.

IO.SYS The hardware dependent MS-DOS module that issues physical data transfer commands.

IP address A 32-bit, dotted format number that indicates the address of a device or a node on the Internet.

IPV4 The current Internet protocol standard.

IPV6 The new proposed Internet protocol standard that increases the number of address bits to 128, significantly increasing the number of unique addresses that can be used.

IPX A Novell NetWare protocol that occupies the Internet layer of the TCP/IP model and the network layer of the OSI model. IPX addresses and routes packets from one location to another.

ISA (industry standard architecture) A standard I/O bus that links slower devices such as the keyboard and the mouse to many microcomputer systems.

Itanium The Intel 64-bit architecture.

Job A unit of work consisting of one or more job steps or tasks.

Job control language (JCL) A batch, command-based user interface that allows a programmer to identify a job, specify to the operating system the programs to be run, and specify the peripheral devices to be allocated in support of those programs.

Job management Under IBM's MVS, the routines that dispatch, queue, schedule, load, initiate, and terminate jobs or tasks.

Journaling file system A file system that uses a log to keep track of changes to the metadata in an effort to improve recoverability.

KDE (K-Desktop Environment) A popular Linux graphical user interface.

Kernel (1) The core of the operating system. (2) The resident operating system.

Kernel mode A Windows operating mode in which kernel mode processes have access to the entire system memory and all processor instructions and can bypass Windows security to access objects.

Kernel-space driver Under Mac OS X, a device driver that resides in kernel space.

Key (1) A value that identifies a specific record in a file. (2) A value that converts a general encryption algorithm into a specific rule for encrypting and decrypting a particular message.

Konqueror The KDE file system.

Konsole The KDE shell, a line command interface.

Last mile problem The problem associated with linking a home or office to the telephone service provider's local central office. The problem is caused by the enormous speed disparity between a local line and a long distance line.

Layering The process of adding onto or tapping into an existing infrastructure.

Leaf object A network resource that is defined at the end of a hierarchical tree structure.

Library An organized collection of data or software.

Line command A cryptic command that is typed on a single line.

Line printer daemon *(lpd)* The standard Linux/UNIX printer server.

Linear address The offset (from 0) in a flat memory model address. The actual physical address.

Linear address space A byte addressable address space in a flat memory model.

Linux A version of UNIX developed by Linus Torvald. The source code is posted on the Internet, making Linux an example of open-source software. Over the years, it has been refined and modified and today incorporates contributions from hundreds of software developers around the world.

Linkage editor A transient system routine that prepares a complete load module and copies it to a load module library for immediate or eventual loading.

Linked list A list in which each node contains data plus a pointer to the next node.

List A data structure in which each entry is called a node, and each node holds a single data element or data structure.

Load module A complete, ready-to-execute program with all subroutines in place.

Local area network (LAN) A set of computers located in close proximity, for example within the same building.

Logical address A relative address that consists of a base address and an offset from the base address.

Logical I/O (1) The programmer's view of I/O. (2) The set of data that supports a single iteration of a program. (3) A request from an application program for a single logical record.

Logical record The unit of data requested by a logical I/O operation.

Logical volume manager A Linux service that allows a user to combine two or more physical disks to create a volume group, a virtual disk that can be partitioned into logical volumes upon which file systems can be built.

Login name A series of characters that uniquely identifies a user.

Long file name A file name that can be up to 255 characters in length.

ls, or list directory A UNIX command that lists the contents of a directory.

Mac OS X Release X (10) of Apple's Macintosh platform operating system.

Mach 3.0 Under Mac OS X, the Darwin kernel's lowest layer.

Machine check interrupt On an IBM mainframe, an interrupt that occurs when the computer's self-checking circuitry detects a hardware failure.

Machine cycle The process of fetching and executing a single instruction.

Machine language The binary instructions the processor actually executes.

Main memory *See* memory.

Make directory (MKDIR or MD) command An MS-DOS command that creates a directory.

Malware Intentionally destructive software.

Management services A set of services that support network management.

Mapped drive A convenient way to reference a particular subdirectory on the network with a single letter.

Master file table (MFT) On a Windows XP system, a master directory that contains information about each file on the volume.

Master scheduler The IBM MVS dispatcher.

Media access control (MAC) address The physical address of an interface card.

Media services An optional module that can be used to configure Windows 2003 Server as a streaming server.

Medium The path over which a message flows. Sometimes called a line, a channel, or informally a pipe.

Member server A server that is in the same domain as a domain controller but does not have an active directory database.

Memory, or main memory The computer component that holds currently active programs and data.

Memory management A set of operating system services concerned with managing the computer's available pool of memory, allocating space to application routines and making sure that they do not interfere with each other.

Memory mapping A technique for minimizing the number of physical I/O operations by (in effect) storing an image of the file in virtual memory.

Memory object Under Mac OS X, a specific source of data, such as a file. Logically, a repository for data upon which various operations (read and write) can be performed.

Memory protection An operating system routine that intervenes if a program attempts to modify (or, sometimes, even to read) the contents of memory locations that do not belong to it and (usually) terminates the program.

Menu A list of available options.

Menu bar A bar at the top of a window that displays key words that activate pull-down menus.

Menu interface A user interface that presents the user with a list of available options.

Message (1) A unit of communication consisting of a header, a body, and a trailer. (2) In object-oriented software, a communication between objects. (3) Under Mac OS X, the unit of task-to-task communication.

Message (or Messaging) port The endpoint of a logical (program-to-program) connection. A port (usually implemented in memory) that links two logical software routines.

Method A process that accesses and manipulates an object's data.

Microcode A layer of circuitry that lies between memory and the processor. Instructions are converted to microinstructions, which are executed in microcode. Sometimes called firmware.

Microkernel A compact version of a kernel that implements a limited number of specific tasks and serves as a base for supporting any of several operating systems.

Middleware (1) A class of software that helps with the translation of messages and communications between a client and a server or between two servers. (2) Any set of routines or functions that allow two dissimilar programs to interoperate.

mkdir, or make directory A UNIX command that creates one or more directories.

MMX technology A set of extensions built on top of the Intel Architecture that enhance the performance of multimedia applications such as video, audio, and 3D graphics.

Modem Acronym for modulator/ demodulator. A device used to connect a computer to a communication line.

Module A software component that provides a set of services to the rest of the system.

MORE filter An MS-DOS filter that sends output to the terminal one screen at a time.

Motherboard A metal framework that contains a series of slots linked through a bus to a processor. Memory and interface boards are plugged into the slots.

MS-DOS A command-driven operating system that allows users to issue cryptic, single-line commands through a command interface.

MSDOS.SYS The hardware independent MS-DOS module that implements logical I/O.

Multiple-bus architecture A design in which a computer system's primary components are linked by multiple buses.

Multiprocessing Two or more processors that share the same memory and are capable of executing instructions simultaneously.

Multiprogramming A processor management technique that takes advantage of the speed disparity between a computer and its peripheral devices to load and execute two or more programs concurrently.

Multitasking Executing two or more programs (or tasks) concurrently.

Multithreading Concurrently executing more than one thread.

MVS Acronym for multiple virtual systems. A traditional IBM mainframe operating system.

My Computer A Windows tool that shows the files in one folder at a time.

Namespace The set of all names that are unique within a network.

Navigation panel *Konqueror's* left panel, which displays a hierarchical view of the directory structure.

NetWare A commonly used networking operating system on local area networks. A product of Novell.

NetWare control protocol (NCP) A Novell NetWare protocol that runs at the application layer.

NetWare file system Novell's traditional file system.

NetWare loadable module (NLM) An object module linkable at run time.

NetWare partition A disk partition that stores the system files using the traditional file system.

Network Two or more computers linked by communication lines.

Network access layer Under TCP/IP, the physical connection between two nodes. Equivalent to the OSI physical layer.

Network access point (NAP) An Internet backbone node at which the network service providers are interconnected and exchange data.

Network client, or network provider A subset of Novell's NetWare that runs under the client computer's primary operating system.

Network device interface specification (NDIS) A Windows 2003 Server protocol that communicates with network card drivers, translating between the drivers and the transport protocol. NDIS allows network card vendors to ensure that their drivers are compatible with Windows.

Network driver A file system driver that redirects an I/O request from a client to the appropriate server machine and receives data from the remote machine.

Network File System (NFS) Under Linux/UNIX, a virtual file system that directs read or write requests from applications to the appropriate file system.

Network layer (1) The OSI layer just above the data-link layer that routes packets. (2) Another name for the TCP/IP Internet layer.

Network operating system A set of system software routines that help to manage a network.

Network server (1) The computer that controls a client/server network. (2) A computer that controls a resource needed by a client in the client/server model.

Network service A service that supports a system task over a network.

Network service provider (NSP) An organization that maintains and leases access to one or more of the high-speed communication links that define the Internet's backbone.

New PSW On an IBM mainframe, a permanent storage location that holds the address of an interrupt handling routine in the operating system.

Node A single computer, router, or terminal on a network.

Nonprocedural language A programming language in which the programmer simply defines the logical structure of the problem and lets the language translator figure out how to solve it. Sometimes called a fourth-generation or declarative language.

Nonrepudiation The security criterion that requires that the sender cannot deny that he or she sent the message.

Notification area A portion of the bottom bar on a Windows XP desktop that displays important information such as the current time.

Novell directory services (NDS) A method of storing and retrieving service and other information in a distributed database.

Novell distributed print services (NDPS) A set of print services that allow a Novell network administrator to manage network printing more efficiently than queue-based services.

Novell Storage Services (NSS) A Novell storage service that enables the management of large files, volumes, name spaces, and storage devices.

Novell storage services partition A Novell disk management partition.

NTFS The Windows/NT file system. NTFS not only manages files, handles large disk spaces, and so on, but also incorporates robustness features required by corporations and businesses.

Nub Under Mac OS X, an object that acts as a bridge or communication channel between two drivers (hence two families).

Nucleus The resident operating system.

Object A thing about which data are stored and manipulated.

Object manager The Windows XP executive service responsible for creating, destroying, and granting access to an object's services or data.

Object module A machine-level version of a programmer's code that can be loaded into memory and executed.

Object-oriented An approach to software development in which the software is designed and written as a set of independent objects linked by signals.

Object rights A set of rights that control what the user can do with an object, such as browse, create, rename, supervise and so on.

Old PSW On an IBM mainframe, a permanent storage location that holds the PSW that was active at the time an interrupt occurred.

Open The act of establishing a link with a physical device or file. For example, when a file is opened, the file system reads the directory, finds the file's directory entry, extracts the file's start address, and (sometimes) reads all or part of the file.

Open source Software, such as an operating, system, that features open, published source code that can be modified by anyone.

Open Systems Interconnect (OSI) A seven-layer model for computer-to-computer communication proposed by the International Standards Organization (ISO).

Operand (1) The portion of an instruction that specifies the memory locations or registers holding the data to be manipulated. (2) On a JCL statement, a field that specifies a detail about the job, job step, or data definition, one of a series of parameters separated by commas.

Operating system A set of system software routines that sits between the application program and the hardware. The operating system serves as a hardware/software interface, performs common shared services, and defines a platform for creating and running application programs.

Operation An external view of the object that can be accessed by other objects.

Operation code The portion of an instruction that specifies the function to be performed.

Ordinary file On a UNIX system, a data file.

OS X Release X (10) of Apple's Macintosh platform operating system.

Output (1) The act of sending data or information out from a computer. (2) The results of that action.

Overlay A memory management technique in which a program is broken into logically independent modules and only the active modules are loaded into memory. When a module not yet in memory is referenced, it replaces (or overlays) a module already in memory.

Packet switching A communication technique in which a message is divided into a set of small blocks called packets. The packets are transmitted independently and reassembled at the receiving end of the line.

Page directory On an Intel Pentium (or Windows) system, a table containing entries that point to a page table.

Page directory entry (PDE) A page directory value that specifies the address of the appropriate page table.

Page fault An event that occurs when a virtual address points to a page that is not in real memory (an invalid page).

Page pool On a virtual memory system, the transient program area in real memory.

Page table A table that lists the (absolute) entry point address of each of a program's pages.

Page table entry (PTE) A page table value that contains the actual physical address of the page that holds the referenced code or data.

Pager A task that is used to move data between the backing store (usually disk) and physical memory.

Paging A memory management technique in which a program is broken into fixed-length pages and the pages are loaded into noncontiguous memory.

Panel Under KDE, a window that displays system information.

Parallel port A connection point for a parallel device such as a printer.

Parameter A field in a JCL statement, a command, or an instruction that specifies a relevant detail.

Parent A UNIX process that creates another process (the child).

Partition (1) A fixed length unit of memory defined when the operating system is first generated or loaded. (2) The act of distributing application logic over two or more computers. (3) Under Novell NetWare, a logical division of the NDS tree that contains one or more complete branches.

passwd A UNIX utility that allows a user to change his or her password.

Password A series of characters used to authenticate a logon ID.

Path A list of all the subdirectories (and, possibly, other elements) one must navigate to get to a specific file.

Path name, or pathname A name that identifies the directory and all the subdirectories one must navigate (the path) to get to a specific file.

PCI (peripheral component interconnect) A local I/O bus that links high-speed peripherals, such as a disk, to many personal computer systems.

Peer-to-peer (peer-peer) network A network in which there is no dedicated server, every computer can be a server and a client, and each user can decide to share his or her hard disk files or printer with any other user.

Personality identifier A Linux feature that allows Linux to emulate the behavior of other versions of UNIX (such as System V Release 4) and allows these other versions to run under Linux without modification.

Physical address A memory address defined by counting the bytes sequentially, starting with zero (0). Also known as an absolute address and a real address.

Physical I/O The act of physically transferring a unit of data between memory and a peripheral device.

Physical layer (1) In the OSI model, the medium of transmission. (2) In the TCP/IP model, another name for the network access layer.

Physical record The unit of data transferred by a physical I/O operation.

Pipe An operator that causes one command's standard output to be used as the standard input to another command.

Pipelining A processor technique that allows multiple instructions to be processed simultaneously to obtain an overall execution rate of one instruction per clock cycle.

Plain old telephone service (POTS) The traditional, wire-based telephone network.

Plain text The form of an unencrypted message.

Platform A combination of hardware and software (usually, an operating system) that defines a base for writing and executing application programs.

Pointer (1) A symbol, often an arrow, that shows the current position of the mouse. (2) An address, often stored in a register or on a stack, that points to a specific unit of data or a specific software routine.

Polling (1) A network management technique in which the network server sends a signal to each workstation in turn and messages are transmitted only in response to the signal. (2) A dispatching technique in which the dispatcher checks a priority table to determine which program the processor will execute next.

Port (1) An access point for attaching a peripheral device to an interface card or board. (2) The endpoint of a logical (program-to-program) connection. (3) Under Mac OS X, a secure channel for intertask or interprocess communication.

Portability The ability to run a program on multiple platforms.

Portal An access point to the Internet or a private network.

POSIX The acronym for Portable Operating System Interface for UNIX, a standard application programming interface.

Post Office Protocol (POP) A protocol that allows a user to download messages from or upload messages to a server.

Postscript A device independent page description language that specifies the layout of the text and graphics on the page.

Postscript Printer Description (PPD) A simple text file that describes device-dependent features and contains commands that a Postscript printer understands.

Preemptive multitasking A form of multitasking in which each thread or process is given a set amount of time called a quantum to access the processor. Once the quantum has expired, the thread is interrupted to let another thread with the same priority access the processor. Additionally, if a second thread with a higher priority is ready to execute, the operating system interrupts the currently executing thread to let the higher priority thread run.

Pre-forking model A robust Apache server model that creates in advance a main parent process and several child processes to handle client requests.

Prepaging Predicting the demand for a new page and swapping it into memory before it is actually needed.

Presentation layer The second highest OSI layer, which is concerned with differences in data representation or syntax.

Primitive A low-level operation that tells a peripheral device to perform a single task.

Print queue A subdirectory on a print server where the data are stored while waiting to be sent to a printer.

Print server A network computer that manages printers.

Print services A set of services that support network printing.

Priority A value that specifies a task's execution order.

Priority bands Under Mac OS X, a set of the four priority levels. Each thread is classified into one of those four bands.

Privacy The security criterion that requires that the contents of the message be known only to the sender and the recipient.

Private key In public key encryption, the key that is kept private.

Privilege level A number that indicates a program's memory protection rights. A program executing at a lower privilege level cannot access a segment or page associated with a higher privilege program.

Privileged instruction On an IBM mainframe, an instruction that can be executed only by an operating-system routine.

Problem state The state of an IBM mainframe that is executing an application program.

Process (1) On a Windows XP system, an object that consists of an executable program. (2) On a UNIX system, the execution of an image.

Process file table A list of open files stored within a process's system data area. The

process file table entry points, in turn, to an i-node in the system file table.

Process id (pid) A process number assigned by UNIX when the process is created.

Process manager The Windows XP module responsible for creating and deleting processes and threads.

Process table A UNIX table created by *fork* that contains one entry for each process. Each entry contains all the data needed by UNIX when the process is not active.

Processor The computer component that manipulates data. Also known as the central processing unit (CPU) or main processor.

Processor or process management A set of operating system services concerned with efficiently managing the processor's time.

Program A series of instructions that guides a computer through a process. Each instruction tells the computer to perform one of its basic functions: add, subtract, multiply, divide, compare, copy, start input, or start output.

Program interrupt On an IBM mainframe, an interrupt that results from an illegal or invalid instruction.

Program request block (PRB) An IBM MVS control block that holds information to support an active task.

Program status word (PSW) An IBM mainframe's instruction counter.

Prompt A symbol or symbols displayed by the operating system to indicate that the command processor is ready to accept a command.

Property rights A set of rights that control access to information fields that define an object, such as supervise, read, write, and so on.

Proprietary Closed. Made, sold, and/or licensed by an entity that retains exclusive rights to do so.

Protected mode An Intel Pentium execution mode that provides programs with code and data protection.

Protection key Under MFT, a 4-bit key stored in the PSW that uniquely identifies a partition or region.

Protocol A set of rules for initiating a connection and exchanging information.

Proxy server An intermediate server located on the client side of the connection that accepts a transaction from a user, forwards it to the appropriate server, and returns the response to the originator.

Pseudocomputer On a UNIX system, an imaginary, private personal computer running under control of a simulated command-driven operating system on which it appears an image is executed.

Public key In public key encryption, the key that is published.

Public-key cryptography An encryption algorithm that uses two keys, a public key to encrypt and a private key to decrypt a message. Also called asymmetric encryption.

Queue A type of linked list in which insertions occur at the rear and deletions occur at the front. Access to a queue is controlled by two pointers.

Queuing routine An operating system routine that places programs on a queue as they enter the system.

QuickTime The Mac OS X multimedia component that allows a user to play back audio, video, graphics, and animation.

Random access Processing data without regard for their physical order. Also known as direct access.

Read memory A nondestructive operation that extracts the contents of memory but does not change them.

Read after write A fault tolerant technique in which data are kept in the buffer after a write operation has completed. The data are then read again and compared against the buffer. If an error occurs, the data are rewritten.

Ready state The state of a program that is in memory and ready to resume processing.

Real address mode An Intel Pentium execution mode in which the processor is treated as a high speed 8086.

Real computer A physical computer.

Real memory Main memory, directly addressable by the processor.

Receiver The destination or recipient of a message.

Recovery The security criterion that requires that procedures are in place to quickly get the system back on line after a security breech has occurred.

Recycle bin A folder in which deleted files are retained for possible recovery.

Redirection The act of changing the default input or output device by adding parameters to a command.

Reentrant A program or program module that does not modify itself.

Region A variable length unit of memory allocated when the application program is first loaded.

Regional ISP A service that operates a statewide or regional backbone and (typically) connects to the Internet by leasing bandwidth from a network service provider.

Register Temporary storage located in the processor that holds control information, key data, or intermediate results.

Registry A database used by Windows XP to keep track of hardware and software settings within the computer.

Relative address An address expressed relative to some base location.

Relative record number The location of a record relative to the beginning of a file.

Remote management A network management technique that allows the network administrator to control the user's workstation remotely from his or her desktop to troubleshoot a problem.

Remote procedure call (RPC) A facility that allows structured data to be passed between application processes.

Remove directory (RMDIR or RD) command An MS-DOS command that deletes a directory.

Replication The act of storing of a copy of a file or a partition on a different server.

Request block An IBM MVS control block, spun off the task control block, that describes the contents of a given partition or region.

Reserve The act of setting aside a block of memory for a process to use. Generally, the reserved memory does not count against the process until commit time.

Resident A routine that occupies memory at all times.

Restart interrupt On an IBM mainframe, an interrupt that allows an operator or another processor to start a program.

Ring network A network in which the connections form a ring and messages move around the ring from machine to machine.

Roll-in/roll-out A memory management technique in which a given user's workspace can be rolled out to secondary storage, making room for another application in memory. Later, when the first user's next transaction arrives, his or her workspace is rolled back into memory. A common memory management technique on time-sharing systems.

Root directory The lowest-level directory on a secondary storage device. Often created by the format routine.

Routing The process of selecting the next node or set of nodes for transmitting a message.

Samba The SMB (Server Message Block) server for the UNIX and Linux world.

Scalar A chip that uses a single pipeline.

Scheduler An operating system routine that selects a program from the queue and loads it into memory.

SCSI (small computer system interface) An external bus for linking such parallel devices as printers and external disk drives to a personal computer system.

Secondary storage A fast, accurate, inexpensive, high-capacity, nonvolatile extension of main memory; e.g., disk.

Secret-key cryptography A symmetric technique that uses the same key to both encrypt and decrypt a message.

Secure sockets layer (SSL) A protocol that runs in the context of the standard TCP/IP protocols, uses public-key encryption to exchange the secret key, and establishes a secure symmetric secret key connection between a client and a server for the duration of a session, thus ensuring the integrity and privacy of the messages.

Security Hardware, software, and procedures designed to protect system resources from unauthorized access, use, modification, or theft.

Security database A Windows 2003 Server database that contains information on users and resource security.

Security services A set of services that support or enable system security.

Segment descriptor A value in a segment table that holds a segment's base address.

Segment selector A pointer in a segmented memory model that identifies the segment.

Segment table A table that lists the (absolute) entry point address of each of a program's segments.

Segmentation A memory management technique in which programs are divided into independently addressed segments and stored in noncontiguous memory

Segmentation *and* paging A memory management technique in which addresses are divided into a segment number, a page number within that segment, and a displacement within that page. Normally, pages are loaded into noncontiguous memory.

Segmented model A memory model in which memory is pictured not as a continuous address space but as a group of independent address spaces called segments.

Sequential access Processing data in physical order.

Serial port A connection point for a serial device such as a mouse.

Server In a client/server network, the computer or software routine that controls access to a resource and services client requests.

Server Message Block (SMB) A client/server protocol for file sharing, printing, and login services that is commonly found in Windows.

Server process A server-side process that is run as a service.

Service (1) A specific task, often a system task, that supports another program. (2) Under Windows XP, a Win32 program (such as event log, spooler, and so on) that is run automatically at startup.

Session A relatively brief series of related transactions with a clear beginning and a clear end.

Session layer The OSI layer just below the presentation layer that establishes a connection with another computer, keeps the line open for the entire session, recovers the connection if necessary, and terminates the session.

Shadow copy A backup facility that allows users to see all previous versions of their files and restore a previous version if necessary.

Share A server resource such as a file or printer that is made available to SMB clients for network sharing.

Shared folder A folder that is shared by multiple users on a network.

Shell (1) A set of services that provides a mechanism for the user and application programs to communicate with the operating system and request operating system support. Also known as the user interface. (2) The line command interface.

Shell mode The UNIX system user interface state when the shell is active.

Shell script A file that consists of a series of shell commands. A shell script is executed by entering the file name.

Shortcut An icon or button that provides quick access to files that are accessed frequently.

Signal (1) A response to an event that activates an object. (2) The form in which a message is transmitted over a communication line.

Simple Mail Transfer Protocol (SMTP) A protocol that transfers mail from the sender's host computer and delivers it to the receiver's mailbox on a different machine using a standard TCP connection.

Simple Network Management Protocol (SNMP) A popular network management protocol.

Single-bus architecture A design in which all a computer's components are linked to a common bus.

Single system image (SSI) A form of distributed computing in which multiple heterogeneous resources such as networks, distributed databases, or servers appear to the user as one, more-powerful, unified resource.

Slot A connector for plugging a memory card or an interface board into the system bus.

sort The UNIX sort filter.

SORT filter A filter that accepts data from the keyboard, sorts the data into alphabetical or numerical sequence, and outputs the sorted data to the screen.

Source code Instructions written by a programmer in a programming language.

Spanned record A single logical record that extends over two or more physical records.

Special file On a UNIX system, a file that represents a block or character device.

Spooling The act of copying input data to a high speed device such as disk for subsequent input or writing output data to a high speed device for eventual output.

SPX A Novell NetWare protocol that occupies the transport layer of both the TCP/IP model and the OSI model and provides a virtual circuit or connection oriented service.

Stack A type of linked list in which all insertions and deletions occur at the top. Access to the stack is controlled by a single pointer.

Stack segment A segment of a UNIX image that holds a memory stack. The stack segment holds addresses, pointers, and so on.

Star network A network in which each host is linked to a central "star" machine.

Start **button** A button at the lower left of a Windows screen that allows a user to access a series of menus that lead to numerous support functions and programs.

State Status. The state of an executing program is often defined by a snapshot of essential operating information such as the values of key control variables, a list of open files, a list of active print jobs, and so on.

Streaming server A server designed to broadcast live information (music, sound, video) in real time, encoding, compressing, and transmitting the information at a constant, predictable rate so that playback glitches (like dropped phrases and broken or frozen images) can be minimized.

Structured program A program that consists of a series of logical modules linked by a control structure.

Subdirectory A special file that holds pointers to other files. Think of a subdirectory as a file folder that allows a user to group related files and thus organize the disk.

Super block On a UNIX disk, a region that identifies the disk, defines the sizes of the disk's regions, and tracks free blocks.

Superpipelining A processor chip that uses more than four stages to complete an instruction and thus support additional levels of pipelining.

Superscalar A processor chip that uses more than one pipeline and thus allows more than one instruction to be executed simultaneously.

Supervisor The resident operating system.

Supervisor call (SVC) interrupt On an IBM mainframe, an interrupt that originates when a program executes an SVC instruction.

Supervisor request block (SVRB) An IBM MVS request block that indicates that a supervisory routine is active in support of a task.

Supervisory state The state of an IBM mainframe that is executing a supervisor routine.

Swapping The process of moving program instructions and data between memory and secondary storage as the program is executed.

Switched line A temporary communication link that is established for the life of a single message or a series of related messages.

Symmetric multiprocessing (SMP) system. A system that runs system and application processes on any available processor, ensuring that all available microprocessor resources are used at any given time.

System data segment On a UNIX system, a process segment that holds data needed by the operating system when the process is active.

System file table A UNIX table that holds the i-nodes of all open files. Also known as the i-node table.

System management mode An Intel Pentium execution mode used primarily for system security and power management.

System process A process (such as the logon facility that accepts user logons and authenticates them) that does not run as a service and requires an interactive logon.

Task (1) A unit of work that the processor can dispatch, execute, and suspend. (2) A single program or routine that has been loaded on the computer and is ready to run. (3) The basic Mac OS X resource allocation unit.

Task control block (TCB) An IBM MVS control block that holds key control information for a task.

Task execution space On an Intel Pentium system, a unit of memory space that holds a program's code, stack, and data segments.

Task management Under IBM's MVS, the routines that support a program it as it runs, primarily by handling interrupts.

Task state segment (TSS) An Intel Pentium control block with entries that point to the segments in the task execution space.

Taskbar A bar at the bottom of a Windows or KDE screen that displays one button for each active program.

TCP/IP model The model that defines the Internet's standard protocols. Also known as the Internet model.

telnet A program that allows a user to connect to another computer (host) and enter commands as though he or she were on the host system.

Text segment A segment of a UNIX image that holds executable code.

Text table A UNIX table that lists each current text segment, its primary and secondary addresses, and a count of the number of processes sharing it.

Thrashing A problem that occurs when a virtual memory system finds itself spending so much time swapping pages into and out from memory that little time is left for useful work.

Thread A unit of work that can execute sequentially and is interruptible.

Thunk A piece of coding that provides an address.

Time-sharing A processor management technique in which multiple, concurrent, interactive users are assigned, in turn, a single time-slice before being forced to surrender the processor to the next user.

Time-slicing A processor management technique in which each program is limited to a maximum slice of time.

Token passing A network management technique in which an electronic signal (the token) moves continuously around the network and a computer is allowed to transmit a message only when it holds the token.

Transient A routine that is stored on disk and loaded into memory only when needed.

Transient area The portion of memory where application programs and transient operating system routines are loaded.

Transmission control protocol (TCP) The Internet protocol that guarantees delivery of the complete message to the destination.

Transmitter The sender or originator of a message.

Transparent Hidden. Not visible.

Transport driver interface (TDI) A Windows 2003 layer that provides a common interface that file system drivers and network redirectors use to communicate with network protocols.

Transport layer (1) The OSI layer just below the session layer that ensures successful end-to-end transmission of the complete message, from start to finish. (2) The TCP/IP layer that performs the same function.

UFS (UNIX file system) One of the Mac OS X primary file systems.

Uniform resource locator (URL) A World Wide Web page's unique address.

UNIX An operating system developed at Bell Laboratories designed to provide a convenient working environment for programming. Today, it is an important standard that has influenced the design of many modern operating systems.

USB (universal serial bus) An external bus used to connect such serial devices as a scanner, a mouse, and a modem to a personal computer system.

User Datagram Protocol (UDP) A connectionless Internet protocol that works at the transport layer. Faster than but not as reliable as TCP.

User interface A set of services that provides a mechanism for the user and application programs to communicate with the operating system and request operating system support.

User mode A Windows operating mode in which user applications and a collection of subsystems execute.

User-space driver Under Mac OS X, a device driver that occupies user space.

Utility A system software routine that performs a specific support function but is not part of the resident operating system.

Valid page A page that resides in physical memory.

Vector On an Intel Pentium system, an identification number associated with an interrupt.

vi A UNIX command that launches the visual editor.

Virtual 8086 mode An Intel Pentium execution mode in which an 8086 processor is simulated in a separate protected memory space, which allows 8086 applications to execute while still enjoying the full benefits of the protection mechanism.

Virtual cluster number (VCN) A number that is mapped to a logical cluster number to identify a file on disk.

Virtual desktop Under KDE, one of several concurrently active desktop environments.

Virtual file system (VFS) A Linux kernel feature that allows processes to access all file systems uniformly.

Virtual machine A simulated computer with its own virtual operating system and its own virtual peripherals that runs on a real computer. Often, two or more virtual machines are run concurrently on a single real computer.

Virtual machine concept The act of multiprogramming or time-sharing at the operating system level.

Virtual memory A model that simplifies address translation. The resident operating system is stored in real memory. Application programs are stored on the external paging device and selected pages are swapped into real memory as needed.

Virtual memory manager (VMM) The Windows XP module that allocates memory to processes and manages system memory.

Virtual memory (VM) module A machine independent module that runs in the Mac OS X kernel and is responsible for processing page faults, managing address maps, and swapping pages.

Virus A program that is capable of replicating and spreading between computers by attaching itself to another program. A common carrier for malware.

Virus signature A code pattern that uniquely identifies a particular virus.

VM object An object associated with each region in the virtual address space by the Mac OS X kernel.

Vnode Under Mac OS X, a file representation structure used to support operations on a file within the virtual file system. There is a unique vnode for each active file or folder.

Voice-activated interface A user interface that utilizes natural-language processing. Key elements include voice recognition and voice data entry.

Volume (1) A physical disk pack or reel of tape. (2) A portion or portions of one or more physical disks.

Volume header A header stored on an HFS+ volume that contains information about the entire volume, including the number of files stored on the volume, the date and time the volume was created, and the location of other key structures.

Vulnerability A weakness in a system that allows a hacker to gain access.

wait A UNIX utility that suspends execution of a process until a particular event occurs.

Wait state The state of a program that has been loaded into memory but is unable to continue executing until some event occurs.

Web-based A Web application designed and built specifically to take advantage of the Internet and the World Wide Web.

Web-enabled A non-Web application, often a legacy application, to which a Web interface has been added, thus enabling a level of Web interactivity.

Web-form interface A user interface that follows the metaphor established by the Internet and the World Wide Web.

Web information system An information system that relies on communication between asynchronous client-side and server-side application routines.

Web page The basic unit of information on the World Wide Web.

Web server A server-side application that manages, retrieves, and serves Web pages.

Web services A set of services that support retrieving Web pages in response to a request from a client, running scripts on both the client side and the server side, and similar tasks.

Web site A set of closely related Web pages that are interconnected by hyperlinks.

who A UNIX utility used to identify users currently logged on a system.

Wide area network (WAN) A network that links geographically disbursed computers. Generally, at least some of the communication takes place over long distance lines.

Wild card A character (usually * or ?) that represents one or more characters in a file name.

Window A box that occupies a portion of the desktop and displays information associated with a program or file.

Windows A family of Microsoft operating systems that allows a user to access a computer through a graphical user interface.

Windows Scripting Host (WSH) A Windows tool that allows users to take advantages of scripting languages to exploit the functionality of Windows.

Wireless A communication medium in which there is no physical connection between the transmitter and the receiver. Examples include radio, television, cellular telephone, WiFi, microwave links, satellite links, and infrared beams.

Word A group of bytes that is treated as a unit of memory. Often holds a number or an address. Word size is a key element in computer design.

Worker process Under Windows 2003 Server's World Wide Web Service Administration and Monitoring (W3SAM) feature, a process that hosts and executes the middleware routines.

Workgroup A peer-to-peer network in Windows 2003 Server terminology

Working directory The user's current default directory.

Workstation An end-user computer through which people access a local area network.

Workstation management The ability of the user's desktop to follow the user.

World Wide Web, or Web A client/server application layered on top of the Internet that provides simple, standardized protocols for naming, linking, and accessing virtually everything on the Internet.

Worm A program that is capable of spreading under its own power. A common carrier for malware.

Write memory A destructive operation that records new values in memory, replacing the old contents.

Zero Effort Networks (ZENworks) The part of NetWare that supports desktop management.

Index